Otherworlds

Psychedelics and Exceptional Human Experience

David Luke

First published by Muswell Hill Press, London, 2017

www.muswellhillpress.co.uk.

British Library CIP Data available

ISBN: 978-1-90899-514-8

Printed in Great Britain
by xxx

Otherworlds

Psychedelics and Exceptional
Human Experience

To all the psychedelic shamans, explorers, discoverers, psychonauts, scientists and researchers who have followed the Promethean fire. To all the species; flora, fauna and fungi, that have shone their light into our darkness. This book is for the benefit of all beings.

Contents

Acknowledgements

With thanks to the following for helping in the preparation and publication of the original articles (in approximate chapter order): Ross Heaven, Juan Alecco, Fabio Eduardo da Silva, Michael Winkelman, Michael Baillot, Natalie Godward, Sarah Poland, Danny Diskin, Anna Hope, Jack Hunter, Devin Terhune, Shelly Morin, Drew Littlebury, Michael Thalbourne, Paul Devereux, Robert Wallis, Peter Lloyd, Gyrus, Hannah Gilbert, Mark Schroll, Jon Hanna, Mike Crowley, Stephan Beyer, Stanley Krippner, David Jay Brown, Marios Kittenis, Debra Weiner, Nicola Holt, Harris Friedman and Adam Rock, as well the following organisations for their support; the Multidisciplinary Association for Psychedelic Studies, the Society for Psychical Research, the Parapsychological Association, the Beckley Foundation, the University of Greenwich, and Tim Read, Ayam Nostaw, and Nikki Wyrd for help with preparing this book. I am also very grateful to Dean Radin for taking the time to write the foreword.

Thanks also to Maura Holden for her exceptional artwork on the cover, and to Devin Terhune, Aldo, Luke Brown, James Jacobs, Naoto Hatorri, Tendzin Yongdü, Stephen Beyer, Mike Crowley, René de Nebesky-Wojkowitz, Alex Grey, Malcolm V. Jones, Roger Heim, R. Gordon Wasson, Dave Curtis, Ede Frecska, and Chris Timmerman for the images used within the book.

The original articles for this collection came from a wide range of publications and I am grateful to the publishers, where applicable, for their permission to reprint these articles here as chapters. I am especially grateful to Devin Terhune for his permission to reproduce and expand the review article on synaesthesia appearing in chapter 3, which he originally co-authored with me. All of the articles have been edited to varying degrees, and updated to some extent, but the main body of those papers remains. Where necessary sections have been removed to minimize repetition between chapters. Chapter 7 combines elements from two papers; the section from Krippner & Luke (2009) was the author's own contribution only, although I am indebted to Stanley Krippner for inviting me to contribute the section available here and co-author the final paper with him. The original articles, when they were first published, are listed here:

Section 1
Chapter 1:

Luke, D. (2012). Notes on getting cactus lodged in your reducing valve: San Pedro and psychic abilities. In R. Heaven (Ed.). *Cactus of mystery: The shamanic powers of the Peruvian San Pedro cactus* (pp.167-195). Rochester, VT: Inner Traditions.

Chapter 2:

Luke, D. (2014). Psychedelic possession: The growing incorporation of incorporation into ayahuasca use. In J. Hunter and D. Luke (Eds.) *Talking with the spirits: Ethnographies from between the worlds* (pp.229-254). Brisbane, Australia: Daily Grail Publishing.

Chapter 3:

Luke, D., & Terhune, D. B. (2013). The induction of synaesthesia with chemical agents: A systematic review. *Frontiers in Psychology, 4,* 753.

Chapter 4:

Luke. D. P. (2010). Rock art or Rorschach: Is there more to entoptics than meets the eye? *Time & Mind: The Journal of Archaeology, Consciousness & Culture, 3* (1), 9-28.

Chapter 5:

Luke, D. (2011). Discarnate entities and dimethyltryptamine (DMT): Psychopharmacology, phenomenology and ontology. *Journal of the Society for Psychical Research, 75,* 26-42.

Chapter 6:

Luke, D. (2008). Disembodied eyes revisited. An investigation into the ontology of entheogenic entity encounters. *Entheogen Review: The Journal of Unauthorized Research on Visionary Plants and Drugs, 17* (1), 1-9 & 38-40.

Chapter 7:

Krippner, S., & Luke, D. (2009). Psychedelics and species connectedness. *Bulletin of the Multidisciplinary Association for Psychedelic Studies, 19* (1), 12-15.

Luke, D. (2013). Ecopsychology and the psychedelic experience. *European Journal of Ecopsychology, 4,* 1-8.

Section 2

Chapters 8-14:

Luke, D. P. (2012). Psychoactive substances and paranormal phenomena: A comprehensive review. *International Journal of Transpersonal Studies, 31,* 97-156.

Luke, D. (2015). Drugs and psi phenomena. In E. Cardeña, J. Palmer, and D. Marcusson-Clavertz (Eds.), *Parapsychology: A handbook for the 21st century.* (pp.149-164). Jefferson, NC: McFarland.

Foreword

Blasting Open the Doors of Perception

David Luke's delightful one-liner about his book is that it's "… about weird people in weird places taking weird substances doing weird things and, importantly, having weird experiences." This sounds like you're about to enter a bewildering realm of seemingly meaningful but brightly colored nonsense.

On reflection, it's much more profound than that.

The usual connotation of the word *weird* is uncanny, disturbing, or supernatural. But *weird* was derived from the Old English word *wyrd*, which means fate, fortune, or destiny. Today's eerie subtext can be traced to the way that the Fates – the three sisters of Germanic mythology who controlled destiny – are commonly portrayed in Shakespeare's play, Macbeth. The sisters are typically depicted as foul witches, not as beautiful starlets. Fate has become frightful and menacing.

So this book is really about understanding our fate, which we perceive through our worldview – that set of commonly agreed-upon principles and concepts that define who and what we are, and what we may be capable of becoming. Today's scientific worldview presents a nihilistic, pointless, utterly meaningless reality. No wonder we fear it. We're trying to see our world and understand ourselves through a murky window. We need a window-washing.

There are two time-honored ways of cleansing the doors of perception. The gentlest method for parting those doors, which must be pulled rather than shoved, is meditation. But for those with less patience or discipline, there's a faster, harsher technique that can blast the doors open. The explosive is psychedelics.

Why "doors" of perception? We see through windows, not doors.

One of the pioneers of "psychedelic rock" in the 1960s, the *Doors*, took their name from Aldous Huxley's book, *The Doors of Perception*. That book described Huxley's experiences with mescaline. Huxley entitled his book based on a line in William Blake's, *The Marriage of Heaven and Hell*: "If the doors of perception were cleansed, everything would appear to man as it is: Infinite." Perhaps Blake imagined doors of glass. As a poet he didn't feel it necessary to explain everything. But his idea is basically the same as Plato's allegory of prisoners in a cave.

As Plato's story goes, these prisoners spent their entire lives chained up in a cave in such a way that all they could see was the cave wall in front of them. They couldn't see that a fire was glowing behind them, nor that actors were holding up puppets and casting shadows on the wall. For the prisoners, their entire world consisted of the shadows. One day a prisoner was released from the cave and taken outside. At first blinded by the light, after a while his eyes adjusted to the brilliance of the colors and depth of "real" reality. His former ideas about the world were shattered, and when he was allowed to return to the cave he tried to explain to the other prisoners that their shadow existence was a pale illusion of reality. Of course, the other prisoners thought he had gone mad.

Plato's allegory was a way to describe the difference between the everyday *appearance* of the world versus the world *itself*. Plato, like most of the ancient Greek philosophers, had attended the Eleusinian Mystery School, which scholars believe involved the use of psychedelics to break open the doors of perception. Plato's mystical concepts were encapsulated in Western esoteric history in the form of Neoplatonism, but his basic idea that common sense reality is just a slice of a larger Reality can be found in all mystical traditions.

Huxley encapsulated a synthesis of the world's mystical literature in his book, *The Perennial Philosophy*. His conclusion was that consciousness writ large is fundamental; more fundamental than the everyday physical world. He also deemed that our individual sense of self-awareness is *the same* as a universal consciousness. Under ordinary circumstances, we filter out awareness of the rest of the universe and narrow our perceptions to the immediate here and now. Psychedelics smash that filter, revealing to our startled eyes the thrilling and terrifying face of naked reality. That unadorned realm is constantly shimmering behind an exceedingly thin veil of normality. Just a few molecules of the right form, and in the right place, can shatter the veil.

Huston Smith, the eminent scholar of religion, wrote about the life-altering religious significance of these shattering experiences in his book, *Cleansing the Doors of Perception*. Modern clinical trials confirm that psychedelics can stimulate profoundly transformative spiritual experiences. The 2016 movie, *Dr. Strange*, a visual homage to psychedelics, is based on the Marvel Comics series by that name, and co-authored by Stan Lee. A cameo scene in the movie shows Stan Lee reading Huxley's *The Doors of Perception*.

Those doors are cracked open in this book. But naked reality is not for the faint-hearted, as David Luke cautions: "The ominous luminous voluminous numinous had proceeded to let me know that I should not be there."

But the Fates have determined that you *are* here.

So weird reader, forge ahead without fear.

Dean Radin
March 25, 2017

Preface

Despite the introduction of severe legal punishments and the prohibition of psychedelics first in the USA and then globally at the beginning of the 1970s, the public's use of psychedelics never diminished. Rather it has steadily grown, although prohibition was effective in stopping all official human research until the recent psychedelic scientific renaissance this millennium. So while prohibition continues there are currently an estimated 32 million people in the USA alone who have used psychedelics in their lifetime (Krebs & Johansen, 2013), with around one in six adults reporting use.

Given that about half of all psychedelic users report some kind of so-called paranormal experience under the influence (Luke & Kittenis, 2005) then we probably have about 16 million people, just in the USA, that have had a psychedelically induced experience that defies the general scientific consensus on what is possible. That's a lot of people having very weird experiences, be that telepathy, clairvoyance, precognition, synaesthesia, entoptics, extra-dimensional percepts, entity encounters, interspecies communication, possession, out-of-body experiences, near-death-like experiences, and so on; the experiences covered in this book.

This book is all about weird experiences: Weird experiences with weird substances. Most of the little that we know, intellectually, about these experiences comes from desktop and, occasionally, laboratory research. But to do the deepest research in this field also requires the researcher to eschew the comfort of one's armchair, desk and laboratory and seek out those far-flung communities where these experiences are common, such as with archaic psychedelic-using shamanic tribes in remote locations.

So, this book is also about weird people in weird places taking weird substances doing weird things and, importantly, having weird experiences. People like shamans, and psychedelic parapsychology field researchers. But, when you go and spend time with such people, such as the Wixáritari (Huichol) in Mexico (Luke, 2012b) – possibly one of the oldest psychedelic using communities on the planet with continuous use probably going back five millennia or more (El-Seedi et al., 2005) – such psychedelically induced paranormal experiences are actually quite normal, not weird. They are in fact very much intrinsic to their culture.

How to find an appropriate term to use for such experiences? What's weird to one culture is acceptable to another, what's paranormal somewhere is normal somewhere else. The term paranormal itself applies to phenomena that are not currently understood or accepted as possible within science; however science has, as yet, not got all the answers, given that most of the universe, the dark matter, dark energy and consciousness for instance, remains a mystery.

So, as science progresses what we term paranormal should manoeuvre itself into the realm of the normal once we begin to understand it, whether it eventually turns out be mere hallucination or something much more subtle and sublime. Nevertheless, the word hallucination itself is typically used within medicine and academia as a wastebasket term for any experience that sits outside of the basic range of consensus waking state reality, and so this term obfuscates our understanding of all experiences in altered states. Therefore we should strive to be neutral and open minded in our approach, as science is intended to operate, and seek to understand such experiences rather than exile them. That is the aim of this book.

For want of a neutral term for all these weird things that occur on psychedelics – and indeed in all other states, especially altered ones – the least encumbered word to transport them all effortlessly together might be 'exceptional'. Because they are exceptional in that they don't tend to occur very often, at least in an ordinary state of consciousness, and they are exceptional in that they are atypical, and they are exceptional in that they are extraordinary. Often they are too extraordinary for people to believe, so they are put into shadow, kept secret, made taboo, and ostracized to the far reaches of the academy.

But these exceptional human experiences shouldn't be so shunned, because potentially they have a lot to tell us about our own nature and the nature of reality itself (Moreira-Almeida & Lotufo-Neto, 2017). Indeed, any psychology that does not include the full range of human experience is incomplete. As the father of American psychology, William James (1902/1985, p283), once said, "our normal waking consciousness, rational consciousness as we call it, is but one special type of consciousness, whilst all about it, parted from it by the filmiest of screens, there lie potential forms of consciousness entirely different." So by studying these exceptional experiences what we might learn about our selves, about consciousness, and even about reality may be the exception that proves the rule; that the universe is not only stranger than we imagine, but stranger than we can imagine.

Exceptional Psychedelic Experience

The parapsychologist Rhea White (1997) can be credited with coining the term exceptional human experience (EHE), which she defined as, "anomalous experiences that transform the individual who has them so that they are engaged in a process of realizing their full human potential" (White 1999).

The term 'anomalous', somewhat broader and less freighted than the term 'paranormal', here refers to "…an uncommon experience (e.g., synaesthesia), or one that, although it may be experienced by a significant number of persons (e.g., psi experiences), is believed to deviate from ordinary experience or from usually accepted explanations of reality according to Western mainstream science" (Cardeña, Lynn & Krippner, 2014, p.4). More simply, "anomalous experiences… are distinct from our ordinary state of awareness or contravene assumptions about reality" (Holt, Simmonds-Moore, Luke & French, 2012, p.2).

However, for White, anomalous experiences themselves are only the seed of an EHE, but for these experiences to be fully exceptional they also have to be transformative, that is, they morph from being merely extraordinary or parapsychological to being 'transpersonal'. Transpersonal psychologist Mike Daniels (2005) defines transpersonal as "…beyond (or through) the personal and includes experiences, processes and events in which the normal limiting sense of self is transcended and in which there is a feeling of connection to a larger, more meaningful reality." As a subject, transpersonal psychology is defined by Lajoie and Shapiro (1992) as being "…concerned with the study of humanity's highest potential, and with the recognition, understanding, and realization of unitive, spiritual, and transcendent states of consciousness." No more definitions in this preface, I promise.

At its core transpersonal psychology is concerned with human transformation and the psychology of exceptional human experience, be that paranormal experience or mystical experience or states of deep empathy, ecstasy, love and compassion. As a psychology it is scientific, but emphasizes understanding and interpretation of the human condition and our highest potential, and it is normative rather than merely descriptive, in that its researchers not only study transformation but actively engage it. As Harman (1993) warned, "the scientist who would explore the topic of consciousness … *must be willing to risk being transformed in the process of exploration*" (p.193, italics in original). Indeed, the discoverer/inventor of LSD, Albert Hoffman, echoed this and amplified it when he said that, "…any scientist who is not a mystic, is no scientist" (Hofmann, Broeckers & Liggenstorfer, 2009, p.1).

Nevertheless, returning to our position of neutrality, while exceptional human experiences with psychedelics can be potentially transformative, they may merely remain anomalous; strange curiosities to be to viewed with intrigue from the safe seat in the audience. Such a position sits well within the field of anomalistic psychology, which considers all such experiences as being due to mundane causes within the sphere of current mainstream psychological thinking, such as via misperception, misreporting, memory errors like confabulation, or merely chance coincidences (Pekala & Cardeña, 2000).

The approach favoured in this book certainly incorporates and considers such anomalistic psychological explanations carefully, and gives them primacy, but does not assume as a starting point that all EHEs necessarily have such mundane causes. As Sherlock Holmes was fond of saying, "Once you eliminate the impossible, whatever remains, no matter how improbable, must be the truth" (Conan Doyle, 1890, p.111). We are a long way off excavating the 'truth' of the type of experiences explored in this book, but we should avoid the folly of presuming to know we have the answers all too prematurely.

In this sense then I am agnostic, and value the approaches of anomalistic psychology for its groundedness, parapsychology for its open minded and yet critical incisiveness, and transpersonal psychology for its encouragement of potential growth and transformation. All these approaches combined, along with support from the humanities, human sciences, and indeed folk and indigenous perspectives, provide the road map here for exploring exceptional human experiences with psychedelics.

Otherworld Cartographies

This book is a journey out to the far reaches of this ordinary world, and on, perhaps, into other worlds, to terra incognita, to the place on our maps marked "here be dragons." We'll be intrepid though, and earnestly don our pith helmets as we leap off the fence at the borders of our collective fields of expertise, and we'll stitch together whatever scraps of intelligence we have gathered to guide our way on.

So what maps do we have? Rhea White catalogued all the variety of Exceptional Human Experiences she encountered from a large body of literature and correspondence from experiencers, and identified over one hundred different types of EHE (White & Brown, 1997). White and Brown also painstakingly qualitatively analysed those multitudinous experiences and plotted a consistent trajectory that people steer following an EHE, and the reader is recommended to explore their work further to understand the psychological effects of EHEs more generally. The current book, however, focuses on only a few example experiences, mostly quite common to the psychedelic user, and utilizes these as a means of penetrating the psychedelic EHE by exploring both variety and depth, thereby slicing the onion as well as peeling it.

Given that we are not exploring EHEs per se, but exceptional psychedelic experiences, perhaps the most accomplished cartographer of these realms is Czech psychiatrist and co-founder of the field of transpersonal psychology, Stanislav Grof. As a pioneer of psychedelic psychotherapy Grof conducted more than 4000 therapeutic sessions over a 20-year period (before prohibition) and reported observing patients having psychedelically-induced EHEs on a daily basis. He mapped these experiences and catalogued 45 different types belonging to three basic ontological categories (Grof, 2000):

i) Experiential extension within space-time and consensus reality (e.g., planetary consciousness, embryonal, foetal and phylogenetic experiences)
ii) Experiential extension beyond space-time and consensus reality (e.g., mental mediumship, entity encounters and cosmic consciousness)
iii) Transpersonal experiences of a psychoid nature (i.e., having apparent physical concomitants, e.g., physical mediumship, UFO phenomena and yogic siddhis).

Those in the third category are the rarest, and arguably the hardest to understand or explain. They are also almost entirely absent from this book because they are so seldom reported with psychedelics (in the scholarly literature at least) and almost never researched. The majority of experiences explored in this book belong to Grof's second category, with the exception of synaesthesia, which, if anywhere, falls into the first category, but is nonetheless anomalous by standard definitions so warrants inclusion in this collection. If nothing else, psychedelically-induced synaesthesia gives us an opportunity to explore a weird phenomenon of psychedelic use that doesn't defy consensus reality when taken at face value. From there on in, it gets much weirder.

A Strange Journey on a Crooked Path

In some sense then it would be logical to start this book by exploring the experience that least challenges the standard 'scientific' worldview, by looking at psychedelic synaesthesia, but that wouldn't be much fun, and besides the nature of the chapters begs an alternative route. That's because this book is comprised of nine previously published articles by the author, that have been edited and updated here and there, and sprinkled with fresh commentary, and the style and content of each of these articles suggests a different order. Nevertheless *Otherworlds* needn't be read in order and each chapter also stands alone. Spanning seven years of publication (2008-2014) in edited books, scientific journals and magazines, the chapters vary in style from essay to review.

The chapters in the first half of the book each take on a different EHE, whereas the second section (chapters 8-14) presents an in-depth yet concentrated and comprehensive review of the research on so-called paranormal phenomena and psychedelics, covering everything from neurochemical models, through anthropological reports, to surveys and experiments on a range of experiences, though mostly directed at ESP (telepathy, clairvoyance, precognition), out-of-body experiences and near-death experiences, but also touching on sleep paralysis, alien abduction experiences, entity encounters, mediumship and shamanism. This second section of the book is the most technical and detailed and is there as a resource and reference for the most committed scholars, although it will likely bear fruits of insight for even the casual reader.

The first section, then, is a bit more accessible to all readers, but has some serious scholarship too, and mixes essays (chapters 1, 2, 4, 6 & 7) with more in-depth reviews (chapters 3 & 5). It also covers a range of writing styles, academic disciplines and research methods, from ethnographic travelogue and speculative thesis via exotic essay to the sturdy literature review. All this whilst roving from psychedelic parapsychological field experiments, to serious archival research and penetrative analysis, to psychonautic misadventures in altogether esoteric territory. It's what you might (politely) call a mixed bag.

Nevertheless at an antipodean academic archipelago as far from mainstream intellectual terra firma as this, there is good cause for being pluralistic in one's approach. When you don't know where you are going or what you expect to find, there's no good reason to stick to one path. Psychedelics do nothing if they don't challenge our existing beliefs and show us alternative ways forward. Therefore, we need a diversity of data, opinions, explanations, theories and approaches if we are to stand any chance of finding our destination, and recognising that we have arrived when we get there. But we are a very long way yet from understanding the wealth of stupendously sensorial, neurobiologically baffling, ontologically shocking, utterly life changing, potentially intellectually revolutionary, and downright strange experiences that ensue from a gaze into yon shaman's medicine bag.

Having said all that, I like to think that this rag-taggledy book of assembled arcana is the seed to an as yet uninitiated sub-sub-field of several promiscuous disciplines, for indeed it demands to be nothing less than multi-disciplinary, spanning anything and everything from psychology, psychiatry, anthropology, neuroscience, ethnobotany, ethnopharmacology, chemistry, religious studies, cultural history to computational neurobiology. I'm not joking either, I just last week penned an article (with an inky tongue only partially stuffed in my cheek) entitled 'The big dream and archeo-geo-neuro-pharmaco-parapsychological theories' (Luke, 2017).

Perhaps one day in the distant future when robots arc busy running the planet and humans have the time and facility to conduct exotic research, a research centre dedicated to this subject will open up in a prestigious university, stimulating many more, and some will look back on this book and consider it a hefty starting block for what we might more simply (than the alternatives) call parapsychopharmacology, or what the French researcher Larcher (1958) presciently called parapsychochimie (parapsychochemistry). Then again, perhaps not. In any case I hope you find something of interest and/or of use in this somewhat niche book, albeit a book that is likely one of the very few academic tomes, verging on a text book, that speaks to those 16 million US citizens alone who have had experiences of the type that feature within these pages. If you do find something in here that resonates with you, then it will all have been worth it. Either way, remember to keep an open mind on your journey, but not so much that your brains fall out. And, love long and perspire, as they say on Venus.

SECTION ONE

Explorations of Exceptional
Entheogen Experiences

CHAPTER 1

Notes on Getting Cactus Lodged in Your Reducing Valve: San Pedro and Psychic Abilities

I'd spent the best part of a week on rickety buses going up and down mountains, skirting and skooting round precarious precipices, and schlepping back and forth across a number of small towns in southern Ecuador. It had started out as a shamanic healer hunt but was fast becoming a manic wild goose chase. Armed with a few leads – some locations and numbers – I had emptied several bags of coins into phone boxes to little effect, because the healers I was pursuing did not, as a rule, make much use of modern telecommunications. I joked with myself that this forsaking of telephony was possibly due to their mastery over psychic abilities, the likes of which I was hoping to test.

Under the auspices of an ambitious scientific research project, I had travelled to South America in an attempt to conduct controlled experiments with people under the influence of the psychedelic San Pedro cactus, in a bid to test the claim that the use of certain psychedelic substances could induce the ability to transcend space and time, and to know and foresee things through non-ordinary means. In essence, I wanted to know if the use of San Pedro could facilitate clairvoyance, telepathy or precognition, the abilities, respectively, of accessing hidden information, communicating directly with others or obtaining knowledge from the future. Collectively these three supposed phenomena have been termed extrasensory perception (ESP), or simply *psi*.

I finally caught up with a mestizo healer on the second visit to his remote village, and traversed the extra few miles up the mountain with my partner to his secluded wooden shack. No running water, no electricity, no neighbours, just spectacular views out over the Andes. He greeted us very hospitably and we began talking about participating in a San Pedro ceremony with him, and the possibility of conducting some psychic tests, which he happily agreed to. Everything was going well until I pointed out that, well equipped with batteries, I would like to use my laptop computer to do the tests. The healer looked at me sternly and marched me over to the edge of the clearing surrounding his small house. Overlooking the valleys and mountains he told me how his family owned all the land we could see on this side of the mountain and how his ancestors had lived here for hundreds of years, in much the same way as he did now: as part of Nature. Standing behind me he then lifted a huge conch shell to his lips and blasted me with a resonant bombardment of sound. Turning me round ninety degrees with his hand he repeated the sonic assault, doing the same manoeuvre twice more until I had been thoroughly trumpeted in all four directions, and so had greeted the four winds. Sledgehammer for a nut, I got the message: There would be no use of computers during his San Pedro ceremony.

It's thus I found myself some weeks later, rather than testing twenty other people for their possible psychic abilities, holed up in room alone sat in front of a computer for eight hours, deeply nauseous and in a definite altered state of consciousness, doggedly running the twenty psychic tests on myself. I'll return to this odd experiment later on, but will first discuss why anyone should even want to test for the ESP-inducing capabilities of a spiny, succulent-stemmed angiosperm.

Cactus of the Four Winds

According to the archaeological evidence the Andean cactus San Pedro (*Trichocereus pachanoi*) was used as a sacred power plant, i.e., as a sacrament, for at least two thousand years before the Spanish conquistadores arrived in the 16th century, although some finds may be much older. The Peruvian site of Chavín, for instance, home of the Chavín people, has stone etchings that attest to the central role of psychedelic plants in that culture (Burger, 1992) including, but not limited to San Pedro cactus (Jay, 2005). The site itself dates from between 1500 B.C. – 900 B.C. and reverence for the cactus among later Andean cultures, dating from the time of Chavín up and till the arrival of the Spanish, has been identified from ceramics from the Cupusnique, Salinar, Nazca, Moche, Lambayeque and Chimu people (Glass-Coffin, 1999).

Written accounts following the arrival of the Spaniards indicate the way in which the cactus was used by the Pre-Columbian Andean people. Of interest to the project under discussion is that most of these include some report of the parapsychological effects of the plant. Juan Polo de Ondegardo, a sixteenth century Spanish officer stationed in Cuzco, Peru, described how the natives using the cactus "...take the form they want and go a long distance through the air in a short time; and they see what is happening…" (Sharon, 1978, pp.112-3), probably indicating out-of-body experiences and 'travelling clairvoyance'. Juan Polo de Ondegardo added that when they take the plant, "they serve as diviners and they tell what is happening in remote places before the news arrives or can arrive" (Sharon, 1978, p.113), clearly demonstrating de Ondegardo's belief in the healers' cactus-induced psychic abilities.

The following century a number of accounts of San Pedro's use appeared among missionaries posted in the Andes. In 1631 Father Oliva described the ritual use of *achuma* (San Pedro), noting that, "they see visions that the Devil represents to them and consistent with them they judge their suspicions and the intentions of others" (cited in Sharon, 1978). Peruvian healers, called *curanderos*, in recent years continue to consume San Pedro to know people's intentions (Glass-Coffin, 2000). It's clear, though, that at that time such activities were treated as suspicious and sacrilegious by the early missionaries, and in 1653, a few years after Father Oliva's account, Father Cobo (as cited in Sharon, 1978) wrote a somewhat more biased pious report of the effects:

> This is the plant by which the devil deceived the Indians of Peru in their paganism, using it for the their lies and superstitions…Transported by this drink, the Indians dreamed a thousand absurdities and believed them as if they were true.

Such negative reports stemming from the period of the Inquisition between the fourteenth and seventeenth century are hardly surprising, nevertheless the witch hunts did not totally eradicate the use of San Pedro, despite the attempt. In the less punitive years after the Inquisition numerous cases of 'pagan idolatry' can be found in the records, such as the trial of Marco Marcelo in 1768, who described how when he drank the San Pedro brew, "he came into full awareness and patently saw with his eyes the sick person's [bewitchment]… and he also recognized the sorcerer who had done the [harm]" (cited in Glass-Coffin, 1999).

Despite continued persecution for the best part of 500 years, the shamanic use of San Pedro still continues to this day, representing an unbroken magico-religious tradition spanning more than 3000 years (Sharon, 1978). According to Dobkin de Rios (1977) the use of San Pedro as 'a revelatory agent', to determine the source of witchcraft and misfortune affecting a patient, is currently its predominant function, although more recently healers may typically diagnose the cause of illness as being due to the person's thoughts and behaviours rather than external agencies such as sorcery (Heaven, 2009). For instance, a curandera interviewed by Glass-Coffin (2000) saw that those living life without conscious awareness and in emptiness were prone to illness, though she specifically used the word *daño* (harm), which traditionally is associated with an illness caused by sorcerers (*brujos, maleros*) through witchcraft (Sharon, 1978). *Envidia* (envy) is unanimously given as the reason for such witchcraft, possibly as result of the continued post-Columbian poverty, scarcity of resources and subjugation of the Andean peoples by the dominant class, according to the Peruvian psychiatrist Mario Chiappe (cited in Sharon, 1978).

Aside from *daño,* other maladies traditionally diagnosed by San Pedro curanderos include *mal aire* (bad air, usually emanating from tombs or ruins of sacred places) (Dobkin de Rios, 1968), *mal suerte* or *saladera* (bad luck, to the point of lethargy and pessimism) (Dobkin de Rios, 1981), *susto* (soul loss, manifesting as lack of self-efficacy) (de Feo, 1992), *mal puesto* (hexing or cursing), *mal ojo* (the evil eye), and *bilis*, *empacho* and *pulsario* (rage, pain and sorrow, caused by a blockage of energy) (Heaven, 2009). Both diagnoses and treatment for such maladies are made by the curandero under the influence of San Pedro during an all night ceremony, in which the healer enacts magical battles to heal the patient. Typically the patient also ingests the cactus brew (Dobkin de Rios, 1968), as it is also considered a medicine, or even a panacea in its own right and it may also help the patient have revelations regarding their own maladies (e.g., Heaven, 2009; Sharon, 1978), though traditionally such revelations are usually made by the healer.

Once known as achuma, these days the cactus is known by a number of pre- and post-Columbian names, such as *huando hermoso, cardo, gigantón, huachuma* (Sharon, 1978), *chuma, pene de Dios* ('penis of God'), *El Remedio* (Heaven, 2009), and *aguacolla* (Shultes & Hofmann, 1992). First described and classified by the botanists Britton and Rose in 1920, they gave San Pedro its Latin taxonomic name, *Trichocereus pachanoi* and noted that its distribution remained solely within Andean Ecuador. More recently it has been found to be indigenous to Bolivia and northern Peru, typically growing at two to three thousand metres above sea level, although it has also been found in coastal regions (Sharon, 1978) and as far south as Argentina (Shultes & Hofmann, 1992).

Plant Allies and Plant Alkaloids

The main active principle of San Pedro was originally identified by the French ethnobotanist Claudine Friedberg (1959), who found that the fresh plant matter contains about 0.12% mescaline (3,4,5-trimethoxy-phenethylamine), an alkaloid of the phenethylamine family (Shulgin & Shulgin, 1991). Dried *T. pachanoi* is reported to contain about 2% mescaline (Stafford, 1977), although a review of published analyses shows that reports vary from between 0.33% to 2.37% mescaline in the dried plant (Erowid, 2001). Nevertheless, this makes it somewhat weaker than its northern Mexican and southern USA cacti cousin, peyote (*Lophophora williamsii*), which contains about 8% mescaline by dry weight (Bruhn *et al.*, 1978), although some reports suggest that dry peyote only contains between 1% and 6% mescaline (Crosby & McLaughlin, 1973).

Louis Lewin first described the extraction of a mixture of alkaloids from peyote in 1888, but it wasn't until 1895 that Arthur Heffter isolated four pure alkaloids, one of which he called *mezcalin,* now known as mescaline (Ott, 1996b). Then, in 1897, Heffter (1898) did what any great explorer would do and tested the alkaloids' psychoactivity on himself and heroically ingested them, thereby identifying mescaline as the main active chemical because its effects differed little from that of the plant itself. It is this self-experimentation technique that later led Albert Hofmann to discover psilocybin and psilocin as the psychologically active principles of the psychedelic *Psilocybe* genus of mushrooms, a discovery made well in advance of the large pharmacological companies who had already been working on the problem for some time but by only testing the chemicals on animals (Luke, 2006). In 1919, the chemist Späth then identified mescaline's structure as 3,4,5-trimethoxy-β-phenethylamine and confirmed this by synthesising the compound (Ott, 1996b).

Returning to San Pedro, besides *T. pachanoi* there are thought to be more than 25 species of *Trichocereus* that contain alkaloids (Crosby & McLaughlin, 1973), and at least eleven of these species contain mescaline (Ott, 1996b). Most of these close relatives of San Pedro are not used as ethnomedical plants, however, because the alkaloids are in trace quantities, the exception being *T. peruvianus* (Peruvian torch) which is supposedly much stronger and thought to contain almost as high concentrations of mescaline as peyote (Ott, 1996b; Pardanani *et al.*, 1977), although other reports suggest this is an exaggeration because some analyses report no mescaline in *T. peruvianus* and yet more than 2% in some samples of *T. pachanoi* (Erowid, 2001). Nevertheless, despite mescaline being the primary active principle of peyote and both San Pedro and Peruvian torch there are a number of other alkaloids present which are not the same, so although the psychopharmacological effects of these cactus are roughly analogous they are not entirely equivalent (Bruhn *et al.*, 2008).

Peyote is known to contain over fifty alkaloids (Anderson, 1980), mostly mescaline and tetrahydro-isoquinoline alkaloids, albeit in trace quantities, as the total alkaloid content is only about 8% of the dry weight (Bruhn *et al.*, 1978), most of which is mescaline. *T. pachanoi*, alkaloids on the other hand, consist mainly of mescaline and related phenethyl-amines, such as tyramine, hordenine (a stimulant with antibacterial and antibiotic properties, also found in peyote), 3-methoxytyramine, 3,4-di-methoxy-β-phenethylamine, 3,4-dimethoxy-4-hydroxy-β-phenethyl-amine, 3,5-dimethoxy-4-hydroxy-β-phenethylamine, anhalonidine and anhalinine (Crosby & McLaughlin, 1973).

A recent study (Bruhn *et al.*, 2008) has also discovered the presence in San Pedro of three new phenethylamine alkaloids: lophophine (3-methoxy-4,5-methylenedioxy-phenethylamine), which is also psychoactive and is closely related to MDMA (3-methoxy-4,5-methylenedioxy-amphetamine, commonly known as *ecstasy*); lobivine (N,N-dimethyl-3,4-methylenedioxy-phenethylamine), a relatively mild psychoactive compound also related to MDMA; and DMPEA (3,4-dimethoxy-phenethylamine) which is a non-psychoactive compound.

These three new alkaloids were also found to be present in peyote, and at higher concentrations than in San Pedro, yet it is thought that they have very little direct psychoactive effect in the quantities they are naturally found at, relative to mescaline, although they might have a synergistic effect with the mescaline (Bruhn *et al.*, 2008). Demonstrating great insight, having previously synthetically created lophophine, Shulgin and Shulgin (1991) noted its similarities to mescaline and predicted its psychoactivity and its likely presence in peyote (*Lophophora williamsii*), hence the name given to it by Shulgin and Shulgin (1991) even before it was found to occur naturally. This discovery calls into question the *artificial*, rather than *natural* status of designer drugs, like MDMA, many of which have been created by Alexander Shulgin over the years, which, if they might later be found to occur in nature are therefore only potentially artificial, or potentially natural.

Artificial Paradises or Natural Chemical Utopias?

A similar difficulty of distinction arises over whether the states induced by psychedelics are natural or artificial, though early writers clearly placed them in the latter camp, such as the medic Havelock Ellis, who was the first person in the UK to write about his experience with mescaline in an article entitled *Mescal: A new artificial paradise*

(Ellis, 1898). However, these days it is known that there are a number of naturally occurring psychedelic substances in the human body, so experiences such as synaesthesia and clairvoyance that are induced by the ingestion of psychedelic substances like mescaline might also occur spontaneously, as they are known to do, through the action of 'endogenous' (made within the body) chemicals.

It is highly likely that all altered states of consciousness, including potentially ESP-conducive states, involve alterations in brain chemistry, and so psychedelics like mescaline have an important part to play in helping us to understand the neurochemistry underlying those states. Taking this further into the realm of parapsychology, several psyche-delic-neurochemical models have been proposed based upon the specific neurochemical action and the subjective paranormal experiences occurring with certain substances, such as ketamine and DMT (e.g., Jansen, 1997; Roney-Dougal, 2001; Strassman 2001). Advancing on these models it is entirely feasible that genuine paranormal phenomena are mediated in the brain through the action of specific endogenous psychedelic molecules, such as DMT (Roney-Dougal, 2001). This does not simply imply that neurochemicals are the sole cause of paranormal phenomena, but they may rather just be a part of the process. As the novelist Aldous Huxley once said in relation to mystical experiences and the use of psychedelics – they are the occasion rather than the cause.

Cleansing the Doors of (Extrasensory) Perception

Aldous Huxley was also prominent in promoting the influential French philosopher Henri Bergson's (1896) nascent parapsychological theory of the brain as a filter of memory and sensory experience. In this model the brain acts to reduce the wealth of information available to our awareness, lest we become overwhelmed by this mass of largely useless data, irrelevant to the survival of the organism. Bergson suggested that if the filter was bypassed people would be capable of remembering everything they had ever experienced and capable of perceiving everything that is happening everywhere in the universe, i.e. clairvoyance.

After being given mescaline by the pioneering psychedelic researcher Humphry Osmond (who coined the term "psychedelic" in correspondence with Huxley) in 1953, Huxley then applied Bergson's theory to psychedelics by suggesting that these mind-manifesting drugs override the *reducing valve* of the brain allowing man access to both psychic and mystic states. A notion that Huxley (1954) eruditely paraphrased with the quote by the English poet and mystic, William Blake, "If the doors of perception were cleansed, every thing would appear to man as it is, infinite."

Huxley's rather basic conception of the influence of psychedelics on the paranormal function of the brain never received a more formal operationalisation of the specific drug action involved but recent research into the neurobiology of psychedelics lends some support to this simple notion (see Chapter 9 for a review of this). However, that the special neurochemistry of psychedelics is central to psi is supported by a wealth of collectively compelling personal accounts from users as well anthropological, clinical and survey reports. There is also a body of preliminary experimental research that presently remains equivocal and generally methodologically flawed, but nevertheless promising (for a review see Section Two). Of these numerous psychedelics, mescaline is one substance in particular that, according to the historical, anthropological and personal accounts to follow, is known to induce psi experiences.

Putting the Psi Back into Psychedelics

Traditionally, the sacramental use of mescaline-containing cacti was restricted to the New World (i.e., the Americas) where these plants are endemic, and included the use of peyote among the Kiowa and Comanche people of the southern states of USA, through to parts of northern Mexico where the Tarahumara people of the state of Chihuahua and the Wixáritari (Huichol) people, originally of the state of San Luis Potasi, make use of peyote and other putative mescaline-containing cacti (Schultes & Hofman, 1992). Archaeological evidence suggests that the use of peyote has continued for at least 5,000 years in this region (El-Seedi et al., 2005) and ever since the use of peyote was first documented in the mid-16th century by the personal physician of King Philip II of Spain, Dr. Francisco Hernández, it has been reputed to induce prophetic qualities, "It causes those devouring it to be able to foresee and to predict things" (quoted in Schultes & Hofmann, 1992, p.134).

Further south, San Pedro has been used traditionally by the indigenous people of Ecuador, Peru, Bolivia, and even Argentina for the same type of magico-religious practices, such as divination, as those of their northern American cactus-using 'cousins' (Schultes & Hofmann, 1992), as discussed earlier. More recently, anthropological research also attests to the capacity of San Pedro, and therefore probably mescaline too, to induce or facilitate psychic experiences. Sharon (1978, p.45) reports that a Peruvian folk healer (curandero) he studied, and studied with, used San Pedro, like other curanderos, to induce what the healer called, "the sixth sense, the telepathic sense of transmitting oneself across time and matter... It develops the power of perception... in the sense that when one wants to see something far away... he can distinguish powers or problems or disturbances at great distance, so as to deal with them." This psychic enhancement apparently occurs because, "San Pedro is the catalyst that activates all the complex forces at work in a folk healing session, especially the visionary and divinatory powers of the curandero himself" (Sharon, 1990, p.117).

Similar reports of actively using other mescaline-containing cacti for 'psi' (e.g., clairvoyance) also appear in the historical and anthropological literature, as with the use of peyote among the Wixáritari (Slotkin, 1956), Chichimeca, Zacatecan, Tamaulipecan and Tarahumara people of Mexico and among the Apache, Comanche and Kiowa in the US (for a review see La Barre, 1938). This literature is backed up by experiential reports from non-indigenous mescaline-users like that of the French researchers who gave mescaline to six subjects, one of whom temporarily developed very detailed and accurate clairvoyant abilities and was able to describe the contents of a nearby room (Rouhier, 1925, 1927).

Similar reports exist among parapsychology researchers themselves, such as Rosalind Heywood (1961) who, after taking the mescaline given to her by psychical researcher John Smythies, believed that psychedelics could help researchers understand spontaneous psi experiences. The same sentiment was reported by the man who coined the term *psychedelic,* Humphry Osmond, after his own mescaline experiences in 1951. Osmond (1961) also reported that in 1957 he and his fellow researcher Duncan Blewett, both under the influence of mescaline, successfully transmitted telepathic information in an informal experiment to such a degree that an independent observer became acutely panicky at the uncanniness of the event.

Similarly, during mescaline self-experimentation Langdon-Davies (1961) claimed to have demonstrated travelling clairvoyance and successfully identified 13 correct targets from a pack of 25 zener cards, where each pack contains an equal mixture of five distinct symbols. The odds of correctly identifying 13 or more symbols by chance alone are 1 in 2,500, which is quite improbable. Reflecting the growing popularity of psychedelics in 1960s alternative culture a member of The Byrds musical group claimed to have experienced telepathy with other band members under the influence of mescaline (Krippner & Davidson, 1970).

Nevertheless, merely consuming mescaline is no guarantee that an experience of ESP will follow, as the Oxford philosophy professor H.H. Price (1964) aptly demonstrated in a self-experimentation guided by Humphry Osmond. Similarly, parapsychologist Charles Tart described in a letter how, when he was given 500mg of mescaline (a reasonably large dose) by Austrian psychologist Ivo Kohler in 1959 and was supposed to perform an ESP card guessing test, he was far too absorbed in cosmic revelations and the overwhelming beauty of the universe to actually engage seriously with the task (Tart, personal communication, 13th May, 2011). Nevertheless, other parapsychologists have reported personal ESP experiences with the use of mescaline (e.g., Millay, 2001).

Despite there being a good body of survey research to substantiate the induction of paranormal experiences with psychedelics *generally* (see Section Two for a comprehensive review), all but one of these surveys omitted to investigate the effects of mescaline in particular. One in-depth drug/experience survey, however, revealed that mescaline did indeed give rise to reports of telepathy and precognition among those using it, yet the primary 'transpersonal' experiential features of ingesting mescaline cacti were the perception of auras (as also reported by Tart, 1972a), the experience of encountering the plant's spirit, and a sense of unity (Luke & Kittenis, 2005). Other less common experiences reported included dissolving into energy, powerful long lasting religious awakenings, out-of-body experiences, clairvoyance, death and rebirth experiences and/or past life memories, psychokinesis (influencing objects or people with one's mind), encountering a divine being, encountering a (non-animal) intelligent entity, and the sense of the loss of causality (where A causes B) (Luke, 2009a). Many of these experiences have also been reported elsewhere under the influence of San Pedro (Heaven, 2009).

Individual reports and surveys of people having psychic experiences with mescaline under non-experimental conditions may be provocative and interesting but these are scientifically limited given what is known about the ways in which individual paranormal *experiences* do not necessarily indicate genuine paranormal *phenomena*. This is because individual experiences may be prone to instances of misperception, misreporting, memory errors such as confabulation, or may be merely chance coincidences (Pekala & Cardeña, 2000). Nevertheless, these various individual reports collected here may be actual cases of genuine psychic phenomena occurring under the influence of mescaline, but without controlled experimental testing there can be no certainty.

Reviewing the extremely scant experimental literature, then, there are few studies that have been conducted which can be considered. Humphry Osmond's co-worker John Smythies (1960, 1987) reported a preliminary study with one volunteer using mescaline in a psychometry experiment, whereby the task is to describe the unknown owner and their environment when given a personal object belonging to them. Although the participant was unable to discern the targets under adequate blind, 'remote-viewing' style conditions, informal questioning about the target location typical of psychometry tasks elicited promising responses.

Similarly using mescaline, a series of pilot studies with three participants "failed in card-guessing tests but showed encouraging success in tests with free material, particularly token objects" (Rush & Cahn, 1958, p.300). Likewise with mescaline, presumably in self-experiments, Breederveld (1976, 2001) reported success in consistently winning above chance at roulette experiments in casinos using real money, although the mescaline condition was only one of several, mostly successful methods perhaps indicating that either Breederveld's methodology was flawed or that he had some psychic talents anyway.

Nevertheless, Breederveld's success echoes informal reports concerning the pioneer psychedelic researcher, Al Hubbard, who after supposedly developing his psychic ability through the use of LSD (Osmond, 1961; Stevens, 1988) became somewhat notorious for winning on gaming machines in casinos, his reputation being such that he was politely escorted out by the management when he reached a certain limit of earning (Krippner, 2006). Overall, it can be said that the scant research literature is very positive about the informal use of mescaline for inducing ESP, however there are as yet no clear reports of well controlled and statistically sound formal experiments, so it certainly begs further investigation.

Uncorking the Genie's Bottle

It's thus I found myself some weeks later, rather than testing twenty other people for their possible psychic abilities, holed up in room alone sat in front of a computer for eight hours, deeply nauseous and in a definite altered state of consciousness, doggedly running the twenty psychic tests on myself. I had prepared about 30 grams of the dried slices of San Pedro by powdering them in a coffee grinder. The actual mescaline content must have been somewhere between about 100mg and 700mg according to the concentrations reported for *Trichocereus pachanoi* (Erowid, 2001), with about 200mg to 400mg of mescaline considered to be a standard dose (Shulgin & Shulgin, 1991). Effective doses are thought to be in the 150mg to 1500mg range, although the maximum safe dose is proposed to be 1000mg (Ott, 1996b). Once the effects took hold I was quite pleased that that the actual dosage was probably at the weaker end of the possible mescaline content range, due to the necessity to be able to function in this state enough to be able to run my own experiment on myself but still have a visionary experience.

Having prepared the cactus I then prepared myself and the experiment. I had fasted since the previous evening to reduce nausea or vomiting, and to maximise the potency of the plant. I had also organized all the materials I would need for the ESP tests: a pile of questionnaires, a clock, a dictaphone and a laptop with a large collection of pre-formulated video clips.

The procedure was fairly straightforward, once I was under the influence of the San Pedro I would close my eyes and attempt to visualise 'the target', and I would write down anything that appeared in my mental imagery, and any feelings or insights associated with it. At this point I had no idea what the target actually was, of course. Once I had written down my impressions of the target, I would then complete a series of standard scales relating to my state of consciousness: how easy it was to visualize, how confused I was, how paranoid I was, whether I saw bright colours, that sort of thing. I would then turn to the computer, on which I had a large collection of 1-minute video clips from films, which were arranged into a number of pools, each of which contained four clips that an independent researcher had previously selected so that they were as different from each other as possible. I had 20 of these pools lined up and so aimed to run 20 trials of the ESP task. Under the influence of mescaline it really would be a trial too.

After writing down my impressions of the target from my mescaline-enhanced visualisation process it was planned that I would then watch a pool of four video clips for the first time, having no idea what the clips were beforehand. Once I had watched all four it was then necessary to rank them according to how closely they corresponded to the mental images I had just had, which I had written down. Then comes the weird bit, I would then select which of the four film clips was to be the actual target by running a random number generator that would choose a number between one and four, in a manner that, according to ordinary linear conceptions of reality, cannot be predicted.

Thus one of the four clips would become the target *after* I had made my selection, but also completely independently of my selection.

Making the target selection after my attempted divination of it made this psi task a test of precognition – rather than telepathy or clairvoyance – which if successful would demonstrate the ability to access information from the future without recourse to inference or other ordinary means of prediction. This precognitive ability might also be also called prophecy, premonition or prescience. Ordinarily, attempting to guess the randomly selected target from one of four clips would produce a successful rate of target selection of 25% by chance alone, so that only one in every four of the clips I selected would be ranked as the most similar to my mental imagery if purely random processes where at work. Over a series of twenty trials like this it is therefore expected that the correct target would be selected just five times by chance alone.

Skipping breakfast in the morning I prepared the 30 grams of San Pedro for consumption by powdering it. Like peyote, San Pedro is known to taste extremely bitter and very difficult to eat or drink without wanting to vomit. Nature has a way of good way of ensuring that you have to be pretty serious if you want to eat these cacti. Having prepared myself mentally, and made my propitiations to the spirits in my own way, I poured the emetic powder straight to the back of my throat in 5g batches every five minutes or so and washed it down with orange juice as quickly as possible, taking care to get as little of the repulsive pulverulence anywhere on my taste buds. I started at 10:15am and within half an hour I had consumed an entire handful of the green-grey dust without any tears, but was beginning to feel increasingly nauseous. The nausea continued in waves, getting worse for a while and then finally abating so that by 2:30pm, more than four hours in, I finally noted that "less sick now, and actually enjoying this, at last".

Despite feeling sick I began testing at 12:08pm. I would start the experiment with a dummy test run that would not form part of the official count, just to make sure I could function properly and do what was required. Attempts to use the dictaphone left me overwhelmed by the fiddliness of technological endeavour required to actually get it to work that, feeling sick as a parrot, I abandoned it in favour of only a written account. I closed my eyes and let the visions come. A swirling liquid cocktail of imagery poured through my mind, morphing and reforming before I could fully comprehend the scene, constantly coalescing and dissolving again, and then occasionally forming something I could hang on to and actually name. Every time an image formed that was distinct enough to describe linguistically I would open my eyes and write, though my descriptions were pretty much limited to primitive machine gun grunts of nouns. "Ancient Greek scene. Eyes. (visuals too vague and fluid). City at night on a lake."

Given that the mental imagery was getting quite diverse I opted to stop there. Turning to the laptop I then opened the folder for the dummy trial and played the first film clip, wondering what would come up. I leapt, somewhat startled, as the speakers suddenly let rip with a strange animal cry, and the screen displayed a monster swinging a large club towards me. There was the sound of crushing metal as a warrior in a distinctly Greek helmet adorned with a plume of Mohawk-like stiff hair fell backwards, his shield crumpling under the blow of the Minotaur's mace. A fight to the death between the human-bull beast and the hero continued for an intense 60 seconds, ending quite abruptly just short of the decisive moment and recklessly derailing my utter absorption in the scene.

I laughed rapturously as I suddenly remembered what my reason for viewing the clip had been, having been so completely engrossed for the last minute that I had totally forgotten during that time what my sense of purpose was. Oh wow! I really laughed. I would have to watch at least another 80 clips throughout the day, a mind-boggling thought. I then watched the other three dummy clips and wrote "12:22, test run complete, very engrossed in clips, laughing at how lost I am when the clip ends." Looking back at what I had originally written I also saw that although the "city at night by a lake" was absent from any clips the "ancient Greek scene" fitted perfectly with the first clip, and this got me excited enough to almost make the nausea worthwhile. I didn't bother to run the randomiser to see if this was 'the target' this time, being just a dummy run.

Then it was time for the first proper trial. I made a note of my increasing nausea and the fact that my finger tips felt odd, and pressed on. Eyes closed, I dove into the swirling vortex of imagery again and fished around for something tangible. "12:32pm, rotating, like [heli-] copter blades, space, more mechanical stuff, space craft, space skeletons." A pause in imagery occurred, then, "water, submarine, big rig but underwater." Quickly then I completed the measures for gauging my state of consciousness, noting merely that I was 28% of the way between being 'normal' and 'extremely altered', and that my closed eye mental imagery was somewhat increased compared to normal.

Turning then to the video clips I began the judging phase of the first trial. Clip one started. Enter Luke Skywalker and Princess Leia in the classic escape scene from Star Wars. Luke and Leia have gone through a doorway onto a ledge overlooking a large drop inside the Death Star. "How do you get the blast door closed?" says Luke, "they're coming through" shouts Leia, and shuts the blast door, they are suspended on a ledge inside the huge machine that is the Death Star. They look around to try to find a way across the huge vertical chamber in front of them.

Suddenly laser fire comes in from the front, and slightly above. Stormtroopers have appeared at an open doorway across the chamber and are firing on our heroes. Luke shoots one of them and they back off for a moment. "Here hold this!" says Luke, handing Leia the gun. He then pulls out a small metal device on a string from his utility belt as Leia engages the Stormtroopers above in a gunfight. Luke pulls out more and more string from his belt as the blast door behind them begins to open a crack at the bottom. "Here they come!" shouts Leia. Lots of smoke now and more laser fire, Leia shoots one of the Stormtroopers above. Luke steps forward and hurls his metal device and string into the air and a small grappling hook consisting of three metal blades on a metal stem spins around a pole above and secures the end of the string line. Luke pulls the string tight, Leia grabs hold of him with her free arm, gun in the other, and kisses him quickly "for luck" she says, as he looks at her somewhat shocked. They launch into the air as the Stormtroopers behind them start to come through under the blast door on their bellies, shooting as they come through. Luke and Leia glide across the large chamber on the string swing just in time and land safely in another doorway on the otherside, casually tossing the string aside as they run to safety amid a hail of laser fire...

Wow! The clip ends. I must have whooped with excitement a couple of times watching the clip even though I had seen it many times before over the years. George Lucas sure knows how to pack in a lot of action into 60 seconds. A mere minute which actually seemed timeless as I had once again been utterly transfixed.

The next clip two clips were much less intense; a cartoon sequence of hippos dancing a ballet, followed by a clip of a flock of Seabirds flying across a browny-orange sky. Then finally a clip from the film Legend of a large blue and ugly hag emerging from a swamp and proposing to eat our armoured hero (a very young Tom Cruise) who cowers behind his shield and tries to flatter the hag out of killing him "You don't intend to eat me do you" he asks, "oh indeed I dooo" replies the hag. This last one I found particularly intense but as it ended I dragged my self out of my absorption in the story and back to the experiment. I began to review and rate the four clips in light of my prior mental imagery, and rank them in order of their similarity to my visions.

It's then I realized how closely my imagery matched the first clip, thematically at least, and quite literally in some ways too. "Rotating, like [heli-]copter blades, space, more mechanical stuff, space craft, space skeletons. Water, submarine, big rig but underwater." Certainly the association with space, space craft and space skeletons was completely obvious with Starwars, and writing now I see how the

Stormtroopers themselves have helmets that look like futuristic skulls – all white save for the black eye patches and the thin black mouth. Indeed the completely white and chunky uniform gave them a real sense of being some kind of techno or futuristic space skeletons, and I now see that this was probably a guiding principle in their ultimate cinematic design when the film was made.

It doesn't get any better than the Death Star either in terms of "more mechanical stuff" as the whole thing is supposed to be one big mechanical planet. And as for the "rotating, like [heli-]copter blades" the metal grappling hook span round and even looked like helicopter rotors. This was pretty convincing for me, and even though clip one was also like a big rig, and somewhat like a submarine I didn't need to find a match for the other bits of my visualisation, I happily ranked this clip number one, with some sense of confidence (42%). The final elements, "water", and "underwater" tied in with the hag emerging from the swamp clip, which I ranked number two, and the hippo emerging from a paddling pool, which I ranked number three. Having virtually no correspondence with my previous mental imagery I ranked the birds clip fourth.

Now began the moment of truth. I had recorded my choices, I now had to randomly determine which was the actual target clip. I opened the randomisation programme on the computer and ran the automated selection of a number between one and four, corresponding to clip 1, 2, 3 or 4 respectively. The computer presented number one as the target, so Star Wars *was* the target clip! I had got it right and, against the odds, successfully selected the correct clip. I then watched the target clip again, so that my viewing it might echo back in time and help my past self reach forward in time and select the right clip in the future – a kind of paradoxical confidence trick symmetrically across time, to ensure my past self would select the correct video. Riding the increasing wave of nausea, and also now my exaggerated sense of meaningfulness and oddity I was feeling, I was pleasantly surprised and pleased at my performance. Unfortunately, guessing just one clip in a batch of four does not really convince anyone that it was just due to psi though, and so I continued the whole process another 19 times, finally finishing the experiment a whole eight hours after ingesting the first inedible mouthful of purgative powder. This was to be a long and strange trip indeed.

Putting the Cork Back in the Bottle

I won't describe the entire experiment or the details of the results – that will eventually be published in a scientific journal, when I find time – but it is suffice to say that the experiment was a success in the end. By the end of the twenty trials I had successfully selected the target directly in advance 8 times out of 20, which, although better than chance, is not particularly extraordinary. However, the method by which I had planned in advance to analyse the data is slightly more refined. This method considers the rank assigned to each clip in relation to the probability of assigning that rank. In this way it would be expected that, out of a range of between one and four, the target would be ranked as 2.5 on average according to chance. The actual average target rank of all 20 trials was 2.0, indicating that my overall score was safely above chance. The important bit for scientists is that the probability of getting this score is less than 5%, or looking at it another way, less than 1 in 20, which is the level at which scientists accept that the results are meaningful. This means that if I selected my targets merely by chance, we would only expect to get these results if we run the entire experiment 20 times. The thought of this makes me feel quite queasy, anticipating feeling that nauseous for hours on end again another 20 times. So chance must take a back seat to improbability and the results as they are must be considered to be what scientists call 'statistically significant' – that is, the experiment, this time at least, must be accepted as successful in demonstrating precognition.

One problem, however, is we cannot be certain that it was the San Pedro that caused the significant results, because, perhaps, I have reliable precognitive abilities anyway, even without San Pedro. This is a possibility, of course, but it should be noted that my ability to visualise a scene in my mental imagery was definitely enhanced by the cactus, and it was the relationship of this visualisation to the clip that led to my accurate choices. A better experiment would have an identical series of comparison tests where I didn't take San Pedro but rather a dummy version of it – what we call a placebo controlled condition. But that is just wishful thinking because it really isn't easy to fake a San Pedro experience with a non-psychedelic substance. Sure, I could have eaten something to give me stomach cramps, but how to induce the sense of meaningfulness and the increased imagery? I would surely have known that the placebo was bogus.

One possibility, almost never used in research, would be use deep hypnotic suggestion to artificially re-induce the same psychedelic state without the use of the cactus, combined with a suggestion to make me think that I had actually taken the cactus rather than being hypnotized. This kind of hypnotic re-induction of psychedelic states has been demonstrated experimentally at least once (Hastings et al., 2000) but inducing selective amnesia requires especially suggestible participants.

This approach has other problems as well, but I won't continue with this line of attack because ALL scientific research has its limitations, and there are always methodological issues to surmount. What is really required is that somebody else replicates my research findings, otherwise, currently, they can only be considered preliminary at best, but nevertheless very promising.

For me, stepping away from the endless scientific debate that could engulf the experiment I have described, and talking in a purely non-scientific way, the sense of awe and surprise at getting many of the targets correct speaks directly to my sense of truth. It's not just the getting them right either, because improbable statistics alone do not convey much meaning, but rather it was the degree to which my mental imagery under the influence of San Pedro repeatedly matched the specific target for the trial. The Star Wars example is quite typical of the hits I had, for instance, but to give another example, on one occasion I wrote "desert, dunes, sands of time" for one trial, and the actual target, which I had also selected, showed a sidewinder snake elegantly traversing the sand dunes of a desert in its unique and perplexing sideways motion: A good metaphor, perhaps, for the equally sideways movement through time and space that psi embodies. One of the oddest things, though, was that on several occasions I would have an image of something which I would write down in a simple form, such as "broken body", and then three or four of the clips would all have elements clearly related to that specific imagery. On these occasions I tended not to pick the target directly as was hoped, but nevertheless it seemed as though I were visualising all four of the coming clips in some oddly synchronistic and codified way despite their supposedly being selected as a pool of four for being as different from each other as possible.

The mind is certainly a maze to get lost in, and from my own experience I am amazed at the apparent accuracy of some of my imagery and that which can be found reported in the literature from those healers that work with such plants as a way of life. I am no shaman, nor healer, I am just a scientist, but the personal significance to me of this research leaves me indebted to those curanderos, healers, vegetalistas and shamans who have kept these interspecies relationships alive for millennia, in the name of their community and for the sake of their environment (Krippner & Luke, 2009). It would serve us well in the West to remember though that science is only one path to truth, thankfully there are many others, because, as the saying goes, the universe is not only stranger than we imagine, but stranger than we *can* imagine.

CHAPTER 2

Psychedelic Possession:
The Growing Incorporation of Incorporation
into Ayahuasca Use

Sometimes an astonishing discovery can be simultaneously eclipsed by the realisation of something even more astonishing – in this case it was the fact that the discovery was astonishing in the first place. A few years ago, whilst researching the use of the highly psychoactive Amazonian jungle decoction called ayahuasca and its magico-religious use in Brazil I was informed that incorporation rituals had been adopted for use in in recent years within the practices of the Santo Daime church, a syncretic Christian ayahuasca-using group widespread in Brazil.

Brazil is, of course, home to numerous new syncretic Christian Afro-Brazilian religions, such as Umbanda, which combines elements of European, indigenous Brazilian and African diaspora religious influence. One of the core features of Umbanda is the utilisation of trance 'incorporation' – a term preferred by practitioners (e.g., Marques, 2007) and some researchers (e.g., Groisman, 2013) for what has elsewhere been called voluntary possession (e.g., Oesterreich, 1966), or trance or spirit possession (e.g., Bourguignon, 1976; Klass, 2003; Lewis, 1978), although some contemporary writers continue to use the terms interchangeably (e.g., Dawson, 2010, 2011, 2012), whereas others discuss the inherent difficulty in defining such a cross-culturally nuanced phenomenon as possession (e.g., Cohen, 2008).

Slowly, over the last few decades, there has been a growing fusion of these two techniques of magico-religious practice (Dawson, 2011, 2012), with individuals within Santo Daime church combining both incorporation and the ingestion of psychedelic potions within the same ritual, a combination that is appropriately termed *Umbandaime*. On first hearing about this I was astonished because psychedelic possession or incorporation is so rarely discussed in the literature, but, then, the more I thought about it, I became increasingly astonished at this fact in itself. The question arose as to why there is an apparent absence of incorpo-

ration with traditional plant psychedelic use, when so many other ostensibly paranormal or parapsychological practices abound with these
substances; be it divination, psychic diagnosis, shamanic healing, mediumship and communication with other spirits, out-of-body experiences
and travelling clairvoyance, and so on (see Section Two). This lead to
further questions, such as how incorporation became incorporated into
ritual ayahuasca use, and what this in itself signifies.

Before proceeding, however, a note here is required to indicate that
this essay does not explore the ontology (i.e., the nature of the reality)
of the experiences here described, be it entity encounters or possession,
as detailed discussion of the relevant arguments can be found elsewhere
(for possession see, e.g., Bourguignon, 1976; Klass, 2003; Lewis, 1978;
for psychedelic entity encounters see Chapters 5-7of *Otherworlds*). Indeed, Lewis (1978, p.26) notes that, "the majority of anthropological
writers on possession have been...absorbed in often quite pointless de-
bates as to the genuineness or otherwise of particular trance states."

The Growing Incorporation of Incorporation into Ayahuasca Use

While conducting research amongst ayahuasca groups in northern Brazil a few years ago I was surprised to come across a branch of Santo
Daime that utilized incorporation in its ceremonies, and so I conducted an interview with one of the mediums. Having previously trained
in Harner Foundation (non-psychedelic) shamanic counselling in the
US, the medium already had a Native American spirit guide prior to
joining the CEFLURIS Santo Daime church at Mapiá, in the Amazon,
in the 1990s. Curiously enough, the native spirit guide was somebody
who had been friends with the medium before they had died. Working
alongside Santo Daime mediums already utilising the Umbanda spirits
at Mapiá he trained in Umbandaime but continued to use his native
American guide as his main incorporating spirit under the influence
of ayahuasca – even working on one of the lead mediums at Mapiá
and becoming accepted into the circle of practising mediums, consisting only of women. The medium eventually left Mapiá and continued
working in northern Brazil, where we met, and he informed me about
the relatively unknown combination of ayahuasca and incorporation.

Despite the relative obscurity of Umbandaime outside of Brazilian
Spiritist circles, some English language texts are available that plot
the history and contemporary practice of Umbandaime (e.g., Dawson,
2010, 2011, 2012; Marques, 2007; Polari, 1999), and can be consulted

for a more comprehensive account than that given here. Starting with Umbanda, as the oldest branch, its history is somewhat hazy, but it undoubtedly has its origins in the fusion of Afro-Brazilian religious influences and Kardecist Spiritism – a system of belief similar to the Spiritualism of Victorian Britain but which is based on the teachings of the 19th century French spiritual philosopher Allan Kardec. Perhaps the earliest agreed progenitor of Umbanda is a young navy cadet officer called Zélio de Moraes who, in 1920 in the city of São Gonçalo, across the bay from Rio de Janeiro, defied the usual Kardecist Spiritist practices of the day during a séance when he incorporated both indigenous (caboclo) and African slave (preto velho) spirits of the dead, rather than the usual Caucasian ones (Brown, 1994).

Sometime later in the 1920s Moraes set up the first Umbanda 'centro' in Niteroi, which then moved to central Rio where it flourished. Combining Catholicism, Spiritism and Afro-Brazilian influences – especially the incorporation of Orixás (deities, typically of Yoruba origin), pretos velhos and caboclos – and the use of mediumship, Umbanda is also porous to other religious and esoteric influences and fast became popular among the middle classes and the poorer communities alike. It spread widely in Brazil during the 1970s and 1980s and had 17,000 registered centros by 1990 (Brown, 1994) but numbers gradually declined after that.

It was shortly after the formation of Umbanda in the urban sprawls of eastern Brazil that Santo Daime emerged from the jungles of Acre in western Brazil in the 1930s. As a rubber tapper in the forest, the healer Raimundo Irineu Serra (Mestre Irineu) encountered indigenes using ayahuasca in a shamanic manner and developed its use as a sacrament in a Christian-based religion – albeit one without recourse to scripture, and where some importance was given to interaction with nature spirits, though not spirits of the dead (Dawson, 2011, 2012). This first Santo Daime community was called Alto Santo and fractured in the 1970s, following Mestre Irineu's death, when Padrinho Sebastião Mota de Melo broke away and founded the Centro Ecléctico da Fluente Luz Universal Raimundo Irineu Serra (CEFLURIS) branch, which ultimately situated itself in Céu do Mapiá, Amazonas, deep in the jungle.

Other non-Santo Daime churches also appeared in the early years, the two largest surviving ones of which we know being the Barquinha and the União do Vegetal (UDV). Having also practised with Mestre Irineu in Rio Branco, Acre, the ex-sailor Daniel Pereira de Mattos (Frei Daniel) established the Barquinha (little boat) religious community there in 1945, and it never spread much beyond the state of Acre (Labate, 2006). The last of the three ayahuasca religions to be formed, the UDV, began its lineage independently of the Santo Daime and was officially established in Porto Velho (state of Rondônia) in 1965 by the rubber tapper José Gabriel da Costa (Mestre Gabriel), although it was also reputedly founded in 1961 at the Sunta rubber camp on the Bolivian-Brazilian border (Goulert, 2006).

To varying degrees, each of the three groups have clear tri-continental spiritual inspirations. There are European influences, such as Catholicism and Kardecist Spiritism in all three, and even Masonry in the case of UDV. Afro-Brazilian influences from the Umbanda cult, for example, are also apparent in all of them, with elements of the African Casa das Minas and other traditions as well in the UDV (Luke, 2011d). Finally, each group is ultimately defined by its utilisation of Brazilian indigenous practices through the utilisation of ayahuasca itself.

Each of these continental influences provides its own methodology for approaching the divine: Prayer in the case of Catholicism, visionary experience from the indigenes, and incorporation from the African traditions (Araújo, 2006), although it should be noted that the French Spiritist influence also champions incorporation too. Additionally, each technique also offers a different relationship to the spirit world: Prayer facilitates faith in, and a reverence for spirit, visions mediate a direct experience of spirit, and incorporation enables a becoming, or merging with spirit (Luke, 2011d).

In accordance with the doctrinal influences at play in each of the three ayahuasca groups we see varying degrees of recourse to these three spiritual technologies, particularly with regard to incorporation. Despite Mestre Gabriel's prior Kardecist spirit guide incorporations and although heavily influenced by Afro-Brazilian religion, the UDV do not incorporate (Goulart, 2006), whereas the Barquinha do (Araújo, 2006; Groisman, 2013), and probably did so before Santo Daime. Nevertheless, the Barquinha refer to their incorporation mediumship as a less complete embodiment of spirits with the term 'irradiation', in that the spirit radiates through them rather than fully incorporating (Frenopoulo, 2006). Finally, within the Santo Daime – the oldest, largest and most widespread of the three religions – a growing 'Umbandaization' (Dawson, 2012) of the religious practice is evident within the widespread CEFLURIS branch.

The Prepossessing Power of Possession

This synthesized practice initially began in 1977 when Padrinho Sebastião, a Spiritist medium prior to joining the Santo Daime in the mid-1960s, began incorporation of several spirits while suffering an illness that lasted three years, following the murder by daimistas of an apparent Quimbanda practitioner at Padrinho Sebastião's centre in Rio Branco (Marques, 2007). By the time CEFLURIS Santo Daime (hereafter just called Santo Daime) arrived at Mapiá in 1983 the Padrinho and his followers, who now included growing numbers of counterculture itinerants from across Brazil and beyond, had developed a number of rituals utilising incorporation, though their use was limited.

In the early 1980s Santo Daime expanded and two churches opened in Rio de Janeiro, bringing in a further surge of white middle-class followers, and with them came elements of Umbanda, which was extremely popular at that time in Rio. The urban daimistas in turn increasingly reached Mapiá, and by 1990, when Padrinho Sebastião died, the third generation of Santo Daime leadership saw the widespread use of incorporation, which by the late 1990s had become part of their cultic calendar (Dawson, 2011). Currently, according to Dawson (2011, 2012) Umbandaime is continuing to grow in popularity, with increasing numbers of both followers and incorporation rituals and styles within Santo Daime. Curiously, however, the use of ayahuasca, or Santo Daime, is apparently not being adopted in return by Umbanda centros, although some Umbanda followers are joining the Santo Daime churches. Indeed, there is now a church in São Paulo that calls itself a temple of Umbandaime (see www.umbandaime.com.br) and the cult even has its own active Facebook group.

Psychedelic Possession Outside of Umbandaime and Barquinha

In many ways both psychedelic plant practice and mediumship – be it through incorporation or through clairaudience – most likely have their roots in what modern researchers loosely call shamanism. Shamanism, strictly speaking, comes from the Tungusic word šaman and, according to Eliade (1972), it is pre-eminently a religious phenomenon of Siberia whereby the ecstatic state is considered the religious experience par excellence and so, in its simplest sense, shamanism is the mastery of techniques of ecstasy.

The term shaman has since been applied by researchers from various fields to those in other cultures who perform similar functions. Shamanism also utilizes religious, magical, spiritual, healing and trance aspects but is not essentially just any one of these things (Eliade, 1972), and alternatively has been described as comprising "a group of techniques by which practitioners deliberately alter or heighten their conscious awareness to enter the so-called 'spirit-world', accessing material that they use to help and to heal members of the social group that has acknowledged their shamanic status" (Krippner, 2000, p.98). Typical magico-religious techniques for altering consciousness include what may be called 'magical flight' or 'soul flight' and possession (i.e., incorporation), as well as auditory driving techniques (e.g., chanting, singing and drumming), fasting, drugs, austerities, isolation, sleep deprivation, seizures, etc. (Winkelman, 1990).

Thought of by many as the primary magico-religious activity of humans, predating all religions (e.g., Eliade, 1972; Winkelman, 1990), the origins of the practice of both mediumship and psychedelic plant usage are thought to stem from shamanism. However, not all shamanism utilizes psychedelic plants, nor incorporation, so neither practice should define shamanism, indeed a survey by Peters and Price-Williams (1980) of 42 different shamanic-like groups across the globe found a variety of ways in which trance was utilized. Spirit possession, defined as "any altered state of consciousness (ASC) indigenously interpreted in terms of the influence of an alien spirit", was found to be practised solely by 43% of the groups investigated, whereas 24% practised only magical flight, defined as an ASC "interpreted as soul journey to heaven, other worlds, underground, or horizontally" (Peters & Price-Williams, 1980, p.408). A further 26% practised both types of trance, whereas only 7% practised neither, so it can be seen that spirit possession, or incorporation, is widely practised across different cultures, indeed in the majority of those (69%) studied in this survey.

Unfortunately, no evaluation is made by Peters and Price-Williams of the relative number of different ethnic groups practicing shamanism that combine both incorporation and the use of plant psychedelics. However, some simple exploration of the 42 groups in the survey reveals that only 7% of the groups are particularly renowned for making use of psychoactive plants in their typical practices (14% if you include the use of tobacco), and of these only the tobacco-using Akawaio and the *Amanita muscaria* mushroom-using Chukchi engage in spirit possession, accounting for only 7% of those groups using spirit possession.

Lending some support to this supposed capacity of *A. muscaria*, the pioneering psychedelic mushroom researchers Wasson and Wasson (1957) note that while most 'mycophobic' (fungus fearing) nationals, such as the English, traditionally ascribe poisonous qualities to this mushroom, the French historically referred to it as causing demonic possession. Nevertheless, it is clear from these two cases in Peters and

Price-Williams' (1980) survey that the combination of both incorporation and use of psychedelics within shamanism is not common. Indeed, the identified incorporation may not even be typically mediumistic, as with the Akawaio whose incorporation occurs on an ongoing basis with multiple spirits, so that the shaman's body can house his own spirit and numerous others, which stay with him all the time (Butt, Wavell & Epton, 1966) in what Lewis (1978) describes as a constant state of latent possession.

There are also geographical trends in the distribution of indigenous groups utilising plant psychedelics or engaging in incorporation. In a survey of what she called 488 different indigenous 'societies' distributed around the globe, Bourguignon (1976) found that 52% engaged in what she termed possession trance, but that it was far more prevalent in sub-Saharan Africa (66%) than in the Americas, especially among North American indigenous groups (25%). Conversely, the traditional indigenous use of plant psychedelics is far more prevalent in the so-called New World (the Americas), than elsewhere, particularly Africa and Europe (see Schultes & Hofmann, 1992). For example, Luna (1986) indicates that at least 72 indigenous groups in the western Amazon region alone make use of ayahuasca, and this is only one of many ethnobotanical psychedelics in the Americas.

Taking a similar approach to Peters and Price-Williams, by surveying 47 different magico-religious healing practitioner groups, Winkelman (1990) aimed to determine a taxonomy of the different spiritual technicians occurring in the sample. Extracting over 200 phenomenological variables, and reducing and clustering these using various analytic techniques, a number of distinct practitioner clusters emerged. Only those termed shamans or shaman-healers made use of psychedelic plants and magical flight, whereas those termed mediums did not make use of psychedelics and (all but one) engaged in 'possession trance' (incorporation). Different socioeconomic conditions prevailed for these different groups too, with shamans occurring only among nomadic and hunter-gatherer people, shaman-healers among agricultural subsistence people, and mediums typically occurring among more politically integrated and sedentary cultures. Additionally, whereas shamans and shaman-healers were typically selected by illness, involuntary visions, dreams or vision quests, the mediums were selected on the basis of their spontaneous possession experiences (Winkelman, 1990).

Applying Winkelman's (1990) grouping to the shamanic cultures selected in the Peters and Price-Williams (1980) survey would surely lead to a reclassification of many of the purely spirit possession shamanic groups to the status of mediums, rather than shamans. Perhaps most importantly, what we find from Winkelman's research is that the use of psychedelics and incorporation tend to occur separately in distinct magico-religious practitioner categories, as largely supported by the statistics above that emerged *post hoc* when I explored Peters and Price-Williams' survey data, and to some extent by global geographical trends too.

Of course, there are some examples of indigenous groups who utilise psychedelic plant shamanism in conjunction with incorporation, but these seem to be the exception rather than the rule. Reference to such pharmacologically aided incorporation is occasionally made in texts on possession (e.g., Bourguignon, 1976; Klass, 2003; Sargant, 1973), but typically without recourse to good evidence, authoritative references or even identification of the substances or peoples involved. It would take a thorough and massive research undertaking to make a comprehensive analysis, but based on a preliminary review of a good number of relevant texts it proved difficult to discover much reference to both practices among the same people.

Two exceptions, besides those mentioned above, are the Yanomami of Venezuela (e.g., Jokic, 2008b) who utilise 'epena' or 'yopo' snuff (usually derived from *Anadenanthera peregrina* seeds), and incorporate various hekura spirits. The other is the Mitsogho people of Gabon who utilise both iboga (*Tabernanthe iboga*) and incorporation in their rituals (Maas & Strubelt, 2003), although this is apparently reserved for female Ombwiri (or Ombudi) trance possession initiates only, who may use the iboga to assist in their vision of the healing genies (Goutarel, Gollnhofer, & Sillans, 1993).

Any Body for Anybody: Shape Sharing or Shape Shifting?

Despite identifying their incorporation, Jokic (2008b) notes that the Yanomami retain both consciousness and control over their actions during hekura spirit incorporation, and relates it to the state of shamanic transformation, metamorphosis or shapeshifting into a spirit animal, which is prevalent among psychedelic plant shamanic groups. Indeed the experience of shapeshifting into an animal under the influence of psychedelic substances is relatively well known.

In a recent survey (Luke & Yanakieva, 2016) of 150 Euro-American psychedelic enthusiasts some 10% of LSD and 27% of ayahuasca users reported the experience of transforming into another species, whereas a survey of 26,121 mostly Euro-American psilocybin users found 15% of the sample reporting this experience (Carbonara, Johnson & Griffiths, 2017).

Elsewhere, the particular experience of transformation into large felines is conspicuous, as has been reported by more than one anthropologist experimenting with large doses of LSD (Masters & Houston, 1966; Rätsch, 2004), a psychologist experimenting with ayahuasca (Shanon, 2002) and a psychotherapist experimenting with harmaline (a typical chemical constituent of ayahuasca) (Naranjo, 1973a), and which is also a known myth or experience of indigenous ayahuasca shamanism, such as among the Cashinahua (Lagrou, 2000), the Sharanahua (Siskind, 1973), and the Shipibo-Conibo (Harner, 1973a) of Brazil and Peru, and the Tukano of Colombia (Reichel-Dolmatoff, 1975).

Indeed, Stone (2011) notes that shamanic transformation into a jaguar is still a widespread belief in the Amazon. However, it has been noted that, unlike mediumistic incorporation per se, shamanic incorporation – if that is what it is – of animals is not of a specific deceased animal but of the spirit of the "tiger-in-general" (Gauld, 1983, p.17).

In his assessment of psychedelics in European witchcraft, Harner (1973b) presents evidence that the solanaceous plants (such as mandrake, henbane, belladonna and datura), were supposedly favoured by witches for shapeshifting activities and were the source of reports of lycanthropy, which were in truth only lycanthropy experiences rather than actual objective shapeshifting phenomena. Additionally, Harner (1973b) notes from his anthropological fieldwork in Ecuador among the Shuar (inappropriately termed the Jivaro), that they use both solanaceous and non-solanaceous psychedelics in their shamanic practices, but they only use the solanaceous datura privately for vision quests because it is so strong as to prevent the shaman from performing their normal (e.g., under the influence of ayahuasca) ritual activities.

In regards to shapeshifting then, Yanomami incorporation by hekura spirits does not map directly to the mediumistic incorporation by personified Orixás or the spirits of slaves as found in Umbanda, but seems to be more of a general animal spirit transformation or incorporation. However, beside the jaguar spirit noted by Jocik (2008b) examples of some of the hundreds, or perhaps thousands (Chagnon, 1992) of hekura that exist include the moon spirit, the darkness spirit, the spirit of the whirlpool, and the Milky Way spirit (Lizot, 1991), so such incorporation is neither standard mediumship nor all shapeshifting it would seem. Furthermore, it's a moot point whether a line can be drawn between incorporation by the spirits of the deceased and the spirits of nature with the Yanomami.

One further thing to consider is that, with the incorporation of hekura spirits, the shaman sings the spirits - which are between a few millimetres and a couple of inches in size - into their chests where they can be commanded, either to be sent to harm one's enemies, or to help cure sick kinsman (Chagnon, 1992). Perhaps the difference between this and typical shamanic control of spirits, as opposed to mediumistic incorporation, is that the Yanomami shaman keeps his numerous spirits under control in his chest, instead of externally as with other shamans – though the notions of things internal and external to one's body is somewhat arbitrary with the concept of magical flight, where the body remains where it is but one's consciousness 'travels'. In any case it is the issue of control and command that is crucial here, as Lewis (1978) notes, although they are also possessed by the spirits, the Tungus shamans say that they themselves possess the spirits in return.

With the possible exception of the Yanomami then, and perhaps the Chukchi and the Mitsogho (and neighbouring Fang), and the Akewaio – if you include tobacco as a psychedelic, which it can be with high enough doses of nicotine – there are few apparent shamanic groups that mix plant psychedelics with incorporation, with the spirits of deceased humans at least. The question remains why this is so. Psychedelic explorer and bard Terence McKenna offers an insight into this by suggesting that shamanism transcends mediumistic incorporation as it aims to command rather than merely communicate with spirits:

> The essential and defining element of shamanism is ecstasy. The shaman is a specialist in the sacred, able to abandon his body and undertake cosmic journeys "in the spirit" (in trance). "Possession" by spirits, although documented in a great many shamanisms, does not seem to have been a primary and essential element. Rather, it suggests a phenomenon of degeneration; for the supreme goal of the shaman is to abandon his body and rise to heaven or descend into hell – not to let himself be "possessed" by his assisting spirits, by demons or the souls of the dead; the shaman's ideal is to master these spirits, not to let himself be "occupied" by them (McKenna, 1992, p.58).

Indeed, Eliade (1972) earlier asserted this position by stating that the primary phenomenon of shamanism is magical flight to the heavens or the underworld, not incorporation and even though this latter phenomenon is universally distributed in its use by shamans it does not necessarily belong to shamanism – although others disagree (for a discussion see Lewis, 1978; Peters & Price-Williams, 1980). One instance of possible support for Eliade's position comes from Jocik's (2008a) research with Buriat shamans. Following years of suppression under Soviet anti-religious ideology, traditional Buriat shamanism all but died out but is now being revived, except that shamans now practice a kind of amnesic incorporated mediumship, and indicate that they have not yet developed the skills required to attain the amnesic-less trance magical flight state of their forebears. Jocik argues that the lack of shamanic flight and memory is a side effect of the lack of inherited initiation into shamanic practice and represents an impoverished form of shamanism. In any event, whether incorporation is separate to shamanism or not, psychedelic incorporation, in particular, seems very much the exception rather than rule given that the two practices are seldom elsewhere combined but, independently, are both globally widespread.

Psychedelic Possession Outside of Shamanism, and Inside Ordinary People

Outside of the anthropological literature there are a few isolated cases of psychedelic-induced incorporation or possession, of course, but 'few' is very much the operative term here. For example, the original discoverer/inventor of LSD, the chemist Albert Hofmann, describes the initial stages of his first accidental LSD trip thus:

> All my efforts of will seemed in vain; I could not stop the disintegration of the exterior world and the dissolution of my ego. A demon had invaded me and taken possession of my body, my senses, and my soul. A terrible fear that I had lost my mind grabbed me. I had entered another world, a different dimension, a different time (Hagenbach & Wertmüller, 2013, p.43).

However, as the first person ever to take LSD, nay, to spike himself unwittingly with LSD, Hofmann was perhaps scratching around and seized the notion of possession as a trope within which to couch his experience, for certainly there was no wealth of well-voyaged psychonautical log books or psychedelic language available upon which to draw in 1943 when Hofmann's surprise trip occurred. Undisputedly, though, he had no control of the experience and, at times, of his body, and while he looked on as his ego dissolved he felt he had become possessed, and yet the kind of demonic possession to which Hofmann refers is rarely reported, and indeed Hofmann's trip ended somewhat less fearfully and he returned to normal. It is possible that Hofmann was speaking metaphorically, or that he feared he had been possessed, for bad trips had no cultural context at that time, and he reports none of the behaviour of possession, only the lack of ordinary control, though nothing else, demonic or otherwise, compelled him in lieu of his own volition.

Nevertheless, in the course of my research into psychedelics and ostensible paranormal phenomena (Luke, 2012d) I have received two first-hand accounts of supposed spontaneous (involuntary) incorporation with MDMA, both benign, and a further second-hand account where a witness believed a person under the influence of LSD was possessed, and which involved some violence and self harming. However, these isolated cases come from encounters with many hundreds of people who have taken psychedelics, with many having done so thousands of times, so the incidence of this phenomenon would seem very low. Indeed, even for those who are experienced in incorporation the use of psychedelics is not an incorporation trigger, at least in the case of the Voodoo mambo that anthropologist Francis Huxley (1966) gave LSD to, as she ended up having a conversation with one of her loa rather than being incorporated by them. As such, though without much evidence, possession researcher Bourguignon, is of the opinion that, "possession trance is not induced by drugs, alcohol or other biological or biochemical factors" (Bourguignon, 1976, p.41).

While Huxley's mambo is an isolated case it points to something extraordinary about the use of psychedelics, and that is that encounters with supernatural entities are relatively common, or at least they may be relatively common with the right set, setting and substance. In some cases, however, only the substance in the right dosage is necessary. Giving the endogenous psychedelic compound N,N-dimethyltryptamine (DMT) to research volunteers, psychiatric researcher Strassman (2008) reported that over half of the high dose participants had at least one entity encounter experience, though possession was not reported. Survey data from non-clinical users and non-users of psychedelics also supports this (Luke & Kittenis, 2005) with 32% of those using psychedelics reporting entity encounter experiences occurring under the influence of psychedelics, compared to 2% of those under the influence of non-psychedelic psychoactive drugs (e.g., alcohol, prescription drugs). In the same survey, encounters with divine beings under the influence of psychedelics was reported by 28% of illicit drug users, compared to 0% of non psychedelic-users while under the influence of non-psychedelic psychoactive drugs.

And yet despite these relatively high rates of supernatural entity encounter experiences with the non-indigenous non-clinical use of psychedelics, reports of possession are scarce – in fact practically the only references to psychedelic drug possession in the literature relate to the legalities of having a psychedelic substance in one's possession. So, to add to Eliade's (1972), McKenna's (1992) and Winkelman's (1990) assessment that, in the encounter of spiritual entities, shamanism primarily entails magical flight and not trance possession – psychedelics themselves tend to lead those using them towards entity encounter experiences rather than entity incorporation experiences, and so traditionally psychedelics best serve a possession-less shamanic spirit encounter, as in magical flight, rather than a full blown possession experience. Among occultists this distinction reflects the difference between evocation and invocation, and the use of drugs is generally only advised for the former (e.g., Carroll, 1987), although some modern occult psychonauts, presumably previously practised in spirit invocation, do occasionally attempt intentional incorporation (i.e., invocation) under the influence of psychedelics (e.g., Xeper, 2005), though such accounts are rare and come with a disclaimer.

So Why is Umbandaime on the Rise?

Buried within this question lies its opposite, why isn't traditional psychedelic shamanism particularly engaged in incorporation? Could it be that the Yanomami, Chuckchi, Akawaio, Fang and Mitsogho shamans are playing a dangerous game by utilising both powerful mind altering substances and somewhat risky spirit possession? Perhaps - though both paths separately have their own challenges and dangers, but relative risk assessments are not meaningful or possible within the scope of this essay. One thing to note is that the incorporation is conducted by specialist mediums in the case of the Fang and Mitsogho, and with the Yanomami and the Akawaio it often involves the control of multiple spirits simultaneously rather than the simple 'one host one spirit' typical of ritual incorporation practices, so such psychedelic possession is apparently not straightforward even when it is practised.

So, too, Santo Daime and the derivative Umbandaime are practices likewise not typically shamanic, but instead somewhat divorced from the shamanic ayahuasca practice from which they were themselves derived. It is not clear which indigenous group was first encountered by Mestre Irineu in the jungles of Acre that then lead to his discovery of ayahuasca and the formation of the Santo Daime church – perhaps it was the Kashinawa – but typically among Amazonian tribes, non-shamans may drink ayahuasca within a ritual or healing context, but, traditionally, it is not taken in a regimented religious manner as it is with Santo Daime.

Drawing upon Winkelman's (1990) taxonomy of magico-religious practitioners, it is apparent that the use of ayahuasca was adapted from hunter-gatherers, most likely, and slowly reinvented for the sedentary politically integrated people of Brazil. Initially these early daimistas were the poor, racially mixed working-classes of the sparsely populated state of Acre, but increasingly these became predominantly more the white middle-class professionals of the Brazilian mega-cities (Dawson, 2011, 2012). And as the religion's demographic shifted this way so too did its attitude towards mediumship, increasingly conforming to Winkelman's classification of mediumistic, not shamanic, practice. Nevertheless, besides the drinking of ayahuasca itself, Santo Daime still retains some shamanic elements, such as soul flight, at least for those few daimistas who perceive it that way (Dawson, 2012).

As a consequence of this apparent 'religionising' of a shamanic practice, the somewhat distinct role of shaman has become diluted. For despite having a padrino in the Santo Daime *works* (ceremonies), there is no one person who takes the sole shaman role and many within the work adopt the role of shaman-healer, ultimately leading to the addition of 'trance possession' to the practice as the system evolves in the manner in which Winkelman (1990) envisages that shamanism changes with increased socioeconomic development. Indeed, with all of the established congregation having a role – a vast increase in the number of roles available within the Umbandaime setting relative to the traditional shamanic use of ayahuasca – the whole evolutionary chain of Winkelman's magico-religious practitioner taxonomy is represented in one sitting, with everything from shamanism to incorporation being performed.

A good example, from elsewhere, of this possible evolution of shamanism towards mediumship via modernisation comes from Harner's (1972) fieldwork with the Shuar. Harner is informed by Shuar shamans that the Canelos shamans upriver, who are more integrated with foreign missionaries than the Shuar, are said to possess the "white man's" tsensak (spirit) and can perform feats not possible for other shamans in the region, such as the ability to become possessed with the souls of the dead and to act as oral mediums. Similarly, some researchers (e.g., Dobkin de Rios & Rumrrill, 2008) consider that the influx of "Western" ayahausca tourists in Peru is likewise breaking down the traditional craft of psychedelic shamanism, so that ayahuasca shamanism is becoming commercialised in Peru as much as Santo Daime has partially religionized ayahuasca shamanism in Brazil and beyond. Indeed, evidence of this religionization is apparent from some Amazonian Brazilian indigenous groups of Kashinawa and Apurinã who have recently been converting to Santo Daime (Labate, 2006).

Nevertheless, numerous researchers assert that Santo Daime practices remains shamanic (for a review see Labate, 2006), though many of these researchers were writing before the period in which Umbandaime began flourishing. Alternatively Cemin (1998) views shamanism as only involving 'ex-corporation' (i.e., magical flight) and so the incorporation practices of CELFURIS render this branch of Santo Daime not shamanic, whereas the original Alto Santo branch remains shamanic, though Labate (2006) suggests this is more an artefact of Cemin's theoretical model than an empirical fact. Ultimately, however, whether Santo Daime retains shamanic elements within its practices or not, it is de facto an organized religion with a large body of followers and includes many non-shamanic, mediumistic and religious elements – rather than being the magico-religious practice of an individual working alone for the benefit of their community.

Shamanic... or Individualistic, Pluralistic, Consumerist and Technologized?

In the view of Dawson (2011, 2012) the specific type of incorporation that is becoming most popular reveals a great deal about the cultural direction in which the religion is being pulled. Accordingly, Dawson, somewhat functionalistically, posits that the use of incorporation in Umbandaime takes three forms; private possession and expressive possession – both of which are types of individual possession – and interactive possession.

Private possession is the incorporation of spirits in such a way as to not distract others during the work, and provides an opportunity for daimistas to exert their ability to remain disciplined, firm and focused in the face of the challenging circumstances of being under the influence of ayahuasca, and in praying with the less evolved spirit that they are hosting.

Expressive possession involves the incorporation of the classic Umbanda spirits, such as the coboclos and pretos velhos, and despite a traditional resistance to incorporation by Orixás these too are also now increasingly appearing in daimista trances (Dawson, 2012, 2012). This rather more theatrical kind of possession, according to Dawson (2011, p.155), "appears to have no obvious ritual function other than the dramatic externalisation of the incorporating spirit's presence."

Finally, interactive possession is utilized only by trained mediums who incorporate suffering spirits of the dead in order to help them, usually through the assistance of other mediums – who sometimes incorporate higher spirits to help them. This kind of possession is a work of charity, and allows mediums to distribute healing energy to others and to act in an oracular manner to advise others in the group. This latter type of possession is performed almost entirely by women.

In categorising the different types of Umbandaime possession Dawson notes that expressive possession is the type that is becoming most popular amongst the growing urban-professional daimistas. Available to all Umbandaimistas, not just trained mediums, the theatrical expressive possession meets the demands of the "self assertive and expressive preoccupations of the late-modern individual" (Dawson, 2011, p.160), and characterises the 'new era spectrum' urban professional, who typically embody an individualistic, pluralistic, consumerist and technologized worldview. In the view of Dawson, the Umbandization of Santo Daime, in effect, is a direct consequence of modernisation, urbanisation and gentrification, thereby somewhat indirectly supporting the mapping of Winkelman's (1990) evolution of magico-religious practitioners, as outlined earlier.

Synthesis and Analysis

Incorporation as a practice is no stranger to shamanism, and is fairly common in various indigenous groups across the globe, particularly in Africa. However, some researchers argue that magical flight, as opposed to incorporation, is the defining mode of spirit contact in shamanism, and according to Winkelman's data-driven classification of magico-religious practitioners, shamans and incorporating mediums belong in distinct categories and generally have different lifestyle modes and exist in different socio-economic strata. The use of psychedelic plants for spirit contact is also fairly widespread within global shamanism, and is especially prevalent in the Americas, where shamanic incorporation is less apparent.

Even though there remains a possibility that psychedelic possession is relatively common – but for some reason goes largely unreported – there is good reason to accept that the use of psychedelic plants combined with incorporation is uncommon within shamanism, particularly in public healing rituals. Furthermore, although supernatural entity encounters are fairly widespread among non-indigenous, non-clinical, psychedelic users there remains an apparent lack of reports of spontaneous possession, or even intentional incorporation with these substances, somewhat matching the trends in the shamanic use of psychedelics. It would seem, then, that psychedelics are better suited to magical flight than incorporation.

One theory put forward for the apparent preference for magical flight over incorporation among shamans is that shamanism is not about relinquishing control to the spirits but about controlling them so they can do one's bidding. Possible gender explanations probably deserve exploration in this regard too, as mediumistic incorporation is typically performed by women (Kehoe & Giletti, 1981) whereas shamans, who engage in the ex-corporation of ecstatic magical flight, are typically men, as many tribes prevent or restrict female shamans, such as the Yanomami (Chagnon, 1992), whereas it appears that the reverse is true in far fewer tribes, such as the Mapuche of Chile. However, the apparent gender difference between mediumship and shamanism deserves further research, is outside the scope of this paper, and is debatable.

Given the apparent divergence of practice of psychedelic use and incorporation within shamanism, the report of a growing utilisation of these techniques in concert within the ayahuasca-using Santo Daime church warrants explanation. To this end a number of factors seem feasible, such as: the explicit eclectic nature of the CEFLURIS lineage and the latent mediumistic heritage of its leaders; the changing demographic of the followers and their changing needs towards a more expressive religious practice; the modernisation, urbanisation and gentrification of the religion; and, ultimately, the religionising of the shamanic practice of ayahuasca use along the dimension, delineated by Winkelman, that occurs as shamanism moves from nomadic and hunter-gatherer groups towards sedentary politically integrated 'mega-citizens.' Given that population growth and urbanisation are increasingly increasing, the question arises as to whether Umbandaime is the prototype supersyncretic suburban shamanism of the future? Only time will tell.

Postscript: Flying High with Goose and Crow

Shortly after writing this article concerning the wild practices of distant tribes and exotic churches, I realized I had gravely overlooked one fine example of psychedelic possession from my own locality; the tale of John Crow, the Winchester Geese, and the accidental re-exhumation of the forgotten Crossbones cemetery in south London.

The story goes that on the 23rd November 1996 in his flat in Southwark, London, the playwright John Constable, in a trance, adopted his shamanic alter-ego John Crow and was given ('channelled') by the spirit of a medieval whore a series of extended poems, which later became an entire play and book entitled *The Southwark Mysteries* (Constable, 1999). The poems, play and book explore the lives of the bawdy Shakespearian era prostitutes, known as the Winchester Geese, who lived and worked in the stew houses (brothels) on the south bank of London that were owned by the Bishop of Winchester. Unbeknownst to John, at that time, below the streets he lived on, work had just stopped on the new Jubilee line underground train line because engineers had encountered a number of human remains. The bodies turned out to belong to the forgotten Crossbones cemetery, a unconsecrated pauper's graveyard for the Southwark underclass, such as prostitutes – the irony being that although the Bishop had owned the stew houses, the Geese were consigned to an unconsecrated grave and became the outcast dead at Crossbones.

John's timely reception of The Southwark Mysteries at the time when this ancient cemetery was accidentally rediscovered is a deeply poetic mediumistic journey into his local psychogeography. The play had its opening night on St George's Day (and Shakespeare's birthday/deathday) in the year 2000 at Shakespeare's Globe and was later even performed at Southwark Cathedral.

What wasn't publically known though, although he had told me as his friend, was that John had been under the influence of a heroic dose of LSD when he received the poems and play. Subsequently John told the full entheogenic entity embodiment tale of John Crow and the Southwark Goose at the biennial psychedelic research conference, Breaking Convention, that myself and colleagues organized at Greenwich University in 2015. The video of that lecture *Acid Mediumship: Goose and Crow* is available online (vimeo.com/137474332). It was somewhat remiss of me to omit such a locally grown tale of psychedelic possession from a friend on my own doorstep, but the story needed telling publically by John first, so I'm pleased to be able to include it here now. A further historical and anthropological exploration of John Constable's Southwark reclamation and protection of the Crossbones graveyard from developers through monthly ritual and protest is provided in Hausner's (2016) book dedicated to the subject. Ultimately though, John's unorthodox poetic inspiration remains a rather unique technique and further highlights the exotic and uncommon nature of psychedelic possession, here in the UK, or anywhere.

CHAPTER 3

The Induction of Synaesthesia with Chemical Agents: A Systematic Review (with Devin Terhune)

Synaesthesia is an unusual condition in which a sensory stimulus will consistently and involuntarily produce a second concurrent experience (Ward, 2013). An example includes grapheme-colour synaesthesia, in which letters and numerals will involuntarily elicit experiences of colour. Synaesthesia qualifies as an anomalous experience due primarily to its uncommonness, being estimated to occur in some form in up to 4% of the general population (Simner et al., 2006), and despite some researchers once doubting it as a genuine perceptual experience it is now considered to be real, i.e., some people really do see sounds or taste colours (Marks, 2014). As such it is only an anomaly in prevalence but not anymore an anomaly in its deviance within Western mainstream science.

Furthermore, save for the possible association between synaesthesia and aura vision (Milán et al., 2012) – an experience reported to occur under the influence of psychoactive drugs by 46% of users (Luke & Kittenis, 2005) – this is possibly the only professed spiritual dimension to the seemingly mundane, albeit odd, experience of synaesthesia. Nevertheless the report of synaesthetic experiences in the general population is correlated with other self-reported anomalous or paranormal experiences, although in a synaesthete vs non-synaesthete ESP task experiment there was no significant differences between groups (Simmonds-Moore, 2013)

Most likely psychedelic synaesthesia would fall within Grof's (2000) first transpersonal category, of 'experiential extension within space-time and consensus reality', if at all. Nevertheless, synaesthesia-like experiences occur quite widely across psychedelic users and across different substances, to follow. One good example comes from Owsley Stanley, the first sound engineer of the proto psychedelic rock band Grateful Dead. Stanley was also one of the 1960s' most pioneering underground LSD chemists and would combine his interests, and consequently his senses, leading him to see the waves of sound coming out of the speakers, and so he arranged the sound system spatially as well as auditorily to maximize the visual effect of the music (McKenna, 1992). So even if the Grateful Dead didn't sound good (my opinion) they probably looked great under the influence of LSD, which was usually given out free at their concerts.

There is emerging evidence that congenital synaesthesia has a genetic basis (Brang & Ramachandran, 2011), but that the specific associations that an individual experiences are in part shaped by the environment (e.g., Witthoft & Winawer, 2013). Further research suggests that synaesthesia emerges at an early developmental stage in infants, but there are isolated cases of adult-onset synaesthesia (Ro et al., 2007) and it remains unclear whether genuine synaesthesia can be induced in non-synaesthetes (Terhune, Luke & Cohen Kadosh, 2017).

Despite the consensus regarding the developmental origins of synaesthesia, the transient induction of synaesthesia with chemical agents has been known about since the beginning of scientific research on psychedelic drugs (e.g., Ellis, 1898). Since this time, numerous observations attest to a wide range of psychoactive substances that give rise to a range of synaesthesias, however there has been scant systematic quantitative research conducted to explore this phenomenon, leaving somewhat of a lacuna in our understanding of the neurochemical factors involved and whether such phenomena constitute genuine synaesthesia.

A number of recent theories of synaesthesia implicate particular neurochemicals and thus the possible pharmacological induction of synaesthesia may lend insights into the neurochemical basis of this condition. For instance, *disinhibition* theories, which propose that synaesthesia arises from a disruption in inhibitory activity, implicate attenuated γ-aminobutyric acid (GABA) in synaesthesia (Hubbaard, Brang & Ramachandran, 2011), whereas Brang and Ramachandran (2008) have specifically hypothesized a role for serotonin in synaesthesia. Furthermore, the chemical induction of synaesthesia may permit investigating experimental questions that have hitherto been impossible with congenital synaesthetes (see Terhune et al., 2017).

Despite the potential value in elucidating the induction of synaesthesia with chemical agents, there is a relative paucity of research on this topic and a systematic review of the literature is wanting. There is also an unfortunate tendency in the cognitive neuroscience literature to overstate or understate the possible induction of synaesthesia with chemical agents. The present review seeks to fill the gap in this research domain by summarizing research studies investigating the induction of synaesthesia with chemical agents. Specifically, our review suggests that psychoactive substances, in particular those targeting the serotonin system, may provide a valuable method for studying synaesthesia under laboratory conditions, but that methodological limitations in this research domain warrant that we interpret the chemical induction of synaesthesia with caution.

Methods

A literature search in the English language was conducted using relevant databases (PubMed, PsychNet, Psychinfo) using the search terms synaesthesia, synesthesia, drug, psychedelic, LSD, psilocybin, mescaline, MDMA, ketamine, and cannabis and by following upstream the cascade of references found in those articles. Initially a meta-analysis of quantitative findings was planned, however it became apparent that there had been only four *direct* experimental attempts to induce synaesthesia in the laboratory using psychoactive substances, making such an analysis unnecessary.

A larger number of other papers exist, however, describing *indirect* experiments in which participants were administered a psychoactive substance under controlled conditions and asked via questionnaire, as part of a battery of phenomenological questions, if they experienced synaesthesia during the active period of the drug. Whilst these studies provide a non-drug state condition for comparison they did not set out to induce synaesthesia and so are less evidential than experimental studies. There also exist a number of case reports describing the induction of synaesthesia using chemical agents within various fields of study. Under this category, we include formal case studies as well as anecdotal observations. A final group of studies used survey methodologies, providing information regarding the prevalence and type of chemically-induced synaesthesias among substance users outside of the laboratory. Given the range of methodologies and quality of research, we summarize the studies within the context of different designs.

The majority of the studies and case reports relate to just three psychedelic substances – lysergic acid diethylamide (LSD), mescaline, and psilocybin. However, some data is also available for ketamine, ayahuasca, MDMA, as well as less common substances such as 4-HO-MET, ibogaine, *Ipomoea purpurea*, amyl nitrate, *Salvia divinorum*, in addition to the occasional reference to more commonly used drugs such as alcohol, caffeine, tobacco, cannabis, fluoxetine, and buproprion.

The final search identified 35 studies, which are summarized in Table 1. The most salient results from the different studies are reviewed.

Results

Experimental studies
Among experimental studies, a distinction is here made between *direct* and *indirect* experiments as those that explicitly attempted to induce synaesthesia in a hypothesis-driven manner and those that explored the induction of synaesthesia as part of a larger battery, respectively.

Direct experiments
We identified four published experimental studies formally attempting to induce synaesthesia with pharmacological agents (Hartman & Hollister, 1963; Kelly, 1934; Masters & Houston, 1966; Simpson & McKellar, 1955). In the first study (Kelly, 1934) four non-synaesthete participants had previously taken part in a seven-week auditory tone-colour synaesthesia training experiment receiving eight different tone-colour pairings 2000 times. Although they had demonstrated a tone-colour association learning effect no evidence of spontaneous consciously aware colour percepts in response to the tones were forthcoming and so failed to demonstrate a synaesthesia training effect. One week after the last training session the four participants were joined by a fifth who had the day before received 1000 single tone-colour pairings but likewise demonstrated no synaesthesia, and they consumed 15g of (presumably dried) peyote cactus.

Although not specified this amount of peyote provides an estimated dosage of between 0.15-1.2g of mescaline (Bruhn, Lindgren, Holmstedt & Adovasio, 1978; Crosby & McLaughlin, 1973), providing anything from a mild to a very strong dose depending on relative alkaloid content (Shulgin & Shulgin, 1991). One participant took a further 5g after receiving no visual perceptual changes, but to little effect. Although four of the five participants perceived colourful visual imagery, due to the mescaline, none perceived the appropriate colour when the tones were played, however other synaesthesia experiences were reported by these four, including haptic-visual, kinaesthetic-visual (especially colour) and algesic-colour, but not the intended tone-colour association.

The second study (Simpson & McKellar, 1955) included two congenital synaesthetes (auditory-visual and multiple types) with the

Table 1: Summary of studies reporting modulation of synaesthesia through drug use. *Note.* Empty cells indicate that the respective information was not reported in the study.

Author(s) (year)	N	Study design	Stimuli	Drug(s)	Type(s) of synaesthesia	Prevalence of synaesthesia & other results
Hartman & Hollister (1963)	16	Experiment	Pure sonic tones	Mescaline	Audio-visual	Mescaline > no drug
Hartman & Hollister (1963)	16	Experiment	Pure sonic tones	LSD	Audio-visual	LSD > no drug
Hartman & Hollister (1963)	16	Experiment	Pure sonic tones	Psilocybin	Audio-visual	
Masters & Houston (1966)		Experiment	Objects	LSD	Music-visual, colour-taste, colour-sound, sound-taste, music-smell	
Simpson & McKellar (1955)	4	Experiment	Various	Mescaline	Auditory-visual, kinaesthetic-visual, tactile-visual, olfactory-visual, algesic-visual, thermal-visual, olfactory-tactile, visual-thermal	
Hollister & Hartman (1962)	18	Experiment	Pure sonic tones	Mescaline	Audio-visual	10%
Hollister & Hartman (1962)	18	Experiment	Pure sonic tones	LSD	Audio-visual	15%
Hollister & Hartman (1962)	18	Experiment	Pure sonic tones	Psilocybin	Audio-visual	11%

(Contd.)

Author(s) (year)	N	Study design	Stimuli	Drug(s)	Type(s) of synaesthesia	Prevalence of synaesthesia & other results
Dobkin de Rios & Janiger (2003)	930	Experiment		LSD	Auditory-visual &auditory-colour-tactile-kinaesthetic-emotion-concept	
Carhart-Harris et al (2011)	9	Experiment	Ordinary environment	Psilocybin	Sound-vision	
Lahti et al (2001)	18	Experiment		Ketamine	(Not specified)	
Riba et al. (2004)	18	Experiment		Ayahuasca	Audio-visual	28%
Savage, Harman & Fadiman (1969)	22	Experiment		*Ipomoea purpurea*	(Not specified)	
Studerus et al (2010)	327	Experiment		Psilocybin	Sound-vision	37%
Studerus et al (2010)	102	Experiment		MDMA	Sound-vision	10%
Studerus et al (2010)	162	Experiment		Ketamine	Sound-vision	27%
Studerus et al (2011)	110	Experiment		Psilocybin	Sound-vision	Linear, dose dependent induced synaesthesia
Studerus et al (2012)	261	Experiment		Psilocybin	Sound-vision	Induced synaesthesia predicted by drug dose, *Tellegen Absorption Scale* (Tellegen & Atkinson, 1974), alcohol consumption, sociability, emotional excitability, and activity
Brang & Ramachandran (2008)	2	Case report		Fluoxetine		Inhibition of congenital synaesthesia

Author(s) (year)	N	Study design	Stimuli	Drug(s)	Type(s) of synaesthesia	Prevalence of synaesthesia & other results
Brang & Ramachandran (2008)	1	Case report		Buproprion		Inhibition of congenital synaesthesia
Brang & Ramachandran (2008)	1	Case report		Melatonin	Grapheme-colour	Consistent induced synaesthesia
Breslaw (1961)	1	Case report	Various	Psilocybin	Sound-smell, colour-sound, taste-semantic	
Ahmedi, Keshtkar & Priidmore (2011)	1	Case report	Visual stimuli	Meth-am-phetamine	Colour-voices	Inhibited by electroconvulsive therapy
Cytowic (1993)	1	Case report		Amyl Nitrate	Taste-tactile	Enhancement of congenital synaesthesia
Cytowic (1993)	1	Case report		Alcohol	Taste-tactile	Enhancement of congenital synaesthesia
Cytowic (1993)	1	Case report		Amphet-amine	Taste-tactile	Attenuation of congenital synaesthesia
Cytowic (1993)	1	Case report		Alcohol cessation		Inhibition of congenital synaesthesia
Cytowic & Eagleman (2009)	6	Case reports		LSD		33% enhanced
Fotiou (2012)	1	Case report	Music	Ayahuasca	Music-visual	

(Contd.)

Author(s) (year)	N	Study design	Stimuli	Drug(s)	Type(s) of synaesthesia	Prevalence of synaesthesia & other results
Klüver (1966)		Case reports		Mescaline	Audio-visual, audio-tactile, visual-tactile, colour-gustatory, visual-audio, concept-olfactory, audio-somatic, visual-somatic, audio-shape, audio-tactile, visual-tactile, visual-thermal, haptic-visual, audio-visual-somatic, audio-visual-somatic-algesic, visual-tactile-conceptual-visual-gustatory-olfactory-entoptic	
La Barre (1975)		Case report		Mescaline	Visual-audio	
McKellar (1956)	1	Case report		Mescaline	Auditory-gustatory	
McKenna (1982)	1	Case report		LSD	Auditory-shape	
Pahnke & Richards (1966)		Case reports		LSD	Music-colour	
Popik, Layer & Stolnick (1995)		Case reports		Ibogaine	Auditory, olfactory and taste	
Smythies (1953)		Case reports		Mescaline	Sound-vision, sound-emotion	
Hofmann (1983)	1	Case report		LSD	Sound-vision	
Ward (2008)	1	Case reports		LSD	Visual-breathing	
Shanon (2003)		Case reports		Ayahuasca	Auditory-visual, olfactory-visual, tactile-visual	

Author(s) (year)	N	Study design	Stimuli	Drug(s)	Type(s) of synaesthesia	Prevalence of synaesthesia & other results
Cytowic & Eagleman (2009)	1279	Survey		Alcohol		9% enhanced, 6% reduced
Cytowic & Eagleman (2009)	1279	Survey		Tobacco		1% enhanced, 1% reduced
Cytowic & Eagleman (2009)	1279	Survey		Caffeine		9% enhanced, 3% reduced
DeGracia (1997)	62	Survey		Multiple psychedelics	Sound-visual, music-visual, Vision-sound. vision-taste, sound-somatic, colour-smell, sound-colour, sound-shape, sound-form, sound-touch, sound-smell, sound-taste, vision-music, colour-taste, colour-sound, colour-somat, taste-colour, music-touch, music-somatic, music-shape, music-colour, smell-taste, smell-vision	50% (all types)
Addy (2010)	30	Survey	Ordinary environment	*Salvia divinorum*	Visual>kinaethetic/ propioceptive/somatic/tactile	57% (all types), 23% (visual>tactile)
Kjellgren & Soussan (2011)	25	Survey		4-HO-MET	Taste-sound & sound-visual	
Tart (1975)		Survey		Cannabis	Music-colour	56% (all types)

researchers acting as non-synaesthete controls (McKellar, 1957). Participants were administered four mescaline doses between 0.3-0.5g (considered strong doses, Shulgin & Shulgin, 1991) on separate occasions. During the active effects of the drugs, participants were presented with a variety of sensory stimuli (visual, auditory, tactile, gustatory, olfactory, kinaesthetic, thermal, and algesic). Participants reported several distinct types of novel synaesthesias: auditory-visual (all 4 participants), kinaesthetic-visual (3), tactile-visual (2), olfactory-visual (2), algesic-visual (2), thermal-visual (1), olfactory-tactile (1), visual-tactile (1) and visual-thermal (1), with a relatively equal ratio of novel synaesthesias (10:7) between synaesthetes and non-synaesthetes. In addition, one of the congenital synaesthetes reported enhancement of their usual auditory-tactile and visual-thermal synaesthesias, suggesting that mescaline can both induce synaesthesia among non-synaesthetes and enhance synaesthesia among congenital synaesthetes.

A third study by Hartman and Hollister (1963; see also Hollister & Hartman, 1962) compared the effects of mescaline (5mg/kg), psilocybin (150mcg/kg), and LSD (1mcg/kg), considered to be light to moderate doses, administered under blind conditions. A total of 18 participants took both substances one week apart and received auditory stimulation from 16 pure sonic tones before and after drug administration. Overall, participants reported significantly more colours and other auditorily-driven visual effects (brightening of the visual field, shattering of patterns, and patterning of form) compared to baseline whilst under the influence of both LSD and mescaline, but not psilocybin, although there was a non-significant increase in such experiences with the latter. Fewer than 50% of the participants (exact proportion not reported) experienced auditorily-induced synaesthesia under the influence of the three psychedelics.

A fourth experimental study is described in Masters and Houston (1964), but only minimal details about the methodology and results were presented. Specifically, they report a series of informal experiments and interviews conducted with 214 participants in 204 sessions in which psychedelic drugs were consumed. In the course of this work the authors report successfully intentionally inducing colour-sound and auditory-gustatory synaesthesia with LSD, but there is no information regarding the proportion of participants reporting such effects, the dosage, or other results. Insofar as few details are provided about this study, it is difficult to critically evaluate its methodology and results, but the reported results do converge with the two previous experimental studies.

These four studies suggest that synaesthesia can be induced in a controlled environment using chemical agents. Nevertheless, they suffer from a large number of limitations including a lack of placebo control, double-blinds and randomized allocation. The absence of these experimental controls warrant concerns about demand characteristics (Orne, 1962) – participants may have expected to have synaesthesia under the influence of the drugs, thereby inflating their tendency to endorse that they had experienced synaesthesia. In addition, the studies identified the experience of synaesthesia using self-reports rather than behavioural measures of automaticity (the concurrent occurs spontaneously in the presence of the inducer) or consistency (a specific inducer generates the same concurrent experience each time)(for a review, see Ward, 2013).

Indirect experiments

Despite the lack of direct experiments in the last 50 years, we identified nine studies that investigated the psychological effects of psychedelic drugs under controlled conditions, including placebo controls. As part of a broad assessment, these studies included questions regarding the experience of synaesthesia during the active period of the drug.

Studerus (2013) reviews data from several studies (Studerus, Gamma, Kometer & Vollenweider, 2012; Studerus, Gamma & Volleenweider, 2010; Studerus, Kometer, Hasler & Vollenweider, 2011) that included nearly 600 psilocybin, MDMA, and ketamine test participants. Studerus (2013) provides prevalence rates of induced auditory-visual synaesthesia (only), with sounds as inducers, for these substances (MDMA: 10%; ketamine: 27%; psilocybin: 37%) and demonstrates its linear dose-dependent nature with psilocybin, the most studied substance in this context.

Averaged across studies, the percentage of positive responses to questionnaire items relating to auditory-visual synaesthesia induced by psilocybin ranged from 0% for placebo and 45mcg/kg doses, up to 50% for the highest psilocybin dose of 315mcg/kg. The linear dose-synaesthesia relationship with psilocybin is also supported by independent data on synaesthesia as one of a number of visual effects in a similar indirect experiment (Griffiths et al., 2011) and tallies with earlier reports of less than 50% of participants experiencing experimentally-induced auditory-visual synaesthesia with 150mcg/kg of psilocybin (Hartman & Hollister, 1963).

A notable finding of these studies is that psilocybin-induced auditory-visual synaesthesia is predicted by different demographic and individual difference variables, most notably *absorption*, the tendency to experience all-encompassing attentional states characterized by intense affective and imaginative involvement in an activity (Tellegen

& Atkinson, 1974). Thus, individuals high in absorption appear to be more prone to drug-induced synaesthesia. Other studies administering psychedelics experimentally also report the prevalence of synaesthesia, usually defined as auditory-visual synaesthesia only. These studies have found prevalence rates ranging from 10 to 37% with various substances including ketamine, psilocybin, ayahuasca, and *Ipomoea purpurea*, a plant containing LSD-like alkaloids (Carhart-Harris et al., 2011; Lahti, Weiler, Michaelidis, Parwani & Tamminga, 2001; Riba, Anderer, Jané, Saletu & Barbanoj, 2004; Savage, Harman & Fadiman, 1969).

Indirect experimental studies largely corroborate the results of the experimental studies. These studies possess a number of the same limitations, most notably the absence of behavioural measures to corroborate synaesthesia. In addition, they are exploratory in design and most studies only report on the prevalence of auditory-visual synaesthesias thereby obscuring our understanding of the types of synaesthesias induced by the chemical agents studied. However, some of the studies (Carhart-Harris et al., 2011; Griffiths et al., 2011; Lahti et al, 2001; Riba et al., 2004; Studerus, 2013) benefit from the inclusion of placebo controls, which in part circumvent confounds pertaining to demand characteristics.

Case reports

We identified 17 case reports exploring the apparent induction of synaesthesia with chemical agents. The majority of the case studies simply report the form of synaesthesia that is induced, adding only to the known types that may be reported (see Table 1), but a few studies provide further details regarding phenomenological characteristics of synaesthesia or information regarding chemical agents that can modulate congenital synaesthesia.

One notable finding among case reports is Klüver's (1966) observation of variability in the perceived visuospatial location of visual concurrents in auditory-colour synaesthesia. Specifically, he reported that some participants would experience concurrents as endogenous mental images or representations whereas others would experience concurrents as though they were localized in space. This variability closely mirrors individual differences among synaesthetes.

In particular, there is evidence that one subset of grapheme-colour synaesthetes experience colours as mental representations (*associators*) whereas another experiences colours as spatially co-localized with the inducing grapheme (*projectors*) (Dixon, Smilek & Merikle, 2004; Ward, Li, Salih & Sagiv, 2007). Klüver (1966) further noted that mescaline-induced synaesthesia can sometimes lead to quite complex fusions of several sensory percepts and may even produce associations between abstract concepts (e.g., negation) and visual images (e.g., a white square metal plate).

One case report describes the apparent consistent induction of grapheme-colour synaesthesia with melatonin, the veracity of which was supported with a behavioural measure of texture segregation (Brang & Ramachandran, 2008).

Of special interest are case reports describing the modulation of congenital synaesthesias with chemical agents. Brang and Ramachandran (2008) described the inhibition of an unspecified form of congenital synaesthesia with two types of antidepressant: the selective serotonin reuptake inhibitor, *fluoxetine*, and the substituted amphetamine, *bupropion*. The former result provides further support for the role of serotonin in the induction of synaesthesia and thus complements direct and indirect experimental studies pointing to serotonergic agonists as reliable inducers of synaesthesia in non-synaesthetes.

As Shanon (2003b) notes, case reports of chemically-induced synaesthesia are typically of the auditory-visual variety, particularly auditory-shape and auditory-colour, as occurs with mescaline (Klüver, 1966; Marks, 1975; Smythies, 1953), LSD (Hofmann, 1983; McKenna, 1982; Pahnke & Richards, 1966), cannabis (Marks, 1975), and ayahuasca (Fotiou, 2012; Shanon, 2003b). Such auditory imagery is sometimes reported to be dynamic in nature fluctuating with the sounds as they change (e.g., Hofmann, 1983; Pahnke & Richards, 1966), as when listening to music.

Surveys

A small number of surveys report on the prevalence and type of chemically-induced synaesthesias. These reports are typically indirect, sampling substance users and reporting on synaesthesia as one of a number of phenomena occurring under the influence of different substances.

In one study (DeGracia, 1995), psychedelic substances in general were reported to induce synaesthesia in 50% of users with 62 respondents reporting 23 different types of synaesthesia, the most common of which was auditory-visual (52% of those reporting synaesthesia), including music and voice inducers. Similar prevalence rates are found in surveys of 30 *Salvia divinorum* users (57%), although with visual-somatic synaesthesia (23%) being the most common (Addy, 2010), and with cannabis users (56%) who predominantly reported music-colour synaesthesia (Tart, 1975).

Even surveys of users of obscure psychedelic substances like 4-HO-MET have reported the induction of synaesthesia, although prevalence rates are not reported (Kjellgren & Soussan, 2011). Notably, lifetime prevalence of chemical induction of synaesthesia is relatively higher than for those induced in individual experimental trials, as might be expected.

We found one study that surveyed synaesthetes regarding the impact of chemical agents on congenital synaesthesia (Cytowic & Eagleman, 2009). This study reports on the relative effects of commonplace drugs among 1279 verified grapheme-colour synaesthetes. Alcohol and caffeine tended to enhance (9% both drugs) or reduce (3% caffeine, 6% alcohol) synaesthesia to relatively comparable degrees. Cytowic and Eagleman (2009) also report that of six synaesthetes ingesting LSD, two (33%) reported enhancing effects with the remainder reporting no effect. Although preliminary, these results suggest that LSD has stronger effects than commonplace psychoactive substances.

Types of synaesthesias
All but a small number of the studies reporting induction of synaesthesia in non-synaesthetes specified the inducer-concurrent associations (see Table 1 & Figure 1). The most commonly reported type was

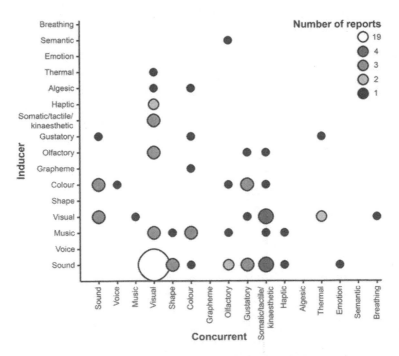

Figure1: Number of reports of particular inducer-concurrent associations in chemical-induced synaesthesias.
Smaller, darker markers reflect fewer reports.

overwhelmingly auditory-visual (19 reports; 23%). In turn, the most frequent inducer was auditory stimuli including music and voices (39 reports; 47%), and the most frequent concurrents were visual experiences (43 reports; 52%).

However these figures are somewhat exacerbated by the exclusive reporting of auditory-visual synaesthesia in the indirect experimental studies. Cumulatively, these results suggest that non-synaesthetes report similar forms of synaesthesia whilst under the influence of certain drugs as congenital synaesthetes, but also other inducer-concurrent associations that to our knowledge have not been reported in research studies of congenital synaesthesia, such as visual-thermal associations.

Discussion

These studies strongly suggest that chemical agents are capable of producing synaesthesia-like experiences. Crucially, there is large convergence across studies with different methodologies in terms of the prevalence of chemical-induced synaesthesia, the types of drugs (and neurochemical mechanisms) involved, and, to a lesser extent, the types of synaesthesias reported. There is also preliminary evidence that the same drugs have compatible effects on congenital synaesthesia. In what follows, the limitations of these studies, the types of chemical agents implicated, and the types of synaesthesia reported are considered. The discussion concludes by considering whether these phenomena are comparable to congenital synaesthesia and offer suggestions for future research.

Study limitations
Despite the importance of convergent results, this research literature suffers from a number of substantial limitations, which need to be considered when interpreting the veracity of the chemical induction of synaesthesia and any implications this research has for the neural mechanisms underlying congenital synaesthesia.

First, there is a relative paucity of experimental studies. Of these, relatively few included placebo controls and some may be contaminated by demand characteristics. The absence of placebo controls in these studies is especially crucial because there is evidence that various psychedelic drugs enhance suggestibility (for a review, see Whalley & Brooks, 2009) and thus may augment participants' susceptibility to demand characteristics.

Furthermore, relatively little information is available regarding dosage, which may be crucial (Studerus, 2013), or the time course of the phenomenon (i.e., onset and duration). There is also considerable variability across participants with only a subset reporting chemical-induced synaesthesia. This variability may be explained in part by individual differences in absorption (Studerus, 2013), but has been largely ignored by researchers. The majority of the reviewed studies describe case reports and surveys. These types of studies are valuable at suggesting research avenues and possible mechanisms, but are not sufficiently rigorous to enable firm conclusions regarding the veracity of the effects.

The most severe limitation of the reviewed studies is that all but one (Brang & Ramachandran, 2008) relied on self-reports of experiences of synaesthesia. Although reports by congenital synaesthetes have been consistently validated by behavioural measures (Ward, 2013), it cannot be assumed that experiential reports among non-synaesthetes under the influence of chemical agents would translate to similar behavioural response patterns as congenital synaesthetes.

Across studies, synaesthesia may not have been properly defined to participants or authors may have been using different definitions. Relatedly, some of the reported forms of synaesthesia (e.g., semantic-olfactory (Klüver, 1966); gustatory-semantic (Breslaw, 1961) closely resemble states of absorption (e.g., feeling cold when viewing a picture of an iceberg) (Ott, 2007). Given these limitations, caution must be exerted regarding the interpretation of the chemical induction of synaesthesia until these phenomena can be verified using more rigorous behavioural measures in studies with stronger experimental controls.

Types of chemical agents
The studies reviewed here suggest that a wide range of drugs can produce synaesthesia-like experiences, even in controlled settings. Most of the research has included LSD, mescaline, psilocybin, ayahuasca, or MDMA. A notable commonality among these substances is that they are all serotonin agonists (e.g., Nichols, 2004), specifically serotonin 2A subtype agonists, although some non-serotonergic substances have been reported to induce synaesthesia, such as ketamine (Lahti et al., 2001) and *Salvia divinorum* (Addy, 2010).

Few studies have included rigorous comparisons of these different drug classes, but the available evidence suggests that the prevalence rates for synaesthesia under the influence of serotonin agonists is greater than for drugs that do not target serotonin (Luke, Terhune & Friday, 2012; Studerus, 2013). Furthermore, Simpson and McKellar (1955) reported that serotonin agonists both induced synaesthesia in non-synaesthetes and enhanced existing synaesthesias in congenital synaesthetes. This result was recently replicated in a survey of psychedelic users and congenital synaesthetes (Luke, Terhune & Friday, 2012). Cytowic and Eagleman (2009) also reported the enhancement of congenital synaesthesia with LSD. Cumulatively, these results clearly implicate serotonin in synaesthesia and warrant further research on the role of this neurochemical in synaesthesia.

Nevertheless, other non-serotonergic compounds can also induce synaesthesia, although the most prevalent ones are typically also psychedelic in character, such as ketamine, *Salvia divinorum*, cannabis, nitrous oxide, datura, and dextromethorphan (Addy, 2010; Lahti et al., Luke, Terhune & Friday, 2012; Studerus, 2013; Tart, 1975). These divergent chemical compounds act primarily on different neurochemical systems to each other and yet they all provide profound changes in consciousness and somewhat similar phenomenological syndromes, such as the experience of synaesthesia.

Given that there are currently around 350 known psychedelic chemicals and potentially 2000 untested ones (Luke, 2012d) all with different modes of action, understanding exactly what neurochemical processes are responsible for the different experiential effects is a complex conundrum that remains to be disentangled by psychopharmacologists (Presti, 2011). Nevertheless, systemic taxonomical research that relates specific chemicals to particular experiences could illuminate the neurochemistry involved (Luke, Terhune & Friday, 2012).

Types of synaesthesia
There was consistent evidence across studies that auditory-visual synaesthesia was the most commonly experienced form of synaesthesia under the influence of drugs. In turn, auditory stimuli and visual experiences were the most common inducers and concurrents, respectively. However, there is also considerable variability across studies in the types of chemically-induced synaesthesias reported by participants. The source of this variability is at present unclear and may be driven by variability in the types of stimuli presented to participants and environment variability (most studies were not conducted in controlled laboratory environments).

The preponderance of sound and music as inducers is likely due to the fact that participants commonly listen to music whilst consuming drugs. A number of studies also report only the prevalence of auditory-visual synaesthesias thereby inflating the differential prevalence rates between this type and other types of synaesthesia. Some phenomena labelled synaesthesia may actually be the result of other factors associated with the drug. For instance, there are examples where drug-induced hallucinations (e.g., Cooles, 1980) lack an unequivocal inducer-concurrent association pattern are incorrectly interpreted as synaesthesias (Ballesteros, Ramon, Iturralde & Martinez-Arrieta, 2006; see also Terhune & Cohen Kadosh, 2012).

Finally, an increase in suggestibility following the ingestion of psychedelic drugs (Whalley & Brooks, 2009) may account for the occurrence of synaesthesia-like experiences that appear to be the product of absorption.

A common critique of this literature is that drug-induced synaesthesias tend to differ from congenital synaesthesias (Hubbard & Ramachandran, 2003; Sinke et al., 2012) in terms of the complexity and types of inducer-concurrent associations. The present review only partly supports this conclusion. On the one hand, there are reports of chemically-induced synaesthesias with unusual inducer-concurrent associations that, to our knowledge, have not been reported by congenital synaesthetes. One striking example is Klüver's (1966) report of a complex visual-tactile-conceptual-visual-gustatory-olfactory synaesthesia following the ingestion of mescaline. Similarly, we do not observe any reports of particular well-documented types of synaesthesia such as spatial-sequence synaesthesia (Cohen Kadosh, Gertner & Terhune, 2012).

On the other hand, there are examples of types of induced synaesthesia that are well-documented in the literature including grapheme-colour (Brang & Ramachandran, 2008; Luke, Terhune & Friday, 2012) and auditory-colour synaesthesias (e.g., Hartman & Hollister, 1963). As an aside, it is especially noteworthy that auditory-visual is the most frequently reported drug-induced synaesthesia as well as the most common acquired form of this condition (Afra, Funke & Matsuo, 2009). The under-representation of specific types of synaesthesia (e.g., grapheme-colour, spatial-sequence) may reflect a lack of exposure to alphanumeric stimuli during drug consumption or, alternatively, may suggest that such types of synaesthesia require exposure to particular associations (e.g., Witthoft & Winawer, 2013) and/or take time to develop (e.g., Simner et al., 2009).

Criteria of synaesthesia

An open question is whether chemically-induced synaesthesias are equivalent to congenital synaesthesias. Consensus has yet to emerge regarding the principal characteristics of synaesthesia and the ways by which ostensible synaesthesias can be confirmed as genuine. Nevertheless, there is considerable agreement that inducer-concurrent associations are automatic, consistent, specific, and accessible to consciousness (Deroy & Spence, 2013; Terhune, et al., 2017; Ward, 2013; Ward & Mattingley, 2006). This review uses these criteria and other characteristics of congenital and chemically-induced synaesthesias to briefly consider the extent to which these two phenomena are similar.

Considered against these criteria, the available evidence indicates that chemically-induced synaesthesias do not as yet qualify as genuine synaesthesia. There is as yet no clear evidence that chemically-induced synaesthesias are automatic as all studies to date have relied on self-report except for one study (Brang & Ramachandran, 2008). The same goes for the criteria of consistency and specificity. There is one study that confirmed the consistency of melatonin-induced grapheme-colour synaesthesia (Brang & Ramachandran, 2008), which is suggestive, but far from conclusive.

The last criterion, accessibility to consciousness, however, appears to be overwhelmingly met by chemically-induced synaesthesias. These results clearly present a mixed picture but it should be noted that almost none of the studies have actually attempted to validate induced synaesthesias. Accordingly, any strong judgments regarding the veracity of chemically-induced synaesthesias in our opinion remain premature (for a different view, see Hochel & Milán, 2008).

Further evidence points to similarities and differences between congenital and chemically-induced synaesthesias. As previously noted, some researchers have emphasized that congenital synaesthesias tend to be relatively simple associations (Sinke et al., 2012; Hubbard & Ramachandran, 2003) whereas induced synaesthesias are often complex and sometimes reflect inducer-concurrent associations not observed in congenital synaesthesia. As observed in this review, there is considerable heterogeneity in the types of chemically-induced synaesthesias. As noted above, this variability may arise from different factors associated with the respective drug and environmental influences. Although the complexity and dynamism of psychedelic-induced synaesthesia is evident in some reports (e.g., Klüver, 1966) it is not mandatory (e.g. Simpson & McKellar, 1995), and indeed as Sinke et al. (2012) note, the complexity of the visual concurrent experience is related to dose and time from dosing (i.e., the intensity of the drug experience).

It is notable that grapheme-colour synaesthesia, the most well-studied form of congenital synaesthesia, was also reported by approximately 1% of recreational psychedelic tryptamine (e.g., LSD, psilocybin) users in an online survey (Luke, Terhune & Friday, 2012). Furthermore, music and other auditory stimuli, the most common inducers across the studies reviewed here, function as inducers in more than

25% of cases of congenital synaesthesia (Hochel & Milán, 2008)(see above).

Other notable similarities include individual differences in the visuospatial phenomenology of colour concurrents in chemically-induced (Klüver, 1966) and congenital (Dixon et al., 2004; Ward et al., 2007) synaesthesias. Finally, the result that individuals high in absorption are more prone to chemically-induced synaesthesias (Studerus, 2013) is notable because absorption is indiscriminable from fantasy-proneness (Rhue & Lynn, 1989) and the fantasizing component of empathy is elevated among congenital synaesthetes (Banissy et al., 2013). Thus, individuals who are prone to chemically-induced synaesthesia may have a similar cognitive perceptual personality profile as congenital synaesthetes.

To summarize, chemically-induced synaesthesias do not as yet meet accepted criteria for genuine synaesthesia, although no study has attempted to rigorously investigate this question (although see postscript to this chapter). Induced synaesthesias do, however, display a number of striking similarities to congenital synaesthesias that warrant further attention.

Future directions
The present review shows that there is convergent evidence that particular chemical agents produce synaesthesia-like experiences. However, the studies conducted to date suffer from numerous limitations and many questions remain unaddressed. Here we briefly outline further directions for research on the chemical induction of synaesthesia.

Future research on chemically-induced synaesthesia will need to utilize up-to-date methodologies to confirm that induced-synaesthesias are not the product of demand characteristics. In particular, there is a strong need for placebo-controlled, double-blind studies of these phenomena. There is consistent evidence that chemically-induced synaesthesias are more common with serotonin agonists, but experimental studies that directly compare a range of chemical agents are required before firm conclusions can be made.

Future studies will also need to include established measures to verify the occurrence of synaesthesia such as measures of the automaticity (e.g., Dixon et al., 2004) and consistency (Eagleman, Kagan, Nelson, Sagaram & Sarma, 2007; Rothen, Seth, Witzel & Ward, 2013) of inducer-concurrent associations, rather than relying solely on self-reports as is the norm in the studies to date. Elsewhere, we have noted that some criteria (e.g., consistency) may not be applicable to genuine synaesthesia at an early stage because the associations may have yet to undergo consolidation (Terhune et al., 2017). Specifically, consistency of inducer-concurrent associations in congenital synaesthetes may arise through a consolidation process wherein the inducer and concurrent are repeatedly paired and the association is strengthened and becomes more specific over time. This hypothesis is consistent with research showing that inducer-concurrent consistency increases over time in children with synaesthesia (Simner, Harold, Creed, Monro & Foulkes, 2009). This should be considered when assessing the veracity of chemically-induced synaesthesias.

Future studies would also benefit from the inclusion of more comprehensive phenomenological inventories in order to identify the similarities and differences between congenital and induced synaesthesias. Finally, it would be valuable to determine using transcranial magnetic stimulation whether drug-induced synaesthesias are dependent upon similar cortical structures (e.g., parietal cortex) as congenital synaesthesias (Esterman, Verstynen, Ivry & Robertson, 2006; Muggleton, Tsakanikos, Walsh & Ward, 2007; Rothen, Nyffeler, von Wartburg, Muri & Meier, 2010). Pursuing these lines of investigation will help to elucidate whether chemically-induced synaesthesias are similar to congenital synaesthesias and thereby greatly inform further research on the neurophysiological and neurochemical mechanisms underlying congenital and chemically-induced synaesthesias.

Summary and conclusions

Although it is nearly 170 years since the first report of the pharmacological induction of synaesthesia (Gautier, 1843), research on this topic remains in its infancy. There is consistent, and convergent, evidence that a variety of chemical agents, particularly serotonergic agonists, produce synaesthesia-like experiences, but the studies investigating this phenomenon suffer from numerous limitations. The wide array of suggestive findings to date are sufficiently compelling as to warrant future research regarding the characteristics and mechanisms of chemically-induced synaesthesias.

Postscript: A Placebo-Controlled LSD-induced Synaesthesia Experiment

Since the review was published in 2013 there have been a number of psychedelic research studies published (not listed) which have also reported synaesthesia, but indirectly as part of a broad assessment as questions regarding the experience of synaesthesia during the active period of the drug, and so these are yet more indirect experiments.

To the author's knowledge only one direct experiment has been conducted and was instigated by the author along with the co-author of this review, Devin Terhune, in combination with synaesthesia researcher Prof. Jamie Ward. The Beckley-Imperial research team in London were conducting an LSD pilot with 10 participants and an opportunity arose, for the first time in decades, to assess LSD-induced synaesthesia in humans (Terhune et al., 2016). This was the first such study conducted in 50 years and, unlike previous direct experimental studies (Hartman & Hollister, 1963; Kelly, 1934; Masters & Houston, 1966; Simpson & McKellar, 1955) this study explored drug-induced synaesthesia for both consistency and inducer specificity using behavioural measures in a controlled manner. Furthermore, this was the first direct psychedelic synaesthesia experiment to employ a blind placebo-controlled design.

Unfortunately that study did not produce evidence to support the existence of consistency or inducer specificity of LSD-induced grapheme-colour and sound-colour synaesthesia. This does not rule out that such consistency and specificity is possible with psychedelic-induced synaesthesia, as occurs with congenital synaesthesia, but that the current methodological approach did not support this, perhaps due to the simplicity of the stimuli used, which may be dissimilar to those occurring naturally. However, participants did report more spontaneous synaesthesia-like experiences (concurrent visual movements, experiences of touch and entoptic patterns) occurring with the visual and, especially, the auditory stimuli under LSD than compared to the control condition. Although it should be noted that colour concurrents were not explicitly observed, perhaps indicating why the experiment was not successful in producing LSD-induced consistency and inducer specificity of grapheme-colour and sound-colour synaesthesia.

In any case, as indicated earlier, it is probable that with congenital synaesthesia both consistency and specificity arise from the consolidation of inducer-concurrent pairings over time (perhaps years) and so are not evident in short-lived substance-induced instances. If this is the case then psychedelic-induced synaesthesia would be unlikely to ever produce consistency and specificity effects in tests, unless the experience was especially prolonged. It is hard to speculate how long someone would need to be tripping for to achieve such an effect, given that evidence suggests that congenital synaesthesia seemingly begins development as an infant. One possibly is to test those rare people reporting hallucinogen persisting perceptual disorder manifesting as synaesthesia-like symptoms. This has never been explored, although I now have three case studies with people who report long term (several years) persistent synaesthesia experiences, previously absent, after taking large recreational doses of psychedelics (LSD, 2C-B, and 2C-T-7), and in time I intend to pursue this line of research further. But, so little time, so much to research!

CHAPTER 4

Rock Art or Rorschach: Is There More
to Entoptics Than Meets the Eye?

The recourse to entoptic phenomena as an explanation of certain geometric rock art has generated considerable debate among archaeologists and anthropologists of consciousness, and even among neuropsychologists, to a lesser degree. Surprisingly little has been discussed concerning the philosophical location of this debate in relation to the mind-body problem of consciousness, however, and a new perspective presented here on the experience of form constants challenges current thinking.

Considering the neuropsychological-shamanistic theory of Paleolithic rock art in light of visionary experiences among both the blind and the sighted, and under different states of altered consciousness, such as with psychedelics, an argument is presented that form constants are not actually entoptic as they are currently defined, that is, made within the eye and the visual cortex. It is suggested that the entoptic rock art model is swayed by philosophical biases that force theorists to see what they want to see, somewhat like a Rorschach ink blot test, when, rather, it actually appears that there may be more to entoptics than meets the eye.

Revolutionizing the field of rock art research by offering a novel shamanistic approach to the discipline, the publication of "The Signs of all Times: Entoptic Phenomena in Upper Paleolithic Rock Art" by Lewis-Williams and Dowson (1988) has fuelled a lively debate kept active throughout the last three decades (Dowson, 2007). The authors advance a neuropsychological model for analyzing the motifs of parietal and mobile art of this period, proposing that the non-figurative images are in fact artistic representations of universal optical patterns, intrinsic to the human visual system, once perceived by our shamanic ancestors during altered states of consciousness (ASCs).

These *entoptics* (meaning "from within vision") seen in the visual field and heightened by the darkness of the cave recess would then literally be traced onto the rock surface and mobile art pieces, thereby representing a neurological imprint of our Paleolithic forebears. Assuming that there is little structural difference between modern brains and those of the Upper Paleolithic period, the neurological basis of these so-called entoptics means that they are a universal phenomenon still observable today.

Lewis-Williams and Dowson (1988, p.202) define *entoptic phenomena* (derived from *entoptical phenomena* by Helmholtz, 1925) as "visual sensations derived from within the optic system anywhere from the eyeball to the cortex". The term covers two classes of typically geometric percept: *phosphenes* (Savigny, 1838), which are entopthalmic ("within the eye") (Walker, 1981) and can be induced by physical stimulation, such as via pressure on the eyeball (Figure 2); and *form constants* (Klüver, 1926, 1966/1928), which derive from within the optic system and are speculated to originate from beyond the eye.

Both classes are distinguished from visual *hallucinations*, such as iconic visions of culturally controlled items (e.g., animals) also represented in rock art, which they consider to lack any foundation in the visual system. Consequently, the generic term entoptic phenomena is restricted to the largely geometric visual percepts observed.

Lewis-Williams and Dowson's model essentially rests on several assumptions, which include (1) entoptic phenomena occur universally in altered states; (2) our ancestors used one or more techniques for altering consciousness (e.g., psychedelic plants or fungi, hyperventilation, rhythmic movements, sensory deprivation, etc); (3) a sufficient

Figure 2: Artistic depiction of a phosphene (by Aldo, used via creative commons). Phosphenes are geometrical percepts that can be induced by physical stimulation of the eye, such as by pressing on the eyeball with a finger.

quantity of Upper Paleolithic rock art represents the entoptic phenomena experienced during ASCs; (4) the explicit visual content of the ASC experience may vary with the cultural context but the basic features of the experience (such as geometric visual percepts) are repeated and are "hardwired" into the human nervous system.

Elsewhere the debate has raged over the first three of these assumptions (e.g., Bahn, 1988; Bednarik, 1988, 1990) and, although these arguments are interesting, this part of the debate will not be tackled here and the model will be assumed to be sufficient on these grounds for our purposes. However, surprisingly little has been raised concerning the latter hardwiring assumption.

This lack of critical analysis of the continued assertion that the geometric visual phenomena of altered states are "hardwired" into the optic system (Lewis-Williams & Pearce, 2005) appears to stem from intellectual neglect: those discussing the archaeological and anthropological aspects of the model are not concerned with the mind-body problem per se (e.g., Bahn, 1988; Bednarik, 1988, 1990), although some have criticized the model generally for being reductionist (e.g., Wallis, 2009), whereas those tackling the neurological assumptions generally assume a de facto materialist-reductionist position on brain-mind interaction in their approach (e.g., Bressloff et al. 2001).

Additionally, few commentators appear to be addressing the assumptions about ASCs from an experiential position. Consequently, there has been little challenge to the notion that the geometric forms perceived in ASCs are in fact entoptic, as that word is defined by Lewis-Williams and Dowson. However, some under-explored corners of phenomenological research into geometric imagery in altered states offer accounts that are perpendicular to this assumption. Specific features of some rock art may indeed be representations of geometric percepts from altered states, but are those percepts merely generated by neurochemically induced misfiring in the optic system?

Entoptics as Hallucinations and Projections: Both, Either, or Neither?

In his myth-busting paper on research into hallucinations Shanon (2003a, p.6) writes that, "It is my firm belief that just as one cannot talk of music if one had not experienced music first-hand, one cannot seriously discuss the phenomenology of the so-called altered states of consciousness without actually having had a first-hand feel of the non-ordinary experiences with these states."

Drawn to the literature on ASCs, entoptic phenomena and rock art my reactions upon reading various papers on the topic matched those of Shanon, having had numerous experiences in altered states – via breathing techniques, sensory deprivation, yoga, lucid dreaming and various other means, particularly through the ingestion of certain psychedelic substances. These substances include the mushrooms of the *Psilocybe* genus (containing the psychoactive molecules psilocybin and psilocin) and the Amazonian jungle decoction ayahuasca.

Used widely in the Amazon basin and across much of South America, ayahuasca, which means "the vine of the spirits" in Quechua, is usually a combination of at least two plants, one of which contains harmala alkaloids – such as the ayahuasca vine (*Banisteriopsis caapi*) – and the other of which contains *N,N*-dimethyltryptamine (DMT), such as the chacruna bush (*Psychotria viridis*) (Shanon, 2002). The ancient use of the ayahuasca vine goes back to at least 500-1000 C.E. in Andean Chile, as confirmed by archaeological hair samples (Ogalde, Arriaza, & Soto, 2008).

My own experience consuming DMT-containing substances and mixtures has provided me with a host of geometric visual phenomena of such exquisite complexity, seeming impossibility and baffling multidimensionality that it seems difficult to believe that "the patterns of connections between the retina and the striate cortex and of the neuronal circuits within the striate cortex determined their geometric form", nor that "people [perceiving entoptic phenomena following the ingestion of psychotropic substances] are seeing the structure of their own brain" (Lewis-Williams, 2002, p.126).

Indeed, the mescaline and perception researcher Smythies (1953, p.346) had difficulty enough mapping the visual system to merely three-dimensional percepts, "how may these visions be related in their internal three-dimensional spatio-temporal structure to the electrical patterns in the cortex, which possesses an entirely different spatio-temporal structure determined by the complex convoluted shape of the cortex?" So how is it that a tangle of neurochemical "wiring" (a term used *ad nauseum* by Lewis-Williams) can be mapped to what I have personally perceived as a non-ordinary extra-dimensional geometric vision?

Approaching entoptic phenomena, then, from a first-hand phenomenological position there is good reason to agree with Shanon (2003a, p.6) about his observations from his own ayahuasca experiences when he further states that, "to a great extent, most scientists... who talk of hallucinations do not know what they are talking about and that, in fact, what they say is more a reflection of their conceptual presuppositions with regard to this subject matter than a fair characterization of the psychological phenomenology at hand."

It is proposed in this chapter that Lewis-Williams and colleagues, by drawing on a reductionist neuropsychological perspective, have merely imposed their rational materialist philosophical
assumptions on the data without actually experiencing such states
and experiences first-hand. This situation has comparisons with the
leading academics of late 19th century rock art research refusing
to visit the caves of Altamira, which contained the most ancient
art discovered at that time, merely because of intellectual prejudice
(Bahn, 1997).

As much as the ancients supposedly projected their visions onto
the rock surfaces and painted or engraved them (Figure 3), so too
have various researchers projected their beliefs about psychoactive
substance-induced visual percepts onto the phenomena. Rather like a
Rorschach inkblot projective test, rock art has once again been used as
an ambiguous pattern on which to superimpose one's subjective intellectual viewpoints – in this case *a priori* speculations about the brain-
mind. So, are supporters of the neuropsychological assumptions of the
entoptic model just seeing what they want to see, and is there actually
more to entoptics than meets the eye?

Multidimensional Form Constants

Following his experimentation with the psychedelic mescaline-containing cactus, peyote (*Lophophora williamsii*), Klüver (1926, 1966/1928)
originally conceived form constants to fall into four different geometric categories: lattices, cobwebs, tunnels, and spirals. Later researchers used cocaine, LSD and cannabis, as well as a variety of non-drug
means of inducing geometric visual percepts, including transcranial
magnetic stimulation (see Billcock & Tsou, 2012; Dronfield, 1996)
and they defined similar categorizations which Lewis-Williams and
Dowson (1988) finally combined to make six entoptic forms: grids,
lattices, dots, zigzag lines, nested curves and filigrees. More recently
Dronfield (1996) opted for seven.

Renderings of these geometric percepts on paper obviously look
two-dimensional, but using mathematical operations the various patterns can be inferred from the various cortical mechanisms used to
process edges, contours, surfaces and textures (Ermentrout & Cowan, 1979). This model is "based on the assumption that the form of
the retino–cortical map and the architecture of [the visual cortex re-
gion] V1 determine their geometry" (Bresloff et al, 2002, p.474). Nevertheless, it has been noted that, "the experience of mental imagery

Figure 3:   Shamanic rock art from Fremont archeological culture, eastern Utah, USA. (Photo: Copyright by J. Q. Jacobs, jqjacobs.net used under creative commons)

is qualitatively different from the experience of seeing a 2D picture" (Froese, Woodward & Ikegami, 2013, p.205). Furthermore, these psychedelic geometrical percepts have the tendency to appear to belong to the external objects in view and follow their contours rather than just free-floating idly as hallucinatory optic system percepts might be expected to. Indeed, experimenting with mescaline Klüver (1926, p505) observed that "the designs [as on rugs] seem to be localized on walls, on the floor, etc." as did Smythies (1956, p.81) who noted that the "hallucinations are spatial and coloured entities and may possess not only a high degree of internal organization, but may also be closely integrated into the 'veridical' remainder of the visual field in which they occur."

On tryptamine-based psychedelics, such as DMT, such geometric patterns may take the same form (frequently hexagons in this author's own experience) but, unlike mescaline visions, can assume extra-dimensional qualities the likes of which do not ordinarily occur in waking reality. One of the most prominent researchers writing on their own tryptamine experiences, McKenna (1991, p.35), supports this assertion, "there is an immense vividness to these interior landscapes, as if information were being presented three-dimensionally and deployed fourth-dimensionally, coded as light and as evolving surfaces."

The geometric visions of psychedelic states, such as those of Klüver's (1926) peyote experiences, may be depicted in two-dimensional form so that they resemble some rock art patterns of the Upper Paleolithic period, but both renderings, if indeed they are depictions of psychedelic-induced visual patterns, are merely that which can be drawn in a simplified form on paper or rock. To think that these renderings represent the dimensionality of what may actually be perceived in such states would be to confuse the map with the territory.

To support this view a number of first-person accounts are presented from others, of their experiences with psychedelic substances. Considering ayahuasca first of all, the prevalence of extraordinary visual phenomena, such as geometric forms, is quite widespread and were experienced by 64% of first-time ayahuasca users in one study (Barbosa, Giglio & Dalgalarrondo, 2005). Furthermore, the cognitive psychologist Shanon (2002, p.88) considers such visual patterns "reminiscent of those defined by Klüver", but, in support of their non-entoptic origins reports that, "at times, the geometric patterns may seem to defy ordinary real-world Euclidean geometry; some persons that I interviewed made reference to higher orders of spatial dimensionality". Reports of similar, seemingly impossible, multidimensional patterned visual displays are also extant elsewhere within the ayahuasca print literature.

> I saw an image of the Great Spiral and had a sense of moving within it… The Spiral changed into an incredible area of third/fourth dimensional energy (S, 1999, p.171-172).

> The room erupted in incredible neon colors, and dissolving [sic] into the most elaborate incredibly detailed fractal patterns that i [sic] have ever seen (Cott & Rock, 2008, p.363).

> Everything was moving around me. I saw energy as small circles pulling in the direction of the bigger circles, external to their rays, and, at the same time, toward the smaller circles that coexisted in their interior to infinity. And that's how it went, from there to infinity and from infinity to the center of the star of David, where the last circle disappeared and began again (Polari de Alverga, 2000, p.147).

The Extra Dimensions of Cyberdelia

Full written reports of psychedelic experiences in published books and journals are relatively sparse and remain widely distributed, and by far the greatest resource of such accounts can be accessed easily online from the *Vaults of Erowid* (www.erowid.org) where a large collection of *trip reports* has been amassed.

This website is an online library containing 51,542 pages related to psychoactive substances and has 56,015 daily visitors (Erowid,

2008). As of November 2008, the Erowid *Experience Vaults* had a total of 17,898 pseudonymous experience reports covering 314 psychoactive substances (Erowid, 2008). At this time there were 142 ayahuasca trip reports, of which 30 contained the search term "dimension", and 5 of these discussed extra-dimensional percepts (3.5 percent of all ayahuasca reports). Of the thousands of trip reports submitted by readers less than 20% get published on the site, and at least two trained volunteers grade the reports for accuracy, believability, interest and quality

Figure 4: Form constants (after Klüver 1966/1928)

before being finally reviewed for publication by an editor (Erowid & Erowid, 2006).

Reports are thus of a high quality but are susceptible to possible bias in their selection, and so may have limited generalizability. Nevertheless, other researchers have used these accounts for phenomenological research purposes (e.g., Addy, 2007) and, further, a small selection of these trip reports reveals a fairly consistent and frequent report of multidimensional – so arguably trans-entoptic – geometric percepts under the influence of ayahuasca and DMT, as just two substance examples. The following quotes are from ayahuasca reports on the Erowid website.

> Now, in the darkness of my mind there was an entirely different world- a digital, multi-dimensional world of infinity (Jungle Girl, 2008).

> After a point i [sic] came to realize that the entire prismatic hyperdimensional wall of images that assailed me was itself one conscious entity (Scotto, 2000)

> Flying through a multidimensional place of pure vision and thought, I saw endless arches of golden salamanders, flowing through the very fabric of space & time, their colors changing and rotating like countless kaleidoscopes (Satori, 2003).

It should be noted that the shapes described in these ayahuasca visions – spirals, fractals, circles, stars, prisms and arches – resemble Klüver's (1926) *form constant* patterns of lattices, cobwebs, tunnels, and spirals (Figure 4), and Lewis-Williams and Dowson's (1988) so-called entoptic phenomena of grids, lattices, dots, zigzag lines, nested curves and filigrees. Such multidimensional geometric percepts are seemingly reported more frequently, however, with the use of the more intense, more visual and much shorter acting DMT, which is considered to be ayahuasca's most psychoactive chemical constituent (McKenna, 2004) and is usually smoked for its effect. This chemical isn't the only psychedelic substance within ayahuasca, however, because subjectively potent brews occasionally do not contain DMT when analyzed (Callaway, 2005).

As part of one research program conducted in the 1990s, more than 60 participants received a combined total of 400 doses of DMT and reported seeing "all sorts of imaginable and unimaginable things" (Strassman, 2001, p.147) that nearly always began with a Klüver-esque kaleidoscopic display of geometric patterns (Strassman, 2008b). Such patterns include beautiful colorful cobwebs and tremendously intricate tiny geometric colors described by many as "four-dimensional" or "beyond-dimensionality" (Strassman, 2001). Inspecting Strassman's

(1994) 100-item Hallucinogen Rating Scale used to survey the phenomenology of such drug experiences (see Strassman, Qualls, Uhlenhuth & Kellner, 1994) it can be seen that item-67, following on from a question about the kaleidoscopic nature of the images, specifically addresses the dimensionality issue.

Respondents to this item of the scale were given a choice of six categories upon which to rate the "dimensionality of images/visions/hallucinations", with options including one labeled "multi-dimensional" and another styled "beyond dimensionality". When asked how his DMT participants responded to this item Strassman (2008a) replied, "It would take some digging around to find out how many volunteers scored 'multidimensional' or 'beyond dimensionality' for Item 67. But, if my memory serves me well, nearly all the high dose session volunteers marked either one or the other response for this item."

Much like Lewis-Williams' (e.g., 2002) suggestion that there are three levels to the ASC, another cartographer of psychedelic spacetime has suggested that there are three levels to the DMT experience, however, the third and deepest of these reportedly involves "three or higher-dimensional space" (Meyer, 1994). Further, a quick search on the internet archive of Erowid for DMT experiences (up until November 2008), revealed a pool of 191 trip reports, of which 63 contained the search term "dimension" and 29 of these (15% of all DMT reports) specifically discussed extra-dimensional percepts, supporting Strassman's assertion. The following quotes represent a sample of these DMT accounts.

> Many-dimensional starflake prisms collide and explode in color and beauty! (Psychedelicious, 2008).

> The space behind my closed eyes becomes almost immediately multi-dimensional. I can clearly see a [sic] animated, domed, geometrically patterned visualization, largely made of colored & patterned equilateral triangles… the geometry's [sic] of the structure taking place around me were not so simple, not so kiddy-math… I have done some minor readings on sacred geometry and it had always just struck me as something that was neat math that could produce intricate and beautiful patterns, but faced with these kinds of structures [I seriously doubted this], built literally out of all of these geometries in ways that boggle the mind (Bong Man, 2006).

> Apparent crystallization of matter all around me…felt even, like being within a sentient prism. All spatial perception seems to enfold itself in to a gravity well of such ineffable density that it is like floating on the event horizon of a black hole, a prudent observer to nothing less than a multidimensional miracle (Diamond Joe, 2000).

At this point the glorious geometries transcended what is even vaguely feasible in this three dimensional mundane [reality], constantly concrescing into new and varigated [sic] permutations, exfoliating out of themselves what might be called hyperspherologies of the divine, and to look anywhere was to be shot clean through with scintillating amazement... You have a sense of being swarmed by the whimsical mastermind artforms of an extremely eccentric Boolean contortionist, a diabolical merry go round of linguistic Rubix cubes, 13th dimensional millipedes saying themselves to themselves as they make love, and impossible Gordian knots dancing the jitterbug at a lyrical lightspeed: a gelatinous ballet of endlessly self-juxtaposing pirouettes (SFos, 2000a).

All of the examples above clearly establish that the geometric percepts seen in certain altered states, such as those induced by ayahuasca and DMT, may assume extraordinary dimensional qualities that are virtually ineffable and exceedingly difficult to render in static two-dimensional

Figure 5: Visionary artist Luke Brown's "Vajravision".
According to the artist his intention is to map his hyperspatial
experiences with utmost accuracy as a form of
multidimensional cartography.

art, though some artists have made admirable attempts (Figure 5). Taking this observation a step further, it is suggested that these percepts therefore challenge the received wisdom that Klüver's psychedelic form constants are actually entoptic, that is, derived from within the optic system somewhere from the eyeball to the cortex (e.g., Lewis-Williams & Dowson, 1988).

Not only is there the standard cognitive neuroscience miracle of electromagnetic impulses somehow becoming converted into the three-dimensional percepts of the outside world – a feat still not satisfactorily explained by neuroscientists or philosophers (e.g., see Velmans, 2009) – but the mind is apparently also capable of multidimensional geometric perception beyond what is ordinarily perceived in the normal waking state. Positing that visual perception can function beyond what neuroscientists understand to occur in the striate and extrastriate cortices (e.g., Bresloff et al., 2001), what further evidence is there, then, that such seemingly trans-entoptic perception genuinely occurs?

Turning a Blind Eye to Entoptic Phenomena

Both studying visual perception as a psychologist and participating in psychedelic experiences it has long been of interest to know what blind people make of psychedelic experiences: do the blind *see* geometric imagery on psychedelics too, and if so how come? Research giving LSD to totally blind participants suggests that some of these participants do indeed perceive visual "hallucinations" (Krill, Alpert & Ostfeld, 1963) although those doing so had also experienced some visual phenomena in normal life, and none of the four congenitally blind people given LSD reported visual hallucinations.

The findings of this research seem to suggest that a working retina isn't necessary for LSD-induced visual hallucinations to occur, but a normally functioning occipital lobe (absent in those congenitally blind) may be, although these findings are not conclusive. LSD also provides a subjectively different experience to DMT, and while no experiments giving DMT to the congenitally blind have been conducted to the best of my knowledge, such a study has been performed with two 7-year old monkeys blind for one year, and the animals demonstrated a dramatic increase in visual behaviour (e.g., exploration) on both LSD and DMT (Siegel, Brewster, Johnson & Jarvik, 1976). Nevertheless, research into the effects of psychedelics on the human visual experience in the blind is presently inconclusive.

And above humane flight dost soar aloft
With plume so strong, so equal, and so soft.
The Bird nam'd from that Paradise you sing
So never flaggs, but always keeps on Wing.
Where couldst thou words of such a compass find?
Whence furnish such a vast expence of mind?
Just Heav'n thee like Tiresias to requite
Rewards with Prophesie thy loss of sight.

John Milton, *Paradise Lost*, 1667

A new body of evidence is emerging, however, that tentatively indicates that even congenitally blind people can have visual experiences during other states of altered consciousness, such as during a near-death experience (NDE) (somewhat like Tiresias, the underworld blind seer of ancient Greece in the poem above). A study into the visual experiences occurring during the life-threatening incidents of 31 blind or severely visually impaired people indicates that they may have the same type of near-death experience as the sighted, despite not ordinarily having visual experiences (Ring & Cooper, 2008).

Interviews with those both congenitally and non-congenitally blind having NDEs reveal reports of veridical out-of-body experiences (OBEs), often *seeing* the scene of their drama from a disembodied perspective (in 67% of cases), as well as having visual life reviews, meetings with other beings (spirits, angels, religious personages, etc.), and traveling down a tunnel. Of the sample 80% had visual aspects to their experience, including 64% of the 14 congenitally blind participants.

For example, one congenitally blind interviewee who had had two NDEs recalled that, "those two experiences were the only time I could ever relate to seeing and to what light was, because I experienced it" (Ring & Cooper, 2008, p.26), and she went on to describe an OBE as part of her experience, "the first thing I was aware of is that I was up on the ceiling looking... I looked down and I saw this body, and at first I wasn't sure it was my own. But I recognized my hair" (p.28).

How is it then that a person who has never experienced sight, let alone a sense of visual space, can have a veridical visual experience during an ASC in the absence of a normally functioning visual system (both retinal and cortical)? Ring and Cooper (2008) don't pretend this type of vision is the same as true ordinary seeing, but instead consider it as a kind of transcendental awareness which they call *mindsight*. The evidence from blind people for this type of seeing is not conclusive, because inference from the other senses cannot be entirely ruled out, but this wears thin as a counter argument because of the extraordinary detail and verification of the accounts by other witnesses. Subsequently, the mindsight proposition still deserves attention. For example, further evidence for supposed mindsight is apparent from highly detailed and acute observations made by others during NDEs, such as a poorly sighted woman seeing dust on the light fixtures from the perspective of the ceiling, "From where I was looking, I could look down on this enormous florescent light… and it was filthy. And I remember thinking, 'got to tell the nurses about that'." (Ring & Cooper, 2008, p.105). The evidence, therefore, suggests that a functioning optic system is not required to generate mindsight, offering some support for the concept of trans-optic percepts.

Omni-Directional Perception

This kind of veridical visual phenomena seen from a disembodied perspective occurs with normally sighted individuals having NDEs as well, of course. However, there are also accounts of people having other extraordinary visual experiences in such near-death states that further challenge the notion, proposed by Lewis-Williams and Dowson (1988), that entoptics are made within the visual system, such as a woman nearly dying of Asian flu virus having, "a fourth-dimensional rather than a three-dimensional experience" (Corazza, 2008, p.27), along with the omni-directional perception of a woman having an NDE caused by pneumonia during pregnancy:

> I glanced down at the stretcher, knew the body wrapped in blankets was mine, and I didn't really care… I could see everything. And I do mean everything! I could see the top of the light on the ceiling, and the underside of the stretcher. I could see the tiles on the ceiling and the tiles on the floor, simultaneously. Three hundred sixty degree spherical vision. And not just spherical. Detailed! I could see every single hair and follicle out of which it grew on the head of the nurse standing beside the stretcher (Ring & Cooper, 2008, p.107).

A similar account of omni-directional vision is also provided by a poorly-sighted (20/200 uncorrected vision) optometrist during another type of ASC, meditation.

> I could suddenly see everything - the whole room and myself in it - and I couldn't tell where I was seeing from! I wasn't seeing from my eyes or from any single point of view. I seemed to be seeing everything from everywhere. There seemed to be eyes in every cell of my body and in

every particle surrounding me. I could simultaneously see from straight on, from above, from below, from behind, and so on (Liberman, 1995, p.47).

Such omni-directional visual experiences also occur with ayahuasca and DMT (respectively), corroborating the trans-optic nature of visual experiences in such ASCs.

Dimensions expanded, my closed eye range of vision became 270 or so degrees... I started hallucinating intensely... there was a light behind the flowing geometric patterns over everything... it was absolute, unadulterated madness... awe-inspiring, transcendent, and profoundly disturbing" (Reverend Raw, 2009).

Taking part as volunteer subject in a recent DMT brain imaging study in the UK in December 2016, I too had this experience of my visual percepts surrounding me, so that I was able to perceive my vision above and behind me and simultaneously in front. Here follows another account.

I then tried to imagine what it would be like to see in every direction at once, i.e., what would a ball look like if you could see every side of it at once? I could sense it but not imagine it in my mind. So this is the challenge I set myself [for the DMT experience]. It not only seemed to work... but it did so immediately. I rushed upwards into this superspace that was a spun galactic ecology of stars, a swarming hive of dragonfly constellations... This was very profound (SFos, 2000b).

Paranormal Visual Perception

The experiences related here, incorporating multidimensional vision, eyeless sight in the blind, and omni-directional perception could arguably challenge materialist-reductionist views of the capacities of the mind in general, and of the neuropsychological assumption that entoptics are made within the visual system, in particular. Constructivists on the other hand might argue that such reports do not actually represent genuine trans-entoptic phenomena but rather reflect culturally mediated linguistic devices used to try and communicate complex experiences.

Nevertheless, some light may be shed on the genuineness of these extraordinary experiences, with research findings from within the field of parapsychology, which does not *a priori* reject such experiences on materialist-reductionist or other philosophical grounds as some disciplines do but, rather, tests the paranormal hypothesis empirically under tightly controlled conditions. The phenomena of clairvoyance, which literally means "clear seeing" is defined as the "paranormal acquisition of information concerning an object or contemporary physical event... [whereby] the information is assumed to derive directly from an external physical source... and not from the mind of another person" (Thalbourne, 2003, p.18).

One such clairvoyance-type category of research is known as *remote viewing* (or *remote perception*), which requires accurately describing the physical (usually visual) characteristics of a distant location by mental means only, without ever having visited the location. At one point during the 1990s both the CIA and the DIA in the United States joint-funded a $20million research project into remote viewing under the codename STARGATE, which returned highly significant results overall when reviewed by two independent scholars. Of which, one said the research provided good evidence of paranormal perception (Utts, 1995a, 1995b) whereas the other (particularly skeptical) scholar said that the highly significant results needed replicating (Hyman 1995).

Other large-scale remote viewing research studies, however, have also returned positive findings (e.g., Targ 1994; Dunne & Jahn, 2003). The evidence for genuine so-called paranormal visual perception seems relatively good, albeit with a signal to noise ratio that is impracticably low for everyday conscious awareness. Further evidence for genuine paranormal visual perception is also forthcoming from reviews of research from other areas too, such as dream ESP (Ullman, Krippner & Vaughan, 2002; Sherwood & Roe, 2003) and image-guessing experiments into clairvoyance and precognition (literally "prior knowing", or seeing future events) (Honorton & Ferrari, 1989; Steinkamp, Milton & Morris, 1998). In such research, attempts are made to select a target image from among a range of decoy images based on the similarity of the selected image to the participant's mental imagery, either produced in dreams or through conscious intention.

Returning to psychedelics, ayahuasca use is frequently accompanied by out-of-body experiences (e.g., Devereux, 2008) and ostensibly telepathic or clairvoyant visions (e.g., Luna & White, 2000), as is DMT (Luke & Kittenis, 2005). For instance, Kensinger (1973, p.12) reports that, "on the day following one ayahuasca party six of nine men informed me of seeing the death of my chai, 'my mother's father.' This occurred two days before I was informed by radio of his death." Surveys typically reveal that under the influence of psychedelic substances there is a distinct increase in the experience of paranormal events, such as ostensible clairvoyance and precognition, and out-of-body experiences (Luke, 2008; Luke & Kittenis, 2005; also see Chapter 11 for a review).

Attempts to experimentally verify the genuine nature of this surveyed increase in *psi* (an umbrella term for clairvoyance, precognition, telepathy and psychokinesis) brought about by psychedelics have so far been inconclusive – primarily due to poor methodology and a relatively small number of studies – however the results are at least suggestive of the genuine induction of psi with these substances (see Section Two). These findings further challenge the assumption that visual percepts witnessed in ASCs are generated by the visual system and the brain generally, because materialist-reductionist conceptions of the brain-mind have a hard time accounting for distant mental information transfer. Consequently, proponents of this philosophical position generally just disregard the evidence for psi instead of trying to account for it. As Radin (1997, p.263) notes, "the persistent controversy over psi can be traced back to the founding assumptions of modern science. These assumptions have led many scientists to believe that the mind is a machine, and as far as we can tell, machines don't have psi."

Conclusions: Cleansing the Doors of Misperception

Arguably, the visual experience, particularly in altered consciousness, can provide percepts that defy the standard materialist conception of the capacities of the visual system: as a transducer of light that produces a kind of virtual reality perception of the three-dimensional world occurring immediately in front of the eyes. The examples provided in the present paper rather suggest that some visual perceptions have trans-optic origins, so how can these observations be accounted for?

There are a number of steps on the way to answering this question that beg consideration. First, the limitations of the evidence need to be considered. First-person phenomenological reports are often treated with suspicion (e.g. Dennett, 1991), occasionally justified, however, in consciousness research the experience itself is the object of study and so such experiences are valid by definition (assuming the honesty of the subject). With the current observations in hand it would indeed seem dishonest to consider so many corroborative reports of extra-dimensional perception, mindsight, and omni-directional vision as deluded and untruthful, so such experiences should probably be taken seriously, despite their perplexing nature. What these experiences actually are is a matter of further debate. Nevertheless, the wealth of well-controlled parapsychological research, once fairly appraised, should be considered supportive of a general non-ordinary type of perception requiring a non-ordinary explanation.

In seeking such an explanation, the materialist-reductionist assumptions about the function of the visual system should not be taken for granted, and so – with regard to the archeology and anthropology of consciousness – the aspects of Lewis-William and Dowson's (1988) neuropsychological model that relate to the philosophy of mind should be reevaluated critically. Clearly the data presented here do not fit the current theories on entoptics.

In reevaluating the model it would seem prudent, then, to take an approach to the study of altered states that was proposed over 40 years ago, albeit one which has not as yet received the attention it deserves: scientific research and theories concerning altered states of consciousness should be researched from the first-person perspective at least as much if not more so than they are from supposedly objective perspectives. Such an approach gives rise to the long overdue methodology of a *state-specific science* (Tart, 1972b, 2000), whereby the phenomenology of ASCs are researched on their own terms. As Shanon (2003a) notes, one cannot hope to talk knowingly about music if one has not heard music. The same applies to the phenomenology of consciousness and its altered states.

Furthermore, accessing particular states of altered consciousness within the domain of a state-specific science might allow for the direct experience and understanding of intellectual concepts that ordinarily lay beyond the grasp of those few who originate such theories. For instance, Jansen (1999) supposed that the use of the psychedelic anaesthetic, ketamine, which was developed at about the same time (1962) as Bell's (1964) theorem of nonlocal space-time was proposed, enabled some to report the experiential equivalence of the concept. Similarly, it has been proposed that the use of psychedelics can help one's understanding of psi phenomena because they allow the mind access to nonlocal space-time (Millay, 2001). Furthermore, it has been suggested that DMT can activate quantum states in which the ordinary perceptual-cognitive-symbolic mode of thinking and perceiving is replaced with a direct-intuitive-nonlocal mode, enabling access to extradimensional connections within the multiverse (Frecska, 2008).

Indeed after listening to a lecture on space-time and consciousness recently by a professor of cosmology I presented to him a similar idea about the 11 dimensions of space-time conceptualized in M-theory (e.g., see Carr, 2008), suggesting that perhaps those people taking DMT who report multidimensional percepts, often geometrical, are actually witnessing such a concept first-hand. The professor kindly explained, however, that only mathematicians can really conceptualize such a thing as 11-dimensional space-time, and then only mathematically, not visually of course. I wonder. Maybe a combined research approach by both physicists and psychonauts could help to unravel the complex puzzles of string theory or some such conundrums of physics.

Whether or not this phenomenon can give insights into theoretical physics and vice-versa the 80-year old categorization of form constants presented by Klüver (1926, 19966/1928) certainly needs updating to incorporate the full spectrum of ASC-induced geometric percepts and their apparent dimensions. This is particularly pressing for those percepts arising from psychoactive substances besides just those provided by researchers working with LSD, cannabis, cocaine and mescaline between the 1920s and the 1970s.

Finally, the other step that needs to be taken on our journey, inching towards a way out of the neurological maze of geometric ASC percepts, is the incorporation of an alternative conceptual map on which these extraordinary experiences can be located and navigated theoretically, rather than being conspicuously omitted. Several workable candidates look much better designed for the job than the dominant neuropsychological "meat computer" (Minsky, 1987) conception of the brain-mind.

One such plausible contender is Lommel's (2004) analogy of the brain as a television set or other worldwide communication device, in which the mind is analogous to the television show, which does not originate from within the television set but is received by it. According to this view, much like the electromagnetic field that carries the television's information signal, minds are not confined to the insides of heads either but extend outwards in a field-like manner, even communicating directly with other minds and information sources beyond the limitations of space and time. Certainly the radical conception of the brain as a receiver of consciousness, rather than the inadequate materialist notion of it as a generator of consciousness, is likely a more satisfactory concept within which to incorporate the experiences described in this paper.

Similarly to Lommel's analogy of the brain as a television, but coming from a psychedelic perspective, Huxley (1954) promoted Bergson's (1896/1990) theory of the brain as a filter of memory and sensory experience. Bergson viewed the brain as an organ that acts to reduce the wealth of information available to awareness so as to avoid becoming overwhelmed by a mass of largely useless data, irrelevant to the ordinary survival of the organism. The French philosopher, Bergson, further suggested that, if these filters were bypassed, humans would be capable of remembering everything that had ever been experienced and of perceiving everything that has happened everywhere in the universe (e.g., as in clairvoyance). After taking mescaline Huxley added psychedelics to the theory and suggested that these mind-manifesting drugs override the "reducing valve" function of the brain, allowing humans access to both psychic and mystical experiences (a deeper exploration of Huxley's psychedelic filter model appears in Chapter 9).

What then of Lewis-William and Dowson's neuropsychological theory of shamanic rock art if the mind is considered capable of being more than just the brain? The model would mostly still stand: our ancestors would still be considered to have actively engaged in pursuing ASCs; certain rock art would still be considered to represent geometric percepts from these ASCs; and the geometric percepts themselves would still be considered to be universally perceived phenomena in ASCs. *Only the source of these percepts* would need reevaluating, assumed to derive from our physical visual system by Lewis-William and Dowson.

It is hoped that this essay has cast sufficient doubt on the standard neuropsychological assumption that the brain generates the percepts of altered states of consciousness, and it is further hoped that Lewis-William's (e.g., 2002) robotic *a priori* view that form constants are "wired" into our brains is not taken for granted. This may be a rather too optimistic ophthalmologistic hope, however, because the mainstream neuroscientific enterprise has so far generally proved to have tunnel vision on the brain-mind issue, particularly where visual perception is concerned. On the (extra-dimensional?) surface of it, when we pool the reports together, there certainly appears to be more to entoptics than meets the eye, but are there other researchers willing to look any further into it?

Postscript: Hurling Algebra at the Hard Problem of Consciousness to Obscure Absurd Infinite Regress

Ultimately, the experience of such 3D-defying geometries, albeit uncommon, seems to be in little doubt. The problem remains of how, informed by a flat sphere retina, essentially a 2D plane, misfiring neurons that code for edges, contours, surfaces and textures can give rise to percepts with more than three spatial dimensions, given that it is not possible to imagine greater than three-dimensional space (the tesseract being insufficient) let alone perceive it in ordinary states of consciousness. The solution to this problem is also embedded in an even greater mystery relating to the mind-body problem; that of understanding how light, coded as electrochemical signals in the brain, gives rise to a functionally veridical 3D percept of the world.

Despite Ermentrout & Cowan's (1979) elegant computational model of form constants, no amount of mathematics can sidestep this conundrum either, for the 'hard problem' of consciousness cannot be solved algebraically. As Cowan (2013) finally admitted after a very lengthy lecture explaining the mathematics of his model of 2D geometrical percepts to neuroscientists, "you're basically seeing your own visual architecture," leading to the absurd infinite regress that something within the visual system sees itself. This seemingly impossible perceptual feat, which presumes meta-optic systems within the optic system itself, is what Froese et al. (2013) apparently unironically yet understatedly call the "*strange subjective experience* of looking into oneself, where the patterns we see directly expose the underlying operation of our brains" (p.207, italics added).

However, given the nature of apparently veridical vision in congenitally blind individuals having near-death experiences, termed *mindsight* (Ring & Cooper, 2008), and the report of the direct perception with psychedelics of events that are not within view, such as molecules or absent relatives, could vision in extreme altered states of consciousness be informed by a kind of clairvoyance? This issue will be evaluated in further detail in Section Two, but meanwhile the perception of apparently 4D+ spatial arrangements begs some questions about the nature of exceptional psychedelic vision and even ordinary perception.

CHAPTER 5

Discarnate Entities and Dimethyltryptamine (DMT): Psychopharmacology, Phenomenology and Ontology

The highly psychoactive molecule *N,N*-dimethyltryptamine (or simply DMT), is found naturally occurring in the brains of humans, mammals, and some other animals, as well as in a broad range of species of the plant kingdom. Although speculative, neurochemical research suggests that DMT may be made in the pineal gland, and it is hypothesised that, as much as melatonin helps activate sleep cycles, DMT activates dreaming, and may also be implicated in other natural visionary states such as mystical experience, near-death experience (NDE), spontaneous psi and psychosis. Amazonian shamans have made use of this chemical for its visionary properties for thousands of years, most likely, and take it as part of a decoction frequently called *ayahuasca*, which translates from Quechua as "vine of the spirits" or "vine of the dead".

The psychedelic brew is taken because it gives rise to extraordinary mental phenomena that have shamanic and supposed healing qualities, such as synaesthesia, ostensible extra-dimensional percepts, out-of-body experiences, psi experiences and perhaps most commonly, encounters with discarnate entities. When described by independent and seemingly naïve DMT participants the entities encountered tend to vary in detail but often belong to one of a very few similar types, with similar behavioural characteristics. For instance, mischievous shape-shifting elves, preying mantis alien brain surgeons and jewel-encrusted reptilian beings, who all seem to appear with baffling predictability. This opens up a wealth of questions as to the reality (i.e., the ontology) of these entities.

The discussion of the phenomenology and ontology of these entities mixes research from parapsychology, ethnobotany and psychopharmacology – the fruits of science – with the FOAMY CUSTARD of **fo**lklore, **a**nthropology, **my**thology, **cul**tural **s**tudies and **r**elated disciplines. Hopefully however, given the broad range of intellectual interests of psychedelic scholars it won't prove to be a trifle too inter-disciplinary.

Rarely does any one molecule excite as much sense of intellectual possibility as that of DMT: A psychedelic indole-alkaloid of the tryptamine family, much like its more notorious cousin LSD, but one which is found naturally occurring in trace quantities in the human body, as well as in many plants and animals – such that McKenna (2018) states that "Nature is drenched in DMT" – and, unlike LSD, DMT also has a long history of shamanic use among many indigenous cultures, particularly in South America.

When administered by Amazonian shamans it is usually ingested orally from stewed plant matter and gives rise to a 4-6 hour intoxication (Shanon, 2002). When smoked, DMT is generally more intense and extremely fast acting – taking only a matter of seconds to act – and makes extremely profound temporary changes to consciousness, lasting about 12-15 minutes (Strassman, 2001). Zen philosopher Alan Watts, smoked DMT to demonstrate his ability as a monk to maintain rational control and verbal fluency in the most exotic states of consciousness, but failed and commented afterwards that it was like attempting to give, "..a moment-to-moment description of one's reactions while being fired out the muzzle of an atomic cannon with neon-byzantine barrelling" (Leary, 1966, p.84). Similarly, someone recently suggested to me that smoking DMT was, "like God punching a hole in the back of your head."

The extraordinary phenomena reported by users includes extra-dimensional geometric visions, synaesthesia, out-of-body experiences, psi (particularly telepathy and clairvoyance), and encounters with discarnate entities. The parapsychological and transpersonal experiences reported by users are increasingly becoming the focus of research and DMT neurochemistry has been called on in the explanation of phenomena such as psi (e.g., Roney-Dougal, 1991) and NDEs (Strassman, 2001). Currently, however, there exists no published review of DMT in relation to encounters with ostensibly discarnate entities, so the current chapter is overdue in presenting an, albeit brief, overview of the psychopharmacology, phenomenology and ontology of such DMT encounters.

History of DMT Biochemistry

First synthesized in the lab in 1931 by the Canadian chemist Jeremy Manske, DMT was then initially isolated from a plant source (*Mimosa hostilis*) in 1946 by the Brazilian chemist and ethnobotanist Gonçlaves de Lima (Shulgin & Shulgin, 1997). In 1965 a German team published an article in *Nature* announcing the discovery of DMT in human blood, and in 1972 the Nobel-prize winner Julius Axelrod reported finding DMT in human brain tissue (Strassman, 2001), clearly establishing DMT as an endogenous chemical (i.e., made within the body).

Its identity as an endogenous 'psychedelic' was discovered by the Hungarian chemist and psychiatrist Stephen Szára, who synthesised DMT in his lab and injected it into himself in 1956, afterwards describing his "hallucinations" that "consisted of moving, brilliantly coloured oriental motifs" that completely filled his consciousness (Szára, 1957). Szára went on to give DMT to his medical colleagues, one of whom reported that, "the whole room is filled with spirits... I feel exactly as if I were flying...", while another noted that, "In front of me are two quiet, sunlit Gods" (Gallimore & Luke, 2015).

The Speculated Psychopharmacology of DMT, its Related Compounds and the Pineal Gland

The production of DMT in the body is speculated to occur through the conversion of the simpler molecule tryptophan into tryptamine and then into DMT (Mandel, Prasad, Lopez-Ramos & Walker, 1977), the tryptophan being available from the diet as an essential amino acid. Such biosynthesis has been observed in plants and is speculated to occur in humans (Mandel et al., 1977) given that all the necessary chemical building blocks and enzymes are available, but it remains unknown where, for certain, this biosynthesis occurs. One hypothesis holds that DMT manufacture occurs at the pineal gland (e.g., Strassman, 2001), although Hanna (2010) reminds us that the pineal-DMT hypothesis remains unproven despite the tendency of many, less-informed psychedelic commentators to assume it to be true. An in-depth evaluation of the evidence for the DMT-pineal hypothesis is given in Chapter 9.

Neurochemical Action of DMT

In terms of the neurochemical *action on* the brain, DMT, like other psychedelic tryptamines, is only very partially understood. Until recently DMT was considered to be similar in action to the classic serotonergic psychedelics, LSD and psilocybin (for a review see Nichols, 2004,

2016), by acting primarily as a $5HT_{2A}$ (serotonin subtype) agonist and, to some extent, $5HT_{1A}$ too. However, a recent review of 35 psychedelic compounds and their affinities for 51 different receptors, transporters and ion channels shows many psychedelic substances to be particularly 'promiscuous' and they share affinities for many receptor types and sub-types (Ray, 2010). Ray demonstrates DMT to be especially promiscuous having the greatest affinity with $5HT_7$, $5HT_{1A}$, $5HT_{1D}$ and $5HT_{1E}$ out of any of the 35 psychoactive chemicals tested, and also having affinity with a range of serotonin subtypes, some alpha adrenergic receptor subtypes, trace amine-associated receptors (Carbonaro & Gatch, 2016), and the sigma-1 receptor – implicated in clinical depression and schizophrenia – for which DMT is the only known endogenous ligand (Fontanilla et al., 2009).

Prior to the discovery of the unique endogenous role of DMT as a sigma-1 receptor agonist the natural concentrations of DMT in the body were throught to be too low to have any pharmacological effects (Carbonaro & Gatch, 2016), but it is now speculated that this mechanism gives DMT a neuroprotective role in immunoregulation (Frecska et al., 2013). Nevertheless, Nichols (2016) argues that the relevance of sigma-1 receptor activiation to the psychedelic effects of DMT is questionable, at best.

DMT is also unique in having the greatest affinity for any single dopamine (D_1) receptor of any psychedelic compound tested in Ray's (2010) review, although the effects of DMT on dopamine receptors is throught to be indirect (Carbonaro & Gatch, 2016). Nevertheless, it could be said that DMT is far from selective in its action and is a potent and broad-acting neuromodulator. However, as a caveat, the receptorome study by Ray did not explore the functional effects of the 35 psychedelic substances reviewed, thereby leaving uncertain the relevance of the high receptor affinity substances (Nichols, 2016), such as DMT.

Trying to unpack the neurocognitive implications of this pharmacologically limited database and yet extremely complex assortment of neurochemical activities is no simple job and is still very much a nascent endeavour. Wallach (2009), for one, suggests understanding the biological function of DMT is as elusive now as it has ever been. Furthermore, Wallach (2009) speculates that DMT's extraordinary visionary phenomena are actually mediated by its recently discovered action upon the "mysterious" trace amine (e.g., p-tyramine and tryptamine) receptors (not reviewed by Ray, 2010) rather than the serotonergic receptors, as previously thought (e.g., Nichols, 2004). The individual neuroanatomy and neurobiology of these implicated receptor systems is altogether another discussion, but see Nichols (2004) and Wallach (2009) for a limited overview, and Carbonaro and Gatch (2016) for a review.

Phenomenology of the DMT Experience

Since the informal DMT administration studies conducted by Szára, during the 1950s and onwards, few scientific inroads have been made into the DMT experience. By the early 1970s DMT had become a scheduled drug in the severest category, despite demonstrating little potential for abuse, and so scientific research ceased. Medical doctor Rick Strassman has been one of the few researchers to work directly with DMT in humans since then and administered over 400 intravenous doses to more than 60 volunteers throughout the 1990s as part of a clinical investigation into its effects.

Following injection, the effects began in seconds, peaked at about 2 minutes, and by 12-15 minutes had subsided to the point were the participant was able to speak again. Physiological changes generally involved a rapid increase in pulse, up to 150bpm, and blood pressure, but both fell as quickly as they rose once the peak of the trip had been reached at about 2 minutes. Sharp but not prolonged increases in the blood levels were also observed for beta-endophin, vasopressin, prolactin, growth hormone and corticotrophin, possibly leading to some psychological effects. Melatonin concentrations in the blood, interestingly enough, fell. Pupils dilated and body temperature rose after a delay of 15 minutes, and was still climbing at 60 minutes (Strassman, 2001). The physiological changes accompanying the use of ayahuasca are similar but less immediate and more prolonged, and also include vomiting due to the purgative effects of the harmala alkaloids (e.g., see McKenna, 2004).

These physiological changes, however, are experienced subjectively far less than the intense immersive shift in consciousness of the DMT itself. The experience begins with an immediate 'rush', felt as a sense of urgency and departure, often accompanied by "high-pitched," "whining and whirring," or "chattering" sounds as the effects begin (Strassman, 2001, p.148). Intense physical vibrations were commonly experienced, though not objectively observed, usually as a sense of "powerful energy pulsing through them at a very rapid and high frequency" (Strassman, 2001, p.146). Given that such sounds and vibrations are common to out-of-body experiences (e.g., Irwin, 1985) it is perhaps not unsurprising that dissociation from the body was common, with experients feeling they no longer had a body, and, often, that it had dissolved and they had become pure awareness (Strassman, 2001).

In a survey of psychedelic transpersonal experiences (Luke & Kittenis, 2005), two of the three most common reports for DMT were being out of one's body but in another dimension and dissolving into pure energy. The other common experience in Strassman's research was the encounter of entities. Such an intense and swift onset was often accompanied with some fear and anxiety, which generally passed after a few seconds of deep breathing, though on occasion the negative affect became almost unbearably bad. Other feelings experienced include elation, euphoria, excitement, revelation and a sense of timelessness (Strassman, 2001).

Mental Imagery

Visual, or rather mental imagery was the predominant experiential effect for DMT participants, and closely resembled those of ayahuasca users also (e.g., see Beyer, 2009; Luna, 2008; Metzner, 2005b; Shanon, 2002). Indeed, in one study, 63% of first time ayahuasca users reported seeing extraordinary visual phenomena including kaleidoscopic lights, geometric forms, tunnels, animals, humans, and supernatural beings (Barbosa, Giglio & Dalgalarrondo, 2005). At higher doses nearly all of Strassman's DMT participants beheld mental imagery, and saw much the same with their eyes open or shut, except that when open the vision overlaid the contents of the room so volunteers generally closed their eyes for less disorientation.

Initially, imagery usually took the form of kaleidoscopic geometric patterns, which have been referred to as *entoptics* (perhaps erroneously) or *form constants* (e.g., Klüver, 1926; Lewis-Williams and Dowson, 1988) because they are considered to be universally experienced in altered states and supposedly conform to a few specific types of patterning (see chapter 4 for a discussion of entoptics and geometric DMT imagery). Certainly, colourful geometric patterns, which may be called form constants, are experienced as a consequence of factors such as ingestion of certain psychoactive drugs, sensory deprivation, auditory driving and hyperventilation (for a review see Lewis-Williams & Dowson, 1988), as well as hypnogogia (Mavromatis, 1987), and deep hypnosis (Cardeña, 2009).

Under the influence of DMT the colours of this geometry tend to exceed what are usually perceived with the eyes, and were "brighter, more intense, and deeper than those of normal awareness or dreams"

(Stassman, 2001, p.147). The dimensions of the geometric patterns often surpass normal percepts too, and were consistently categorized as "four-dimensional" or "beyond dimensionality" at high doses (Stassman, 2008, personal communication, 6th October), with similar reports occurring for ayahuasca too (Luna, 2008), giving rise to reservations about the supposed physiological origin of such visions (see chapter 4): the optic system seemingly belonging to only three dimensions. The DMT imagery also appears as iconic forms, often becoming incorporated into the aforementioned geometry in a somewhat ineffable manner, as best described by this DMT experient:

> At this point the glorious geometries transcended what is even vaguely feasible in this three dimensional mundane [reality], constantly concrescing into new and varigated [sic] permutations, exfoliating out of themselves what might be called hyperspherologies of the divine, and to look anywhere was to be shot clean through with scintillating amazement ... You have a sense of being swarmed by the whimsical mastermind artforms of an extremely eccentric Boolean contortionist, a diabolical merry go round of linguistic Rubix cubes, 13th dimensional millipedes saying themselves to themselves as they make love, and impossible Gordian knots dancing the jitterbug at a lyrical lightspeed: a gelatinous ballet of endlessly self-juxtaposing pirouettes (Sfos, 2000).

Iconic images seen may take the form of tunnels, stairways, ducts (Strassman, 2001); symbols and scripts; incredible landscapes and cities of alien worlds (Shanon, 2002), the inner workings of fantastic machines, computers, internal organs and bodies; and, commonly, DNA double helices (Strassman, 2001). The anthropologist Narby (1998) also found DNA was a frequent feature in the ayahuasca visions of Amazonian shamans, but often 'represented' by two intertwined snakes. A possibly apocryphal and certainly controversial story shortly after Francis Crick's death suggests that the geneticist was under the influence of LSD when he envisioned the double helix structure of DNA in 1953, for which he was jointly awarded the Nobel Prize (Rees, 2004).

Prior to the Crick news report, Narby (2000) took three molecular biologists to Peru for their seminal trips up the Amazon and on ayahuasca. All three scientists received valuable information from their visions that helped inform their research, and which ultimately changed their worldview. For instance, "the American biologist, who normally worked on deciphering the human genome, said she saw a chromosome from the perspective of a protein flying above a long strand of DNA" (Narby, 2000, p.302).

Similarly, but previously, the biochemist, Kary Mullis, who received the Nobel Prize for inventing the polymerase chain reaction (PCR) – making possible the human genome project and forensic DNA testing – said that taking LSD had been invaluable in helping him visualize sitting on a DNA molecule and watching the polymerase go by (Mullis, 1998). Clearly LSD is not the same as DMT, but as a psychedelic tryptamine it has some similar neurochemical properties and, in auspicious circumstances, both substances seem capable of inducing microscopic molecular visions, particularly of DNA. Whether such feats are due to the imagination or clairvoyance remains unclear, but support for the latter is abundant, albeit inconclusive.

DMT and Veridical Visions

When the harmala alkaloid now called *harmine*, the first psychoactive compound isolated from ayahuasca, was discovered by Zerda Báyon (1912) it was named *telepathine*. Zerda Báyon illustrated the psi-inducing power of telepathine with the case of Colonel Morales who, after ingesting ayahuasca, beheld a vision of his dead father and his sick sister. About one month later he received the same news by messenger. It seems unlikely that the news could have arrived first by non-paranormal means, as the group was deep in the jungle 15 days' travel from the nearest communications outpost. Indeed, beholding visions of distant dead or dying relatives – who were not known at the time to be ill or dead – is an ayahuasca story that has emerged repeatedly in the writings of South American explorers during the last 150 years (for a brief review see Luke, 2010a).

Many more published accounts of such apparent ESP occur in Luna and White's (2000, 2016) anthology of classic ayahuasca experiences, as well as elsewhere (for summaries see Luke & Friedman, 2010; Shanon, 2002). Survey respondents also reported DMT and ayahuasca as inducers of spontaneous psi-type experiences, although these were more conspicuous with certain other psychedelics (Luke & Kittenis, 2005). Nevertheless, the only two published experiments to attempt to test for psi under the influence of DMT, in this case ayahuasca (Don, McDonough, Warren & Moura, 1996; Tinoco, 1994), both failed to elicit it, though this may well be due to the arduous and boring testing deployed. In one study the participant complained that experiencing the visions was far more interesting than testing for psi, and both studies lacked control conditions to compare against (for a review see Section Two).

Phenomenolgical Cartography of the DMT World

Considering the phenomenology of the DMT experience several researchers have attempted to map the psychic topography of the DMT space. Meyer (1994), probably the first researcher to write specifically about DMT entities, characterized the deepening levels of the experience – somewhat like Lewis-Williams and Dowson's (1988) stages of altered states of consciousness – as:

Level I: Threshold experience; an interior flowing of energy/consciousness

Level II: Vivid, brilliantly coloured, geometric visual patterns; geometries are basically two-dimensional but may pulse

Transitional phase: Tunnel or breakthrough experience; passage through an entrance into another world

Level III: Three- or higher-dimensional space, possible contact with entities; a sense of being in an "objective" space and of meeting intelligent and communicating entities.

Level IV: The white light.

The cognitive psychologist Shanon (2002, p.293) has a similar, albeit more refined system for the stages of the ayahuasca experience, framed around the predominant visual or visionary phenomena:

1. Bursts, puffs and splashes of colour
2. Repetitive, multiplying non-figurative elements
3. Geometric designs and patterns
4. Designs with figures
5. Rapid figural transformations
6. Kaleidoscopic images
7. Well-defined, stable, single figurative images
8. Proto-scenes
9. Full-fledged scenes
10. Interactive scenes
11. Scenes of flight
12. Celestial and heavenly scenes
13. Virtual reality
14. Supreme light

Like Meyer's four DMT stages, Shanon's fourteen ayahuasca stages begin with colourful geometry, pass through fully immersive other worlds and terminate in experiences of euphoric light, though it should be noted that not all experiences 'go all the way'. Ayahuasca cartographer Beyer (2009), prefers to characterize the experience into just three chronological stages, the first two of which map closely to those of Shanon and Meyer: First is the geometric pattern phase, second is the "contact with the spirit world" phase – incorporating entity encounters and corresponding to Meyer's *Level III* and Shanon's *9th-13th stages* – whereas the third and final stage is a recovery phase, of pleasantness, lassitude, fading visions and decreased intensity. Alternatively, Strassman (2008) takes a categorical rather than a stage approach to classifying the different DMT experiences, into three types:

Personal: Encounters with one's own personal issues, often difficult to accept

Transpersonal: An experience novel in intensity and quality but formed from the subject's previous experience. May be a mystical or near-death type experience.

Invisible worlds: Encounter with autonomous, freestanding realities sometimes appearing to be inhabited by alien beings capable of interaction.

At least half of the volunteers taking a high dose of DMT had a minimum of one 'invisible world' experience (Strassman, 2008b). That is, that pure DMT can reliably induce an entity encounter experience in a good proportion of volunteers.

Discarnate Entities

Perhaps one of the most striking, common and therefore unique features of the DMT or ayahasuca experience is the encounter with seemingly sentient discarnate beings, which are often described as being more real than anything ever experienced (Cott & Rock, 2008). Commonly they were described as "entities," "beings," "aliens," "guides" or "helpers," and would appear something like "clowns, reptiles, mantises, bees, spiders, cacti, and stick figures" (Strassman, 2001, p.185), as well as dwarves, elves, imps, angels, spirits, gods, or just as a presence, the latter four of which were commonly supremely powerful, wise, and loving.

Encounters with serpents and large felines, particularly black pumas are much more typical on ayahuasca (Shanon, 2002): In traditional ayahuasca mythology the serpent is considered to be the spirit of ayahuasca and the feline is considered to be the power animal of the shaman, and on occasion the ayahuasca drinker feels themselves transformed into this creature. Besides visionary encounters with people, animals and other ordinary things (not typical of DMT), the kinds of supernatural beings encountered on ayahusaca are classified by Shanon (2002) thus:

1. *Mythological beings*: Such as gnomes, elves, fairies, and monsters of all kinds.
2. *Chimeras or hybrids*: Typically half-animal half-human (e.g., mermaids), or transforming or shapeshifting beings, for example from human to puma, to tiger, to wolf.
3. *Extraterrestrials*: These are particularly common for some experients and may be accompanied by spacecraft.
4. *Angels and celestial beings*: Usually winged humanlike beings that may be transparent or composed of light
5. *Semi-divine beings*: May appear like Jesus, Buddha, or typically Hindu, Egyptian or pre-Columbian deities
6. *Demons, monsters and beings of death*: Such as the angel of death

A similar classification might also be applied to DMT entities. In a qualitative analysis of interviews with 19 DMT users (Cott & Rock, 2008), a common theme emerged of entering other realities and having what the user experienced as real encounters with sentient beings. Of note, the entities tended to impart insightful information about themselves and the universe in which they were inhabited, much like the positive performative role played by the apparently sentient beings encountered in near-death experiences, typically identified as being deceased persons (Cott & Rock, 2008).

In addition another category, of plant teachers or plant spirits, should be added to Shanon's list, because these are regularly encountered on ayahuasca according to interviews with shamans and surveys of users (see Luke, 2012d). Further, a sub-category to Shanon's bestiary might be added to the extraterrestrial category, that of insectoid-, and especially praying mantis- aliens (Luke, 2008b). Ever since Leary's (1966) account of his DMT encounter with metallic and bejewelled Venutian crickets, reports abound of mantid-like creatures performing exotic surgical operations and probe insertions on DMT experients, as well as those on psilocin (4HO-DMT), in a manner reminiscent of alien abduction cases (e.g., Kottmeyer, 1999; Mack, 1999). Indeed one close friend naïvely reported a mantis encounter on their first DMT trip and another naïvely experienced full blown "psychic brain surgery" from a mantis on their second ayahuasca session (Luke, 2013b).

Concurrently, though probably starting somewhat later with Strie-ber (1987), mantises became a growing motif in the alien abduction literature, and one assumes that this was virtually independent from the DMT literature at this time – at least no one appears to have joined up the dots on DMT versus spontaneous alien abduction insectoid encoun-ters until Pickover (2005). For example, there was an article about the increasing presence of praying mantises in alien abduction cases in the 1990s, which were dubbed the 'greying' mantises as they appeared so often in people's abduction experiences (Kottmeyer, 1999). Notably, this pre-millenium article was essentially entirely naïve to the DMT literature of this era, or at least it appears so, and yet we find a con-cordance between the alien abduction and DMT experiences, not least with this motif of the praying mantis, and with the elf-like characters too.

Psychedelic explorer McKenna (1991) posited that the visions of 4HO-DMT (psilocin) and of aliens and UFOs originated from the same source. Strassman (2001) developed this further and suggested that spontaneous endogenous DMT fluctuations could be at the root of alien abduction experiences as they share the same newly found fear-lessness of death and visions of energy tunnels, or cylinders of light, in common with DMT experiences. Following the use of ayahuasca Severi (2003) also noted the similarity between NDEs, traditional psy-chedelic-induced shamanic initiations, alien abduction experiences, and heightened psychic sensitivity, as have previous researchers (e.g. Harvey-Wilson, 2001; Ring, 1989).

However, Barušs (2003) notes that, despite the similarities, DMT and alien abduction experiences lack specific commonalities, such as the absence with DMT of the classic *grays* (alleged small gray aliens). Nevertheless, Hancock (2005) argues that there are substantial simi-larities between aliens and 'elves', whether induced through DMT or else appearing in historic-folkloric legends and testimonies, speculat-ing that the latter also have a DMT-induced etiology and, adopting the theory proposed by Vallee (1969), that these elves are the prototype en-counter/abduction experiences. It should be noted that few experienc-ers ever doubt the reality of their encounters with either aliens (Mack, 1999) or DMT entities (Strassman, 2001).

Ontology of DMT Beings

Encounters with elves, gnomes, pixies, dwarves, imps, goblins and other 'little people' (though clearly not human people), are extremely prevalent. Indeed on my first experience with DMT, unaware of virtually all lore associated with it, I found myself, eyes closed, being stuffed full of light by what I can only describe as little elves. I thereafter discovered a similar account reported by Meyer (1996) and so was struck by the coincidence. It's the seeming reality of the experience at the time, and the similarity of such encounters with those of others, that have led many to seriously ponder the ontology of these beings.

Similar 'elven' characters once reappeared on an ayahuasca trip but disturbed me even more because this time they appeared in front of me, interacting with me, with my eyes open. These little people, perhaps due to their prevalence, have long been at the spearhead of the debate on the reality of DMT beings, and have been popularly dubbed the "self-transforming machine elves" (McKenna, 1991, p. 16).

Initiating the debate, Meyer (1996) indicates that, under the influence, the independent existence of these beings seems self-evident, but suggests that there are numerous interpretations of the entity phenomena. Meyer's and others' interpretations fall into three basic camps:

I – *Hallucination*: The entities are subjective hallucinations. Such a position is favoured by those taking a purely (materialist reductionistic) neuropsychological approach to the phenomena. One particularly vocal DMT explorer who adopted this neuro-reductionistic approach, James Kent (Pickover, 2005, pp.104-105), appears to have taken a more ambiguous stance recently (Kent, 2010) by considering the entities simply as information generators. For Kent (2010), the question of the entities' reality is redundant given that they generate real information, and sometimes this seemingly goes beyond the experient's available sphere of knowledge. Nevertheless, according to Kent the entities cannot be trusted to always tell the truth and must be regarded as tricksters.

II – *Psychological/ Transpersonal*: The entities communicated with appear alien but are unfamiliar aspects of ourselves (Turner, 1995), be that our reptilian brain or our cells, molecules or sub-atomic particles (Meyer, 1996). Alternatively, McKenna (1991, p. 43), suggests "We are alienated, so alienated that the self must disguise itself as an extraterrestrial in order not to alarm us with the truly bizarre dimensions that it encompasses. When we can love the alien, then we will have begun to heal the psychic discontinuity that [plagues] us."

III – *Other worlds*: DMT provides access to a true alternate dimension inhabited by independently existing intelligent entities. The identity of the entities remains speculative, but they may be extraterrestrial or even extra-dimensional alien species, spirits of the dead or time travellers from the future (Meyer, 1996). A variation on this is that the alternate dimension, popularly termed *hyperspace* (e.g., Turner, 1995), is actually just a four-dimensional version of our physical reality (Meyer, 1996). The hyperspace explanation is one of the conclusions drawn by Evans-Wentz (1911/2004, p.482) following his massive folkloric study of 'the little people' (i.e., elves, pixies, etc):

> It is mathematically possible to conceive fourth-dimensional beings, and if they exist it would be impossible in a third-dimensional plane to see them as they really are. Hence the ordinary apparition is non-real as a form, whereas the beings, which wholly sane and reliable seers claim to see when exercising seership of the highest kind [perhaps under the influence of endogenous DMT], may be as real to themselves and to the seers as human beings are to us here in the third-dimensional world when we exercise normal vision.

Clearly, no amount of speculation will reveal the true nature of such DMT 'visions' nor their entities and the ontological debate remains wide open without a scientific approach. At this juncture, parapsychology, and psychical research in particular, can lend over a century's worth of similar such enquiry to the issue. A case in point comes from a proposal by computer scientist Rodriguez (2007) to experimentally prove or disprove the entities' existence. Grossly simplified, Rodriguez (2007) suggests obtaining from the entities solutions to complex mathematics puzzles that are unknown to the DMT participant communicating with them. Regrettably, this ingenious method for testing the reality of DMT entity encounters is subject to a number of flaws, aside from the huge assumptions involved in expecting our supposed hyper-intelligent beings having the desire to cooperate and make themselves 'proven'.

The most crippling problem for Rodriguez' test, however, is the *super psi* hypothesis, which has long proved difficult to surmount in parapsychological attempts to validate the existence of discarnate entities considered to be spirits of the dead, e.g. those apparently communicating via trance mediums. The problem is that, because psi has no theoretical or even apparent limits, it remains a possibility that any information provided by ostensibly discarnate entities may actually be due to the 'super' psi of the receiver (e.g., the medium or DMT explorer) receiving the information directly from an earthly incarnate source (e.g., see Braude, 2002, for a comprehensive discussion).

A parallel debate aptly demonstrates how the super psi problem applies to Rodriguez' (2007) proposal. The living chess grandmaster Victor Korchnoi ostensibly played a high level game of chess with the deceased Hungarian grandmaster Géza Marcóczy via a non-chess playing automatic-writing medium (Eisenbeiss & Hassler, 2006). Good evidence was presented that none other than a grandmaster of Marcóczy's standing, of which few if any are living, could have maintained that standard of playing over 47 moves, and so Neppe (2007) dismissed the super-psi hypothesis, but failed to consider the possibility that Korchnoi himself was the (living) source of such psi information (Breederveld, 2008). Surely Occam's razor should prevail in such cases, making 'the survival hypothesis' (of some sort of consciousness extending post-mortem) stand proud, but alas, uncertainty prevails, and a similar curse awaits any such attempts to test the reality of DMT entities through ordinary informational means, be that maths puzzles, chess or otherwise.

One alternative approach to investigating the ontology of shamanic entity encounters considers similarities in independent reports concerning the characteristics of particular entities, especially those encountered naïvely and without any cultural context from which the characteristics of the entity could be derived (see chapter 6). For instance, one such being that commonly appears to naïve DMT users is an entity consisting of multiple entwined serpents covered in multitudinous eyes, often forming a fibbonaci spiral-like geometrical shape. Obscure references to a similar mythological entity, sometimes identified as the angel of death, also exist in various cultural cosmologies, possibly indicating the transcultural nature of this entity (Luke, 2008a).

Such data pose challenging questions as to whether the entity is culturally mediated – which seems unlikely given the obscurity of the cultural references – or a culture-free universal feature of DMT activation (naturally or artificially) in the brain, with possible incorporeal origins. A recent conversation with a 5-year old boy who described this exact entity and its activity in exquisite detail had me wondering whether the boy was a) generating an extremely elaborate spontaneous hoax, b) deeply psychic, or c) had genuinely encountered this entity on a regular basis during dreams and hypnogogia (see postscript to the following chapter).

A similar phenomenological triangulation approach could fruitfully be made with other types of entities commonly encountered with DMT and ayahuasca, such as the bizarre preponderance of praying mantises (Luke, 2008b). It might be possible by such means to determine how statistically improbable is the occurrence of these shared visions. Such a methodology has its limitations, of course, nevertheless upon inspection of the literature it appears that such an approach has rarely been applied to the study of apparently collective visions and may point the baffled DMT ontologist in an enlightening direction.

Nevertheless, to supply enough rope for any attempt to fathom the identity of such entities it would seem beneficial to first demonstrate the authenticity of some less nebulous paranormal phenomena, so as to at least show that extraordinary experiences under the influence of DMT may be genuine. Appropriate directions for such endeavours may include demonstrating the utility of DMT (or ayahuasca) for either inducing psi under controlled conditions (Luke, 2008) or genuine extra-dimensional percepts (Luke, 2010b). An alternative would be the demonstration of the lawful and orderly induction of synaesthetic communications, such as reports of shamans singing while weavers 'see' the sounds and independently weave identical yarn patterns (see Luke, 2012d). These are possible avenues of research but any small miracle these days is a step in the right direction.

The real benefit of this research, of course, is that a deeper understanding of DMT and its discarnate entities may cast some light on the study of all encounter phenomena, be they apparitions, ghosts, poltergeists, aliens, elves, or the kinds of spirits supposedly channelled by mediums. The danger with such information is that even if DMT is implicated in other spontaneous encounter experiences it cannot, by itself, tell us whether such experiences are real or not. Ultimately we remain burdened with an intellectual regress whilst left clutching a neurochemical piece of the jigsaw, though we may not quite be certain where it fits in and, in any case, it seems to make the puzzle that much more perplexing.

CHAPTER 6

Disembodied Eyes Revisited: An Investigation into the Ontology of Entheogenic Entity Encounters

And all should cry, Beware! Beware!
His flashing eyes, his floating hair!
Weave a circle round him thrice,
And close your eyes with holy dread,
For he on honey-dew hath fed,
And drunk the milk of Paradise
Samuel Taylor Coleridge, Kubla Khan, 1797

Figure 6: Image Naoto Hatorri (Virus 025)

All that glitters is not gold. Such a maxim might well serve any psychic voyager on a journey into the weirder realms of psychedelics. After all, out here on the edges there is seldom any firm evidence that the beatific or hellish visions beheld whilst chemically neurohacking your wetware have any basis in consensus reality. Indeed these visions are often so extravagantly strange and terrifyingly ineffable that reminding yourself that they are not real can serve to keep one's sanity on a short leash when madness looms.

Nevertheless, as John Lilly put it, how does one recognize one's in-sanity from one's out-sanity? And in any case how would anyone even begin to try and prove the ontological credibility of the psychedelic experience if they are to visit some other world or meet some alien entity? No one has yet put forward a solid method for testing these supposed realities within the domain of science, despite some admirable but flawed attempts recently (e.g., Rodriguez, 2007), so all we have left to rely on is anecdote and phenomenology. This story lies somewhere between the two but also takes on a new dimension that has urged me to depart momentarily from the fruits of science into the "foamy custard" of folklore, myth, cultural studies and related disciplines, but it seemingly has enough semblance of objectivity to warrant a whisper of truth - whatever that may be.

A Brief Glance at the Truly Forbidden

I'd taken a full dose of DMT (~ 50mg smoked) about forty or fifty times, but always with some trepidation and reverence for its power. True to form I met a variety of extraordinary entities on these excursions (as Terence McKenna once said "you get elves, everybody does") - sometimes unknown God-like beings, sometimes shape-shifting mischievous imps - but increasingly I kept getting the feeling I was intruding upon a cosmic gathering I wasn't invited to. Sometimes, the effects failed to go any further than an ego-dissolution and a wild swim through a fractal geometry of pulsing light with all the usual wild array of colours. Yet, I often felt as though I was being blocked to whatever lurked beyond these multiple geometrical dimensions and to the places I had been to previously. A couple of times I had felt so uninvited and intimidated by the entities I did meet that I did not wish to return, regardless of my curiosity.

On my last DMT session I had been determined to return to the mystic bliss I had once known and I took myself off to a secluded beach on the banks of the River Ganges. I prepared myself with an improvised ritual hoping to gird myself against whatever lay beyond and inhaled a pipe full of the foul plastic-tasting resin. Sucked into the space between the pipe and my brain I found myself breaking through the veil like a gatecrasher at a party of swirling smiling eyeballs all attached to snake bodies, which were as startled to see me as I was to be there. The whole ordered assortment of eyes and snakes acted as one being and in the brief moment before it reacted to my arrival I managed to catch a glimpse over what might loosely be described as the shoulder of this strange being and instantly realized that I had seen something I should not have - a brief glance at the truly forbidden.

Afterwards I could not recall what this was exactly, having some-how blocked it out, but only recall that it was a scene that seemed both ineffable and highly illegal for mortal minds. Then the multitudi-nous eyes of the being before me quite suddenly and quite deliberately blocked my curious consciousness explorations any further by mes-merising me with its squirming rhythmic geometrical eyeball hypnosis. I mean, this thing really scared me! It had acted with utter surprise at my being there and then, alarmed, the ominous luminous voluminous numinous had proceeded to let me know that I should not be there and that I should certainly not be peering into the hallowed space beyond it, which it clearly guarded. I opted not to defy this terrifying entity and attempted to remain as passive as possible while it pulsed and gyrated intimidatingly at me for the next ten minutes, though it seemed like an eon.

I finally came out of it all a bit shell-shocked and decided that this would be my last DMT experience, for a long time at least. [This event actually happened something like 14 years ago and I ventured into my first full DMT voyage since then only last month, as a volunteer subject in a DMT brain imaging study with some colleagues. I lived to tell the tale, but that's another story.]

Like many of my psychedelic encounters with seemingly discar-nate beings I didn't know quite what to make of this experience, but it had rocked me to the core. It wasn't until a few years later that I began to piece it together with some other visionary fragments. In a dream once I had, quite naïvely, had a mind-blowing encounter with Azrael, the Islamic angel of death. The angel had told me its name, though I'd never heard it before, but unfortunately it never showed itself because among Muslims the archangel Azrael is considered to have ten thou-sand eyes, and is the holy psychopomp ushering souls into the realm of the dead.

A similar character, Azrail the god of death, belongs to the Huasa people of western Africa (Besmer, 1983). I also later stumbled across

Ezekial's vision of the cherubim in the bible (Ezekial 10: 12); guarding the ark in the temple of Solomon they too were covered in a multitude of eyes, all over their hands, back, wings, etc., much like the multi-eyed beasts guarding the throne of god in heaven (Rev, 4:6) and this struck a cord of recognition, although the being I had met on DMT had not seemed quite so angelic.

It wasn't until several years after this last DMT event that I made a surprising discovery when I accidentally came across a reference in a book on Tibetan magic and ritual to an ancient deity by the name of Za [gZa' in Tibetan] that is known to appear with half the body of a snake, no less, and is covered in a thousand eyes. Interestingly, like the cherubim guarding the ark, the Tibetan Za functions as a "protector of the law" and is a guardian deity belonging to a class of demon-gods called Lu or Lhamayin (associated with the Indian nāgas), who appear with snake bodies.

Figure 7: The ancient protector Za. From an iconographic sketch
by Tendzin yongdű (Beyer, 1974).

Figure 8: A peaceful lu **and a fierce** lu **of a river.** From an iconographic sketch by Tendzin yongdŭ (Beyer, 1974).

The author, Beyer (1974, p 295), wrote, "These Lu are undisputedly spirits of the underworld, found in places where their realm impinges upon ours, such as in springs, wells, and rivers". This struck an even greater chord when I realized that on that last occasion I had smoked the DMT on the banks of the River Ganges near the Tibetan border, which in retrospect would seem like a sure way to meet this Tibetan deity.

The idea that I had been interloping into the sacred realm of the dead, the underworld, and was blocked by a powerful guardian spirit sat well with my experience, which had me wishing I hadn't turned up uninvited as I was obviously not on the guest list. Knowing I shouldn't be there I clearly recall spending the duration of the trip trying to keep my tryptamined mind inconspicuous and so I focused on the mesmeric rhythmic eyes and nothing more, realising that I had stolen a glance at some holy grail when I had burst through the veil. The entity there responded quickly and I couldn't have been more compelled not to mess with it. This feeling was further corroborated by Beyer (1974, p.54) who wrote that, in relation to Za and the other fierce protector deities, they

> ...are powerful deities who symbolize currents of cosmic force to be tampered with only at one's peril. They constitute the monastic cult [of the Nyingma yogin - the oldest Tibetan sect] because they are best left to the ritual experts. It is not that their cult is particularly secret, just as there is nothing esoteric about the workings of a television set; but in

Figure 9: Tibetan image of Za/Rahu
(from the collection of Mike Crowley).

both instances the forces involved are too potent to be played with by a
layman, and in both instances the same warning applies.

The same sentiment was echoed by the noted scholar of Tibetan
demons, Nebesky-Wojkowitz (1956) who offered that the Nyingmapa
consider the planetary god Za (Rahu) to belong in the highest trinity of
deities and that he "…guards the religious teachings, and his thousand
eyes watch the happenings in the three worlds" (p.260).

Worryingly, Nebesky-Wojkowitz indicates that the elaborate propitiatory dough cake (gtor ma) made to honour Rahu (Za) is constructed
of a large red serpentine pyramid dotted geometrically with numerous

eyes and bearing stakes "…arranged around the base of the 'gtor ma' on which dough effigies of men and animals have been impaled as offerings" (p.353). (Somewhat weirdly this eyed-pyramid bears some resemblance to the be-tentacled pyramidal monster of Robert Anton Wilson and Robert Shea's *Illuminatus* trilogy, the Leviathan). Beyer (1974) even submits that a lama led him to believe that Nebesky-Wojkowitz died accidentally before his time because of his careless interest in these fierce protector deities.

Reading Beyer's account had made me feel particularly alarmed that there had been some objective reality to my encounter and that I had, seemingly, really run into this Tibetan underworld guardian. But these few coincidences barely constitute enough to convince most folk about the objective reality of DMT entities or Tibetan deities, and nor should they, particularly those folk, like James Kent (2004), who argue that these entities are merely the imaginary output of our neurochemical meddlings.

Others have suggested that these entities cannot be considered either real or fictitious but might be better thought of as just a part of ourselves (e.g., Turner, 1995). It might have ended here but, soon after, I discovered that the experience I thought was unique to me was not so unique after all. Alarmingly, this discovery threatened to bolster the tentative argument that our particular DMT entity, who we could

Figure 10: Sketch of red-coloured gtor ma propitiatory dough cake dedicated to Za (Nebesky-Wojkowitz, 1956).

call Za, might have some objective reality, and then so too might all those other beings we encounter along the way to Chapel Perilous, be they mischievous dwarves, machine elves, ancient gods or their praying mantis aliens.

Snake Eyes

Only a few days after reading about Za I chanced across an article by Meyer (1994) on *Apparent Communication with Discarnate Entities Induced by DMT* in which there was the following account:

> I noticed what seemed to be an opening into a larger space, like looking through a cave opening to a starry sky. As I approached this I saw that resting in the opening was a large creature, with many arms, somewhat *like an octopus, and all over the arms were eyes*, mostly closed, as if the creature were asleep or slumbering. As I approached it the eyes opened, and it/they became aware of me. It did not seem especially well-disposed toward me, as if it did not wish to be bothered by a mere human, and I had the impression I wasn't going to get past it, so I did not try [my emphasis].

That this creature was also quite intimidating and appeared to be guarding the way to something beyond matched my own experience, but it doesn't end here. I was conducting a web-survey of paranormal psychedelic experiences at the time (Luke & Kittenis, 2005) and found that one of my respondents had also had a similar experience, but with psilocybin rather than DMT:

> I was convinced I was dying, I saw another dimension, one filled with eyes in a fibonacci vortex/dome… I've explained this to so many people and regardless of how many things I see, be it in art or biblical references, they all say I'm nuts.

Encouraged by finding these chance reports I then began searching through psychedelic journals and on the internet for similar stories and found a few more corresponding accounts. This first one occurred with psilocybin-containing mushrooms and is from the *Entheogen Review* (Owl, 1995):

> I began seeing a peculiar phenomenon during low dose mushroom sessions: a pattern of threatening eyeballs. I intuited that the mushroom was trying to scare me, and I marveled at the workings of the mind, feeling humored rather than frightened. … In spite of my scientifically-orientated worldview, I was being visited by a spirit which seemed to be anticipating a deeper encounter.

...I took about five grams... This is when I felt the strange spirit enter me: the many eyed apparition that had already been haunting my consciousness. The difference was that this time the "creature" seemed to be inside of me. ... I immediately began questioning its intentions – who was it, what did it want, and was it a demon? I received no answer, and so, not being certain that it belonged in my head, forcefully commanded it to leave, which it apparently did. ...I had the creepy feeling that I was either going crazy or was infected with a spooky denizen of hyperspace... Perhaps like an insect under a magnifying lens, I have difficulty fathoming this mysterious being of a thousand eyes. Interestingly enough, one of my companions later commented that at one point he perceived my forehead to be covered with eyes.

This next one, from the web-based *Vaults of Erowid*, actually occurred on LSD (Trip333, 2007):

Countless numbers of eyeballs were looking at me. They were the most evil things I have ever seen. They were all on these snakelike bodies that were weaving back and forth. I reopened my eyes and saw the eyes and the worms all over me and on the ground.

Although I only found these three isolated reports on LSD and psilocybin, I found numerous DMT reports that mentioned eyeball-riddled snake entities in variously weird or disturbing sequences. I needn't quote them all as this last one offers some kind of "radical empirical" (James, 1912/2003) mystical triangulation of my own experience and a tentative interpretation of it (Pup, 2006):

I remember the veil, like rubber, or the surface of jelly stretched in front of me. ...I leaned forward to touch the surface of the membrane and then what happened next I swear nearly killed me from its sheer bizzarity. ...A creature emerged. It was not a happy, smiley elf. ...It had inumerable tentacles, like a cross between some weird octopus or jellyfish...and the EYES! OH MY GOD THE EYES!!!

I froze on the spot thinking 'shit that's it. I've gone and done it now. I'm fucking toast'. I never believed. I should have believed. And now. Now I am at the mercy of something much, much, bigger and complex, and clever and definitely malevolent than myself. I asked it its name. I wish I had not asked. It's voice utterly destroyed me. It was like being caught in a storm of psychic noise - a whirlwind of deadly electrical shrapnel. ...With its innumerable eyes, It gazed at me steady and extended a tendril. At the same moment it fired a beam of light directly between and above my eyes. The alien laser was pinkish-green. It hurt. I begged it to stop. I whimpered 'please stop. You're hurting me. I'm fragile. Please be careful - I am sentient and mean you no harm...'

It seemed to consider this; the laser was withdrawn but the tendrils (there were more now) still held me in place. I was trying to make out details of its shape or structure but the closer I looked, the more it slipped away from me. It seemed to tell me in some weird non-verbal fashion not to struggle and to stop making noise with my eyes. I took this to mean 'Be calm, do not struggle. Clear your head. See but don't look'.

Then it became a little clearer. It seemed to be cloaked in some way - some sort of organic hood and covering was wrapped around it - some sort of armor or protection. The tentacles had no substance as we know it and the eyes were the most awe-inspiring/terrifying thing I have ever beheld. They defied counting. They defied reason. The whole thing was too much and I felt myself losing my mind.

I...JUST...LOST...IT...goooooooooonnnnnne [all emphasis original].

I guess this account really did it for me. There really seemed to be some degree of objective reality to all these experiences, including mine, because they had historical precedent, shared experience and, perhaps most importantly, some apparent meaning. On a level-playing field of explanation, where all theoretical perspectives hold equally convincing, or perhaps equally unconvincing positions, the notion of *meaning* can provide the greatest intuitive appeal to one's understanding. For instance, a physiological, or neurotheological explanation might suggest that the highly similar visions are due to similar neurochemical reactions, but this devalues the complexity and cultural significance of the experience and also extends itself much further than the current explanatory power of neuroscience.

Alternatively, a parapsychological explanation might suggest that these similar visions all belong to a particular morphogenic field (a field of consciousness that contains imprints of past experiences that can be experienced by others) activated by chemically-induced near-death-type experiences. Yet there is little understanding or evidence for morphogenic fields of this kind, even though they may be possible in principle (Sheldrake, 1988), [although Sheldrake (2018) explores this notion in more detail].

Any number of other theories might be put forward but, with all such explanations appearing as equally uncompelling, the possibility of this entity somehow being real as an independently sentient discarnate being – whatever that may be – has comparable explanatory power. However, beyond other ontological speculations this level of explanation – an acceptance of the experience at face value – also has esoteric and cultural *meaning* because it fits with a mystical understanding of the universe in which the existence of supernatural beings is accepted.

Sentient Entities

That said, I have little problem, then, assuming that entities - be they dream angels, DMT encounters, or mythical beings – have at least the *possibility* of independent sentience or some kind of objective reality, because I don't confine myself ultimately to any one ontological perspective. So, as clearly as I can make sense of it, it seems that smoking DMT can lead temporarily to some kind of death realm - an idea championed by Rick Strassman (2001) and supported by shamanic concepts of ayahuasca states – and in such a place the traveller might encounter one of the (one could say 'archetypal') guardian deities of the underworld. One such guardian is the angel of death, who appears with thousands of eyes, much like Alex Grey's painting of *Dying*. Yet it seems that sometimes this multi-eyed being also assumes the tentacled

Figure 11: Dying (1990) by psychedelic artist Alex Grey,
www.alexgrey.com

or snake-bodied appearance of Za. And like a guardian of the underworld no doubt should be, this being is not to be trifled with and holds
whoever encounters it in the grip of utter fear and the urge to obey its
hypnotic glare – to just "see but don't look" – because it seemingly
guards the sacred way on after death.

On reflection, my encounters with both Za and Azrael have resonance with each other and possibly represent the same psychic atavism
or Jungian archetype, albeit an archetype which may have independent
sentience, that may become activated by tryptamines, such as DMT, or
by dreaming or other altered states. This entity is the archetype of the
guardian of the realm of death and the doorway to occult knowledge.
In considering this I was lucky enough to find a book by two occultists
(Jackson & Howard, 2000) that made some sense of this. They offer
an argument that the Islamic Azrael, the angel of death, is synonymous
with the Hebrew Azazel, the fallen angel of light and the serpent of
the Tree of Knowledge who, as the Promethean prototype, stole the

Figure 12: Azazel also appearing with numerous eyes, from
The Sandman (Gaiman, et al, 1991)

gnostic fire from God and gave it to man – in much the same way that psychedelics can. They also associate the Persian fallen angel Azza, or Shemyaza with the Luciferian Azazel, who in similar Promethean style swapped the name of God for sexual favors with the mortal Ishtahar making her immortal.

Jackson and Howard likewise associate Azazel, the great watcher, with the Persian dragon serpent Azhadaha, the black serpent of light and leader of the Inri, the fallen angels – known appropriately as the watchers. Interestingly, they link the etymology of the common root *az* with the Hebrew letters *ayin* (or *ain* in Arabic) meaning eye, and *zayin* (*zain* in Arabic) meaning sword, which represent the all-seeing eye and the flaming sword of initiation, the guardian of the garden of Eden in biblical and kabalistic tradition. Jackson and Howard note that "The secret significance of the Zayin Sword is typified by Azazel as Master of Metals and Lord of the Forge" (p.92) because smithcraft and fire-working were the crafts first taught to humans by the watchers, much like the myth of Promethcus. They note that (p. 92):

> The Hebrew letter-form of Zayin, ז, the sword blade, is the supracosmic fire that, like a shining lightening flash or thunderbolt, 'cuts' through the veil of material nescience.

Assembling all these links it didn't take a huge cognitive leap to also associate the Tibetan eyeballed serpent of my DMT encounter, Za, with these anarchic archangels of other cultures. Without making any great claims to the exclusive resemblance of any of these myths to each other - for the different legends have both similarities *and* differences - further comparisons to Za and Azrael from elsewhere can also be made. Such as the Persian Zahhāk, also known in Iranian mythology as Aži Dahāka the serpent or dragon, who was struck down by the divine Frēdōn and snakes issued forth from the wounds (Boyce, 1975). Like Prometheus he was condemned to be chained to the side of a mountain for eternity. The likely etymological link here between the interchanged ayin (a) and zayin (z) of *za* and *az* is itself compelling, especially in the case of the Zahhāk / Aži Dahāka, but the myth story of Za himself has further resonance with the other fallen archangel and Promethean myths.

In Tibetan mythology, Za (known as Rahu in the Indian tradition) features in the *Dri Med Zhel Phreng* version of the Buddhist "churning of the oceans" story about the origins of the original entheogenic ambrosia par-excellence, amrita, or soma (Crowley, 1996). Having been left in charge of the Buddhas' newly made water of life – the amrita – before its supposed dissemination to humanity, Vajrapani (associated

with the great soma-fiend, Indra) carelessly left the sacred amrita un-
guarded and returned to find the demon Za, the Lhamayin, had drank
it. In further offence to the gods Za urinated what remained of the pro-
cessed amrita back into the vessel, and as penance Vajrapani was made
to drink what had now become poisonous and so turned permanent-
ly blue as a consequence. The similarities here between the methods
of enjoying amrit and psychedelic *Amanitas* have not gone unnoticed
(Crowley, 1996), and furthermore the link here between the psychedelic and the Promethean features of the myth is clear.

As just punishment Varjapani finally caught up with Za and
wounded him many times and then sliced him in two with his vajra, the
lightning bolt, but because Za had drank the amrita, the water of life,
he survived; Amrita translates literally from Sanskrit as deathlessness
and it seems appropriate that this guardian of the underworld himself
should become "deathless". But as further punishment the Buddhas replaced Za's severed legs with the tail of a serpent or dragon (much like
the Iranian Aži Dahāka above) and fixed eyeballs upon his numerous
wounds giving him his unique appearance.

Its here that I saw a further transcultural myth story emerging with
the legend of the Greek Lamia, the serpentine daimon and prophetess.
Lamia is somewhat similar in name and character to the Lhamayin, the
class of Tibetan serpent spirits to which Za belongs. However there is
some contention, not least from the Tibetan scholar, psychedelicist,
and etymologist, Mike Crowley (personal communication, Dec 2005),
that the Tibetan language has no roots in Middle-Eastern and Mediterranean languages because it is uniquely related to Mongolian. Nevertheless, in the same vein with which Robert Graves (whom we can
credit for tipping off Wasson to re-discover psychedelic mushrooms
anyway) makes more poetic than precise associations between cultural myths there is a resonance between the legend of Za - the Tibetan
serpentine Lhamayin - and the Greek serpentine Lamia, whom we may
also associate with Python, the serpentine prophetess of Delphi.

Accordingly, Python was responsible for maintaining the secret
of prophecy, the wisdom of the underworld and, similarly to Za, was
struck down by the sun-god Apollo, thereby heralding what Graves
(1961) describes as the usurpation of the Goddess for the rights over
divinatory power, and henceforth recasting Python in the role of demon. Something similar also resounds in the Greek myth of the Me-
dusa and Perseus, and perhaps with the Luciferian Norse Loki and the
Assyrian-Babylonian Zu (or Azu) too - who was struck down by a
lightning bolt for stealing the tablets of destiny from Tiamat the dragon
queen - but that's another story.

With the dawning of the age of patriarchal theism that occurred two to three thousand years ago the Promethean-type tale of the Python retells the same story of the divine maverick: A chthonic being betwixt this world and the underworld, the all-seeing serpent divinity holding the key to man's enlightenment who steals that wisdom or shares it with mankind and then becomes re-branded as a demon, a fallen angel, a trickster or a deceiver, much like Za, Azazel, and the rest. The Aryan demon Rahu (Za) had once been a Dravidian god and it's clear that an old culture's gods often become a dominating culture's demons, and the archaic tools with which the old culture accessed their divine, be they psychedelic or otherwise, become heretical.

Subsequently, the old chthonic sacramentals, such as amrit, or henbane – called "pythonian" by the ancient Greeks in honour of Python (Rudgley, 2000) – fell out of grace as easily as Lucifer fell from heaven, or Adam and Eve fell from the Garden of Eden. But like poor old Frank Olsen (who was supposedly the first LSD user to try and fly from a window, but years later was discovered to have been murdered by the CIA), did they fall, or were they pushed? The identity of amrit was almost completely lost, and remains a matter of debate, and although few soma hunters have proposed tryptamines as the culprit (save perhaps McKenna, 1992, who championed psilocybin-containing champignons, and Matthew Clark, 2017, who argues for an ayahuasca analogue), what the Tibetan lama Chogyom Trungpa (p.236) says about it fits happily with the various tryptamine visions mentioned above:

> ...amrita is the principle of intoxicating extreme beliefs, belief in ego, and dissolving the boundary between confusion and sanity so that co-emergence can be realized.

Perhaps a report of a multi-eyeballed Za-like entity being induced by *Amanitas* might say something more for the usual favored identity of amrit, and yet, even though there's some certainty that the ancients of the East never smoked DMT, perhaps any old entheogen will do [though see Clark, 2017].

But is there anything that can be found in this wayward meandering through myth and vision that offers a case for the genuine reification of 'the other' encountered in that psychedelic space on the far side of the psyche? Knowing that speculation is the vice of the precise and yet the virtue of the poetic I am in no doubt that those wearing their right brain today will already have departed company with me somewhere along the line here. As a scientist myself I have deeply questioned this temporary departure from so-called rational thought, but as an explorer of the weirder realms of the mind I have also been forced occasionally to leap the fence at the edge of my field of expertise and traverse unknown territory. I don't offer any of this as 'fact' beyond the phenomenological, but merely as 'possibility' in a psychic landscape as 'off the map' as that provided by DMT. Indeed, here be dragons, and, yes, beware that among the dragon's treasure all that glitters is not gold. Yet who can resist inspecting a few gems occasionally in case they are of any real value?

Figure 13: Many-eyed dragon drawn by a psilocybin subject in Paris. (Note the similarity to the depiction of Azazel shown earlier) Image taken from Heim & Wasson's 1965–1966 book *Les Champignons Hallucinogènes du Mexique*.

Postscript: More Fishy Than the Greenwich Pie n Eel Shop

Once I had assembled the various images together for this piece, but too late for the 2008 publication, I began studying the shape of pine-cones and noticed the resemblance to its shape in the multi-eyed beings of Figures 10, 12 and 13. Things got much weirder when I discovered that the end of the pinecone forms a Fibonacci spiral, identical in form to the eyes in Alex Grey's *dying* image (Figure 11). Indeed the entire pattern of the scales on a pinecone forms a Fibonacci sequence, much like DNA. The most curious part about this, however, is that the pineal gland is named as such because it resembles a pinecone, and further-more endogcnous DMT is speculated to be made in the human pineal (see chapter 9 for a full discussion). It is also speculated that this sup-posedly nocturnally produced pineal DMT might be responsible for dreams, which was the other altered state that I had an encounter expe-rience with the (this time unseen) multi-eyed empyrean entity Azrael.

Figure 14: Greenwich Pie n Eel shop

Upon realising this I found myself in a mind-boggling mental bootstrapping exercise and pondered the possibility that myself and other psychonauts and artists where somehow perceiving our own (DMT-producing?) pineal glands in such states, which was somehow given sentience and perceived as the guardian on the threshold. A threshold to what though? Insanity perhaps, following such lines of thought, ending up a psycho-nut rather than a psychonaut (Salway, 2015). Nevertheless, the aim here is to be agnostic about even the most strange of propositions.

The plot got even more esoteric after discovering that the pinecone was a sacred object to many ancient deities, and is seen in ancient artwork being held prominently by gods from numerous ancient cultures, such as the Sumerian, Egyptian, Mithraic, Roman, Mayan and Greek, to name a few. Significantly, often the pinecone forms the tip of the staff held by certain deities, such as with the thyrsus, the staff of the ancient Egyptian deity, Osiris (the lord of the underworld no less), which is entwined by two serpents, as is the staff, called the caduceus, of Hermes, the psychopomp who conducts the souls of the dead through into the afterlife. Osiris' thyrsus also appears somewhat transformed with a pinecone atop but only one snake around the staff for the Greek god Asclepius. Also a psychopomp, Asclepius is god of dreaming and healing, and his temples were the antecedent institutions for medical colleges, hence Asclepius' staff is still used as the symbol for medicine (Luke, 2012a).

Is it possible that the ancients knew about the function of the pineal, considering it important for dream and other altered states, especially those giving rise to psychopompic and underworld experiences. Like Osiris' thyrsus, on the Indian subcontinent the concept of one's kundalini energy is depicted as a central column (approximate with the spine) entwined by two serpents rising up. The central shaft of this kundalini ends at the ajna chakra, which is the etheric counterpart of the pineal gland, and is considered the power source for psychic abilities (siddhis)(Satyananda, 1972,1996). It seems apparent that both the tantric system of South Asia and the mythology of the ancient Mediterranean cultures seem to point to the importance of the pineal gland, the pinecone and serpents in embracing all things post-mortem and otherworldly.

Since publishing the *Disembodied Eyes* article I also keep coming across psychedelically inspired artwork that depicts multitudinous eyes, often in a Fibonacci sequence. It's as though no psychedelic visionary artist is bono fide these days without such a piece in their portfolio. They are so numerous, in fact, that without searching for them

Figure 15: Argus, by Dave Curtis

I have now amassed several dozen such art pieces, some of which were made before my article was published, and some since. It's debatable as to whether or not the later ones have been made naïvely though the artist's direct experience, or have been influenced by the publishing of this article. Its not that I hope to claim any credit for the inspiration, rather, it is impossible to really know which art made post-2008 has been culturally-mediated, consciously or unconsciously, now that I've set loose the psychedelic multi-eyed serpent beasty meme.

One possible insight comes from some research that was conducted in Brazil by the Hungarian psychiatrist, psychopharmacologist and DMT researcher, Ede Frecska. I met Ede in Brazil whilst visiting Luis Eduardo Luna's home, Wasiwaska, where he runs the Research Centre for the Study of Psychointegrator Plants, Visionary Art and Consciousness. Ede had just finished collecting data from ayahuasca participants who had been given several creativity tasks before and after drinking the psychedelic jungle decoction (the main active ingredient of which is DMT). One of the tasks was to merely draw whatever they felt inspired to draw inside a number of presented circles.

Discussing my experiences within this chapter with Ede he announced that he had expected people to draw more classic entoptics immediately after the ayahuasca but that he was surprised to find that a large number of his participants spontaneously drew eyes, so much so that he created a new category for them in coding the data. However, he hadn't yet analysed their frequency so we sat down together and did the analysis there and then and found that, despite his small sample, there was a significant increase in the number of circles depicting eyes after drinking ayahuasca than before.

Unfortunately, when the final paper was published it only discussed the spontaneous generation of entoptic art among participants, not eyes (Frecska, Móré, Vargha & Luna, 2012). In any case, the widespread reporting of multi-eyed multi-serpent/worm/tentacle beasties

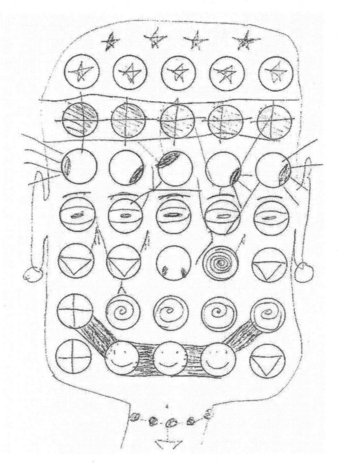

**Figure 16: Post-ayahuasca creativity task output,
from Ede Frecska study**

akin to my own experience prior to the publishing of the article in this chapter seems to suggest that these experiences are relatively common on psychedelics, especially with DMT and related compounds. What the nature of these visions is remains a mystery.

A few final notes probably deserve adding here too, although from here on in it starts to get really weird. Near the start of a talk on entoptics I was giving at a festival a few years ago I was holding up an entoptic-rich ayhuasuca-inspired Shipibo yarn picture to the audience when a small boy interjected. I recognised him to be the 5-year old son of a friend of mine. He said that he saw a similar pattern as he was going off to sleep but that he saw the same but inverted pattern when he wakes up. I wasn't surprised at the phenomenon occurring, having recently just read about entoptics appearing during hypnogogia (Mavromatis, 1987), which is how I responded, although I *was* surprised that a boy so young would interrupt my adult lecture with such an intelligent comment.

I sought him out afterwards to talk to him some more and he soon began to blow my mind. He told me that once every eight days as he was going to sleep he would see these geometric designs and would enter into this special world, where he would meet the same character each time, and then he would re-emerge through the inverse of the pattern again at the end of his nocturnal adventure. Its when he started describing the character encountered that I was astonished, because he described this multi-serpent being covered all over in eyes. He said he met him a lot! Well every eight days anyway. And he would hang out with him all night. I listened intently, intrigued, suspicious (in case I was being duped), amazed and baffled, and I asked him several very clearly non-leading questions to see where it would go.

He said that the multi-eyeball multi-serpent being would sometimes appear as one creature and sometimes it would send its wiggly snakes out in different directions to do things. Mostly what they did was usher round spirits of the dead, according to the boy, and he said that 'the man' was very busy – although he was able occasionally to stop to make the boy laugh with a joke or silly multi-eyed multi-serpent daft pose – and that sometimes he would get the boy to help him.

Mr Za, as we proceeded to call him (my suggestion), was a very busy man indeed, and the boy said in describing him how, "he has a near-infinite number of eyes, because he has a near-infinite number of souls to look after!" – I practically fell off my chair at this point. How many five year olds know what infinity is let alone near-infinity, and then I thought about; if this hypothetical lord of the underworld did look after all the souls that had ever lived then that would approximate nicely to a near-infinite number one presumes.

All this could have been made up of course (though why he would do this, and how so convincingly, boggles the mind), perhaps as some kind of elaborate set up by someone (an adult presumably) who knows me and my writing – although that seems too paranoid. But what he said next took it to the next level. He told me how when he was helping Mr Za round up the lost souls, they were quite scary and he didn't like them getting close to him, so Za had given him some special silver 'ghost string', as he called it, to lasso the souls with and lead them off. What he said stopped me in my tracks because the boy was describing the very same thing that happened to me in my extremely intense dream of many years ago. A dream I had told but only a handful of people close to me. This following direct unedited excerpt is taken from a private journal I wrote in 2004.

> "*I am in some old derelict Tudor monastery-type building, there are a number of lost dead spirits present that appear as people, but either with highly distorted and deformed faces, or with no face at all. I am trying to move the six of them on through into the next world, but one in particular is causing a lot of difficulty and is being very stubborn. I understand from this spirit that he was previously a murderer when alive (a long time ago), but is unwilling to depart this plane of existence. It takes all my effort just to stop this spirit from attacking me. Suddenly the space is filled with an immense, intense, and huge presence, I do not see a form or a face, and it does not speak, but telepathically I am told the great being's name. The form gives me a set of angelic wings, feathered and white like that of some huge bird, but big enough to lift me easily into the air. With this new advantage I am able to take to the air and subdue the troublesome spirit, entwining it in some ethereal binding, I lash it to the rafters and fly around effortlessly rounding up the rest of the spirits to be ushered through into the next plane.*"

I awoke suddenly with the name *Azrael* on my lips. I found the whole experience completely amazing and wrote it down. I was quite surprised to have been given the name of the angelic being. Numinous dreams, although uncommon, are one thing, but being given something tangible like a name is another. I was astounded. Once again, I consulted my good friend and mystic advisor and described the dream to him. At first, I did not give him the name. He asked me if the name was one of the four archangels; Gabriel, Ariel, Michael, Raphael. But no! So he suggested it was one of the ten holy angels of the Qabalah, which, although I knew very little of the Qabalah at this point, this proposition intuitively appealed. Checking the names with the ten angels of the Qabalah, which includes Gabriel and two of the other three archangels, there was no Azrael amongst them.

I was a bit perplexed, and thought maybe I had got the name wrong, though really I knew it was this name that was inked indelibly on my mind (and my dream notes). The experience stayed with me, but it wasn't until about two weeks later that I found an explanation, although I hadn't been looking for the answer. Casually browsing through someone's bookshelf I came across a book called 'the little book of angels' and flicking through it, to my complete astonishment, I found a couple of pages referring to Azrael, as the Angel of Death! I was quite amazed. That seemed like quite a hefty title, but I was more amazed when I read that the angel of death, called the archangel Azrael by Muslims, not Christians, has a thousand eyes and a thousand wings and would occasionally employ people in the enormous task of gathering in all the souls of the departed. Holy shit! I had been given a job working for the Angel of Death. That was going to look a little bit deranged on my CV!

I think the thing that really struck me by this event was that, I had no knowledge of this angel, or its name before the dream. Nor would I have had much likelihood of coming into contact with this divine character, who was only known to Muslims, because I had very little knowledge of Islam and didn't even have any Muslim friends [such was provincial life!]. Yet, my dream experience, which had been incredibly vivid, numinous, and powerful, had perfectly matched the habits and activities of this divine being.

Perplexity took another step towards the incredible. In such cases, where something seemingly unknown is revealed to the conscious mind there is always the possibility that the information was already lurking hidden and unremembered in the subconscious. Is it possible that I already knew about Azrael, the angel of death, his many wings (spares, perhaps?), and his employment of earthly characters for gathering souls, etc? This would be known as 'cryptamnesia' or hidden memory, and although it has been shown by psychologists that people may be able to process information without consciously remembering it, this explanation is all too often wheeled out by skeptics as a frail old argument to account for spontaneous psychic experiences involving clairvoyant information.

And so it was that the young boy spoke of being employed as a psychopomp, seemingly by the lord or guardian of the underworld, and in his fear of the old lost souls he had been given some ghost string to help bind them and move them on. And when he said it I knew exactly what he was talking about and couldn't have found a better phrase to use than ghost string to describe my own 'ethereal binding'.

It's at this point that I thought he would have to be bluffing or cold reading extremely hard to have come up with that – despite my non-leading questioning and retention of my own information. In all my readings of Azrael and the other seemingly mythical incarnations of 'him' I had never come across this reference to psychopompic ghost string for 'his' assistants. Its then I seriously doubted that he was taking me for a ride, which could leave two plausible explanations. Either he was extremely telepathic and was just extracting my deepest secrets from me, or… he really was having these experiences with such resonance to my own.

And yet I had had this psychopompic experience once, in a dream (an extremely powerful dream nonetheless) and had pieced all the other fragments together over the period of some decade or so of mystical jigsaw puzzling, whereas this boy said he had these experiences all night, every eight nights. It had been one of my most profound life experiences that dream and the later discovery of Azrael as the 'hand of God', and yet here was a five-year old boy who fuses all the disparate pieces of my jigsaw together, and some, in just 10 minutes, who was virtually an apprentice to the Angel of Death, cracks jokes with him, and says things like "he has a near-infinite number of eyes, because he has a near-infinite number of souls to look after." Well it's one eye for every soul I suppose, but that must take a strain, so even the angel of death needs a hand now and then.

Its heading back on the train home from the festival that I remember my journey there. On the way to the festival the train had been packed and I was having to stand and was leaning over a young boy who happened to be reading a Terry Pratchett book. I had looked on fondly recalling my own joy at reading Pratchett in my youth. But it was the book he was reading that then came back to me, a book called *Mort*, about an ordinary young boy, Mortimer, who becomes an apprentice to Death! Some synchronicities are just too uncanny.

So what to do with all that information? I decided to mine it further and resolved that I must go and visit the boy and his mother, who I knew only by association. I'd never been to visit them at their home, and it was a couple of hours drive away, but I would have travelled any distance to find out more. I arranged to go to their house and immediately the boy got me to work 'playing'. This was no ordinary play though (for me at least), he said he was a black belt Jedi and that he would train me if I was worthy, so we spent the next two or three hours with him and I running around fighting kung fu style and performing feats of derring-do.

Luckily I was quite athletic and acrobatic at the time and was able to impress him with my finest moves, and now and then he would upgrade me to the next level belt. My disappearing trick (using misdirection and then diving over a low wall) had impressed him enough for him to make me red belt, one below him, and I felt I had now won his trust enough to finally begin the conversation I wanted to have, which he had seemed unmotivated to give me. A natural pause came in our game and, with my dictaphone ready in my pocket, I looked to him and asked him directly to tell me some more about Mr Za, the many-eyed multi-serpent. He stood motionless and said nothing, his face screwing up with disappointment. Then, from out of nowhere, he swiftly kung fu punched me with all his might straight in my groin and I doubled up in agony on the floor, incapacitated. It was certainly one way to tell me that he would say no more on the subject. And he wouldn't. Not one peep.

This (serpent's) tale could probably end here, but recently, a few weeks either side of the 2016 Autumn equinox two friends, independently of each other, and without knowing each other told me that they too had had a terrifying encounter with a multi-eyed, multi-serpent being on their last toke of DMT. One knew my story, the other didn't. Both had had the prior experience with DMT of being told by the entities that they encountered there that there was nothing more for them to learn from going to the DMT 'world' and they shouldn't return, and both had nonetheless returned and meet our ostensible

Figure 17: DMT brain imaging study participant drawing following injection, December 2016 (from Chris Timmerman, Imperial College)

**Figure 18: DMT brain imaging study participant drawing
following injection, December 2016**
(from Chris Timmerman, Imperial College)

Za. For both of them, this had also been the last time they smoked
DMT, as it had been for me. At least it was for about 14 years until I
was a subject in a DMT brain imaging study last month. I was injected
with DMT rather than smoking it, but it was still my first full hit in
14 years since my seeming Za encounter. One day I'll tell the story of
what happened when I did return to DMT, but for now, well, I'm not
actually allowed to say publically until the research has been published
by my colleagues. I guess there has to be some mystery left with this
myth story; my story.

The night has a thousand eyes,
And the day but one;
Yet the light of the bright world dies
With the dying sun.

The mind has a thousand eyes,
And the heart but one;
Yet the light of a whole life dies
When love is done.

Francis William Bourdillon, *Light*, 1873

CHAPTER 7

Psychedelics and Species Connectedness

Turning Topiary

On my travels in Mexico many years ago, last millennium in fact, I came across a psychoactive plant, known locally as 'the shepherdess', which was used by indigenous people for divination and healing. I was given the opportunity to try this foreign foliage and doing so had an incredible and entirely unexpected experience. Within moments of consuming the herb a strange sensation began seeping through my toes and fingertips and moved towards my core turning me rapidly into some kind of thorn bush. The metamorphosis spread quickly up my arms and legs, across my body and up to my head until I found myself completely transformed into a small spiky shrub. I was quite literally rooted to the spot and could not move.

Simultaneous to this, all the trees and all the plants, in fact every blade of grass across the large field within view, began laughing hysterically. Anything and everything before me that photosynthesized was in side-splitting fits and they were all cracking lines like "now you know what it's like to be a plant, ha, ha, ha", swaying back and forth, shrieking and howling with laughter. I didn't find this particularly funny though, because I was absolutely convinced of my transmutation, and furthermore believed it to be permanent. Oh how the plants laughed. Then a disembodied voice spoke. Loud, deep and stern. A woman's voice. She said something like, "you stupid humans think you run the show around here, you're so arrogant, but you haven't got a clue." And then she proceeded to lecture me on species-centrism and our lack of harmony with others on Earth. I was terrified and 'bewildered' – in the literal sense too – for although I had hypothetically reasoned that everything might be inherently conscious, I had never expected to be chastised by the spirit of Nature or publically ridiculed by grass.

The experience, mercifully, only lasted ten minutes, and quickly subsided as the voice drifted away and I turned back into a slightly more aptly named *Homo sapiens* than before. The immediate psychological effects had gone, but the ontological shock remained indefinitely. I would say that this was my first serious shamanic experience with plant (or fungal) psychedelics, and since then I have never considered ecology in quite the same way as before. So what then of psychedelic experiences and species connectedness?

Ecodelia

The fact that a large portion of this essay was originally published in a special issue of the *MAPS Bulletin* (Brown, 2009) given over solely to ecology would seem to suggest that at the very least the consumption of psychedelic substances leads to an increased concern for Nature and ecology. On one level we can understand that this may be due to a basic appreciation of place and aesthetics that accompanies the increased sensory experience, or that psychedelic plants come from Nature and so we are forced to enter her realms when we search them out. However, on a deeper level we can also appreciate that a communication with Nature may on occasion occur through the mystical experience of the psychedelic state.

With the aid of mescaline Aldous Huxley came face to face with such a mystical experience, even though the Oxford Theologian R.C. Zaehner (1957) denigrated his experience of nature mysticism as somehow inferior to the 'genuine' theistic mystical experience. Yet the irony remains that the very split from Nature in the mind of theologians that occurred in the Garden of Eden probably lies at the heart of many people's current sense of separateness from our ecology, whereas psychedelics are seemingly capable of augmenting that reunion. Despite Zaehner's derisions Huxley (1954, p.4) witnessed this reunion through mescaline, "I was seeing what Adam had seen on the morning of creation — the miracle, moment by moment of naked existence."

It is this naked experience that reconnects the environ to the mental capacities of those psychedelically-inspired that, at its best, forges an environmental way of thought and action. For some – often the pioneers of psychedelic discovery such as our shamanic predecessors or the odd chemist – the process occurs the other way around. The patriarch of psychedelia, Albert Hofmann, demonstrated this by believing that a mystical nature experience he had had when he was young prefigured his discovery-cum-invention of LSD. He states that, "…my mystical experience of nature as a child, which was absolutely like an LSD-experience… this oneness with Nature. I believe I was in some fashion born to that" (Hofmann, Broeckers & Liggenstorfer, 2009, p.2).

Throughout his long life Hofmann increasingly drew upon the great hope that psychedelics were the key to this reconnection for others too. When asked about the role that LSD had played in brining people back to Nature, he said, "It has given many people good ideas, and those who have gone back to Nature have been saved. Many people, however, are still stuck in technological Hell and cannot get out. Nevertheless, many have discovered something which hardly exists in our society any longer: the sense of the sacred" (Hofmann et al., 2009, p.6). Always vocal on ecological issues, Hofmann recalls that among his most beautiful experiences were hearing young people say things like "I grew up in the city, but once I first took LSD, I returned to the forest" (Hofmann et al., 2009, p.4).

Providing us with an insight into the cause of this yearning for a return to Nature, based on their extensive experiential research with psychedelics, Masters and Houston (1966) noted that, "...the [psychedelic] subject, almost from the start, already has achieved a kind of empathy with his surroundings as a whole... That is to say, nature seems to the subject a whole of which he is an integral part, and from this characteristic feeling of being a part of the organic "body of nature" the subject readily goes on to identify with nature in its physical particulars and processes." But if man is empathizing with Nature in this state, whose feelings is she or he feeling? The notion that something is empathized with implies that the thing itself has emotions, and the idea forms that Nature itself and the beings who inhabit it – be they animal, vegetable or perhaps even mineral – are also conscious.

Shamanism, Animism and Animaphany

We find that such animism is at the root of all shamanic religions, which, as Jeremy Narby notes, involve a communication with the spirits of plant and animal species, "Shamanism is all about attempting to dialogue with nature" (Narby, 2006, p.16). In shamanism, of course, this communication is frequently achieved through the ingestion of psychedelic plants. As a nature religion Shamanism is ecological to its core, as the shaman is a caretaker of Nature and a negotiator between people and "other-than-human persons", as Graham Harvey calls them in his recent animist manifesto. For Harvey, its our fungal friends themselves that get the idea of Animism across the best, "Maybe sometimes the mushrooms just want to help us join in the big conversation that's going on all around us" (Harvey, 2005, p.128).

Expert mycologist Paul Stamets also finds that mushrooms have a hidden agenda to bring us into communication with other species. In studying the taxonomy of the *Psilocybe* genus Stamets notes how these psychoactive mushrooms proliferate particularly in the wake of human destruction and the taming of the land, such as through "…chopping down trees, breaking ground to create roads and trails, and domesticating livestock" (Harrison, Straight, Pendell & Stamets, 2007, p. 138). By this means, Stamets believes, the mushrooms become available to those who most need to speak to Nature through them. For Stamets, when this dialogue is engaged the message "…is always that we are part of an 'ecology of consciousness,' that the Earth is in peril, that time is short, and that we're part of a huge, universal bio-system", but Stamets isn't alone because, "many people who have taken these substances report receiving the same message" (Harrison et al., 2007, p. 138).

Recent research backs up Stamets' assertion that it isn't just him and Harvey either who are receiving mycelial messages from Nature. A survey into people's exceptional experiences with psychedelics found that encountering the consciousness of the ingested plant/fungus was the most widely reported of a range of 17 paranormal and transpersonal type experiences occurring with those taking psilocybin-containing mushrooms (Luke & Kittenis, 2005). According to the respondents this encounter also occurred quite frequently and was the second most prevalent experience with any one substance, after experiences of unity consciousness on LSD. Additionally, the plant consciousness encounter was the most widely reported transpersonal event for several other plant substances too, such as ayahuasca, *Salvia divinorum*, and the *Amanita muscaria* mushroom (Luke & Kittenis, 2005). If Harvey's Animist manifesto is to be taken seriously then the plants, and especially the mushrooms it seems, are clearly trying to tell us something.

These findings were extended in a later survey I conducted (Luke & Yanakieva, 2016) on the contribution of psychedelic experiences to eco-consciousness. Nearly 80% of the 150 psychedelic-using respondents reported that their use of psychedelics had increased their subsequent degree of interaction with nature, with almost none saying it had reduced their interaction. Indeed all of the respondents reported that their connection with nature had increased following their use of psychedelics, and more than 60% said that their concern had also increased. These figures compare quite well with respondents in a different survey (Ring, 1992), that found that 70-80% of those having near-death experiences, and 80-86% of those having UFO encounter and/or alien abduction experiences experiences had increased ecological concerns following their experience, giving some support to notion that there is an overlap between NDEs, traditional psychedelic-induced shamanic initiations, alien abduction experiences, and heightened psychic sensitivity (Harvey-Wilson, 2001; Ring, 1989, 1992; Severi, 2003). Interestingly, the substance most commonly reported to increase connection was psilocybin-containing mushrooms, which resulted in increased eco-connectedness in almost half of all mushroom users. Furthermore, approximately one third of magic mushroom users reported encounter experiences with the spirit or intelligence of the ingested mushroom.

Interpreting man's many dialogues on the mushroom experience, expert mycophile Andy Letcher (2007) calls these mushroom-mediated encounters with discarnate spirit entities the 'animaphany'. He warns us, however, that these experiences largely go ignored because, in a Foucauldian sense, they offer a resistive discourse to that of the societally legitimated explanations of what occurs under the influence of such plants, in the West at least. Being based solely on the effects of mushrooms on others these legitimated discourses typically take a pathological, psychological or prohibitory stance, and so this subjective animaphany appears to transgress a fundamental societal boundary, by communicating with spirits, and becomes labelled as "madness". But which is the more mad, communicating with the spirits of Nature or sitting back while Earth's ecological system descends rapidly into the greatest wave of mass extinction in 65 million years, which at some estimated rates (Pimm, Russell, Gittleman, Brooks, 1995) would see all species on Earth extinct within the next 70 years?

Interspecies Communication

It appears that the plant/fungus entities aren't the only ones getting in on the apparent conservation conversation either, as such pharmacologically-induced trans-species communications also engage the animal kingdom. Through the use of psychedelics, particularly LSD and ketamine, the scientist John Lilly (1978) apparently began communicating telepathically with other species and consequently made an ethical U-turn in his highly invasive animal research (such as involving the death and dissection of a dolphin) to increasingly involving consensual peer-to-peer exchanges with other-than-human species. If other species are conscious and can communicate with us then perhaps the best way to do this would be directly through our own minds, in a language that transcends physical restrictions. If this telepathic communication requires changing our consciousness to do so then plants are expertly disposed to begin this dialogue through their potent and often ancient psychoactive compounds.

Ever since Albert Hofmann (e.g., 2005) had an out of body experience on his first accidental LSD journey, and Gordon Wasson's photographer Allan Richardson had a prophetic vision on their seminal mushroom trip in Mexico (Richardson, 1990), psychedelic explorers the likes of Huxley and Osmond have been intrigued by the apparent stimulation of so-called paranormal faculties with these psychoactive substances. A review of the parapsychological literature (see Section Two) indicates that while the issue still requires further research there is good reason to consider the possibility that psychedelics might actually promote psi phenomena such as telepathy. However, the kind of species centrism that *Homo sapiens* are prone to tends to promulgate the view that animals and especially plants are not conscious, but, given that they might be sentient, direct communication with them shouldn't be ruled out either, and should probably be encouraged instead. Psychedelics, especially those coming from plants/fungus, would seem well suited for that task.

The question still remains to be answered why plants/fungus even produce highly psychedelic alkaloids in the first place. Is it just an accident that certain plants produce such supposedly toxic compounds that have no apparent benefit to the plant/fungus and yet interact so sophisticatedly with our own minds, especially given that Nature (apart from man perhaps) isn't disposed to wasting resources without good reason? On the contrary, evidence is now emerging that our brains actually developed in co-evolution with psychedelic plants (McKenna, 2018; Winkelman, 2008), although we may well ask for what purpose?

Psychedelic shamanism might be thought of primarily as a communication with Nature, for instance by asking the plants directly which ones can heal a particular illness, or by asking the plant spirit to teach them, or by using the plant in aiding the psychological metamorphosis into a plant or animal familiar (Dobkin de Rios, 1996). Given that shamans have most likely been communicating with Nature in this way for thousands of years (Devereux, 2008) then it might well be asked what can be gained for man's relationship with the ecosystem from such a dialogue and, more importantly, how can Nature benefit from it?

One thing that seems apparent now since conducting the first survey exploring psychedelic-induced changes in eco-consciousness (Luke & Yanakieva, 2016), – now that there is some data on the subject rather than just anecdote – is that, according to self-report, psychedelics do indeed tend to increase users interaction with, connection to, and concern for Nature. Further to that, these psychedelically induced changes in attitude (especially via organic substances) also often have subsequent changes in eco-orientated behaviour. In our survey, the majority of psychedelic users reported changing their diet (presumably towards organic, raw, vegetarian or vegan) and increasing gardening. Many also reported becoming more actively engaged in ecological activism, and 16% reported changing their careers to more eco-oriented ones, such as switching to studying PhDs in botany (reported by two people in the sample). In a time of such global ecological crisis psychedelics might just have an essential role in literally saving the planet, and the importance of interspecies relationships in this endeavor should not be overlooked.

SECTION TWO

Do Psychedelics Like Psilocybin Really Cause Psi?

CHAPTER 8

Psychoactive Substances and
Paranormal Phenomena

Ever since the beginning of the 20th century when Western scientists and academics began earnestly turning their attention to psychedelics there has been a clear association between the use of these substances and the transpersonal or paranormal experience. Indeed, those people most readily associated with the discovery and popularization of psychedelics also witnessed and explored both the transpersonal and the parapsychological dimensions that these substances induced, such as Albert Hofmann, Humphrey Osmond, John Smythies, Aldous Huxley, Gordon Wasson, Timothy Leary, Ken Kesey, Duncan Blewett, Walter Pahnke, James Fadiman and Stanislav Grof, to name but a few (Luke, 2006; Stevens, 1988). The overlap between transpersonal and paranormal experiences is apparent (e.g., Daniels, 2005), but while a great deal has been written in recent years about psychedelic experiences from the transpersonal perspective, a comprehensive review of the parapsychological literature relating to psychedelic experiences is long overdue.

This half of the book investigates the relationship between psychoactive substances and so-called paranormal phenomena falling within the study of parapsychology. It is primarily concerned with extrasensory perception (ESP) - telepathy, precognition, and clairvoyance - as well as out-of-body experiences (OBEs) and near-death experiences (NDEs). Psychokinesis (PK), aura vision, encounter and alien abduction experiences, kundalini eperiences, and sleep paralysis only make a very limited contribution to this review as they are seldom related to psychoactive drugs within the parapsychological literature.

This section borrows widely, but by no means exhaustively, from parapsychology as well as transpersonal studies, anthropology, ethnobotany, phytochemistry, psychiatry, psychotherapy, psychopharmacology, and neurobiology. It is organized into neurochemical models of paranormal experience (chapter 9), field reports of intentional and spontaneous phenomena incorporating anthropological, historical and clinical cases, and personal accounts (chapter 10), surveys of paranormal belief and experience (chapter 11), experimental research (chapter 12), and a methodological critique of the experimental research with recommendations for further work (chapter 13), ending with a summary and concluding comments (chapter 14).

This review focuses primarily on the class of psychoactive substances that largely induce visionary and trance-like experiences. For the purposes of the present review this includes drugs and sacraments such as mescaline, lysergic acid diethylamide (LSD), psilocybin, ayahuasca, *N,N*-dimethyltryptamine (DMT), marijuana (which is treated as a psychedelic in the current review), and ketamine, but not opiates or cocaine.

This class of visionary substances has been termed differently by different authors, usually dependent upon the connotation they wish to convey about the psychoactive effects or how the substance is used. Within the literature of the present review, they have been termed "mind-expanding" (e.g. Palmer, 1979), "psychotropic" (e.g. Irwin, 1994), "psychodysleptic" (Cavanna & Servadio, 1964), "hallucinogenic" (e.g. Blackmore, 1992), and even "entheogenic" (Ruck et al., 1979), meaning bringing forth the divine within, which is a useful term to convey the apparent divinatory and visionary nature of these substances (for discussions see Letcher, 2004; Ott, 1996a; Smith, 2000), although they might be more correctly termed "potential entheogens" as they do not automatically produce such experiences (Krippner, 2006b, p.1). Finally, there is the most frequently used term, "psychedelic", which was created in 1956 by Humphry Osmond and means "mind manifesting" (Osmond, 1961a, p.76). Where specified, the original term used by the authors will be preserved to reflect their orientation to the issue. However, elsewhere, where appropriate, the more widely used term psychedelic will be used.

For the purpose of the present review, with some caveats, a psychedelic drug is:

> ...one which, without causing physical addiction, craving, major physiological disturbances, delirium, disorientation, or amnesia, more or less reliably produces thought, mood, and perceptual changes otherwise rarely experienced except in dreams, contemplative and religious exaltation, flashes of vivid involuntary memory, and acute psychoses. (Grinspoon & Bakalar, 1998, p. 9)

The earliest parapsychology experiments with psychoactive substances were conducted with simple stimulants and depressants, such as caffeine, amphetamine, alcohol, amytal, and quinal-barbitone (e.g. Averill

& Rhine, 1945; Cadoret, 1953; Huby & Wilson, 1961; Murphy, 1961; Rhine, 1934; Rhine, Humphrey, & Averill 1945; Soal & Bateman, 1954; Wilson, 1961, 1962; Woodruff, 1943). This work is not included here (for reviews see Palmer, 1978; Ramakrishna Rao, 1966) as this review is instead focused on the visionary substances, which are seemingly more favourable to the production of psi, that Braud (2002) suggests primarily cause qualitative, rather than just quantitative alterations to the user's state of consciousness, However, Rock and Krippner (e.g., 2012) argue that (altered) states of consciousness may be more accurately described as (altered) states of phenomenology. Some earlier reviews of psychedelics in parapsychology are available and have been incorporated into the present investigation (Blewett, 1963; Gowan, 1975; Krippner & Davidson, 1970, 1974; Luke, 2008b, 2012d, 2015; Luke & Friedman, 2010; Parker, 1975, Rogo, 1976, Wilson, 1949).

There are good theoretical reasons for investigating psychedelics as a means of inducing ESP and other paranormal experiences or phenomena. Given that an altered state of consciousness (ASC) is assumed (for a discussion see Storm & Rock, 2009) to be a common feature in the occurrence of subjective paranormal experiences (Alvarado, 1998; Barušs, 2003; Honorton, 1977; Parker, 1975) and has often been incorporated into experimental attempts to induce ESP (see Luke, 2011a; Palmer, 1978, 1982; Schmeidler, 1994), then visionary drugs are, potentially, a reliable means of accessing such a state. Several researchers have documented some of the mind-altering features of the visionary-drug experience that are considered conducive to the production of parapsychological experiences and phenomena (see also Braud, 2002). These have been categorized thus:

1. Increase in mental imagery, in both vividness and quality, and the dreamlike state (Blackmore, 1992; Osis, 1961a, 1961b; Progoff, 1961; Tart, 1968, 1994)
2. Altered perception of self-identity, such as unity consciousness: The mystical experience of becoming one with everything in the universe (Krippner & Fersh, 1970; Nicol & Nicol, 1961; Osis, 1961a; Pahnke, 1968; Tart, 1994)
3. Altered body perceptions and dissociation (Blackmore, 1992; Tart, 1994). This is of particular interest with respect to the out-of-body experience (OBE)
4. Distorted sensory input (Blackmore, 1992)
5. Increased absorption and focused attention (Millay, 2001; Tart, 1968, 1994)

6. Increased empathy (Blewett, 1963; Nicol & Nicol, 1961; Tart, 1994). This is of interest to telepathy, and indeed, elevated empathy is associated with use of psychedelics generally (DeGracia, 1995; Lerner & Lyvers, 2006)
7. Emotional flexibility (Blewett, 1963), which may also assist in negotiating the fear of psi (Tart, 1994)
8. Increased alertness and awareness (Huxley, 1961a; Nicol & Nicol, 1961; Osis, 1961b; Tart, 1994)
9. Increased inwardly focused attention and awareness, and decreased external and bodily awareness (Dobkin de Rios, 1978)
10. Increased spontaneity (Osis, 1961a)
11. Sensitivity to subtle changes (Parker, 1975) and intensity of feeling (Osis, 1961a)
12. Physical relaxation (Blackmore, 1992), although Tart (1968) questions its occurrence
13. Increased suggestibility (Huxley, 1961a; Tart, 1968)
14. Increase in intuitive thought processes (Tart, 1994)
15. Reduced critical conscious faculty and increased optimism towards impossible realities (Nicol & Nicol, 1961; Osis, 1961b; Tart, 1968, 1994)
16. Increased openness and extroversion (Rogo, 1976)
17. Release of repressed and unconscious material into the conscious mind (Rogo, 1976)
18. Complex distortions, and transcendence, of space and time (Garrett 1961b; Nicol & Nicol, 1961; Tart, 1994; see also Dawson, 2005; Mayhew, 1956; Shanon, 2001; Whiteman, 1995)

This last feature of the psychedelic experience is probably of paramount importance for the experience of ESP when it is considered that precognition, telepathy, clairvoyance, and possibly OBEs all represent radical departures from Newtonian concepts of time and space. Smythies (1983) has suggested that the psychedelic experience originates from the 'collective unconscious' outside of space and time, to which Jung agreed with Smythies' idea. Millay (2001) offered that psilocybin and similar substances are important for studying psi because they allow us access to nonlocal space-time. Jansen (1999) also supposed that the same might be possible of ketamine, which became popularly used at the same time as Bell's theorem of nonlocal space-time was becoming seriously considered, enabling some to report the experiential equivalence of the concept.

Indeed, the Berkley-based Fundamental Fysiks Group that formed in the 1970s experimented with psychedelics to inspire their investigations of both psi and Bell's theorem – neglected as it was by mainstream physics at that time – which eventually lead to the birth of what is now the multi-billion dollar research enterprise of quantum information science (Kaiser, 2011).

More recently, something akin to this may also be evident with the psychedelic substance DMT, which sometimes provides users with the perception of many more than the usual four space-time dimensions, perhaps comparable to what physicists discuss in M-theory (Luke, 2010c). Keeping with the times ketamine is also now reported to induce such extra-dimensional percepts too (Newcombe, 2008), as is the semi-synthetic psychedelic salvinorin B ethoxymethyl ether (Mercury & Feelodd, 2008).

In addition to these temporary alterations that occur during the psychedelic experience, it is arguable that long-term ideological alterations may occur that might also be psi-conducive. For example, enduring changes in concepts of reality may occur with the use of psychedelics (Conway, 1989; Strassman, 2001), such that optimism about unseen realities, both during and after the experience, leads to a greater openness to, or belief in, psi and the paranormal.

In a follow-up survey of 113 LSD-psychotherapy clients (with an 82% response rate) 78% reported an increased tendency to view telepathy and precognition as possibilities warranting investigation (International Foundation for Advanced Study, 1962). It has even been stated that the psychedelic experience is itself, by common consent, paranormal (Unger, 1963).

Furthermore, the distinguished medium and psychical researcher Eileen Garrett asserted that the use of LSD had made her a better, more accurate sensitive (Garrett, 1961b) and she related certain psychedelic states to the mediumistic pre-trance state of euphoria, although she specified that the LSD experience was not the same as the mediumistic trance (Garrett, 1961a). Huxley (1961a) proposed that LSD is invaluable in training participants to use their subjective faculties to enhance their psi ability.

Besides the subjective aspects of the psychedelic experience, there are other theoretical reasons for investigating paranormal phenomena with drugs: Because paranormal phenomena are brain-mind experiences, neurochemicals - and therefore psychoactive drugs - would be expected to be involved in the process. It is also highly likely that all ASC, including potentially ESP-conducive states, involve alterations in brain chemistry. Indeed, several psychedelic-neurochemical models, discussed in the following chapter (also see Luke & Friedman, 2010), have been proposed, primarily based upon subjective paranormal experiences occurring with certain substances and their specific neuro-chemical action.

It is entirely feasible that genuine paranormal experiences are me-diated in the brain through the action of specific endogenous (made within the body) molecules (Larcher, 1958; Roney-Dougal, 1991; Strassman, 2001; Vayne, 2001). This does not simply imply that neu-rochemicals are the sole cause of paranormal phenomena, but they may rather just be a part of the process. As the novelist Aldous Huxley once said in relation to mystical experiences and the use of psychedelics – they are the occasion rather than the cause. .

CHAPTER 9

Psychedelic/Neurochemical Models of
Paranormal Experience

Brain as Filter

Aldous Huxley (1954) was also prominent in promoting Henri Bergson's (1896/1990) theory of the brain as a filter of memory and sensory experience, acting to reduce the wealth of information available to awareness lest people become overwhelmed by a mass of largely useless and irrelevant data not needed for the survival of the organism. It was Bergson who suggested that, if these filters were bypassed, humans would be capable of remembering everything that had ever been experienced and perceiving everything that has happened everywhere in the universe (e.g., as in clairvoyance).

It was also Huxley who applied this theory to psychedelics by suggesting that these mind-manifesting drugs override the "reducing valve" of the brain (Huxley, 1954, p.12), allowing humans access to both psychic and mystical experiences. A notion that Huxley (1954) eruditely paraphrased with the quote by the English poet and mystic, William Blake (1906/1793), "If the doors of perception were cleansed, every thing would appear to man as it is, infinite."

Huxley's (1954) rather basic conception never received a more formal operationalization of the specific drug actions that may be involved, but research into the neurochemistry of psychedelics lends some support to his notion. For instance, Vollenweider and Geyer (2001) proposed that information processing in cortico-striato-thalamo-cortical (CSTC) feedback loops is disrupted by psychedelics via 5-HT (serotonin) receptor agonism (specifically 5-HT_{2A} receptors), thereby inhibiting the "gating" of extraneous sensory stimuli and inhibiting the ability to attend selectively to salient environmental features.

Furthermore, psychedelics are also thought to induce presynaptic release of glutamate from thalamic afferents, leading to a simultaneous overload of internal information in the cortex. It is thought that these combined information overload effects are at least partly responsible for the "hallucinogenic" experience with these drugs, which are known to induce greatly altered or amplified incoming sensory information, as is indicated by an increased startle effect (Vollenweider, 2001).

Research into the neurobiology of psychedelics in humans has only just resumed after decades of dormancy, so the current understanding of the action of these substances in the brain remains limited. One of the first studies to have been conducted, however, also offers some unexpected support for Huxley's reducing valve theory. Looking at the blood flow around the brain following the ingestion of psilocybin, it was expected that certain regions of the brain would have more activity, given the overwhelming intenseness of strong psychedelic experiences, and yet, counter-intuitively, there was no single brain region that increased in activity, and the brain's activity was reduced overall (Carhart-Harris, 2011; Carhart-Harris et al., 2012).

The main areas demonstrating reduced cerebral blood flow were the cerebral hub regions of the thalamus, anterior and posterior cingulate cortex (ACC & PCC), and medial prefrontal cortex (mPFC). Significantly, the usual positive coupling between the mPFC and the PCC – which forms part of the default mode network thought to be important in introspection and high level constructs such as self and ego – was reduced leading to "a state of unconstrained cognition" (Carhart-Harris et al., 2012, p. 2138).

This psychedelic disruption of the sensory gating function discussed by Vollenweider (2001), and the reduction of activity in the default mode network discussed by Carhart-Harris (2011) could also underpin the neurochemistry of ESP, whether elicited with any number of psychedelics or, indeed, without the intervention of such exogenous chemicals (though perhaps via endogenous chemicals such as DMT). Indeed like psychedelics, psi experiences and events have variously been conceptualized in relation to an inhibition of the ordinary sensory inhibition, often in conjunction with elevated psychosis and creativity, such as with the concepts of latent disinhibition (Holt, Simmonds-Moore, & Moore 2008), transliminality (Thalbourne, 2000; Thalbourne & Houran, 2005), boundary thinness and schizotypy (Simmonds & Roe, 2000), and self-expansiveness (Friedman, 1983; Pappas & Friedman, 2007). It may be noted that psychedelics have also been long associated with both creativity (e.g., Dobkin de Rios & Janiger, 2003; Krippner, 1985) and psychosis (Osmond & Smythies, 1952).

Despite the simplistic appeal of the anti-reducing valve action of psychedelics as a neurochemical model of psi, considerable gaps still remain in our current understanding of the neuropharmacological action of psychedelics in humans. Since the early 1970s, until relatively recently, practically all psychedelic research has been conducted with animals and there remain no definitive generalizations that can be made about the main neurotransmitter receptor sites involved, as psychedelics vary considerably in their chemical makeup and their affinity (Ray, 2010) for ligands (a ligand is a molecule, such as a neurotransmitter, that triggers a response in a target protein).

For instance, dissociative anaesthetics such as ketamine are commonly N-methyl-D-aspartate (NMDA) receptor antagonists, whereas the simple tryptamines, such as psilocybin, are apparently 5-HT_{2A} agonists. Speculations about the cause of the hallucinogenic effects of psychedelics generally include the activation of 5-HT_{1A}, 5-HT_{2A}, 5-HT_{2C}, dopamine, and glutamate pathways, although it is generally believed that classic psychedelics primarily work by stimulating 5-HT_{2A} receptors, particularly those expressed in the neocortical pyramidal cells (Lee & Roth, 2012; Nichols, 2004, 2016), although this is certainly not the case for all psychedelics (e.g., mescaline; Ray, 2010).

Electrophysiology and receptor studies have revealed that both NMDA antagonists (e.g., ketamine) and classic serotonergic psychedelics (e.g., LSD) may actually enhance glutamatergic transmission via non-NMDA receptors in the frontal cortex. This may indicate a common mode of chemical action in the brain responsible for such similar experiences with these divergent molecules (Vollenweider, 2004); this serotonin/glutamate receptor-complex model of drug action is receiving high-profile attention again for psychedelics as a possible comparative model of psychosis (e.g., González-Maeso et al., 2008).

Despite the lack of understanding of the neurobiology of psychedelic action, and lack of generalizability across so many diverse substances, recent advances would appear to support the Bergson-Huxley notion of brain as a filter capable of being deactivated by chemicals and other techniques of inducing altered states, such as ayahuasca, hypnosis, meditation and mediumistic trance (Brewer et al., 2011; Garrison et al., 2015; McGeown, Mazzoni, Venneri & Kirsch, 2009; Palhano-Fontes et al., 2015; Peres et al., 2012). Furthermore the brain as filter concept, including the parts pertaining to ESP, is now gaining ground once more among theorists of consciousness (e.g., Kastrup, 2012). Indeed, recent theoretical developments (Smythies, 2011) suggest that NMDA antagonism, such as via ketamine, bypasses the reducing valve/filter action of the brain (ketamine-NDE section below for a discussion).

β-carbolines, Tryptamines, and Psi

Advancing on earlier suggestions about the pineal gland's involvement in psi (e.g. Miller, 1978; Sinel, 1927), Roney-Dougal (1986, 1989, 1991, 2001) has developed an endogenous neurochemical-perspective of psi based on the action of the pineal and several hallucinogenic substances found in ayahuasca, the visionary Amazonian brew reported to induce a range of paranormal experiences. The common neurotransmitter serotonin is known to be most active in the pineal gland, where it follows a circadian rhythm and is converted at night into melatonin (5-methoxy tryptamine, or 5MT) and the β-carboline, pinoline (6-methoxy tetrahydro-β-carboline, or 6-MeO-THβC), which regulate sleep cycles.

The pineal may also create other β-carbolines, such as 6-methoxy-harmalan, a harmala alkaloid. These β-carbolines block the neuronal uptake of serotonin making it available for use, and inhibit the enzyme monoamine oxydase (MAO), which breaks down certain tryptamines such as N,N-dimethyltryptamine (N,N-DMT, or simply DMT) and 5-methoxy-dimethyltryptamine (5-MeO-DMT). MAO inhibiters, such as pinoline or the harmala alkaloids, make serotonin available at the pineal where, with the aid of pineal enzymes (methyl transferases), it can also be converted into 5-MeO-DMT, DMT, and bufotenine (5- hydroxy-N,N-dimethyltyptamine, 5-HO-DMT), which are endogenous visionary substances also found in certain ingredients (such as *Psychotria viridis)* of ayahuasca brews and other shamanic visionary substances, even some of animal origin (e.g. the Sonoran desert toad, Rudgley, 2000). In vivo biosynthesis of DMT might also occur through the conversion of the common, nutritionally essential, amino acid tryptophan (Jacob & Presti, 2005; Shulgin & Shulgin, 1997).

However, these endogenous visionary tryptamines are not orally active, as they are denatured by the MAO enzymes present in the stomach, but ayahuasca brews also contains plant additives (such as *Banisteriopsis caapi*) containing a range of harmala alkaloids that inhibit MAO and allow the complementarily ingested visionary tryptamines to be active in the brain. It is this action of the β-carbolines (particularly harmine) in ayahuasca that is these days considered their primary purpose as admixtures in the brew (e.g. McKenna, 2004), though this may not always be the case as subjectively potent ayahuasca decoctions occasionally do not actually contain DMT when analyzed (Callaway, 2005). Nevertheless the harmala alkaloids are also known to induce visions themselves and Roney-Dougal (1986, 1989, 1991, 2001) originally implicated β-carbolines, such as the endogenous pinoline and the exogenous harmala alkaloids, as inducing psi-conducive states, either naturally during dreams (Callaway, 1988) or artificially by causing waking dream states.

Roney-Dougal (2001) also later acknowledged that the β-carbolines may exert their visionary effects by potentiating the effects of ingested visionary tryptamines like DMT or 5-MeO-DMT when consumed in combination with them, as in ayahuasca. Further to Roney-Dougal's proposals, it is my speculation that the β-carbolines may also induce visions by contributing to the endogenous manufacture of visionary tryptamine substances, either when taken alone or in combination with such tryptamines, perhaps even indicating endogenous DMT or related tryptamines as the primary or even sole cause of such visions. This may account for why harmala alkaloids are less effective and slower than DMT at inducing visions (see Shulgin & Shulgin, 1997).

In essence, ayahuasca contains two types of visionary chemicals, one type (β-carbolines, e.g., harmine) that helps to both create and potentiate the effects of the other type (tryptamines, e.g., DMT), potentially mimicking the nocturnal chemistry of the pineal and its supposed control over natural visionary states, such as dreams (Callaway, 1988), mystical experiences, and NDEs (Strassman, 2001).

Roney-Dougal (1989, 1991, 2001) suggested that the pineal gland and its neurochemistry is important in the occurrence of psi phenomena and points to the association made by yogis between the pineal gland and the ajna chakra, the yogic psychic center that controls psi-experiences in those with awakened kundalini (Miller, 1978; Satyananda, 1972). Further to this, Naranjo (1987) noted that both kundalini and ayahuasca experiences, being similar in many respects, also feature the same serpentine imagery, further speculating that they probably have the same neurochemistry and result in the same bioenergetic activation.

There is also some possibility that pineal gland activity or DMT production can be stimulated by certain esoteric yogic practices, such as kechari, which involves pressing the tongue into the far rear roof of the mouth to stimulate the production of amrit, a yogic nectar that reputedly causes DMT–like ecstasies, which is supposedly secreted in the brain following prolonged practice (Motoyama, 2001; Satyananda, 1996). Some support for this speculation comes from Strassman's (2001) observation that the pineal gland is formed *in utero* from the tissue of the roof of the mouth rather than in the brain, and later migrates to its unique ventricle position just outside the blood-blood barrier, directly above a critical cerebrospinal fluid byway, and this very tentatively suggests that pineal stimulation via the roof of the mouth may be possible.

Furthermore, manifestation of very specific body vibrations said to be classic kundalini symptoms are supposedly quite reliably induced with substances such as DPT (*N,N*-dipropyl-tryptamine) and 4-Acetoxy-DIPT (*N,N*-diisopropyl-4-acetoxy-tryptamine), which are even more obscure psychedelic tryptamines than DMT, but close relatives of it (Toad, 1999a, 1999b). Similarly, Grof (2001) has reported spontaneous kundalini arousal occurring during psychedelic psychotherapy sessions and surveys of kundalini experiences have found them to be related to drug use (DeGracia, 1995; Thalbourne, 2001).

Roney-Dougal (1989, 1991, 2001) also indicates that the pineal gland is sensitive to – possibly changing its chemical production – the same fluctuations in geomagnetic activity that appear to be associated with spontaneous psi-activity, possibly related to pineal melatonin (Persinger, 1988) or DMT fluctuations (Hill & Persinger, 2003) – for a review see Roney-Dougal, Ryan, and Luke (2013, 2014). That the pineal gland is central to psi is further supported by anthropological research, to follow – although experimental evidence is lacking – that suggests that DMT and the harmala alkaloids found in ayahuasca are psi-conducive, along with clinical research that suggests that pinoline and melatonin regulate sleep cycles and dreaming, during which spontaneous psi experiences most often occur (Roney-Dougal, 1986, 1989, 1991, 2001). Durwin (2001) has further suggested that the total isolation in the dark undergone for either the first 9 or 18 childhood years of the lives of trainee shamans of the Andean Kogi causes pineal gland deformation (presumably by melatonin/pinoline overproduction) that is responsible for their renowned divinatory skills.

Some tentative support for the notion that ESP performance is directly predicted by pineal gland activity is also evident with experimental research that demonstrated prepubescent children score better on ESP tests at 3am, when the pineal's nocturnal chemicals (melatonin, etc.) are supposedly at peak concentrations in the brain, rather than at 9pm (Satyanarayana, Rao, & Vijaylakshmi, 1993). This effect was not evident with a comparable group of pubescent children, which the authors suggest might be expected because the pineal is less active after infancy.

A more extensive follow-up investigated dream-ESP and circadian pineal rhythms among young adults finding a significant improvement in dream precognition scores at 3am compared to 8am (Luke, Zychowicz, Richterova, Tjurina & Polonnikova, 2012) with scores in the same direction but non-significant in a replication study (Luke & Zychowicz, 2014), providing some tentative indirect support for the notion that ESP may be linked to circadian pineal rhythms.

Roney-Dougal (2001) also draws parallels between the ostensibly psi-conducive nature of the shamanic trance state, psychotic states, psychedelic states, and the dream state, which she suggests all belong to the same continuum – perhaps somewhat akin to Thalbourne's (1998) concept of transliminality, the proclivity for psychological material to cross thresholds in or out of consciousness – and that they all show suggestive evidence of being regulated by the same neurochemical processes. Recently, the discovery of trace amine receptors in the brain for which DMT shows greater affinity than does serotonin – its more common neuro-amine cousin – has lead to a resurgence of interest in endogenous DMT in the mediation of mental health (Jacob & Presti, 2005).

DMT, Near-death and Other Exceptional Experiences

After extensive research investigating the phenomenological effects of administering intravenous injections of DMT, Strassman (2001) has independently hypothesized a role for DMT similar to that suggested by Roney-Dougal (2001). Strassman echoed the same neurochemical action of the pineal as Roney-Dougal, and similarly proffered that psychotic, dream, meditation, and mystical states all occur through the overproduction of DMT, implicating DMT as a "reality thermostat" (Strassman, 2001, p.327). However, Strassman indicated the action of DMT, not β-carbolines, as primary in producing these states and alternatively proposed that the pineal gland and endogenous DMT are central during extraordinary events, such as birth, death, and the near-death experience (NDE).

To support this view Strassman noted that the anatomy of the pineal, suspended in cerebrospinal fluid outside of the blood-bathed brain, is independent enough to resist activation by normal stresses and yet is optimally situated to deliver DMT directly to the middle brain regions where DMT-sensitive serotonin receptors are involved in mood, perception, and thought. Furthermore, access to the brain in this way eliminates the need for DMT transportation in the blood – where it would be broken down by MAO enzymes anyway – thereby negating the need for a pumping heart for delivery.

Jacob and Presti (2005) also noted that DMT is virtually unique among endogenous neurotransmitters in that it is a molecule small enough to have blood-brain barrier permeability, and has a unique three-step active uptake into the synaptic vesicles of the brain making it available from peripheral parts of the body (Frecska et al, 2013). That melatonin exerts its influence slowly over a period of a day or more, and so does not need the pineal's unique location, further supports the supposed postmortem function of pineal DMT. Strassman further speculated that the pineal might continue to produce postmortem DMT for a few hours.

Strassman also noted that the NDE has psychedelic and mystical qualities, and that the DMT experience often shares the same features as an NDE. Some of his DMT study participants reported NDEs and death-rebirth experiences, with many others reporting a newfound fearlessness of death. However, that the participants may have been inadvertently primed for these experiences cannot be ruled out because they were told in the briefing to expect feelings of death or impending death. Nonetheless, independent survey research indicates that DMT users sometimes do report death-like and near-death-type experiences (Luke & Kittenis, 2005).

Nevertheless, not all researchers agree that DMT experiences mimic NDEs. Potts (2012) indicates that there are several typical features of the NDE that do not occur with DMT, and vice versa. However Potts' comparison is not based on a systematic review or balanced sample of accounts and many of the features he lists as only occurring in NDEs (e.g., cosmic unity, peace, joy) *are* actually experienced in some DMT (e.g., Strassman, 2001) and ayahuasca experiences (Liester, 2013). Nevertheless, some of the weirder DMT features, such as encounters with clowns, elves and insectoid beings do tend to be absent from NDEs. Regardless, in a systematic analysis of interviews with DMT experiencers one theme to emerge was the entities' tendencies to impart insightful information about themselves and the universe in which they were inhabited, much like the positive performative role played by the apparently sentient beings encountered in near-death experiences, typically identified as deceased persons (Cott & Rock, 2008).

Furthermore, countering Potts' analysis, Liester (2013) conducted a more thorough comparison of experiences on ayahuasca with the nine classic features of the NDE as outlined by Moody (1989), the original cartographer of the NDE and the man who coined the term. Ideally, a systematic prospective study is required, nevertheless Leister determined that eight of the Moody's nine key NDE elements could be found in ayahuasca experiences, although, as with DMT, some of the weirder entity encounters, such as elves and fairies were absent from the NDE cosmology. However, it should be noted that, historically, in folkloric accounts elves and fairies are commonly interpreted as spirits of the dead (Evans Wentz, 1911/2004; Lang, 1893; Luke, 2013b).

Indeed, it was to Strassman's (2001) surprise that many of the participants in his DMT study reported contact with sentient beings during the experience, often described as elves, dwarves, imps, gremlins, clowns, reptilian beings, and aliens, but also as spirits, gods, or just as a presence, which was commonly supremely powerful, wise, and loving. Such prevalent encounter experiences with DMT use (for a review see Luke, 2011b) are seemingly so unique and reliable (e.g., Meyer, 1993) as to have had the impish characters popularly dubbed the "self-transforming machine elves" (McKenna, 1991, p.16), and who's tangible reality has been hotly debated by other DMT-experience researchers (Carpenter, 2006; Gallimore, 2013; Gallimore & Luke, 2015; Kent, 2005, 2010; Luke, 2012c, 2013b; Luke & Spowers, 2018; Pickover, 2005).

Strassman suggested that fluctuations in endogenous DMT levels were also responsible for the frequent reports elsewhere of alien abduction, which share the newfound fearlessness of death and visions of energy tunnels, or cylinders of light, in common with DMT experiences. Following personal experiences with ayahuasca, Severi (2003) likewise noted the similarity between NDEs, traditional psychedelic-induced shamanic initiations, alien abduction experiences, and heightened psychic sensitivity, as have previous researchers (e.g. Harvey-Wilson, 2001; McKenna, 1991; Ring, 1989, 1992).

However, Baruša (2003) pointed out that, despite the similarities, DMT and alien abduction experiences lack specific similarities, such as the absence with DMT of the classic 'grays' (small gray aliens). Nevertheless, Hancock (2005), also having experienced DMT and ayahuasca, argued that there are substantial similarities between aliens and elves, whether induced through DMT or else appearing in historic-folkloric legends and testimonies, speculating that the latter also have a DMT-induced etiology and, adopting the theory proposed by Vallee (1969), that these elves of folklore are the prototype encounter/abduction experiences.

It should be noted that few experiencers ever doubt the reality of their encounters with either aliens (Mack, 1999) or DMT entities (Strassman, 2001), perhaps with the exception of Kent (2005, although see Kent 2010) in this latter category, and most actually consider them to be more real than most ordinary experiences. Additionally, like alien abduction reports, Strassman notes that his DMT study participants reported being probed and having things inserted into them by the beings, however, it should be noted that this might have been induced by the medical nature of his experiments and the use of intravenous injections and equipment for monitoring vital signs.

Incidentally, although neither Strassman nor other researchers originally pointed this out, it is apparent that some of the DMT experiences reported in his study, particularly the negative ones, share several features in common with sleep paralysis (e.g., see Cheyne, 2001), particularly the sense of presence, reports of one's chest being crushed, strange whistling, whining, and whirring sounds, and the terrifying paralysis of both body and vocal chords (Strassman, 2001).

Alien abduction experiences and NDEs are also associated with sleep paralysis (see Sherwood, 2002), and indeed Strassman (2008) later noted the apparent relationship between sleep paralysis and DMT experiences, although caution has been raised about claiming too many anomalous phenomena can be explained by DMT, as this ultimately explains nothing, and further phenomenological analysis is needed (Luke, 2008), such as that conducted by Cott & Rock (2008), although a direct comparison of such experiences is needed. Nevertheless, there certainly warrants something to research here regarding a DMT etiology for sleep paralysis.

Curiously, experiential reports from research programs in the 1950s and 1960s (outlined in Shulgin & Shulgin, 1997; Torres & Repke, 2006), indicate that the endogenous 5-hydroxy-DMT (bufotenine), a very close relative to DMT with similar neurochemistry, is seemingly able on occasion to cause feelings of constriction in the throat and the crushing of one's chest, as well as anxiety and fear reactions, much like sleep paralysis, possibly implicating it as a co-chemical factor in such experiences, along with DMT.

Additionally, in South America and the Caribbean the entheogenic cohoba snuff is made from one of the few traditionally-used plants in which bufotenine is active, *Piptadenia peregrina*, and is used specifically to contact spirits (Cohen, 1970; Torres & Repke, 2006), perhaps somewhat like the sensed presences of sleep paralysis and numerous DMT experiences.

However, Ott (2001) pointed out that the circulatory crises in the earlier bufotenine research were most likely due to psychological factors caused by the enforced nature of the experiments – conducted as they were on psychiatric patients and prisoners with limited consent – because such experiences were absent during Ott's own extensive self-experimentation, and nor do indigenous users of plants containing bufotenine worry about or report respiratory arrest (Torres & Repke, 2006).

In any case the breathing difficulties associated with sleep paralysis may be more to do with the paralysis of conscious bodily functions caused by being asleep, and the inability to inhale at will. Furthermore, sensed presence, as opposed to direct perception of an entity, as often occurs with sleep paralysis, may be more common with other substances, such as *Salvia divinorum* (Aardvark, 2002; Addy, 2010; Arthur, 2010) (meaning something like "diviner's sage"), although systematic phenomenological research is needed.

In evaluation of the role of the pineal gland and endogenous psychedelics in the activation of psi and the NDE, it has yet to be shown that psi can be produced with these substances under controlled conditions. In addition, both psi experiences and NDEs might be induced with other psychoactive substances, as shown in the following sections, although this criticism has been countered by Strassman (2001) with the possibility that other psychedelic substances may also stimulate the pineal and endogenous DMT by their action. However, this proposal is little more than conjecture. Furthermore, although there is good reasoning for the hypothesis that DMT is made in the human pineal, this is yet to be proven and remains speculative, like many of Strassman's and Roney-Dougal's suppositions at the present time.

According to Strassman (2001), although the lungs, liver, blood, and eye all contain the enzymes necessary to convert tryptamine to DMT, the pineal gland is especially rich in them and also has high concentrations of serotonin ready to convert to tryptamine. So while the pineal-DMT hypothesis is currently unproven (Hanna, 2010), it is certainly feasible, especially when it is considered that the chemical conversion of tryptamine to DMT can be demonstrated *en vitro*.

The only attempt thus far to support the hypothesis directly has been Strassman's attempt to isolate DMT from 10 human pineal glands extracted from cadavers. No DMT was detected in the glands; however, neither the bodies nor the glands were freshly frozen and any chemicals present may have degraded before analysis (Strassman, 2001).

Thus far DMT has been found to be naturally occurring in the brains of rodents (Kärkkäinen et al, 2005), and in the highest concentrations in humans in the cerebrospinal fluid (for a review, see Barker, McIlhenny & Strassman, 2012), but not the brain, let alone the pineal. Furthermore, although the pineal contains methyltransferase enzymes, as Strassman (2001) indicated, the particular one thought to be crucial for *en vivo* DMT production (indolethylamine N-methyltransferase, or simply INMT) has as yet not been found in the human pineal gland although, curiously, DMT was found in rabbit brain tissue, despite the absence of INMT (Kärkkäinen et al, 2005), perhaps indicating that INMT is not necessary for the production of DMT. Nevertheless, INMT has been found to have a wide distribution in the human brain, with the highest concentrations in the uncus, medulla, amygdala, frontal cortex, and fronto-parietal and temporal lobes, and is densely located in anterior horn of the spinal cord, implying a wide distribution of human brain DMT (for a review see, Carbonaro & Gatch, 2016).

Furthermore, McIlhenny (2012) pointed out that most INMT mapping research only establishes where enzyme translation is occurring, as they are based solely on INMT mRNA studies. A recent study (Cozzi, Mavlyutov, Thompson, & Ruoho, 2011) using a florescent INMT antibody suggests the presence of INMT in three Rhesus macaque nervous tissues samples, including the pineal gland. Evidence of INMT in primate pineal glands indicates better potential for Strassman's human pineal-DMT production hypothesis, nevertheless direct support is still lacking. However, absence of evidence is not evidence of absence, and the pineal gland is difficult to research *en vivo* and DMT is an under-researched substance, particularly in humans. DMT is also difficult to detect (Barker et al., 2012) and belongs to the most controlled category of drugs in most countries, so, currently, the jury remains out on the pineal-DMT hypothesis. Nevertheless, other researchers sympathetic to the notion of endogenously-mediated spontaneous exceptional DMT experiences (such as NDE), suggest the production of DMT in the lungs, rather than the pineal, as a better candidate location (Frecska et al., 2013).

Overall, despite their incompleteness, the pineal/β-carboline/DMT models of psi and NDE do offer unique neurochemical perspectives on paranormal experience around which further research can be framed. Additionally, although neither author has speculated on the others' ideas, their models are not incompatible with each other; however, they may begin to answer the question of why such visionary molecules as DMT are made within humans at all. For a further discussion of DMT, brain action and exceptional phenomena, see Luke (2011b)(Chapter 7 this book).

Ketamine and NDEs

A proliferation of reported cases of NDEs with the use of ketamine (Jansen, 1997a, 1999, 2001) and the similarity of aspects of the ketamine experience to that of the NDE (Morse, Venecia & Milstein, 1989; Rogo, 1984) – despite Morse's (1997) later contentions that the evidence for this is weak – has led to the development of a neurochemical model of NDE based upon the action of this psychoactive substance (Jansen, 1990, 1997a, 2001). A dissociative anaesthetic – also reported to induce experiences of telepathy, precognition, clairvoyance, psycho-kinesis, communication with the dead, kundalini experiences and an increase in synchronicities (Case, 2003; Jansen, 2001; Luke & Kittenis, 2005; Wyllie, 1981) – ketamine acts by binding to the phencyclidine (PCP) site of the N-methyl-D-aspartate (NMDA) receptor, blocking the action of the neurotransmitter glutamate.

Jansen indicated that potentially life-threatening circumstances (e.g., hypoxia, ischemia, hypoglycemia, temporal lobe epilepsy) can initiate a glutamate flood, which results in neurotoxicity through the over-activation of the NMDA receptors (for further details, see Smythies, 2011). This NDE trigger may be accompanied by a flood of neu-roprotective agents that also bind to the NMDA receptors preventing damage, in much the same way as ketamine. Like Grinspoon and Baka-lar's (1979) speculation that the brain synthesizes a chemical similar to ketamine in times of stress, Jansen proposed that "endopsychosins", which bind to the same receptor site as ketamine, would be discovered as the neuroprotective agents that cause an ASC, like that of ketamine, termed the NDE.

Although parsimonious, Jansen's (1997a) ketamine model of NDE has been both duly criticized and well defended. It has been argued that unlike NDEs, ketamine trips frequently induce fear (Strassman, 1997) and are not considered "real" (Fenwick, 1997). However, as Jansen (1977b) likewise contested, it is becoming increasingly recog-nized now that NDEs are also commonly reported to be distressing or traumatic (Atwater, 1994; Montanelli & Parra, 2000) and, furthermore, ketamine experiences are also more often than not reported to induce a sense of peace and pleasantness (Corazza, 2008; Luke, 2007).

In support of the perceived reality of the ketamine experience, there are documented accounts of people who have had an NDE and then later a ketamine experience, and who reported the experiences being the same (Jansen, 2001). In support of this, Grof (1994) found that several cancer patients had NDEs during psychedelic therapy (most likely with LSD) that were very similar to later spontaneous NDEs.

In further criticism of Jansen's model, it has been argued (Fen-wick, 1997; Greyson, 2000) that the clarity and clear memory of the NDE experience is not consistent with cerebral dysfunction. However, it is arguable that Jansen's model does not stipulate the necessity of cerebral dysfunction for a NDE, merely the threat, or even just the perceived threat of it, and Jansen (1997b, p. 87) points out "there is no reason to suspect that the NDE mechanism would never be acti-vated spontaneously". Furthermore, Jansen (1997b) regarded clarity of consciousness as a nebulous term in the discussion of altered states, as the term is loaded towards the ordinary state of consciousness.

Some researchers (e.g., Greyson, 2000; Smythies, 2011) have further contested that, despite the possibility that the endogenous peptide alpha-endopsychosin is a candidate, no endopsychosins have yet been identified or proven to exist, and Jansen (2001) conceded that this may initially have been a false lead and has suggested a number of alternative endogenous NMDA antagonists as candidates: N-acetyl-aspartyl-glutamate, kynurenic acid and magnesium, all of which protect brain cells from excito-toxic damage (Jansen, 2004). Nevertheless, Thomas (2004), following Jansen in his search, has identified technical flaws with these speculated endogenous "NDE-ogens" and has instead proposed the neuromodulator agmatine as the most likely candidate. The debate continues.

In further criticism of the model, Parker (2001) noted that one-drug/one-experience theories were abandoned in the 1970s and that, along with Greyson (2000), he further noted that ketamine appears to have multiple effects in the brain and multiple experiential features, some of which include those of the NDE. Jansen (1997b) earlier countered this latter criticism with the proposal that factors of set and setting are paramount in determining experience with all ASCs, be they NDEs or ketamine-induced states, so experiences are expected to vary.

Parker (2001), like Siegel (1980), added that other drugs also produce features of the NDE, although Jansen (1997b) has asserted that these NDE-features are typical with ketamine but are not typical with other drugs, except for PCP and ibogaine (Bianchi, 1997; Jansen, 2001) which are NMDA antagonists (or more specifically called NMDA-PCP receptor blockers).

However, in support of Parker's (2001) criticism, Roll and Montagno (1985) have noted the similarity between NDEs and LSD experiences, as reported by Grof (1994). Reports of NDE also occur with the use of other dissociatives, like dextromethorphan (DXM)(White, 1997), and carbogen (Meduna, 1950), as well as with high doses of hashish (Siegel & Hirschman, 1984), tryptamines like 5-MeO-DMT (Shulgin & Shulgin, 1997) and the ayahuasca (meaning "the vine of the dead") derivative, DMT (Strassman, 2001). Yet, Strassman (2001) does not find Jansen's model incompatible with his own DMT model of NDE, but rather asks why a neuroprotective agent like ketamine should also be psychedelic as there is no obvious benefit to the near-death visionary experience, other than enabling consciousness to have awareness of its departure from the body.

More recently, electrophysiology and receptor studies have revealed that both NMDA antagonists, such as ketamine, and classic hallucinogens, such as LSD, may actually enhance glutamatergic transmission via non-NMDA receptors in the frontal cortex. This may indicate a common mode of chemical action in the brain responsible for such similar experiences with these divergent molecules, though further investigation is required (Vollenweider, 2004).

Given the similarities between NDEs, ketamine experiences, and other drug experiences, Rogo (1984) proposed that the NDE-like effects of ketamine are more often interpreted as NDEs because it has so often been used in a medical setting, further suggesting that ketamine-induced NDEs are less prevalent with recreational use than with anaesthetic use, though this has not been systematically investigated to my knowledge.

To our knowledge, the only systematic investigation of the ketamine hypothesis, besides Jansen (2001), is that of Corazza (2008), who compared 36 cases of apparent NDEs induced by ketamine with 36 cases of NDEs reportedly caused by a cardiac arrest or other life threatening circumstances. Both groups showed a high degree of similarity in certain experiential features, with a roughly equal prevalence among the groups of experiences involving altered perceptions of time, speeded up visions, and the occurrence of ESP (25%), but the ketamine group were more likely to report unity with the universe, and the cardiac groups were more likely to report dissociation from the body, visions of light, and encounters with deceased or religious beings. However, Corazza asserted that the evidence indicates that NDEs can be induced through ketamine, although they may not be identical to those occurring naturally.

The study is not without its limitations; however, as outlined by Luke (2009b), as the ketamine participants were recruited on the premise that they felt that they had had an NDE on ketamine, which Jansen (2001) reported only occur to about 12% of ketamine users. Furthermore, it is unclear if the respondents are describing a specific ketamine experience or an experience more generally, as most of the respondents had taken ketamine between 10 and 2000 times, though a similar number of cardiac arrest experiences is very unlikely for the comparison group.

Nevertheless, Corazza and Schifano (2010) acknowledged the limitation that their findings are based on a self-selected, nonrandomized, limited size sample. Subsequently, ketamine can at best be thought of as an occasional NDE trigger or mimic, but is not a wholly repeatable or reliable source of NDEs (Luke, 2009b). Nevertheless, cardiac arrest and the experience that ketamine invokes appear to be similar enough to genuine NDEs that leading consciousness researchers Hameroff and Chopra (2010) have called for its use in prolonging end of life brain activity (by delaying neurotoxicity) to allow terminally ill patients to have more conscious deaths.

More recently, having first researched the parapsychological potential of psychedelics in the 1940s, and still going, Smythies (2011) has identified several apparent flaws with Jansen's K-NDE model. First, an NMDA-antagonist model of NDE is too general because the glutamate receptors can be found in all regions of the brain and yet the NDE phenomena suggest the activation of only specific brain regions, and furthermore ketamine does not appear to produce global brain NMDA-antagonism (although this latter point may argue against the first).

Second, ketamine, Smythies argued, cannot actually stimulate the action potential of the neurons it binds to, but rather affects the modulation of the strength and number of synapses (i.e., the neuroplasticity), so it cannot immediately affect the brain regions required to stimulate the NDE. This second argument, however, seems somewhat contradicted by the phenomenological evidence that suggests that ketamine *can* in fact stimulate NDE-like phenomena and so presumably *does* activate the appropriate brain regions, at least indirectly.

Finally, Smythies (2011), contested that if the NMDA-antagonism explanation for NDEs were true, we would expect to see a relationship between NDEs and *grand mal* epilepsy – during which massive cerebral glutamate overload occurs. However, according to Smythies, the relationship is only apparently reported by one study (Britton & Bootzin, 2004), and is in any case weaker than the relationship between epilepsy symptoms and disturbed sleep patterns, although, in argument against Smythies, this weaker relationship may be accounted for by the infrequent occurrence of NDEs relative to sleep disturbances.

Furthermore, counter to Smythies' conjecture, several other researchers have speculated about the link between NDEs and temporal lobe epilepsy, drawing parallels (Blanke & Dieguez, 2009; Jansen, 2001; Morse, Venecia, & Milstein, 1989; Neppe, 1989; Persinger & Makarec, 1987; Saavedra-Aguilar & Gómez-Jeria, 1989), although admittedly the NDE-epilepsy link is incomplete (Neppe, 1989), and epilepsy might best be thought of as one of several possible NDE triggers, as Jansen (1997a) originally proposed, rather than an explanation for NDEs.

Ultimately, Smythies (2011) proposed that the excitatory NMDA receptor system, which runs continuously even while asleep, actually *is* the Bergson brain filter mechanism (discussed earlier in Chapter 9: Brain as Filter) that ordinarily prevents people from experiencing what Aldous Huxley (1954, p.11) called "Mind at Large": mystical and paranormal consciousness (i.e., an NDE). Consequently, Smythies asserted that NDMA antagonism, such as via ketamine or a natural NDE, bypasses the brain's natural filter action, leading to all manner of paranormal and transpersonal experiences.

Much as Smythies should be applauded for morphing the two theories together, the same might be said for psychedelically induced serotonergic action as for glutamatergic action, so in effect this says little more than what Huxley originally proposed and what we now know about psychedelic neurochemistry (see Chapter 9: Brain as Filter).

Overall, despite over simplification and generalization, the ketamine model of NDE offers the most complete neurochemical explanation of the NDE so far and, as with the DMT model, does not necessarily assume a materialist reductionism to explain the data – unlike Siegel (1980) for example – although some commentators (e.g., Sakellarios, 2005) have erroneously assumed that it does.

Furthermore, the model can be easily tested and refined. For instance, there is evidence to suggest that the non-competitive antagonism at the non-glycine site of the NMDA receptor in particular is linked to the event of dissociative anaesthesia and altered sensory perceptions that are familiar to ketamine. This would indicate that relatively novel substances like HA-966 (1-hydroxy-3-amino-pyrrolidone-2), which acts in this particular neurochemical manner (Bonta, 2004), could induce NDEs in blind conditions comparable to those occurring ordinarily, though this remains to be seen.

In research with monkeys, HA-966 induced EEG patterns characteristic of sleep despite the animals remaining completely alert, which may be related to Jansen's (2004) observation that the same 60% of the population that do not recall their dreams also do not recall their ketamine experiences during anaesthesia, a proportion apparently equivalent to the number of people who do not report having had some kind of NDE. Alternatively, in order to test the K-NDE theory, it has been suggested to administer ketamine to those who have had a natural NDE and compare the two (Kolp et al., 2007). Assuming ketamine NDEs to be genuine, ultimately, however, the question remains of whether chemically induced NDEs utilize alternative pathways or the actual NDE pathway (Fracasso & Friedman, 2011).

Bringing personal observations (Luke, 2005) to the K-NDE debate, it seems apparent that the degree of general anaesthesia induced by ketamine is relative to one's motor control ability and what Grosso (1976) identified as the degree of being out-of-body: Factors which are more pronounced with the positive S-isomer of ketamine rather than the negative isomer (Domino & Warner, 2010), further indicating how entwined these effects are, specific as they are to just one ketamine molecule type. Such relationships between sensory and motor impairment and reported body image have elsewhere been found with local anaesthesia (Paqueron et al., 2003), though obviously not full blown OBEs.

Returning to the personal observations, in repeated ketamine experiences I observed that the initial stages of anaesthesia and out-of-body-ness are accompanied by increasing difficulty in controlling one's body and a growing sense of body dysmorphia, in a non-clinical sense, in that part of one's body may appear longer (macrosomatognosia) or shorter (microsomatognosia), as described by Frederiks (1963). For example, on one occasion I recall being unable to successfully manoeuvre out of the door because my legs appeared to be the approximate distance of an entire football pitch away. It is observed that the relatively changing gradation in increased anaesthesia, body dysmorphia and motor control continues, with a sufficient dosage, as the trip intensifies towards a full-blown out-of-body experience, total anaesthesia, and ultimately no motor control.

Indeed, while some K-OBEs are accompanied by autoscopy, even awareness of one's body can disappear at the peak of a high dose ketamine experience, even to the point of not realizing one actually has a body but is instead just experiencing the present as a single point of consciousness and nothing more. On one such occasion I was seemingly privileged to a view of Earth from space and yet I did not even know who or what I was, let alone that I was human and apparently had a body.

This relatively changing relationship between anaesthesia, motor control, out-of-body-ness, and even body-ownership-awareness is apparent on both entering and exiting the ketamine experience, although seemingly more so in exiting (although in reverse), as the entrance to a ketamine experience can often be abrupt, with a swift and intense onset, whereas the departure is more gradual. Such first-person psychonautics can tell us a good deal about both psychedelic states, especially ketamine states (Newcombe, 2008), and parapsychological phenomena (Luke, 2011c) and such methods are witnessing somewhat of a revival after a long hiatus since the era of William James' (1902) classic experimentation with nitrous oxide – another NDMA antagonist.

Survey research also shows that ketamine induces OBEs and autoscopy far more often than other (non-anaesthetic) psychedelics

(Wilkins, Girard, & Cheyne, 2011), as had been previously speculated (Luke & Kittenis, 2005), the question remains of why anaesthesia should accompany an OBE/NDE: Does the anaesthesia cause the perception of being out of one's body, and therefore leads to a feeling of dying or of having died, or does the near-death experience provoke an OBE and subsequent anaesthesia as a defence against likely pain?

Observing the ketamine experience from the recipient's perspective, it appears that the anaesthesia occurs because one's consciousness is no longer connected to one's body, and certainly the OBE and anaesthesia are intimately connected, but why and how deserve further investigation and may shed light on the neurobiological factors of OBEs and NDEs.

Dopamine and Paranormal Beliefs and Experiences

Taking a purely materialist reductionist view of paranormal experiences by attempting to account for them exclusively in terms of beliefs arising from faulty cognitions - what Irwin (2009) calls the cognitive deficits hypothesis – a loose neurobiological model for the explanation of paranormal beliefs has arisen that posits the dopamine neurotransmitter system as the primary facilitator. Put forward by Krummenacher and colleagues (Krummenacher, Brugger, Fahti, & Mohr, 2002; Krummenacher, Mohr, Haker, & Brugger, 2009) the theory suggests that, although activity of the endogenous neurotransmitter dopamine is classically implicated in *enhancing* cognitive and perceptual decisions by improving the signal to noise ratio of neuronal transmission, paradoxically, hyperdopaminergic activity is associated with psychotic symptoms, schizophrenia and even schizotypy (for a brief review, see Krummenacher et al., 2009). So excess dopamine may be accountable for delusional thinking stemming from an increased tendency to find patterns in apparently random data – what the psychiatrist Klaus Conrad (1958) called apophenia.

According to Brugger and colleagues (e.g., Pizzagalli, Lehmann, & Brugger, 2001) paranormal believers – and so most likely paranormal experiencers too – have been shown to be more inclined towards apophenia than skeptics, thereby accounting for the increased creativity apparently associated with paranormal thinking and its similarity to some psychotic symptoms: A combination of creative and delusional dimensions being indicative of the positive phenomenology of schizotypy (Eckblad & Chapman, 1983).

Direct research into what might be most accurately called the hyperdopaminergia-apophenia hypothesis is somewhat limited at this time, consisting of only two studies, with somewhat mixed results. The first study (Raz, Hines, Fossella, & Castro, 2008) attempted to relate paranormal belief as a phenotype to hyperdopaminergia as a genotype via what Raz et al. (2008) call the "COMT dopaminergic gene", building on preliminary findings in behavioral apophenia dopamine research by Krummenacher et al. (2002) and studies associating schizotypy with dopaminergic genes (e.g., Avramopoulos et al., 2002).

COMT (Catechol-O-methyltransferase) is an enzyme that degrades catecholamines such as dopamine, and the COMT protein is encoded by the COMT gene. Utilizing questionnaire measures of paranormal belief, 107 psychology students were genetically screened for three COMT allelic forms, successfully identifying approximately one quarter of the sample with high COMT activity, a quarter with low activity, and half with intermediate activity.

However, failing to support the hyperdopaminergia-apophenia hypothesis those with decreased COMT activity, and hence greater hyperdopaminergia, reported no more paranormal beliefs, abilities or experiences than the higher COMT activity participants. Undeterred, Raz et al. (2008) pointed to the observation that attempting to unravel links between single gene polymorphisms that influence neurochemical function, and consequently individual differences in cognitive function, may be difficult when using distal phenotypes such as questionnaire measures, and that more proximal measures like brain imaging might be more promising.

Indeed behavioral genetics is in a state of epistemological crisis after the lack of hard findings from the recently completed Human Genome Project (e.g., see Maher, 2008), so it may well be too soon to expect good data relating paranormal beliefs to genes, particularly single genes, even if they are related.

The second study, by Krummenacher et al. (2009), sampled 20 paranormal believers and 20 paranormal non-believers and administered levodopa – an active precursor to dopamine in the brain – in a randomized placebo controlled between-subjects study. Participants were given two signal detection tasks, one with words (tapping left hemisphere processes) and one with faces (right hemisphere), that presented either word/non-word or face/non-face stimulus pairs tachistoscopically for just 140 milliseconds.

Participant responses were assessed for both their tendency to make correct guesses relative to incorrect ones, their sensitivity index (d'), and their tendency to respond with a positive or negative bias, their response tendency (C), both measures being independent of each other. Findings indicate that skeptics had significantly greater sensitivity to signal detection than believers in the placebo condition but, contrary to expectations, increased dopamine lead to a significant *decrease* in sensitivity in skeptics and had no effect on believers.

These findings challenge the view that dopamine generally assists in signal detection, and Krummenacher et al. (2009) suggested that the opposite may actually be true in some cases, especially with presumed *hypo*dominergic individuals (i.e., skeptics). Additionally, the authors argued that the lack of change in sensitivity in believers administered levodopa may be due to a plateau effect caused by high cerebral dopamine baseline levels; however, such a suggestion is somewhat *post hoc* and, even if it were true, the authors do not comment on why the dopamine-enhanced skeptics had lower sensitivity (i.e., greater sensory apophenia) than either believer group.

Whereas the sensitivity measure findings are puzzling, the response bias measure results are somewhat more straightforward, in the control scenario at least. As was expected, in the placebo condition believers had a greater tendency to respond in the affirmative (favoring a Type I error strategy), whereas skeptics had a greater tendency to respond in the negative (favoring a Type II error strategy), the difference between the groups being significant. However, against expectation, in the levodopa condition these tendencies in each group were diminished so that there was no significant difference between skeptics and believers, although the trend remained.

Specifically, compared to their placebo controls, dopamine-enhanced believers were more cautious of making false positive decisions (i.e., more conservative), and skeptics were less prone to make false negative decisions (i.e., more liberal, so that in effect both believer groups were less polarized in their responses. Contrary to the linear dopamine-apophenia relationship originally proposed, these results may indicate differing baseline dopaminergic activity in skeptics and believers and the possibility that there is a non-linear relationship between task and dopamine levels, perhaps an inverted U-shape, possibly modulated by individual differences in belief.

However, these findings should be replicated first and more direct measures of baseline dopamine (e.g., spinal dopamine metabolic marker assay) should be made before these findings and *post hoc* interpretations are given much weight. Furthermore, as the authors noted, use of a between- rather than within-subjects design is far from ideal, leaving too much faith in the randomization of the small groups and no certainty in equivalence of baselines in dopamine responsivity and behavioural performance, and so further studies would benefit from a cross-over design.

Aside from the current lack of research on the hyperdopaminergia-apophenia hypothesis and the somewhat confusing mixed results, this line of research seems worthwhile pursuing further, although it suffers from additional limitations. One is that it aims to boil down paranormal experiences to misperceptions and misjudgments of the pattern recognition type, which, even if we allow for the fact that the authors *a priori* preclude the possibility of genuine paranormal phenomena, this approach does not account for the swathe of other cognitive deficits that are also given to account for paranormal beliefs, such as poor judgments of probability and randomness, egocentric bias, selective remembering, confirmation bias, and more (Brugger & Mohr, 2008).

Indeed a study investigating probability inferences in those under the influence of ketamine, versus matched controls and schizophrenic patients, shows that the ketamine group were no different from the placebo group, whereas the patients were shown to exhibit a jump-to-conclusions response concerning probability inferences (Evans et al. 2012). Although ketamine is primarily an NMDA-antagonist, it also has direct effects on dopamine receptors (e.g., Kapur & Seeman, 2002), and so the lack of probability inference effect with ketamine does not complement a dopamine explanation for paranormal experiences within the cognitive deficits paradigm. Other psychological factors supposedly related to paranormal experiences, such as the propensity for false memories, also show no relationship with self-reported recreational drug use generally (Wilson & French, 2006).

So in this respect the dopaminergic approach does not currently incorporate many of the multitudinous psychological explanations for paranormal beliefs and experiences. Furthermore, the wealth of evidence, to follow, relating increased paranormal experience – and to some extent experimentally controlled production of ESP – to the ingestion of psychedelic substances does not particularly support a dopamine-based theory of paranormality either, as dopamine activation is neither primary nor ubiquitous with psychedelic substances.

Typically, classic tryptamine psychedelics (such as LSD and psilocybin) are thought to exert their effects via serotonin activation, particularly via the 5-HT$_{2A}$ receptor subtype (Lee & Roth, 2012). Nevertheless, it is thought that 5-HT$_{2A}$ receptor stimulation can activate dopamine release (Diaz-Mataix et al., 2005), and Previc (2011) asserted that all the various psychedelic neurochemical pathways to "altered states of consciousness with distorted reality" (p.43) ultimately lead to elevated levels of dopamine in the brain, although such reasoning rather ablates the intricate nuances of psychopharmacology and disregards primary neurochemical pathway activation as in any way important.

Furthermore, although some psychedelic substances (e.g., LSD, psilocin, DMT) do have relatively high affinities for certain dopamine receptors (Ray, 2010), dopamine is rarely considered to be a primary neurotransmitter site for psychedelic effects. Indeed, the primarily dopaminergic recreational drugs, such as amphetamine and cocaine, have been found to be either unrelated or negatively related to paranormal experiences and beliefs (for a review see Luke, 2008b; and see section on survey data, to follow), contradicting the dopamine-paranormal belief/experience hypothesis. Indeed, if Previc were right about psychedelics exerting their effects via the dopamine system, then we would expect amphetamine and cocaine to be psychedelic too, which they are not.

Furthermore there are numerous psychedelics strongly associated with paranormal experiences that do not have dopaminergic action, such as the k-opioid agonist salvinorin A (Ray, 2010) and anticholinergic agents like scopolamine and hyoscyamine – which are found in nightshade family plants like datura (Katzung, Masters & Trevor, 2012). Overall – with scant direct research, mixed and complex findings, and poor generalizability of the hypothesis to a) other psychological explanations and b) most of the psychedelic-parapsychology literature – at the present time, Krummenacher, Brugger, Mohr, and colleagues' (Krummenacher et al., 2002; Krummenacher et al., 2009) dopamine-apophenia conjecture remains very much rudimentary and unsupported.

Overview of Psychedelic/Neurochemical Models of Paranormal Experience

The preceding sections outline five neurochemical models germane to explaining psychic experiences, namely the brain as filter, β-carboline and tryptamine, DMT, ketamine and, finally, dopamine models. Aside from the latter, all of these models draw upon the action of psychedelic substances in particular and remain open to the possibility that psi and other so-called paranormal phenomena may be genuine.

It should be noted, however, that no single psychedelic model may ultimately be the correct one, as psychedelics may work in many ways (e.g., dissociatives are both NMDA antagonists, as well as mu-opioid agonists); nevertheless these models provide important avenues for future research and begin to help develop more complete neurobiological models of apparent paranormal cognition or merely paranormal belief, and, indeed, more complete models of consciousness itself. The importance of understanding the apparent paranormal effects of psychedelics is clear and the evidence in support of this relationship is reviewed and evaluated next.

CHAPTER 10

Field Reports of Psychedelic Paranormal Phenomena

Anthropological and Historical Reports

Despite apparent prejudices by anthropologists against reporting such phenomena traditionally (Winkelman, 1983), the anthropological and ethnobotanical literature remains replete with examples of ostensibly paranormal phenomena occurring with the traditional use of psychoactive plants. Commonly these plants are taken in ritual context for the express purpose of accessing altered states conducive to clairvoyance, precognition, telepathy, out-of-body travel, psychic diagnosis, psychic healing, and spirit communication, which provoked the mycologist Wasson (1964) to label them as the keys to extra-sensory perception.

Archaeological evidence suggests such practices have existed the world over for millennia (see Devereux, 1997). However, the paranormal effects of particular plants are not necessarily arbitrary. Shamans who use the ayahuasca brew in Amazonia report having control over whichever particular paranormal function the brew elicits through the discerning use of psychoactive admixtures that may "make you travel, make you see" or "teach you to heal" (Andritsky, 1989, p.78).

Indeed, when the harmala alkaloid harmine, the first psychoactive compound isolated from the ayahuasca decoction, was discovered by Guillermo Fischer Cárdenas in 1923 it was named "telepathine" (Beyer, 2009) because of its apparent psychical properties, as reported by Zerda Bayon (1912). Zerda Bayon illustrated this with the case of Colonel Morales who, after ingesting ayahuasca, beheld a vision of his dead father and his sick sister. About one month later he received the same news by messenger. It seems unlikely that the news could have arrived first by non-paranormal means, as the group was deep in the jungle 15 days' travel from the nearest communications outpost.

Clairvoyant states induced with the harmala alkaloid-containing *Perganum harmala* shrub in Morocco have also been reported (Rudgley, 2000). Additionally, there are many more accounts of such apparent

ESP with ayahuasca reported in Luna and White's (2000, 2016) anthology of classic ayahuasca experiences, as well as elsewhere (e.g. Beyer, 2009; Bianchi, 1994; Dobkin de Rios & Rumrrill, 2008; Gorman, 1992; Kensinger, 1973; McGovern, 1927; Shanon, 2002; Weil, Metzner, & Leary, 1965; Wilson, 1949).

Typically, the earliest reports from explorers and anthropologists to the Upper Amazon were of either OBEs or experiences of someone discovering via visions that some distant person known to them, usually a relative, had just died (Luke, 2010a). In addition, Naranjo (1967, 1973b) gave harmaline to 30 naïve urban elite Chilean participants who inexplicably reported the same images of snakes and jaguars, or big cats, as are commonly reported in traditional South American ayahuasca visions (Naranjo, 1987; Shanon, 2002).

Visions of jaguars and snakes with harmaline have also been reported elsewhere (Shulgin & Shulgin, 1997) and one second-hand story from late 1960s Haight-Ashbury (the temporal-spatial epicentre of psychedelic counter culture) proffered that someone once experimented giving ayahuasca to Eskimos and, devoid of the cultural milieu typical of ayahuasca use, they still saw huge cats in their visions, although it is unlikely that this research ever took place (Weil, 1980). Furthermore some of the participants in Naranjo's study were convinced they had seen these images by traveling out-of-body in time and space.

Ott (1993) noted, however, that harmaline only occurs in minimal quantities in tested ayahuasca decoctions and so cannot be accountable for the psychoactive effects of the brew. Nevertheless, Strassman (2001) found that administering DMT (the most psychoactive constituent of ayahuasca) induced a similar certainty of space-time travel and resulted in the inordinately frequent occurrence of images of DNA, an image which Narby (1998) found commonly featured in the ayahuasca healing visions of Amazonian shamans, but was most often represented by snakes.

It has been suggested, amid some controversy, that the geneticist Francis Crick was under the influence of LSD when he had a vision of the double helix structure of DNA in 1953, a discovery for which he was awarded the Nobel Prize (Rees, 2004).

Prior to this news report, which came after Crick's death, the anthropologist Narby (2000) took three molecular biologists to the Peruvian Amazon for their first visit there and for their first encounter with ayahuasca. The two female biologists both had encounters with plant teachers whom they perceived as independent sentient entities, and all three scientists received valuable information from their visions that helped inform their research, and which ultimately changed their world view. For instance, "the American biologist, who normally worked on deciphering the human genome, said she saw a chromosome from the perspective of a protein flying above a long strand of DNA" (Narby, 2000, p. 302).

Similarly, the biochemist, Kary Mullis, who received the Nobel Prize for inventing the polymerase chain reaction (PCR) that significantly advanced DNA research, said that taking LSD had been invaluable in helping him experience the mental imagery that allowed him to visualize sitting on a DNA molecule to watch the polymerase go by (Mullis, 1998).

Further reports of the ritual use of psychoactive plants for the induction of paranormal abilities are commonplace among indigenous peoples from every inhabited continent. These range from the use of pituri (*Duboisia hopwoodii*) in Australia (Australian Institute of Parapsychological Research, 2004) to the use of San Pedro cacti (*Trichocereus pachanoi*) in Peru (Luke, 2012c; Sharon, 1990) and peyote cacti (*Lophophora Williamsii*) in Mexico (Slotkin, 1956), *Amanita muscaria* mushrooms by the Ojibwa in Canada (Wasson, 1979) as well as suburban Muscovites and Siberian tribes-people in Russia (Ostrander & Schroeder, 1997; Wasson & Wasson, 1957), the use of datura among the Chumash of California (Driver, 1969), and the use of *Psilocybe* mushrooms (Stamets, 1996; Wasson, 1962) and *Salvia divinorum* by Mazatecs in Mexico (Soutar, 2001) to name but a few.

Indeed, anthropologist Dobkin de Rios (1984, p. 60) has suggested that "the single most important function of plant hallucinogens in the Amazon area is to divine the future." Efforts to document the diversity of these traditional "shamanic" plants indicate there are about 100 distinct genera, let alone species, of such traditional plants that are reported to induce visionary states and are used ethnomedically (Schultes & Hofmann, 1992), with new ethnobotanical discoveries continually being made.

However, few parapsychologists have conducted research with these plants or their users in their traditional environment, although with Wasson, Puharich (1959) attempted a remote viewing experiment with the *Psilocybe*-using Mazatecs in Mexico in 1955, but the experiment was aborted when instead Wasson and his co-expeditioner, Richardson, became the first researchers to be initiated into the mushroom cult. Nevertheless, Richardson reported personally having had an apparently precognitive vision, during what is documented as the first non-indigenous *Psilocybe* genus (i.e., "magic") mushroom trip (Richardson, 1990).

A cross-cultural taxonomical study of shamans, shaman-healers, healers, and mediums, posits that, although these groups share many of the same characteristics, there is a clear division between those who do, and those who do not, use psychoactive plants and the differing paranormal activities they perform (Winkelman, 1989).

Levine (1968) credited the botanist Schultes with the suggestion that the prevalence of vision-inducing plants among the herbarium of "primitive" societies is based upon a differing concept of illness, which has spiritual rather than physical causes. Contrary to Schultes, Winkelman suggested that the difference in the use of hallucinogens was due to cultural and developmental variances.

Shamans from hunting and gathering societies and shaman-healers from agricultural subsistence societies both frequently use hallucinogens for the purposes of healing, divination, hunting-magic, and malevolent acts, whereas healers and mediums from sedentary and politically integrated societies as well as agricultural subsistence societies, do not use hallucinogens to access their altered states, which they use for healing and divination only.

Yet it appears that these cultural differences have occurred only recently in the developed world, as it has been suggested that the ancient Greek oracles, including the Pythia of Delphi - the seeresses that anteceded the divinatory Goddess Python - also used the *solanaceae* family of psychedelic plants (henbane, belladonna, mandrake, and datura) for divination (Masters & Houston, 1966; Parker, 1975; Bibra, 1855/1994). Indeed the ancient Greek name for henbane was "pythonian" (Rudgley, 2000).

It is also well documented historically that Northern European witches also utilized these plants for psychic purposes (see Andrews, 1997; Rudgley, 2000). Indeed, similarly to the Greeks, the Northern Europeans gave the name "alruna" to their visionary seeresses, in common with the German name for mandrake, "alraune", both of which stem from "rune", the Germanic divinatory letter system (Müller-Ebeling, Rätsch, & Storl, 2003).

No doubt, the traditional Northern European practice of pharmacologically accessing visionary states all but died out with the witches during the Inquisition, between the 14th and 17th centuries (Grob & Harman, 1995). It is probable that a combination of changing concepts of illness, the development of a sedentary, politically integrated society, and the influence of the Inquisition or colonization were responsible for the virtual disappearance of the traditional indigenous use of psychoactive plants for paranormal purposes in Europe and North America.

At the end of the 19th century, pioneering psychological explorers in the West rediscovered the vision-inducing qualities of novel plant substances, such as mescaline (Ellis, 1898), whereas others explored new synthetic visionary chemicals like nitrous oxide (James, 1902), with some early psychical researchers dabbling in both (Dunbar, 1905). By the middle of the 20th century the Swiss chemist Albert Hofmann had discovered LSD – experiencing its OBE-inducing properties – and isolated, named, and synthesized psilocybin and psilocin, the psychoactive derivatives of the visionary *Psilocybe* mushroom genus (Hofmann, 1983; Luke, 2006). The ascribing of the word psi to psychic phenomena during this period, however, may only be a coincidence.

By the turn of this millennium there were around 200 psychedelic compounds known to science, a figure estimated to likely rise to 2000 compounds by the year 2050 at the current rate of discovery, increasing exponentially by a factor of ten every fifty years, starting with the two that were known in 1900 (Shulgin, 2004, 2010). Despite the rapidly upwards bending curve of Shulgin's formula, current quantities may even exceed it, as a good guestimate puts the number of *potentially* psychedelic compounds now known to man at about 2000 (Hanna, personal communication, August 12, 2012), given that there are something like 1300 documented phenethylamine compounds *alone* (including substances like mescaline, MDMA, & 2CB) known at the current time (Shulgin, Manning, & Daley, 2011), though they may not all be effectively psychoactive and have not been sufficiently tested as yet.

However, a conservative estimate would put the number of known, tried, and tested psychedelics at between 250 (Hanna, personal communication, August 12, 2012) and 300 to 400 (Shulgin, 2010). Furthermore, a more recent projection puts the total number of undiscovered drugs (not necessarily psychedelic) at 1×10^{60} (Reymond & Awale, 2012), more than visible stars in the sky, and so Brown (2012b) anticipated a near limitless number of psychedelic compounds to arise, especially when factors of nanotechnology, neurostructural engineering, and other technological advances are additionally considered.

Nevertheless, Brown's projection is purely speculative, but it is safe to say that we have not yet discovered all the psychedelic substances that will ultimately be available, and that there may be many more to come, and, with each one offering a different type of ASC, there remain many states yet to be discovered. Brown (2012b) even fancied that specific psi-inducing psychedelics may be intentionally engineered in the future.

Personal Views and Experiences

Since the discovery of psychedelic compounds by the academic community and their popularization among the intelligentsia by the novelist Aldous Huxley (Smythies, 1960), there has been a steadily growing number of reports of paranormal experiences occurring with the use of these compounds. Several parapsychologists and psychical researchers, primarily from the 1950s and 1960s when psychedelic research was at its peak, have endorsed the research of psi with psychedelics (e.g. Assailly, 1961; Broad, 1962; Hoffer, 1961a, 1961b; Johnson, 1955; Kern, 1964; Laidlaw, 1961; Paterson, 1961b; Price, 1948; Thouless, 1960; Tibbs, 1963; West, 1965).

Even J. B. Rhine, the father of modern parapsychology, ran some informal psychedelic sessions in 1961 at the Rhine Research Centre in Durham with the then Harvard psychologists Timothy Leary and Richard Alpert (Black, 2001; Horn, 2009; Stevens, 1988), although there was apparently too much spontaneous laughter erupting for anyone to credibly test for anything (S. Abrams, personal communication, August 14, 2006; S. Krippner, personal communication, January 19, 2006).

Notably, many other parapsychologists have reported personal ESP experiences with the use of LSD (Cavanna, 1961; Garrett, 1961b; Millay, 2001; Osmond, 1961a; Servadio, in Alvarado, 1995), peyote/mescaline (Langdon-Davies, 1961; Millay, 2001; Osmond, 1961a), psilocybin (Cavanna, 1961; Krippner, 1967; Millay, 2001) *Amanita muscaria* (Puharich, 1962), and ayahuasca (Severi, 1996, 1999).

Krippner's apparent precognitive vision of President Kennedy's assassination while on psilocybin serves as a good example (Krippner, 1967, 2006a). Though, of course, merely consuming a psychedelic is no guarantee that an experience of ESP will follow, as Price (1964) aptly demonstrated self-experimenting with mescaline. However, other psychical researchers, sometimes following their own experiences, have noted the apparent tendency for ESP production with the use of psychedelics, including no less than four Parapsychological Association presidential addresses (Dean, 1967; Heywood, 1978; Hastings, 1973; Luke, 2010b; Radin, 1989; Servadio, 1961; Stevenson, 1981).

Furthermore, some have recommended other psi researchers to personally explore psychedelic states of consciousness to aid in their understanding of the concept of psi (Cavanna, 1961; Heywood, 1961). The most highly experienced LSD psychotherapist, Stanislav Grof (1980), also advised that an intimate knowledge of the transpersonal realms created by psychedelics is essential for parapsychologists.

Personal accounts of ESP have also been reported by leading psychedelic mycologists (Stamets, 1996; Wasson & Wasson, 1957).

Beloff (1968) asserted that greater reporting of ESP on college campuses would have been evident if drugs induced psi particularly, to which Tart (in Beloff, 1968) replied that many students took paranormal events in conjunction with psychedelics very matter-of-factly, due to their prevalence. This point was further echoed by the suggestion that users of psychedelic drugs frequently report vivid ESP experiences but that they remain largely unpublished (Stafford & Golightly, 1967).

Yet, Heywood (1961) found several incidences of psi with LSD within the "well-evidenced" SPR spontaneous-case collection. However, more recently, Vayne (2001), echoing Tart, has suggested that among practised users of psychedelics, dubbed *psychonauts*, the telepathic experience is so common that it is hardly remarked upon. Luke (2004c) agreed with Vayne but further offered that, even so, many (less well-evidenced) anecdotal reports could be found on contemporary resources on the internet. Psychedelic drug information sites (such as www.lycaeum.org and www.erowid.org) have amassed a large online archive of experiential psychedelic reports, among which are accounts of ESP experiences with substances as diverse as ketamine, *Salvia divinorum*, *Psilocybe* mushrooms, ayahuasca analogues, and 3,4-methylenedioxymethamphetamine (MDMA, or ecstasy) mixed with baby Hawaiian woodrose seeds, a natural source of lysergic acid (Anonymous, 2004a, 2004b, 2004c, 2004d, 2004e, 2005).

Similar reports of frequent ESP experiences with such substances from within the psychedelic community are also available elsewhere in the literature (e.g., Eisner, 1989; Gaskin, 1990; Krippner, 2006a; Krippner & Fersh, 1970; Lilly, 1967, 1978; McKenna, 1991; McKenna & McKenna, 1994; Millay, 1999, 2004a, 2004b, 2005, 2006, 2010; Osmond, 1968; Saunders, 1993; Scully, 2010; Stevens, 1989; Turner, 1994; Wyllie, 1999; Zelnick, 2005).

Indeed, the notion of experiencing a telepathic group mind, or "tribal telepathic understanding" (Nuttal, 1970, p. 249) through "tripping" became so prevalent among the psychedelic culture of the 1960s that prospective psychedelic users were told they might expect such an experience (Leary, Metzner, & Alpert, 1964) and commonly it became known as "grokking" (Stevens, 1989; Wolfe, 1971).

Currently, the same notion is still apparent among psychedelic users (e.g. MoDu, 2003) and the largest public-edited internet encyclopedia indicates that ESP-type phenomena are a common fourth-level experience on a five-level spectrum of psychedelic experience intensity (Wikipedia, 2005), though clearly this is not academically evidential but rather an indication of commonly held notions, among Wikipedia editors at least.

Notably, PK is seldom reported in the literature, save for the odd exceptional report (e.g. Shulgin, 2004), and it has been suggested among occultists that chemical agents are only useful for "receptive" magic/psychic purposes, such as traveling clairvoyance, divination, and spirit evocation or invocation (e.g. Carroll, 1987; Vayne, 2001; Xeper, 2005). The use of psychedelics for such magical purposes now appears to be growing in popularity among occultists and is seemingly far more prevalent within the literature than it used to be (e.g. see Louv, 2005; Kent, 2010, Vayne, 2017).

Clinical Reports

A review of the literature from the clinical setting reveals surprisingly few published psychiatric inpatient reports, although there are some epidemiological studies (see Chapter 11) relating to psychedelics and paranormal experience. This may be due to any number of factors, such as the lack of any such spontaneous phenomena within the psychiatric population, or the medicalization within psychiatry of paranormal experiences as delusion or hallucination.

Indeed, Mogar (1965) noted that early psychoanalytic and behaviourist researchers using LSD were prejudiced against ESP phenomena. Yet, there is one study, a psychiatric-interview survey with users of LSD (Abraham, 1983), which reports precognitive experiences as one of the symptoms of the LSD flashback phenomena, such as hallucinogen persisting perception disorder (American Psychiatric Association, 2000).

On the other hand, there are many accounts of paranormal experiences with psychoactive drugs from within psychedelic psychotherapy, particularly that involving LSD (Grof, 1975, 1980, 1990, 2001; Harman, 1963; Holzinger, 1964; Levine, 1968; Masters & Houston, 1966; Pahnke, 1968) and psychedelics in general (Eisner, 1995; Laidlaw, 1961; Stolaroff, 2004).

Tart (in Levine, 1968), quoted the International Foundation for Advanced Study, which in the course of between 300 and 400 psychedelic therapy sessions has reported the incidence of ESP with strong evidence seven times, which is a considerably higher incidence of psi than that reported to have occurred in non-psychedelic psychotherapy (Tornatore, 1977a, 1977b). As one specific example of this line of research, the percentage of clients reporting telepathic communication during LSD-assisted therapy changed from 49% in the first psychotherapy session to 80% in the second session (Blewett & Chwelos, 1959).

The psychiatrist Stanislav Grof, generally credited with the most expertise in this field having conducted more than four thousand psychedelic therapy sessions over a two-decade period, reported observing patients experiencing OBEs, ESP (particularly precognition), accurate remote viewing, and space-time travel on a daily basis (Grof, 1975, 1980, 2001). Despite acknowledging that there was a danger of data contamination and a difficulty of verification, Grof contended that the occurrence of ESP was relatively frequent (Grof, 1980) and that LSD could induce states conducive to an unusually high incidence of ESP (Grof, 1975).

Often the reports of telepathy could have been merely self-deception, but other times there was apparently objective verifiable communication at work (Grof, 1980). Grof (1980) further found the common occurrence of OBEs, both within and independent of this physical plane, often with traveling clairvoyance and clairaudience. There were also occasional NDE experiences reported (Grof, 1994). Most frequent was the occurrence of extraordinary coincidences or synchronicities, yet only among those clients who experienced transpersonal breakthroughs within the psychedelic session (Grof, 1980).

Finally, Grof (1990) also reported two events, rare in the literature, of clients under LSD who experienced visions of the dead that provided apparently unknown, but verifiable information. One such event occurred to the wife of the late psychedelic-psychical researcher Walter Pahnke. During an LSD session, Mrs. Pahnke had a vision of her dead husband who requested her to return a book concealed in her attic. Although she claimed to have had no prior knowledge of the book, she managed to locate and return it. Of course, it is possible that the knowledge of the book already lay in her subconscious (Stokes, 1997).

One of the most astonishing reports of psi occurring within the clinical setting came from the psychiatrist Paul (1966), who reported taking the mushroom *Amanita pantherina*. This was her only psychedelic experience and was part of an ESP experiment being conducted by Puharich (see Puharich, 1959, 1962). Paul had an incredibly intense trip, complete with apocalyptic visions followed by salvation through overwhelming love, and was unable to complete the experiment. However, on return to her practice, two of her clients reported extraordinary events at the time Paul had been tripping. One patient had amnesia for the same three hours on Friday evening following the consumption of his first-ever (non-psychedelic) mushroom meal, and upon remembering his experience, recalled that he had experienced the same apocalyptic fears as Paul had experienced.

The other patient could not remember what she had done that evening but on investigation discovered that she had gone to the house of a secret lover and waited outside, love-struck, for two hours, but was prevented from taking any irrational action by her friend, who later informed her of the event. Both patients had a strong bond with the therapist and had expressed an interest in ESP. Paul interpreted the event as a case of spontaneous telepathic tripping, complete with amnesia on the part of the receivers, perhaps demonstrating a certain unpredictability in the experimental induction of psi with psychoactive drugs.

Evaluation of Field Reports

In summary, there is a wealth of reports of the spontaneous occurrence of ostensibly paranormal phenomena with the use of psychedelic substances. Yet this does not mean that these experiences are necessarily genuine paranormal events: Aside from the usual arguments for and against spontaneous phenomena as evidence for the paranormal (e.g., see Pekala & Cardeña, 2000; Stokes, 1997), the fact that respondents had consumed a visionary substance may be reason to question their perception and interpretation of the experiences, at least for those cases which are not substantiated by evidence or independent observers.

Nunn, Rizza, and Peters (2001) have found that cannabis use is related to delusional ideation, although it is not directly related to delusional conviction; however, the relationship between psychedelic use and the propensity for false memory and poor probability judgments has not been established (Kapur & Seeman, 2002; Wilson & French, 2006). Furthermore, Shanon (2003a) pointed out that the usual definitions of hallucination in the psychological literature fail to adequately encompass the diverse and complex nature of experiences that occur with psychedelics, and nor can assumptions be made about the ontology of such psychedelic-induced visions.

Indeed, many people who have had paranormal psychedelic experiences reported how real the experience seemed, often being felt as more real than the ordinary waking experience (e.g., Hofmann, in Grof 2004; Shanon, 2003a; Strassman, 2001). It has also been reported that psychedelic-induced mystical experiences feel no less real than previous spontaneous mystical experiences (Doblin, 1991; Exman, 1961; Greeley, 1974; Griffiths, Richards, McCann & Jesse, 2006; Pahnke,

1966; Pahnke & Richards, 1966; Roberts, 2001; Smith, 2000; Smith & Tart, 1998; Watts, 1968), the same being true for NDEs (Jansen, 2001).

In defence of drug-induced altered states, Devereux (1997, p. 243) has suggested that, "it is a culturally engineered cliché to dismiss such states as being somehow delusional." Furthermore, Smythies (1960, 1983) has taken issue with the concept of dulled and hallucinatory psychedelic states and insisted that these hallucinations are more than just images from a poisoned brain. Additionally, LeShan (1968) has mocked the assumption that ordinary reality is somehow more real than the psychedelically induced ASC, whereas Tart (1977) questioned how natural the ordinary state of consciousness is built through a lifetime of socialization. Tart (1972, 1998, 2000, 2001) further questioned the idea that rationality only occurs in the ordinary state, and proposed the establishment of "state-specific sciences" (for further discussion see Walsh, 2003)

No matter what their epistemological status, however, these experiences do offer a phenomenological spectrum of evidence around which to orientate further research. Furthermore, the similarity in reports between those occurring spontaneously in exploratory, therapeutic, and accidental contexts, and those induced intentionally in the traditional ritual context, gives credence to the shamanic use of these substances for supposedly paranormal purposes.

By contrast, other traditional psychoactive substances, such as alcohol, coffee, and cocaine are not contemporaneously reported to induce spontaneous paranormal phenomena, and neither are there folk beliefs that suggest they do. Nevertheless, Rogo (1975) wondered whether the occurrence of psychedelic-induced ESP experiences exceeded that of normal ESP experiences, a question which may be partially answered by survey research.

CHAPTER 11

Surveys of Psychedelic Paranormal
Beliefs and Experiences

When reviewing the survey research one immediately notices two trends. First, virtually all of the surveys reported here were published since the 1970s, after the period when most psychedelic research was conducted and the unlicensed use of these drugs mostly became illegal in Europe and North America. Secondly, most of the following surveys have primarily focused on paranormal experiences or belief and have only recorded drug use information as one of many possible co-variables, often omitting to distinguish among the different substances. Only a few studies (DeGracia, 1995; Kjellgren & Norlander, 2000; Tart, 1993; White, 1997) have approached users of psychoactive substances as the target sample.

Surveys of Belief in the Paranormal

Investigating belief in the paranormal with the Mental Experience Inventory (MEI), Kumar, Pekala, and Cummings (1992) additionally utilized a sensation seeking scale that included a yes/no question about recreational drug use. Of an opportunity sample of 574 psychology students, drug users reported greater paranormal and psi-related beliefs; however, results were reported in terms of the larger sensation-seeking measure as significant main effects.

In a more direct assessment of the relationship, Gallagher, Kumar, and Pekala (1994) transformed the MEI into the Anomalous Experiences Inventory (AEI) (Kumar, Pekala, & Gallagher, 1994), adding a Drug-use subscale to complement the other four subscales relating to Anomalous/Paranormal Belief, Experience, Abilities, and Fear. The AEI was successfully validated against other paranormal experience and belief scales using an opportunity sample of 400 psychology students.

The AEI Drug-use subscale correlated positively, although only very weakly, with the AEI Anomalous/Paranormal Beliefs subscale ($r = .16$, $p < .01$) and with Tobacyk's (1988) paranormal belief subscales: Belief in Psi ($r = .10$, $p < .05$), Belief in Witchcraft ($r = .12$, $p < .05$), Belief in Superstition ($r = .11$, $p < .05$), Belief in Spiritualism ($r = .17$, $p < .01$), Belief in Extraordinary Life Forms ($r = .13$, $p < .01$), but not Belief in Precognition. Drug use correlated negatively with Traditional Religious Beliefs ($r = -.14$, $p < .01$).

In addition, some items in the AEI Drug-use subscale correlated with Tobacyk's (1988) Revised Paranormal Belief Scale, although only very weakly. Overall, paranormal belief correlated negatively with heroin use ($r = -.12$, $p < .05$) but positively with the use of LSD ($r = .11$, $p < .05$) and mind-altering substances ($r = .15$, $p < .01$). There were no significant correlations found for marijuana, cocaine, or alcohol.

The same correlations were found between the AEI Anomalous/ Paranormal Belief subscale and some AEI Drug-use subscale items (mind altering substances, $r = .18$, $p < .001$; LSD, $r = .15$, $p < .01$), but also including marijuana ($r = .16$, $p < .01$), but not heroin. Additionally, for all categories of drugs except heroin there was a small significant negative correlation with the fear of psi (from $r = -.12$ to $-.24$), whereas alcohol use correlated positively with fear of psi ($r = .13$, $p < .05$).

The lack of a consistent significant correlation between paranormal belief and marijuana use runs counter to Tart's (1993) finding that 76% of marijuana users believe in ESP. This difference may be due to cohort differences, such as culture and their reasons for using marijuana, or that Tart's marijuana sample were mostly also experienced with LSD (72%, with 36% classified as heavy psychedelic users; Tart, 1971), a drug which Gallagher et al. (1994) did find to be related to paranormal belief.

Furthermore, it should be noted that the items of the AEI Drug-use subscale only register nominal yes/no responses, whereas more sensitive ordinal drug-use measures would have been expected to demonstrate stronger correlations, if the relationships were linear. Nevertheless, correlations from this study reported here are uncorrected and should be accepted with some caution because of the use of multiple inferential tests.

Pekala, Kumar, and Marcano (1995a, 1995b) sought to find a relationship between the subscales of the AEI and measures of hypnotic susceptibility and dissociation on a similar opportunity sample of 413 psychology students. Supporting the Gallagher et al. (1994) study findings, the Drug-use subscale correlated positively, and somewhat more strongly, with Anomalous /Paranormal Beliefs ($r = .25$, $p < .001$) as well as negatively with Fear of the Anomalous/Paranormal ($r = .14$, $p < .01$), although no breakdown of the results for the Drug-use subscale was given for the different substances. In addition, overall drug use was found not to correlate with dissociation or hypnotic susceptibility, although marijuana was a special case (see Pekala et al., 1995b).

A later opportunity sample of 107 students (Houran & Williams, 1998) were surveyed using the AEI to explore the equivocal relationship between belief in the paranormal and tolerance of ambiguity. Further support was demonstrated for the small but significant relationships between drug use and anomalous/paranormal belief ($r = .22$, $p < .05$) and fear of the anomalous/paranormal ($r = -.18$, $p < .05$). Tolerance of ambiguity was found to correlate minimally with both paranormal belief and drug use ($r = .23$, $p < .05$), and more so with psychedelic drugs (LSD, marijuana), rather than cocaine, alcohol, or heroin.

Simmonds and Roe (2000) used the AEI in relation to schizotypy, temporal lobe lability and personality correlates with an opportunity sample of 145 psychology students. Similarly to previous surveys, there was a small significant correlation between drug use and anomalous/paranormal belief ($r = .20$, $p < .05$). Drug use was also found to relate to complex partial epileptic signs (CPES) as measured by a subscale of the Personal Philosophy Inventory developed by Persinger and Makarec (1987), which they had predicted would be the case.

However, it is apparent that several items of the CPES are consistent with experiences often reported in other ASCs, drug-induced or otherwise, so such a correlation might be expected anyway. Furthermore, neither of these correlations remained significant when the alpha level was recalculated using a Bonferroni correction for multiple tests, although the relationship between drug use and belief remains consistent with these other surveys, so this correlation is probably genuine, albeit small.

A later survey (Thalbourne, 2001) using the AEI sought to replicate the relationship found by Gallagher et al. (1994) between drug use and belief in the paranormal, and in addition investigated this relationship with respect to transliminality and to kundalini experiences. Transliminality was measured using the 29-item Transliminality Scale (Thalbourne, 1998), before it rasch-scaled for age and gender bias. Using an opportunity sample of 125 psychology students, Thalbourne found a small significant positive correlation between the AEI subscales: Drug-use and Anomalous/Paranormal Belief ($r = .24$, $p < .01$), supporting previous findings.

There was a suggestive but non-significant negative correlation between drug use and fear of the anomalous/paranormal. There was also a significant positive correlation between drug use and transliminality ($r = .29$, $p = .001$) and the New Age Philosophy (NAP) subscale of the Tobacyk's (1988) Revised Paranormal Belief Scale ($r = .23$, $p < .01$). There was, however, no significant correlation with Tobacyk's Traditional Paranormal Beliefs (TPB) subscale, and reanalysis of Thalbourne's data by Houran and Lange (2001) found the difference in reports of drug use in relation to NAP and TPB to be significant ($p < .001$, uncorrected for multiple analyses), reinforcing their argument for two distinct paranormal belief groups. Furthermore, drug-use did not correlate with Thalbourne and Delin's (1993) (non-rasch scaled) Australian Sheep-Goat Scale, a different paranormal belief scale (Thalbourne, 2001).

These findings partially support Gallagher et al.'s (1994) small positive correlation of drug use with the Tobacyk Belief in Psi subscale, yet to what extent is not discernible because Thalbourne's (2001) results were reported in terms of just two collapsed subscales rather than the full seven. The same is also true of correlations between Anomalous/Paranormal Belief and the Drug-use subscale, although of note, very few respondents used heroin ($n = 3$) and cocaine ($n = 6$) compared to LSD ($n = 26$) or marijuana ($n = 61$), indicating that correlations with those reporting drug use ($n = 57$, obviously some of the respondents did not consider marijuana to belong to this category) were largely in terms of psychedelics rather than other drugs.

A *post hoc* analysis of the relationship between transliminality and drug use revealed there were small, but significant, positive correlations (ranging from $r = .20$ to .27) between transliminality and all of the AEI drug-use categories (mind-altering substances, marijuana, LSD, cocaine, and heroin) except for alcohol. Thalbourne (2001) suggested that this relationship may be due to the need to use drugs to escape the unpleasant aspects of the transliminal state, or that drug use may be a means of promoting the psychic phenomena of which high transliminal scorers may have become deprived.

Both of these hypotheses might prove to be somewhat correct, but only for differing substances. It is highly unlikely that psychedelic drugs are used to escape the transliminal state because these substances are actually more likely to cause the opposite effect, although some non-psychedelic drugs, such as opiates/opioids might help to escape transliminality. Indeed, Vayne (2001) has suggested psychedelics are expressly used to access liminal states. Alternatively, Thalbourne has speculated that an "openness to experience" trait underlies the relationship between drug use, transliminality and paranormal experience.

In a follow-up survey (Thalbourne & Houran, 2005), an opportunity sample of 200 psychology students completed the Revised Transliminality Scale (Lange, Thalbourne, Houran, & Storm, 2000), and an extended version of the AEI Drug-use subscale, which included two extra items, one relating to ecstasy (MDMA) and one relating to speed (amphetamines). As previously, though somewhat less so, drug-use was found to correlate marginally, although significantly with transliminality ($r = .21$, $p < .005$, one-tailed).

Furthermore, scores on the Oxford Happiness Questionnaire demonstrated that transliminality was not related to happiness and that the majority of high transliminals were happy, offering support to McCreery and Claridge's (1995) notion of the pathology-free "happy schizotype" prone to paranormal experiences. However, unhappy high-scoring transliminals reported significantly more drug use than happy high-scoring transliminals ($t = 1.98$, $n = 77$, $p < .05$), somewhat supporting Thalbourne's (2001) speculation that transliminality, akin to psychosis, can be a unhappy state that such people attempt to escape from with drugs.

Unfortunately, Thalbourne and Houran's findings sweep several different types of drugs – including psychedelics, narcotics, stimulants and alcohol – together under one umbrella, revealing very little about which of these very different drugs relate to each particular syndrome. For instance, given the system of scoring in this study, it is easily possible that the use of just one drug, such as alcohol, entirely accounts for the differences in substance use between happy and unhappy transliminals, and further research begs more specific analyses.

Here Metzner (2005a) pointed out that, aside from merely varying in how they activate or relax one's nervous system, psychoactive drugs may also be classified along a hedonic continuum of pain and pleasure, reflecting Thalbourne and Houran's (2005) simplified notions about drugs and the quest for happiness.

However, taking a transpersonal approach, Metzner further indicated that drugs may also be considered along a third dimension of consciousness expansion and contraction, such that psychedelics are essentially conscious expanding, whereas opiates, alcohol, cocaine and amphetamines, being focally restrictive and addictive, are consciousness contracting. Thus, a range of drugs can be used when seeking stimulation, sedation, or happiness, but only specific drugs, psychedelics, will lead to consciousness expanding experiences, and perhaps even ostensibly paranormal ones too.

Arguments may prevail over precise definitions and classifications here, but the point remains that psychological research would most likely benefit from a recognition of the experiential differences between drugs rather than just a recognition of their legal status and a crude categorization of them based only on that (Friedman, 2006).

Surveys of Paranormal Experiences

Psychiatric epidemiological samples
Recently, a wealth of epidemiological psychiatric research has surveyed reports of cannabis use and schizotypal symptoms, finding fairly consistent correlations between them (for a review, see Castle & Murray, 2004). Items relating to telepathy and other kinds of thought broadcasting have been often included, and it deserves mentioning that the subscales in which these items appear tend to correlate with cannabis use (e.g., Johns et al., 2005). However, although relevant, this research is largely indirect to the present review as incidence rates for specific types of paranormal-like experiences are rarely reported, but rather form part of more general subscales.

More specifically, in a quasi-experimental design with 196 university students, Nunn, Rizza, and Peters (2001) found that cannabis use, but not alcohol use, was positively related to unusual experiences (such as the possession of special, almost magical powers), but use of either drug was unrelated to depression or anxiety. Furthermore, cannabis use was related to delusional ideation but not distress, further supporting the notion of the happy schizotype, although cannabis and alcohol use combined was related to delusional conviction. Nunn et al. suggested that schizotypal traits may predispose subjects to cannabis use or that cannabis use may result in high schizotypy scores. Although some prospective studies have been conducted in this area, there are often so many possible confounding factors involved in such research that directions and sources of causality remain entirely speculative (see Castle & Murray, 2004).

Clinical populations
Finding numerous paranormal experiences reported in a DXM-users survey (see Chatper 11), White (1997) sought to explain the survey results in terms of temporal lobe dysfunction (TLD). Tentative indirect support comes from a survey of a convenience sample of 100 neuropsychiatric patients where a positive recreational drug-use response was used, among other measures, as a predictor of TLD, with TLD correlating well with reports of subjective paranormal experience (Palmer & Neppe, 2003).

However, the recreational drug-use measure utilized a blanket definition that lumped together the use of a variety of different psycho-active drugs and moreover treated drug use alongside brain injury as causative factors in TLD, although there is no clear reasoning given for doing this. In this study, recreational drug use was taken to be either of the following: prolific marijuana use; the three times use of hallucino-gens, LSD, mescaline, or PCP; or six months use of heroin or amphet-amine. However, it was reported in a later paper that, when gender was controlled, there were no relationships between subjective paranormal experiences and any of the categories of drug use or brain injury with this sample (Palmer & Neppe, 2004), although results may be due to underpowered statistics with only six respondents in this group.

General and student samples.
Several major surveys of psychic experiences have included questions regarding the use of psychoactive drugs. The first series of surveys of this nature utilized a psychic experiences questionnaire created by Palmer (1979) for use in a randomly distributed postal survey. The questionnaire was completed by 354 townspeople (T) and 268 students (S), treated as different samples, with response rates of 51% and 89% respectively.

Those who acknowledged the use of mind-expanding drugs also responded positively to being an ESP agent, having a recurrent sponta-neous PK experience (T only, $p < .01$, although Palmer urges caution with these two results because of low responses), haunting experience (T only, $p < .05$), aura vision (S, $p < .05$), and OBEs (S, $p < .01$). Despite reported drug-use differences between samples, equal propor-tions from each group (T: 29%; S: 28%) reported psi experiences ac-tually occurring during use. Kohr (1980) criticized the analysis for not reporting the chi-squared statistic and for using an underpowered test.

Kohr (1980) surveyed a special sample of self-selecting respon-dents ($n = 406$) from the Association for Research and Enlightenment, an organization whose membership represented those intrigued by the legacy of the renowned psychic and Christian mystic Edgar Cayce. Us-ing Palmer's (1979) questionnaire, Kohr failed to find any association between subjective paranormal phenomena and the use of mind-ex-panding drugs, although figures for drug use were not actually report-ed. It is suspected that the drug use statistics were not reported in this study because its incidence was quite low.

The Kohr sample was both older (61% over 40 years) and marked-ly more religious (40% = very religious) than the Palmer samples (over 40 years, T = 51%, S = 0%; very religious, T = 8%, S = 9%), and, as stated earlier, Gallagher et al. (1994) found traditional religious beliefs to correlate negatively with drug use. Roney-Dougal (1984) surveyed a different special sample, attendees at an occult conference, about their psi experiences. Of the 33 respondents, 30 (91%) reported psi experiences, of which 12 (40%) reported the use of mind-expanding drugs. This indicates both the slightly higher reported use of psyche-delics (36% of the sample) and the greater reporting of paranormal experiences among occultists compared to other populations, though this observation may not be reliable.

Another survey (Usha & Pasricha, 1989a, 1989b) modified Palm-er's (1979) questionnaire, particularly the demographic questions, to suit the needs of an Indian student population ($n = 328$; response rate 79% using opportunity sampling). Use of mind-expanding drugs was reported by 11%, who were also significantly more likely to be Hindu ($p < .05$) or male ($p < .01$), probably largely due to the sacred use of marijuana among many Indian men, mostly Hindus. Of those reporting drug use, 18% reported psi experiences during the drug experience, somewhat less than Palmer's 28–29%.

Similar to Palmer's work, the use of mind-expanding drugs was positively associated (chi-squared) with OBEs ($p < .01$), and addi-tionally with waking ESP ($p < .05$), apparitions ($p < .01$), and déjà vu experiences ($p < .01$). Except for apparitions, these three experiences tended to correlate significantly with other psi-relevant experiences such as lucid dreaming, meditation, and mystical experiences. None of the studies using Palmer's 46-item questionnaire (Palmer, 1979; Kohr, 1980; Usha & Pasricha, 1989a, 1989b) made any corrections for multiple inferential analyses, so results should be accepted with some caution.

Returning to the surveys of paranormal belief among students re-viewed earlier, these studies also investigated anomalous/paranormal experiences, and Kumar et al. (1992) found drug users reported sig-nificantly more of these. The later series of five surveys (Gallagher et al., 1994; Houran & Williams, 1998; Pekala et al., 1995a, 1995b; Sim-monds & Roe, 2000; Thalbourne, 2001), utilizing the Anomalous Ex-periences Inventory (Gallagher et al., 1994), each reported a significant positive relationship between the Anomalous/Paranormal Experience and Drug-use subscales.

Correlations ranged from $r = .13$ (Gallagher et al., 1994) to $r = .29$ (Thalbourne, 2001), and Pekala et al. (1995a) additionally found that drug use was positively correlated with a Shamanic or Encoun-ter-like Experiences subscale ($r = .23$; $p < .001$), which included items relating to OBE and contact with spirits. Furthermore, Pekala et al.

(1995b) reported correlations between the use of certain substances and subjective psychic experiences occurring under the influence of drugs, although results were only given for high hypnotically susceptible participants ($n = 56$) (for the AEI Drug-use subscale $r = .57$, $p < .01$; mind-altering substances $r = .34$, $p < .01$; marijuana use $r = .30$, $p < .05$) and high dissociative participants ($n = 59$) (Drug-use subscale $r = .58$, $p < .01$; mind-altering substances $r = .30$, $p < .05$; LSD $r = .41$, $p < .01$; cocaine $r = .34$, $p < .01$).

Thalbourne (2001) also found a relationship between drug use and kundalini experiences ($r = .28$, $p < .01$) measured using the 32-item Kundalini Scale (Thalbourne & Fox, 1999). It was suggested by Thalbourne that the relationship between paranormal experience, drug use, and the kundalini experience either indicates that certain drugs may trigger a kundalini experience or that the use of drugs may alleviate it. Alternatively, it was proposed that the relationship between these factors may also indicate a need for non-standard sensations, or that the physiological aspects of the kundalini experience were being misinterpreted as paranormal.

This final supposition is not consistent with long established tantric teachings that warn of genuine psychic kundalini experiences called 'siddhis' (e.g. Satyananda, 1996). Furthermore, as an alternative to Thalbourne's interpretations, the results may simply be due to an overlap of subjective psychic experiences common to both the kundalini and the drug experience, as suggested by Naranjo (1987) and demonstrated by DeGracia (1995) in the following paragraph. Perhaps the activation of the pineal gland and its chemistry, as supposed by Roney-Dougal (e.g. 2001) and Strassman (2001), underlies both factors, resulting in subjective paranormal experiences. Indeed, Roney-Dougal (1989, 1991) noted that the pineal gland is considered by some yogis to be primary in the control of kundalini psi experiences, and there is other putative evidence (Chapter 9) that suggests such a link.

Psychedelic-users samples
DeGracia (1995) conducted a self-selecting internet survey with 61 experienced psychedelic users about their experiences of kundalini-like phenomena. Of those responding, 58% had used psychedelics more than 20 times, most frequently LSD (95%), and psilocybin (82%). The respondents revealed a large overlap between reported psychedelic experiences and those experiences commonly arising in spontaneous kundalini awakenings.

Of particular interest, psychedelic drug users frequently reported an enhanced sense of empathy (75%), OBEs (40%), intuition, psychic powers, and the recall of past lives (no statistics given). That the use of psychedelics is related to both paranormal and kundalini experiences is further supported by the survey findings of Thalbourne (2001), as discussed earlier.

One of the first surveys (Ditman et al., 1969) to explore paranormal experiences with psychedelics randomly gave 99 alcoholics receiving treatment one of the following three drugs: LSD (the only psychedelic of the three), methylphenidate (a dopaminergic stimulant, also known as Ritalin), or chlordiazepoxide (the first benzodiazepine, a sedative/hypnotic). Those taking LSD reported significantly more of the paranormal-type phenomena, having more experiences of transcending time and of having an OBE supporting findings with the AEI that dopaminergic stimulants (i.e., cocaine) are not conducive to paranormal beliefs.

A survey (Tart, 1970, 1971, 1993) conducted in California in 1970 with 150 experienced users of marijuana recruited by discrete snowball sampling found even higher reports of paranormal experiences than the student and general samples discussed above. The marijuana-user sample consisted of 76% students, and 72% of the sample had tried LSD, although only 7% had tried hard narcotics (e.g., presumably heroin).

With regard to experiences under the influence of marijuana, 69% reported telepathy (rising to 83% in a later sample), 32% reported precognition, 13% PK (defined as magical operations that cause an effect), and 50% reported seeing auras, with heavier users reporting significantly higher frequencies of these experiences in each category (Tart, 1971). OBEs were reported by 44%, with 53% of this group reporting a least one OBE under the influence (Tart, 1971). In comparison, a later survey (Luke & Kittenis, 2005) found that somewhat smaller percentages of experienced cannabis users (i.e., those using it often or more frequently, $n = 60$) than in Tart's study reported the occurrence of telepathy (20%), precognition (12%), psychokinesis (12%), and auras (22%) while under the influence.

Yet, the percentage reporting OBEs either with or without cannabis (62%) was larger than in Tart's study (44%). The use of Californian students at the epicentre of the psychedelic scene at that time may at least partially account for Tart's heightened findings, perhaps because these respondents were more psychedelically active and responsive, and consuming higher quantities and grades of cannabis than in the 2005 survey.

A survey, similar to DeGracia's (1995) investigation of transpersonal drug experiences, was conducted in Sweden with an anonymous snowball sample of 16 experienced psychedelic drug users (Kjellgren & Norlander, 2000). Of those returning questionnaires (94%), 37% had used psychedelics more than 20 times, mostly LSD (75%) and psilocybin (75%). Respondents indicated the occurrence of OBEs (53%), telepathy (60%), the loss of the sense of a discrete self (47%), psycho-geographical traveling (62%), contact with entities (20%), time-travel (40%), animal shape-shifting (53%), and visions of mythological beings (33%), all under the influence of psychedelics.

All respondents reported having some psi experiences, with heavier users and, similarly to Usha and Pasricha (1989a, 1989b), those practising mind-expanding, spiritual, or ritual techniques or preparation reported more of these experiences than infrequent users. However, significant differences in the quantity of experiences between low and high users only occurred for the experiences of telepathy ($U = 12$, $p < .05$, two tailed) and gaining knowledge of oneself, and for a combined index of all paranormal experiences ($U = 7$, $p < .05$), though uncorrected for multiple analyses. This partially supports the hypothesis that subjective paranormal experiences occur more frequently during the use of psychedelics, although alternative explanations are possible. Furthermore, 31% of the sample reported that their views on life after death have been influenced by their use of psychedelics, and 44% had become less afraid of death through their experiences, although 12% had become more afraid.

In further support of the notion that greater psychedelic use is associated with more paranormal experiences, a limited survey of 67 psilocybin-containing mushroom users found that only 9% of those taking low doses (less than 5 dried grams of *Psilocybe cubensis*) had experiences of telepathy, whereas 28% of those taking higher doses – what McKenna (1991) called a heroic dose – had telepathic experiences (Hurst, 1994).

Of particular interest to the present review are the results of an incidental internet survey (White, 1997) of subjective paranormal experiences with the use of the dextromethorphan (DXM). Commonly used in cough remedies DXM is a synthetic drug that results in similar subjective experiences to other dissociatives, such as ketamine and PCP. White was concerned about the use of DXM and had a "frequently asked questions" report regarding DXM posted on an internet-based psychoactive drug information site (www.erowid.org).

The published survey, unfortunately without statistics or demographics, was the product of reports sent to White from people who had used DXM, often unwittingly as a simple cough remedy, and had experienced a number of subjective paranormal experiences. White was surprised at the reports and was originally very reluctant to take them seriously, until he received so many that he collated, categorized, and published them.

Many of the experiences reported by White (1997) are consistent with experiences common to ketamine use (Jansen, 2001; Corazza, 2002) and include the following: visions of energy ribbons; a disturbing sense of infinity; a sense of presence of a profoundly powerful, loving, and intelligent being (as is also quoted with DMT use, a very different substance – Strassman, 2001); déjà vu; jamais vu; a loss of sense of causality; memory loops; a sense of presence; OBEs (most often to a different dimension but also on the corporal plane outside of one's body); NDEs; contact with entities, spiritual beings, and other free-floating consciousnesses (also reported by Carpenter, 2006; Xeper, 2005); occasional ESP, including clairvoyance; and the intuitive understanding of complex ideas such as a math student understanding Gödel's Incompleteness Theorem for the first time.

Most of these experiences have since elsewhere been reported in an online user journal, *The DXM Zine* (Gelfer, 2007). It is noted there were no reports of PK, although some felt that they could slightly influence the laws of probability. These reported experiences are independently consistent with a psychiatric inpatient report of an apparently accidental overdosing with a cough remedy containing DXM (Price & Lebel, 2000). Reported symptoms included the experience of observing oneself from outside of one's body (OBE), becoming "just thoughts," 360° vision, vision within people, and "delusions" of telepathy, all of which ceased when the DXM wore off.

Taking a more taxonomic approach than earlier research, Luke and Kittenis (2005) sought to determine which of a range of psychedelics are related to which paranormal experiences in particular. The online survey pooled responses from 139 self-selecting respondents recruited via both parapsychology and psychedelic interest groups. The percentage of respondents who had tried an illicit drug even once ($n = 110$) and who reported a psi experience while under the influence (47%) was somewhat higher than the 28–29% and 18% found previously with general and student samples (Palmer, 1979; Usha & Pasricha, 1989a, 1989b), as might be expected from this non-ordinary sample.

The study also corroborated many of the observations made in previous research. For example, supporting Strassman (2001), DMT was widespread in inducing entity contact experiences and OBEs, although primarily to other dimensions, and like 5-MEO-DMT, DMT commonly gave the experience of dissolving into a universal energy. The hypothesis that DMT is fundamental to the NDE (Strassman, 2001) was partially borne out by the relatively widespread reporting of the, albeit generalized, death-like experiences (dying, rebirth, or memory of a past life) although such experiences seemed to be relatively more widespread with 5-MEO-DMT, as observed elsewhere (Luke, 2005; Roney-Dougal, 2001; Shulgin & Shulgin, 1997).

Reports of "sensing an intelligence or spirit being in an ingested plant or substance" were found to be most widespread where respondents were under the influence of plant-based substances: psilocybin-containing mushrooms, ayahuasca, mescaline-containing cacti, and *Amanita muscaria,* but especially with *Salvia divinorum,* as has been documented elsewhere (Aardvark, 2002; Addy, 2010; Arthur, 2010; Doyle, 2012; Horner, 2012; Juszczak, 2012; Miller, 1994; Vayne, 2001). For a discussion of interspecies encounters on psychedelics see Krippner and Luke (2009)(also see chapter 7).

Such plant-spirit experiences also occurred with the use of the cannabis plant, although the most widespread experiences with this drug were clairvoyance and OBEs on this plane and, primarily, telepathy, making this substance a prime candidate for ESP research, as has already been advocated by Tart (1993) for a number of reasons. The dissociative DXM is also a potential candidate for further ESP research, particularly collective ESP experiences, supporting earlier reports of psi occurring with its use (Gelfer, 2007; Price & Lebel, 2000; White, 1997).

There were also relatively widespread reports of telepathy with LSD and particularly with MDMA, a drug, categorized as an empathogen, that is characterized by its capacity to induce empathic experiences and that has elsewhere been reported to induce telepathic experiences (Brown, 2012a; Eisner, 1989; Saunders, 1993). *Psilocybe* genus mushrooms too demonstrated some relatively widespread capacity to accompany psi experiences of all kinds, particularly clairvoyance, but even PK to some extent. However, possibly because of the more infrequent experience of PK, there did not seem to be any one substance that was related to it, with the possible exception of *Psilocybe* mushrooms, mescaline, and LSD, although none of these convincingly.

In keeping with the previous findings of correlations, ranging from $r = .13$ to $.29$, between the occurrence of paranormal experiences (including mystical experiences) and the use of all drugs (excluding prescription drugs) as measured with the AEI (see earlier), the Luke and Kittenis (2005) study also found a positive correlation of $r = .46$, $p < .001$. The greater correlation in this study most likely was due to the use of different sample types, and variations in the questions used. In addition, an overall correlation was calculated between the frequency of paranormal experiences and the frequency of drug use (excluding alcohol and prescription drugs) that gave a small positive value of $r =$ .31, $p <$ .001, supporting Kjellgren and Norlander's (2000) and Tart's (1971) finding that greater psychedelic use is related to more paranormal experiences.

Recently, an analysis of online trip reports posted by psychonauts found that telepathic-like experiences were reported in 25% of *Salvia divinorum* trip reports compared to 10% of LSD trip reports (Juszczak, 2012), giving some unique relative incidence figures of ESP per trip, rather than prevalence rates across the population.

More recently the psilocybin research team at John Hopkins Univeristy (Carbonaro, Johnson & Griffiths, 2017) collated the data from two internet surveys of mystical-type experiences ($N = 1602$) and challenging experiences ($N = 1993$) with psilocybin and combined it with reports from three laboratory studies conducted with healthy volunteers ($N = 126$) who reeived a high dose of psilocybin. Particpants endorsed experiencing loss of usual sense of time 88% (86–90%), entoptic percepts 76% (71–79%), experiences of ESP 36% (33–48%), profound experience of one's own death 29% (22–34%), visions of compassionate deities 25% (13–38%), contact with people who had died 17% (10–27%), sense of becoming a specific animal 15% (10–12%), and past life experience 13% (10–16%). The types of experiences reported from this the largest of all the survey datasets corroborates experiences reported elsewhere, although the prevalence rates are typically somewhat lower.

Surveys and Out-of-body Experiences (OBEs)

The connection between psychoactive substances and OBEs has received special attention. An inspection of the SPR files led Whiteman (1956) to summarize that approximately a third of "separation" (OBE) cases were initiated by physical conditions, including drugs, although which drugs are not specified. Drug type is clearly of relevance, however, as a study experimentally comparing LSD with Ritalin and benzodiazepine experiences also found that LSD induced a significantly greater degree of OBEs (Ditman et al., 1969).

Since the 1950s and 1960s several OBE surveys have incorporated questions relating to drug use. Combining two convenience samples of students ($n = 192$), Blackmore (1982) reported that of the 35 (18%) claiming to have had at least one OBE, 13 (37%) occurred when taking drugs, most often LSD or marijuana. A later questionnaire survey with students (convenience sample, $n = 96$) found 31% claimed to have had an OBE, and they were significantly more likely than those who did not claim to have had an OBE to have taken drugs such as cannabis, LSD, or opium derivatives (Blackmore & Harris, 1983).

In a similar survey of students from an opportunity sample ($n = 200$), Myers, Austrin, Grisso and Nickeson (1983) utilized the OBE question from Palmer's (1979) questionnaire and found a significant, but small, correlation between reported OBEs and the use of mind-expanding drugs ($r = .23$, $p < .001$). Similar to the 18% of Blackmore's (1982) study, 22% of the Myers et al. sample reported the occurrence of OBEs, with 42% of these having used mind-expanding drugs compared to only 20% using such drugs among those not reporting OBEs. Furthermore, 50% of the OBE experience group ($n = 45$) reported some psi-related experiences during drug taking, compared to only 4% of the non-OBE group ($n = 155$), perhaps indicating a commonality in the etiology of drug-induced psi and OBE experiences.

Although these surveys (Blackmore 1982; Blackmore & Harris, 1983; Myers et al., 1983) suggest that the use of psychedelic substances is an important correlate of OBEs in the student population, this relationship is less pronounced in other populations. A later randomized postal study (Blackmore, 1984) with a sample of people who had reported OBEs revealed that only 18% of respondents reported OBEs occurring after taking drugs and medicines (type not specified).

Blackmore (1992) concluded that hallucinogenic drugs undoubtedly help induce the OBE and were more useful for this than other drugs (e.g., stimulants, tranquillizers, sedatives, and alcohol), although she added that OBEs still occur rarely with psychedelic drug use and that there was no specific OBE-inducing drug, despite Lilly's (1978) assertion that ketamine is virtually a chemical road to the OBE. However, Blackmore (2005) later reported an OBE in a self-experiment with ketamine and conceded that, more so than other drugs, ketamine "often involves feelings of body separation" (Blackmore, 2003, p. 356).

The Blackmore OBE surveys (Blackmore 1982, 1984, 1986; Blackmore & Harris, 1983), and that of Myers et al. (1983), support the findings of the earlier survey of psychic experiences by Palmer (1979). In Palmer's study, a higher percentage of the student sample than the townspeople sample reported OBEs (S: 25%; T: 14%; $p < .01$), which Palmer attributed to the likely greater use of mind-expanding drugs among the student sample.

Of the townspeople, 7% reported the use of mind-expanding drugs compared to 32% of the student population, although Palmer suspected that the student figure was a gross underestimate, possibly due to the illegality of drug use or the interpretation of the term "mind-expanding drugs" to exclude marijuana. It is not specified why Palmer should consider the student sample to be less likely to report their drug-use than the townspeople. In addition, 13% of the townspeople and 21% of the students reporting OBEs said that at least one OBE had occurred under the influence of such drugs, figures that compare more similarly to the 18% reported for the general OBE population (Blackmore, 1984) than to the 37% and 42% in the student OBE groups (Blackmore, 1982; Myers et al. 1983, respectively).

In a review of the OBE survey literature, Irwin (1994) agreed with Palmer that the higher reports of OBE experiences among students (20–48% compared to 8–15% in the general population) were probably due in part to students more frequent experimentation with "psychotropic" drugs. However, Irwin suggested that it was probably also due in part to other factors, such as education and familiarity with surveys.

Using Palmer's (1979) questionnaire, Kohr (1980) failed to find any relationship between OBEs and drug use with the members of the Association for Research and Enlightenment – previous criticisms still standing - although Usha and Pasricha (1989a, 1989b) did find such a relationship with Indian students. The occurrence of OBEs in the Indian sample was positively associated with the use of mind-expanding drugs (chi-squared = 6.87; $p < .01$) supporting Palmer's findings, although no proportion was given for comparison.

Tart (1993) also found that 44% of marijuana users reported OBEs, with 58% of these indicating that their OBE occurred since using marijuana, with 54% of those experiencing OBEs reporting at least one experience whilst actually under the influence of marijuana (Tart, 1971). Most of Tart's sample were also students (72%), supporting Alvarado's (2000) suggestion that the relationship linking psychedelics with OBEs shown in student populations is not evident among the non-student populations, although this assertion is arguably too exclusive of non-student drug-users. For instance, in surveys with psychedelic-users, DeGracia (1995) found that 40% had an OBE while under the influence, and in Kjellgren and Norlander's (2000) sample, of which only 25% were students, OBEs under the influence of psychedelics were reported as 53%, a figure comparable to Tart's marijuana group (54%).

Reports of OBEs are also prevalent in other surveys among users of dextromethorphan (White, 1997). The OBE has also appeared within numerous experiential reports of those who have used either nitrous oxide or ether (Crookall, 1961, 1964; Schroll, 2011), LSD (Eastman,

1962; Grof, 1975, 1980; Lilly, 1969; Whiteman, 1965), PCP (Rudgley, 2000), DMT (Strassman, 2001), 4-HO-MET (Kjellgren & Soussan, 2011), *Salvia divinorum* (González, Riba, Bouso, Gómez-Jaraboa, & Barbanoj, 2006), pituri (Australian Institute of Parapsychological Research, 2004), harmaline and ayahuasca (Andritzky, 1989; Bianchi, 1994; Luna & White, 2000; Naranjo, 1967; Roney-Dougal, 1986, 1989), a host of other plant psychedelics (Schultes & Hofmann, 1992), and even certain simple carbon dioxide and oxygen gas mixtures (Meduna, 1950).

That OBEs are also frequently reported to occur with the use of ketamine (Blackmore, 2003; Curran & Morgan, 2000; Jansen, 1997a, 1999, 2001; Lilly, 1978; Muetzelfeldt et al., 2008; Pomarol-Clotet et al., 2006), even apparently veridical ones (Hanna, 2003), is further echoed by a widely distributed UK Department of Health (2004) information booklet, aimed at teenagers, subtitled "Facts about Drugs" that states the primary experiential effect of ketamine is an OBE.

Furthermore, a taxonomic survey of psychoactive substance use phenomenology found that, out of a possible 17 different transpersonal experiences, OBEs (to another dimension) were the primary experience of both DMT use and ketamine (Luke & Kittenis, 2005). Indeed, a recent online survey (Wilkins, Girard, & Cheyne, 2011) of 192 recreational drug users found that ketamine was the primary predictor of OBEs among a number of so-called recreational drugs (alcohol, cannabis, MDMA, amphetamine, and LSD/hallucinogens), though DMT was not listed specifically. It is also documented that the ancient Indian psychoactive sacramental, Soma, was capable of inducing OBEs (Spess, 2000).

Early OBE researchers were well aware of the occurrence of these experiences with psychoactive drugs and categorized them differently from OBEs with "natural" causes, suggesting that they were of a different type (Eastman, 1962) and of inferior quality (Crookall, 1961, 1972). Blackmore (1986) disagreed, suggesting that a distinction between drug and non-drug experiences was not evident.

Similarly, Grosso (1976) stated that both drug and non-drug OBEs have the same characteristics and that the OBE is the extreme manifestation of a normal human process. Grosso further proposed that drug states nicely demonstrated this continuum of out-of bodyness by exhibiting a range of body-image alterations, from feeling taller to being completely bodiless, offering the most promising means of experimental OBE induction (see Chapter 9). Nevertheless at this time, a systemic comparison of the various chemically-induced OBEs and more spontaneous ones is long overdue.

A recent survey substantiates Grosso's (1976) notion by finding that 32% of a sample of 28 first-time users of ayahuasca report alterations in self-body image, ranging from fusion with the environment to the complete separation of the conscious self from the body. All respondents were new members to one of two particular Brazilian syncretic Christian churches that use the jungle decoction ayahuasca as a sacramental (Barbosa, Giglio, & Dalgalarrondo, 2005).

Summary of Survey Research

In summary, the findings from the survey research indicate a small but consistent relationship ($r = .16$ to $.25$) between belief in the anomalous/paranormal and drug use, although the size of this relationship was more pronounced for the marijuana users in Tart's (1993) study. Furthermore, these studies support the hypothesis that psychedelics can induce some paranormal phenomena, although the same arguments for and against the genuineness of field reports (Chapter 10) also prevail here.

In the surveys reported here, with either student or general samples, those reporting ESP, apparitions, and anomalous/paranormal experiences were found to be significantly more likely to use psychedelics. One study found the same for recurrent spontaneous PK (sometimes called poltergeist phenomena) as well, although only tentatively (Palmer, 1979). Furthermore, of those reporting the use of psychedelics, 18–83% reported psi experiences – most commonly telepathy but also precognition – actually occurring during drug use, with heavier users reporting more experiences where specified.

Yet, the occurrence of PK during drug use was only reported among a very small proportion of marijuana, psilocybin, mescaline and LSD users. OBEs are also an occasional or common feature of psychedelic experiences and are reported to occur with a wide variety of drugs and wide variety of users, particularly students.

A weak relationship between paranormal experiences, the use of psychedelics, and kundalini experiences has also been found in two studies, and there is also a weak, but repeated, correlation between transliminality, drug use, and paranormal experience with Australian psychology students. Where specified, the relationship with paranormal experiences, belief in the paranormal, transliminality, and tolerance of ambiguity is reduced compared to psychedelics with respect to cocaine, heroin, and alcohol, perhaps reflecting Metzner's (2005a) classification of these as consciousness-contracting drugs.

The same is also true for the negative relationship with the fear of psi found with psychedelics, which is not apparent with heroin and actually reversed with alcohol, although replication and analyses for specific classes of drugs is necessary. Correlations between self-reports of cannabis use and thought transmission in psychiatric research are apparent, often indirectly, though such experiences are also more widely commonly reported in the apparent absence of pathology, with or without cannabis. Many of the surveys fail to adequately identify which substances lead to which experiences, although a switch in such taxonomic research is now evident (Luke & Kittenis, 2005).

CHAPTER 12

Experimental Psychedelic ESP Research

Several experiments have attempted to elicit psi directly through the controlled consumption of psychedelics. These experiments have been reported quite differently, sometimes as entire monographs in excess of 100 pages or at other times as footnotes within another published report, often without useful details and statistics. The majority of these experiments were essentially pilot studies and were mostly conducted during the psychedelic research period of the 1960s.

Forced-choice Designs

Forced-choice designs are those in which the target is chosen from among just a few known target types, as with the classic Zener cards. Whittesley (1960) reported on the use of LSD (no dose specified) in a forced choice ESP task with 27 participants, using mostly psychiatric outpatients receiving psychotherapy (with LSD presumably). Using ESP cards concealed within opaque envelopes, participants performed two runs of 25 guesses, one before and one after dosing.

Neither performance yielded significant deviations from mean chance expectation (MCE), although a chi-squared analysis of the extent of variance revealed a significant reduction in variance ($p < .001$) for scores in the experimental condition. Under the influence of LSD, participants had reported that the card guessing-task was "ridiculous, petty, mundane, etc." (p. 221), and Whittesley suggested such an exceptional lack of deviation from MCE was due to participants feeling so constrained. Little can be said of the methodological merits of this simple experiment because little detail is given, but it is questioned whether the variance analysis was pre-planned.

Making similar use of ESP symbols, Pahnke (1971) reported a pilot study with five participants given a high dose of LSD (200–400 micrograms) and tested 8–9 hours later. The results did not reveal an increase from pre-drug scores for the experimental condition. Pahnke cited the long delay in testing from dosage and, somewhat similarly to Whittesley (1960), the use of an ESP machine with sterile symbols as counterproductive factors.

Pahnke proposed that future research would benefit from the use of familiar sender-receiver pairs, with both under the influence, and the use of a stimulant (e.g., caffeine or amphetamine) along with a psychedelic such as 3,4-methylenedioxyamphetamine (MDA) or 2,5-dimethoxy-4-methylamphetamine (abbreviated as DOM, but also known as STP). Despite Pahnke's reported failure, the psychiatrist Grof (1970) reported his own experience taking LSD in one of Pahnke's experiments in which Grof successfully described a remote target in each of three attempts. Grof aptly described the dissonance between the task and the experience that occurs to the psychedelic participant, a mixture of both complete acceptance and fear of psi, when he wrote:

> When I got the third correct answer in a row, the feelings [of a universe where no laws of time and space exist] were so powerful that I could not continue. The reason for discontinuation of the ESP experiment was a strange mixture of a conviction that it was absurd to test the obvious and, on the other hand, a metaphysical fear of confusion that would follow if I had to give up the usual concept of time and space and with it all the related reference points we feel so secure with (Grof, 1970, p. 3).

Prior to using free-response procedures with LSD, Masters and Houston (1966) also experimented with an ESP-card guessing procedure. With each participant performing ten 25-card runs, only 4 out of the sample of 27 participants did better than chance. Those few participants performing better were known very well by the trip guide and had reported a high degree of empathy (with the guide presumably). Masters and Houston noted that participants very quickly became bored with the task and complained that it was "psychedelically immoral" (p.90) to have them perform card guessing while tripping.

As part of a larger series of individual ESP tests with 36 participants under the influence of psilocybin, Asperen de Boer, Barkema, and Kappers (1966) found that, in ten 25-card runs, no individual scored significantly better than in their own no-drug control condition. The results of the 29,000 ESP-card trials for the 36 psilocybin and 44 control participants (a few participants did multiple conditions) were significantly above chance ($p < .01$) overall.

However, a closer inspection of the results showed that, when compared as a group, those in the psilocybin condition scored higher (MCE = .2; mean correct = .214, $p < .05$) than the control condition (mean correct = .206, $p = .09$), although the difference between the groups was not significant. However, there is some indication that order effects reduced any difference between the groups, because the psilocybin condition always occurred after the control condition, possibly resulting in test fatigue, as described in later paragraphs.

Kugel (1977) reported very briefly on the results of a telepathy experiment with LSD, in which test scores actually declined under the influence of LSD in comparison to the periods before and after intoxication. Participants had been given trial by trial feedback and it was noticed that there was a very strong tendency for participants to respond to this feedback by responding with the same call after a hit and a different one after a miss, the latter action being known as the gambler's fallacy. Analysis revealed that this feedback susceptibility increased under the influence of LSD, possibly accounting for the poorer test performance. No further details about the methodology or statistical results were provided in this paper.

In an indirect experiment with participants selected for good psi scoring, Palmer, Tart, and Redington (1976) found a positive correlation between scores on an automated ESP-symbol guessing task in the laboratory and the reported frequency of marijuana use outside of the laboratory, with a negative correlation between ESP scores and alcohol consumption (see Tart, 1993). However, a follow-up study (Tart, Palmer, & Redington, 1979) failed to replicate these results, although Tart (1993) suggested that this was due to the difference in sample groups and the rising popularity of marijuana as a social drug rather than as a tool of self-development.

Tart explained this with observation that the subjective effects of marijuana are highly susceptible to changes in psychological set and expectation, echoing Weil's (1972) suggestion that marijuana is primarily just an active placebo. Nevertheless, direct experimental telepathy research with marijuana by the parapsychologist Dr. Thelma Moss was apparently unsuccessful (Rogo, 1976), though no original research papers on this are readily available. Even so, some similar findings to the original Palmer et al. (1976) study were found when scores on a secure non-intentional forced-choice precognition design task with 100 participants (Luke, Delanoy, & Sherwood, 2008) was correlated positively (r_s = .27, p = 008, two-tailed) with the reported number of consumed psychedelics over the lifetime.

Despite earlier cautions (e.g., Masters & Houston, 1966; Pahnke, 1971; Whittlesley, 1960) that ESP-card tests are too boring to those affected by psychedelic drugs, two later studies (Tinoco, 1994; Don, McDonough, Warren, & Moura, 1996) found further support for the forced choice task boredom factor with the use of ayahuasca in Brazil. In a series of 825 ESP-card guessing trials conducted in two 90-minute sessions with one sender and one receiver, both under the influence of ayahuasca, no significant deviation from MCE was found (Tinoco, 1994).

A second automated ESP-card precognition test involved one of the previous participants in 625 trials over two separate sessions lasting one hour and 40 minutes each, the scores of which were slightly below chance but not significantly so. However, it is apparent that no control condition was evident for comparison. As in earlier studies, both participants reported that the tasks were boring and that the tests lost their meaning and importance because it was more important to live the visions of the moment.

As part of a larger investigation into EEG variations with ayahuasca use, Don et al. (1996) similarly found no significant deviation from MCE with a small group of (presumably experienced) participants using an automated ESP task under the influence of ayahuasca, though again, like Tinoco's (1994) study, without non-drug controls. Despite the poor preliminary psi-task results, which Don et al. attributed to methodological factors, the use of ayahuasca was shown to significantly increase 40-Hz (gamma) activity within the occipital-temporal-parietal area, particularly when the participant's eyes were closed.

It was noted that amplification of this kind has often been observed during successful psi-tests in previous studies with gifted participants. Don et al. hypothesized that the reported psychic effects of ayahuasca were due to this particular 40-Hz activity amplifying unconscious psi information to conscious levels; however, an independent ayahuasca-EEG study by Stuckey, Lawson and Luna (2005) failed to replicate the power increases in the gamma frequency range, but instead found increased gamma coherence across the cortex with ayahuasca when compared to control periods.

Study	Substance	N	Type	Control condition	Results	
Forced Choice						
Rush & Cahn (1958)	mescaline	3	ESP	?	ns	
Puharich (1959, 1962)	*A. muscaria*	26	ESP	pre-drug	sig +ve	
Whittesley (1960)	LSD	27	ESP	pre-drug	ns	
Langdon-Davies (1961)	mescaline	1	ESP	no	sig +ve	
Masters & Houston (1966)	LSD	27*	ESP	no	sig +ve	

Study	Substance	N	Type	Control condition	Results
Asperen de Boer *et al* (1966)	psilocybin	36	ESP	no-drug group	sig +ve (ns vs. control)
Pahnke (1971)	LSD	5	ESP	pre-drug	ns
Kugel (1977)	LSD	?	T	pre-drug	ns
Tinoco (1994)	ayahuasca	1	T & C	no	ns
Don *et al* (1996)	ayahuasca	?	C	no	ns
Free Response					
Rush & Cahn (1958)	mescaline	3	P	?	+ve (no stats)
Smythies (1960, 1987)	mescaline	1	P	no	+ve (no stats)
Osis (1961)	LSD	6	P	no	+ve (no stats)
Asperen de Boer *et al* (1966)	psilocybin	36	P & C	no-drug group	sig +ve (ns vs. control)
Rouhier (1925, 1927)	mescaline	6	C	no	+ve (no stats)
Cavanna & Servadio (1964)	LSD or psilocybin	3	C	pre-drug	+ve (no stats)
Wezelman & Bierman (1997)	cannabis	36*	C	no-drug group	+ve vs. control (ns vs. MCE)
Wezelman & Bierman (1997)	psilocybin	6*	C	no	sig. +ve (stacking effect)
Puharich (1962)	*A. muscaria*	4	T	pre-drug	sig. +ve (optional stop)
Asperen de Boer *et al* (1966)	psilocybin	36	T	no-drug group	ns
Masters & Housten (1966)	LSD	62*	T		+ve (no stats)
Bierman (1988)	psilocybin	20*	T	pre-drug	ns
Tinoco (1994)	ayahuasca	3	T	no	ns

Table 2: Summarising all controlled experiments into ESP with psychedelics (from Luke, 2015)

Type: ESP = general ESP card guessing, or not clearly specified; P = psychometry; T = telepathy; C = clairvoyance
* Study reports that participants were experienced with psychedelics

Unlike most of the other forced choice designs, a series of successful experiments were reported by Puharich (1959, 1962), one of which utilized a 10-image unseen picture-matching test with participants who had ingested the psychedelic mushroom *Amanita muscaria*. Preliminary exploratory work had led Puharich to report the subjective feeling of telepathy himself, and one of his gifted participants perfectly matched two sets of ten unseen pictures in 3 seconds. Controlled experimental work with 26 unselected participants in independent trials revealed an overall chance occurrence of hits in the control picture matching series (106/1140; MCE = 114) compared to the experimental group (141 hits; $p < .01$), indicating a positive effect of the mushroom on ESP, later repeated in a telepathy-type design.

Free Response Psychometry (Object Reading) Experiments

Several experiments have opted for a free-response design, which is arguably more conducive than forced choice in eliciting meaningful responses from participants under the influence, and psychometry has been especially popular. In an exploratory study, using a special sample of six mediums, Osis (1961a) administered 100 or 125 micrograms of LSD to each of them prior to a psychometry test. Five performed at chance whereas one was extremely successful.

Although further details were not provided about the successful participant, Osis noted that the others were too absorbed in either the aesthetic pleasure of the experience or the quest for philosophical knowledge. The mediums distinguished the visions from normal perception and stated that the LSD experience was unique and caused a sense of profound unity with the world unlike that occurring during psychic experiences. Osis advised continuing research with drugs where the experiments were brief (only 20 min), as longer sessions appeared impractical and were thought to result in negative scores because participants would lose interest. Limited information is provided about this study, although it is assumed that participants were not experienced with psychedelics.

Smythies (1960, 1987) reported a preliminary psychometry investigation – planned more like a remote viewing task – conducted in 1950 with one volunteer using mescaline. Although the participant was unable to discern the targets under adequate blind, remote-viewing style conditions, informal questioning about the target location typical of psychometry tasks elicited promising responses.

Similarly using mescaline, a series of pilot studies with three participants "failed in card-guessing tests but showed encouraging success in tests with free material, particularly token objects" (Rush & Cahn, 1958, p. 300), though, unfortunately, further details were not given in this paper. Further to these preliminary reports, Marti-Ibanez (1965) gave a second-hand account of success with mescaline in a series of unpublished telepathy experiments conducted at the Pasteur Institute in Paris.

Likewise with mescaline, presumably in self-experiments, Breederveld (1976, 2001) reported success in consistently winning above chance at roulette experiments in casinos using real money, although the mescaline was only one of several mostly successful methods. Nevertheless, Breederveld's success echoes anecdotal reports concerning the pioneer psychedelic researcher, Al Hubbard, who, after apparently developing his psychic ability through the use of LSD (Stevens, 1988), became somewhat notorious for winning on gaming machines in casinos, his reputation being such that he was politely escorted out when he reached a certain limit of earning (Krippner, 2006a).

The most extensive object-reading test of participants under the influence of psychedelics formed part of a battery of ESP tests conducted in a large-scale psilocybin study (Asperen de Boer, Barkema, & Kappers, 1966). In a no-blind repeated-measures design, 44 no-drug control and 36 test participants (30 participants did one of each condition, whereas a few other participants did multiple conditions) given 10 or 20 mg of psilocybin, were individually tested for four hours for ESP performance with ESP-cards, object reading, traveling clairvoyance, telepathy, and clairvoyance tests regarding both people and objects.

Using a complex system for evaluating the success of the free-response tests, the experimenters jointly estimated the degree of probability for each statement given by the participants and then determined the extent to which the probability of correct statements outweighed the number and probability of incorrect statements. All participants were considered to have performed better than chance overall in the object reading, traveling clairvoyance, and clairvoyance-for-persons tests, but those in the psilocybin condition were not considered to have performed better than those in the control condition. However, the free-response results were combined for these three tests so that no separate comparisons between the groups on these tests were reported. Overall performance on the telepathy test revealed 3 hits out of 220 sessions, where 7 were expected by chance, making comparisons between the groups of little relevance, and similarly little success occurred with the clairvoyance-for-objects test.

Asperen de Boer et al. (1966) concluded that it is not possible to induce ESP with psilocybin, although Bierman (1998) argued that their participants should be pitied for having to do such a range of boring and strenuous tests while tripping, a burden unlikely to be imposed in modern research. Parker (1975) also criticized the study for promoting a scientific methodology at the expense of interpersonal factors.

Furthermore, Asperen de Boer et al. made little account for the methodological shortcomings of the psilocybin condition, even though they reported that more than half of the psilocybin participants, mostly drug novices, were distracted by their visions. The authors did note, however, that there may have been some order effects because the psilocybin condition always occurred after the control condition.

Of the five participants who completed two control trials, four did worse in the second trial, possibly indicating fatigue effects independently of the drug. Asperen de Boer et al. also reported briefly on a previous series of more promising unpublished psychometry trials with LSD that were conducted prior to switching to the psilocybin, which they considered to be less distracting. Out of several LSD participants some exceptionally accurate accounts of object reading were given, for which Kappers (1983) later suggested only a paranormal explanation seemed possible.

Other Free Response Clairvoyance Experiments

Perhaps the first psychedelic ESP experiment was conducted by the French researcher Rouhier who gave mescaline to six subjects, one of whom temporarily developed very detailed and accurate clairvoyant abilities and was able to describe the contents of a nearby room (Rouhier, 1925, 1927). The same sentiment was reported by the man who coined the term *psychedelic,* Humphry Osmond, after his own mescaline experiences in 1951. Osmond (1961) also reported that, in 1957, he and his fellow researcher Duncan Blewett, both under the influence of mescaline, successfully transmitted telepathic information in an informal experiment to such a degree that an independent observer became acutely panicky at the uncanniness of the event, though, unfortunately, no formal experiment with a larger sample is reported.

Using the more popular substances of the 1960s, Cavanna and Servadio (1964) reported extensively on a repeated-measures clairvoyance design with the alternate use of LSD and psilocybin in what was primarily an ideographic, psychoanalytic study. In a series of three control, five psilocybin, and four LSD trials, three participants performed in a single-blind (water placebo) free-response clairvoyance test. In each trial there were 10 targets of combined, yet incongruous, elements (e.g., a foot with an eye), which Parker (1975) unduly criticized for being improbable. Only one participant had a positive attitude towards psi phenomena and all were inexperienced with psychedelics.

Participants were given low doses of LSD (40, 50, and 75 micrograms) and psilocybin (10 mg), much criticized by Blewett (1965) for failing to consider the possible dose-dependent nature of psychedelic-induced ESP. Yet despite the low doses and extensive psychological screening one participant had an anxiety attack in the first LSD session, which the authors attributed to demand characteristics expressed through the anxiety and anticipation of the experimenters.

The participants' mentations were rated for correspondences by three experimenters and then independently by two blind judges, with reasonable correspondence between the judging groups, though Blewett (1965) argued otherwise. Compared to the control conditions, the blind judges' results with both the LSD and psilocybin showed a clear improvement in ESP ability, with some accurate correspondence with about one in five of the targets for both drugs.

Notably, no success at all was achieved in the three control conditions, though unfortunately no estimation of the probability of the results was given, nor were inferential statistical analyses possible because the design had no decoy targets in the judging process, as duly criticized by Smythies (1965). Although the results are positive, caution is raised concerning any inferences drawn from so few trials. Cavanna and Servadio (1964) suggested that further research should make use of: stronger emotional targets, greater emphasis on interpersonal relations, and use of free association rather than interview.

A study of some indirect relevance investigated the effects of low-dose LSD (65 micrograms) on apparent subliminal perception with five participants (Freidman & Fisher, 1960). Participants were shown a bold image faded out below the subjective threshold of (conscious) discrimination with several layers of paper and presented after a blank control image in repeated trials. Analysis of free-response descriptions of the hidden image by independent judges revealed that participants gave significantly more accurate descriptions of the target in the experimental condition under the influence of LSD compared to the control condition, and that these participants also performed significantly better with LSD in the experimental condition than they had done six weeks previously without LSD.

The results were interpreted as indicating the enhancement of subliminal perception with LSD; however, they might also be due, partly or wholly, to the enhancement of ESP with LSD. This is because the design mimics an ESP-study design in protocol, and there is some evidence to suggest that ESP is an active factor in subliminal perception research (Stanford, 1990). Alternatively the results may be due to poor methodology, such as order effects, quasi-experimental design, and expectation or other bias due to the lack of blind controls across all conditions and the repeated use of the same subliminal target image. Furthermore, according to Cheesman and Merikle (1986), the mere perception of information from between the subjective and objective threshold, as in this study, is not strictly subliminal perception, but unconscious perception.

Based upon earlier recommendations to avoid boring and repetitive test procedures with participants under the influence of psychedelics, a series of pilot ganzfeld experiments with cannabis (marijuana) and psilocybin were conducted (Wezelman & Bierman, 1997; Bierman, 1998). In the first series, Wezelman and Bierman utilized a no-sender auto-ganzfeld set-up with 40 participants pre-selected for experience with marijuana. In a randomized crossover design, participants performed two trials each, one self-dosing marijuana condition and a control condition.

All but four participants, who became nauseous and dropped out after the first session, completed both trials. A planned mixture of subject judging or external judging was used. The control condition had a hit rate of 15% (MCE = 25%) compared to 30% for the marijuana condition, and Bierman (1998) noted that the score for the marijuana condition was mainly due to the external judges, particularly one experimenter-judge who was also using marijuana. However, scores for the experimental group were not significantly different from MCE.

Wezelman and Bierman (1997) also reported on findings from a no-sender ganzfeld pilot-study conducted with six psilocybin-experienced participants performing two trials each under the influence of psilocybin. There was no control condition. Utilizing a buddy system to deter bad trips, pairs of receivers performed the ganzfeld together. With only subject judging this time, participants in the psilocybin group scored 7 direct hits out of 12 trials (58%), a figure that even with only a few trials is significantly deviant from MCE ($p < .05$), although uncorrected for a stacking effect (see Milton & Wiseman, 1997, p. 93).

Free Response Telepathy Experiments

Bierman (1998) continued with the previous work, this time in a telepathy design using a within-subjects control condition with 20 psilocybin-experienced participants who each performed one control and one psilocybin ganzfeld trial with a sober sender. Participants in the psilocybin condition scored at chance (25%), whereas in the control condition they performed slightly below (20%), with no significant difference between the two. However, a *post hoc* analysis of the results for negative and positive clips revealed an interaction between target emotionality and drug state, with a much higher hit rate for positive clips (44%) than negative clips (8%) in the psilocybin condition and a reversal of this effect in the control condition. This interaction was explained in terms of psilocybin participants possibly detecting the positive ESP targets, but blocking the negative images to deter bad trips, given that participants were tripping alone this time; however, the reverse effects for the control condition are not as easily explicable.

Bierman interpreted this result as suggesting that psychoactive drugs affect psi performance and that target emotionality and the psychological set of the participant may interact to alter the results. It is also worth noting that ganzfeld experiments with psychoactive drugs are likely to induce a unique, possibly combined, state of consciousness, unlike the usual drug or ganzfeld experience alone, given that the ganzfeld environment is considered by many scholars to already induce a unique kind of ASC (e.g., Wackerman et al., 2000). However, this idea needs further verification.

Coming from the field of psychedelic experimentation rather than parapsychology, towards which they reported being skeptical, Masters and Houston (1966) conducted a series of ESP experiments in which they demonstrated a much greater degree than their contemporaries of familiarity with the effects of the drugs being used. They provided an experienced trip guide, with whom most participants were familiar, and utilized experienced trippers as participants.

The study had 62 receivers, with their guide as the sender of the 10 static image targets, and only the receiver under the influence of LSD. Using independent judges, the majority of the 62 receivers (77%) gave free-recall responses approximating the target at least 2/10 times, with five of these participants approximating the target image 7/10 or 8/10 times. The remaining 14 participants (23%), who performed worse, were either unknown to the guide, anxious or primarily interested in their own personal psychological narrative rather than the ESP task, though these observations may be *post hoc*. Sometimes, receiver statements also matched non-target thoughts of the sender. But Parker (1975) noted that non-verbal communication from the guide could not be ruled out.

Once again, no estimation of the probability of describing the target image is known, because no decoy images were used in the judging process and no comparison was made to a control condition to establish if LSD actually improved scores. Nevertheless, accuracy rates were similar to those reported in the clairvoyance procedure of the same nature by Cavanna and Servadio (1964), where LSD and psilocybin scores exceeded those in control conditions. Cavanna and Servadio further reported an exploratory sender-receiver telepathy design with one LSD trial and one control, where only the receiver took LSD. The results indicated accurate comparisons in approximately one in three of the targets for LSD, with a rate of only one in ten for the no-drug control condition.

Following up from a previous forced-choice ayahuasca ESP study (Tinoco, 1994), Tinoco (2011) conducted a free response task in 1995 with three participants under the influence of ayahuasca acting as senders and receivers in a telepathy-type task. No use of decoy targets was made in the judging procedure, nevertheless three independent judges concluded that there was no correlation between the target and the response in any of the 15 trials; however, no exact probability of getting a hit can be calculated with this method, and the interpretations of the judges are subjective. Furthermore, no control group was used for comparison, it is not clear how the targets for sending were initially chosen, and participants complained that they were not getting any visual imagery and, as with the two previous ayahuasca studies, that the task was boring in such a state.

Finally, Puharich (1962) followed up his earlier success at clairvoyance with *Amanita muscaria* with a demonstration for four Los Angeles news reporters, who also acted as participants and who were either skeptical or hostile towards the idea of drug-induced psi. The design relied on a computer-recorded random number-series guessing task with a non-drugged sender elsewhere, though where was not specified so sensory leakage cannot be ruled out. Participants scored at chance in the control condition (35 hits in 297 trials, nonsignificant) and after ingestion of *A. muscaria* repeated the test (average 40 min later) and made a combined score of 65 hits in 432 trials ($p < .005$). Scoring returned to chance after two and half hours, as they had in the previous clairvoyance experiment, although participants still reported feeling that their intuition was active.

Puharich (1962) attributed the results to the neurochemical action of cholinergia heightening the ESP function by activating the parasympathetic functions (slow heart rate, etc.) indicative of the trance state. However, this explanation is somewhat erroneous because the psychoactive principles in *A. muscaria* – muscimol and ibotenic acid – can both calm and stimulate the central nervous system, respectively, whereas the cholinergic chemical, muscarine, is now known to be only a trace and psychologically inactive constituent of the mushroom (Michelot & Melendez-Howell, 2003). There is also the possibility that optional stopping occurred in this latter experiment as indicated by the different number of trials in the control and experimental conditions, and Krippner (2006a) also raised concern that Puharich's research, as with Masters and Houston (1966), was reported in a self-authored book rather than a peer-reviewed journal.

Summary of Experimental Research

Due to the exploratory nature of most of these experiments, it is difficult to fully assess their efficacy using psychedelics to produce ESP (no PK experiments having been attempted). In most cases this could have largely been improved with an adequate control condition without order effects (Palmer, 1978), and the blind use of decoy targets in the judging process. Procedures using subjective probability estimates by experimenters (such as Asperen de Boer et al., 1966) are now virtually obsolete in parapsychology because they are so difficult to assess and are prone to bias (Parker, 1975).

In the one ESP-card experiment to use a control condition, scores in the psilocybin condition were significantly different from chance and were also superior to the control condition, although not significantly (Asperen de Boer et al., 1966). Nevertheless, it is apparent that those experiments using ESP-card type symbol guessing procedures were largely unsuccessful compared to chance expectation.

The use of the symbol-guessing procedure has been widely criticized for being far too mundane under the influence of psychedelics (Grof, 1980; Masters & Houston, 1966; Pahnke, 1971; Parker, 1975; Rogo, 1976; Stafford & Golightly, 1967; Smythies, 1960; Tart, 1968; Whittlesey, 1960). Even so, using *Amanita muscaria*, Puharich (1962) demonstrated that forced-choice procedures could be successful with picture-sorting tasks. More engaging, free-response procedures have demonstrated at least some success in all but one of the studies that have used psychometry, although rarely with any control condition for comparison.

A clearer indication of possible psychedelic-induced ESP, even at times in comparison to a control condition, comes overall from the clairvoyance and telepathy designs, except for the Asperen de Boer et al. (1964), Tinoco (2011), and the marijuana ganzfeld studies (Wezelman & Bierman, 1997). Replication, however, is needed and, in some cases, with better methodology and pre-planned analyses. It remains curious that no formal explicit experiments with precognition or PK have been performed, particularly the former because powers of divination are traditionally attributed to many plant psychedelics.

CHAPTER 13

Methodological Critique of Experimental Research

When consideration is given to what has been learned from these mostly pilot studies, experimenters and commentators alike have highlighted the difficulties involved in attempting to test for psi with participants who have taken a psychedelic. Aspirin de Boer et al. (1964) suggested that the participant's willingness to perform in the task was important, but given that participants have difficulty maintaining alertness, self-control, focus, interest, and orientation to the task (Edge, Morris, Palmer, & Rush, 1986; Millay, 2001; Rogo, 1976), it seems much more important to consider the participant's "capability" to perform in the experiment rather than their mere willingness.

Parker (1975) notes that a participant's increased sensitivity to subtle influences under psychedelics is both a boon and a bane to research. Indeed, using psychedelics to induce psi is a double-edged sword, namely all of the reasons cited in the introduction that make such research alluring also make participants poor test subjects. This is because participants may become engrossed in the experience (Rogo, 1982), the aesthetic rapture (Osis, 1961a; Smythies, 1960), the quest for philosophical knowledge (Osis, 1961a), a deep soul-searching self-examination (Blewett, 1963), one's own personal drama (Millay, 2001; Parker, 1975), and the flow of thoughts (Ryzl, 1968).

In addition, participants may have difficulty communicating because of the lack of adequate language (Lilly, 1969), the overwhelming flood of ideas and emotions (Ryzl, 1968) and the speed of change of the internal experience (Blewett, 1961b, 1963). The experience of dissociation (e.g., with ketamine) can also hinder communication when participants become no longer present or aware of their physical environment and, as Huxley (1961b) pointed out, there is a need to assure participants of their identity once constructs of space and time disappear. Blewett (1961a) further warned of other unwanted psychological reactions that may occur if participants attempt to either escape from or rationalize their experience.

However, it is apparent that these obstacles to research may be greatly alleviated or even eliminated if participants are experienced with the use of psychedelics (Blewett, 1963; Parker, 1975; Tart, 1977). Indeed, about a quarter of inexperienced participants are expected to have intense spontaneous mystical experiences during their first trip (Wulff, 1997, 2000). Yet, very few of the studies reviewed here (only Bierman, 1998; Masters & Houston, 1966; Wezelman & Bierman, 1997) specifically reported the use of participants experienced with these psychedelics, although it is worth noting that those that did were relatively more successful than those that used inexperienced participants.

Further to this, it has been suggested that experienced psychedelic participants can be better trained to stabilize their experience (Millay, 2001; Tart, 1977) and may even naturally train themselves to do so experiences through repeated use (Levine, 1968). Regardless of training, it has been strongly advised that participants be allowed to stabilize their experience before testing begins (Blewett, 1963, 1965; Millay, 2001; Parker, 1975; Tart, 1977). Pahnke (1968) further recommended an 8- to 12-hour pre-dose preparation period when working with terminal cancer patients, although Ludwig (in Tart, 1968) questioned the necessity of this in a parapsychological context.

Stabilization of the experience may even be expedited by inducing hypnosis prior to drug administration (Parker, 1975; Tart, 1968) in what has been called the "hypnodelic" state (e.g. see Levine & Ludwig, 1965; Ludwig 1968; Tart, 1967). Alternatively, Ryzl (1968) reported re-inducing LSD states through hypnosis, as is also reported elsewhere, although it was uncertain how successful this was (Ludwig, 1968), though success inducing other drug states (e.g., MDMA, heroin) has also been reported (Hastings, 2006; Hastings et al., 2000; Ludwig & Lyle, 1964). Similarly, Farber (2000) has described the successful re-induction of psychedelic states using hypnotic anchoring techniques available in neuro-linguistic programming.

Perhaps, the entire psychedelic experience can be stabilized and anchored during test trips with experienced users and then later re-induced, with or without hypnosis, so that no psychedelics are actually taken during the test procedure. Testing for psi under such "controlled flashbacks" may overcome most of the stipulated problems, and have the added advantage of investigating Rogo's (1976) question of whether it is the neurochemical action of the drugs or the state induced that can seemingly produce psi.

Although some researchers (Halliday, 1961; Nicol & Nicol, 1961; Paterson, 1961a; Smythies 1960; Tart in Levine, 1968) suggest that using good-psi scorers, psychics, and mediums in drug studies would improve scoring, Eileen Garrett (1961b) noted that although LSD enhanced her mediumistic experience it would not improve forced choice test-scores. Echoing this, the Osis (1961a) experiment has shown that using mediums did not prove any more successful than the use of normal participants in the other psychometry experiments. This was probably due to all the problems mentioned already that occur more with inexperienced psychedelic users, indicating that sample selection should primarily seek to select experienced users over psi-effective participants, although, presumably, ideal participants would be both, though not necessarily.

Considering aspects of timing, several authors have offered advice, though no formal studies have been conducted. Both Ryzl (1968) and Grof (1980) suggested that the optimum period for testing psi during the LSD session was towards the end when the effects were leveling off, as in the Masters and Houston (1966) experiments, yet Pahnke (1971) disagreed. From extensive personal experience, Copley (1962) suggested testing for ESP once the trip had finished. As regards to the duration of the psi-task, rather than the extended test periods favored by some researchers (e.g. Asperen de Boer et al., 1964; Tinoco, 1995), Osis (1961a) suggested 20 minutes should be the maximum for optimum performance.

Some consideration has also been given to the optimal substance. Pahnke (1971) recommended combining stimulants with psychedelics, whereas Asperen de Boer et al. (1966) chose psilocybin over LSD, due to it being milder, to which Cavanna and Servadio (1964) agreed. Indeed, LSD has a much longer duration of action than psilocybin and as Blewett (1963) noted, 10-hour trips are hard to staff.

Ryzl (1968) also questioned the utility of LSD in psychedelic psi testing and proposed that the ideal substance, if it can be synthesized, should inhibit cortical activity to suppress the stream of thoughts, depress sub-cortical activity to block incoming stimuli and excite spheres of the cortex involved in ESP production, yet maintain rational insight, and increase suggestibility. However, such a designer drug is far in the future, though such psychochemical engineering may one day be possible (Brown, 2012b); moreover, there are an increasing number of ethnobotanical substances becoming known that have traditionally been used for psychic purposes, which have not yet been thoroughly tested, or even tested at all (e.g., *Salvia divinorum*).

Tart (1993) further suggested that marijuana was an ideal substance for psi experimentation because of its wide familiarity within the public, its mild psychedelic qualities and its reputed ability to induce psi, experientially at least. Puharich's (1962) apparent repeated success with *Amanita muscaria* also needs replicating. Furthermore, other non-psychedelic chemical psi research, such as Pablos' (2002) unsuccessful first-person precognitive-dream drug-study, could also be replicated with the use of psychedelic substances that have actually been reported to induce psi in dreams. For instance, there are reports of precognitive dreams, by both traditional users and by modern consciousness researchers, with substances such as *Calea zacatechichi* (Devereaux, 1997; Díaz 1979; Mayagoitia, Díaz, & Contreras, 1986), *Silene capensis* (Hirst, 2000, 2005; Sobiecki, 2008, 2012), and tree datura (*Brugmansia*) (Metzner, 1992; Schultes & Hofmann, 1992).

Other substances seem best suited to other experimental designs too, for example, telepathy-like experiments might also benefit from the empathogenic effect of substances like MDMA, as the one participant under its influence in a remote detection experiment did exceedingly well (Brown, 2012a). The use of a placebo in a double-blind or blind control condition, as in Cavanna and Servadio (1964), is of questionable utility in this type of experiment because at anything less than sub-threshold doses the participant is likely to easily detect the effects of the drug; nevertheless, researchers should be aware that placebo drug effects have been demonstrated in ESP research when coupled with positive false feedback on task performance (Pitman & Owens, 2004).

Several researchers have also commented on the importance of dosage (e.g. Braud, 2002; Levine, 1968). Blewett (1961b) warned that giving participants low doses of LSD may not be sufficient to break through the barrier between the normal and the full-blown psychedelic state and can be merely disorientating rather than transformative, and he later suggested that doses up to 1,500 micrograms of LSD (a very large dose) need investigating, because ESP might be dose dependent (Blewett, 1965). Support for this logic is also evident in escalating dose research with DMT (Strassman, 2001). It is additionally advised that experienced participants control their own dosage (Tart, 1977), as in the experiment by Wezelman and Bierman (1997).

Participant's self-reports of the depth of the altered state were also considered better than dosages as indicators of subjective effects (Tart, 1977). Self reports using the Hallucinogenic Rating Scale were also considered better indicators of dosage than physiological measures (Strassman, Qualls, Uhlenhuth, & Kellner, 1994), though the use of a scale of transpersonal experience, such as the Self-Expansiveness Scale Form (Friedman, 1983; Pappas & Friedman, 2007), would also likely be fruitful in discerning the relevant depth of the psychedelic ASC.

Furthermore, some researchers (e.g. Parker, 1975; Tart 1968, 1977) have noted that the issue of dosage is largely irrelevant in comparison to the influence of the psychological factors of set and setting, as originally noted in psychedelic research by Leary, Litwin, and Metzner (1963). In discussion of this, Vayne (2001) suggested that the influence of psychological factors on psychoactive drugs can vary their effects so much that the drug can be thought of primarily as an experience, composed of set, setting, and substance.

Factors considered important in determining psychological set include the participants' expectations, attitudes towards themselves, idiosyncratic perceptions, and emotional orientation to the experiment (Levine, 1968; Tart, 1968). It is also deemed imperative to engender a sense of self-surrender, acceptance, and trust (Blewett, 1963). Factors considered important in determining psychological setting include those that are ordinarily considered under demand characteristics (Parker, 1975; Tart, 1968, 1977), particularly the experimenter's attitude, which should be warm, friendly, and supportive (Blewett, 1963).

Psychological issues induced through interpersonal relations within the laboratory become magnified when participants are on psychedelics (Blewett, 1963; Parker, 1975). Cavanna and Servadio (1964) highlighted this when one of their participants had an anxiety attack concurrent with their own anxiety, which led them to advise that the experimenters themselves should be experienced users of the psychedelic substance under investigation, as also advised by Strassman (2001).

Tart (1968) also recommended that the experimenter should guide the experience towards the goal of the study, and has criticized previous work for assuming psychedelic states automatically induce psi, because, as noted by Tart, Osmond, and Beloff (in Levine, 1968), and Puharich (1959), in traditional scenarios the shamans who use these substances usually have extensive training and experience. It is further suggested that the experimental task be shaped to the state of the participant, not vice versa (Tart, 1977), and utilize the strong motivation, directed awareness, and complex ritual that is found in shamanism (Copley, 1962; Grof, 1980; Tart, 1968).

Grob and Harman (1995) have also urged the integration of aspects from shamanic practices into scientific procedure so that there is attentiveness to factors of set and setting, such as intention, expectation, preparation, group identification, and formalized structure, as well as the integration of the experience in the following months. Indeed a multi-method approach to studying psychedelic shamanic practices is advised, so that ethnography can inform suitable experimentation (Giesler, 1984, 1985; Luke, 2010a).

Nevertheless, Storm and Rock (2011) pointed out that, in psi research with psychedelics, researchers need to be aware of the difference between shamanic techniques and merely shamanic-like techniques; for example, the latter may lack the purpose of serving one's community. Furthermore, Tart (1977) has recommended the implementation of mutual research, where participants are considered as co-investigators, to reduce experimenter bias and enhance a sense of participation, trust, and motivation.

CHAPTER 14

General Summary and Conclusions on Psychedelic Parapsychological Research

Even though the subjective paranormal experiences, clinical observations and anthropological reports are subject to all the usual criticisms and rebuttals that apply to non-experimental cases (e.g., see Stokes, 1997) there is a growing body of reports, rooted in thousands of years of traditional psychedelic use, that supports the notion that genuine paranormal phenomena do occur. Nevertheless, as evidence this data is not scientifically rigorous, yet it has great value in mapping the phenomenological terrain of paranormal experiences with psychedelics.

This body of reports is further supported by correlations from surveys linking psychedelic use with the increased reporting of paranormal experiences and belief in the paranormal, although again, self-reports have more phenomenological merit than evidential value. Furthermore, even though it can be considered little more than exploratory at this stage, the experimental evidence is more positive than not and proves promising so far, illuminating both methodological pitfalls and possibilities.

It is apparent that parapsychopharmacology is a multidisciplinary endeavour pooling expertise from anthropology, ethnobotany, phytochemistry, neurobiology, psychopharmacology, psychiatry, psychotherapy, transpersonal psychology and indeed parapsychology. It also owes much to the non-academic explorers of consciousness, be they shamans, occultists, or psychonauts. It is a branch of research that is still very much in its infancy, and, along with other fields conducting research with the use of psychedelics, has been operating very quietly since the late sixties until a gentle turn in the tide during the last decade or so has seen experimental research resumed (see Grob & Harman, 1995).

Nevertheless, further experimental research continues to need strict ethical and often governmental approval before it can proceed, requiring lengthy applications (see McKenna, 2004; Strassman, 2001).

Several years ago, Tart (1977) recommended bypassing these difficulties by casually enrolling participants who were already using psychedelics, rather than having the experimenter administering the substances directly. An example of this kind of experiment involved several thousand Grateful Dead fans, renowned for their psychedelic consumption, who acted as senders in a series of dream telepathy experiments with some success (Krippner, 1999; Krippner, Honorton, & Ullman, 1973; Roberts, 2004).

Indeed, taking what Giesler (1984, 1985) calls a psi-in-process approach and keeping naturalistic variables intact, group experiments may be one way to access the kind of group telepathy experiences that people tripping in groups sometimes report (e.g., Grey, 2007; Nuttal, 1970; Stevens, 1989; Wolfe, 1971), especially on DXM (Luke & Kittenis, 2005). However, without the grounded and controlled atmosphere of a concert or shamanic ceremony, psychedelic group ESP experiments run the risk of turning into bacchanalian scenes, as once witnessed by Puharich's wife (Hermans, 1998).

Having now resumed, direct parapsychological research with psychedelics needs expanding beyond the Netherlands and Brazil – the only place where experimental psi-chedelic research has been conducted since the 1970s – and treating these substances like any other drug worthy of investigation within a medical or therapeutic context has recently proven a fruitful means of inquiry for many researchers (Doblin, 2004; Grob & Harman, 1995), although psi research does not readily attract such funding at the present time.

Nevertheless, it should be noted that psychedelics are considered as sacraments by the spiritual and religious groups that use them and they must be utilized and researched with respect. It is also clear that besides trying to replicate the promising free-response studies, further experimental psychedelic research should utilize protocols that maximize psi effects, and this work can then simultaneously enhance process research methodology by indicating optimal conditions for psi through the psychologically magnifying effects of these substances. For instance, Bierman's (1998) psychedelic psi research may have revealed the apparent psychic blocking of negative images, and, from earlier experiments, forced-choice tasks are clearly too mundane. Research should also seek to study these substances in the shamanic context in which they have most effectively been used, designing appropriate test protocols for traditional settings. A recent example of which is Hirukawa et al.'s (2006) apparently successful demonstration of psi using a field random event generator in an ayahuasca ritual with the Santo Daime church in Brazil.

Additionally, following in the footsteps of William James, there has already been some return to self-experimentation with psychoactive drugs by Pablos (2002, 2004), who has developed a viable protocol for testing one's own precognitive dreaming abilities with drugs, which might easily be adapted to waking experimentation as well. All experimental research should also be designed and conducted with an appreciative consideration of Tart's proposals for the creation of state-specific sciences (Tart, 1972b, 1998, 2000, 2001).

In the future, parapsychologists might ask their participants about their drug use, and researchers investigating the use of psychedelics might once more include questions relating to paranormal experiences (e.g., Echenhofer, 2005). Furthermore, with an ever growing number of substances being discovered and a large natural data pool of psychedelic users, there is a need for more thorough and focused phenomenological research that investigates and identifies the types of paranormal experience that occur through the use of each of these diverse psychedelic substances (Luke, 2004a, 2004b, 2004c; Luke & Kittenis, 2005).

Finally, there is much that can be offered to transpersonal studies from the investigation of parapsychopharmacology, and vice versa. Certainly it is clear that no study of the extraordinary phenomena of the psychedelic state would be complete without the insights and perspective of transpersonal psychology. Indeed, many of the exceptional experiences encountered with psychedelics involve parapsychological elements and yet they also go beyond the ordinary scope of parapsychology into the wider transpersonal realms (Luke, 2012d), such as entity encounters (e.g., Luke, 2011b) and profound mystical experiences (Luke & Kittenis, 2005).

It's also somewhat inevitable then that this course of research is as likely to culminate in transformation for the researcher as it is in evidence for the genuine existence or otherwise of psychedelically induced paranormal phenomena (Luke, 2011c). It is also illuminating at this point to consider this research in terms of Tart's (2002) evaluation of these related fields of enquiry, where parapsychology is to transpersonal psychology what physics is to engineering: One researches the fundamental technical nature of the subject matter so that the other may apply it. In the current case a great deal can be learned, as Tart reminds us, about the fundamental nature of mind through the study of parapsychology and – by looking to the psychedelic dimension – about the neurochemical mediation of exceptional aspects of consciousness in particular. Ultimately, however, it is down to transpersonal psychologists how they use this knowledge and apply it, though, fortunately, the history here tells us that wisdom usually prevails.

Afterword

Pulling Magicians out of a Rabbit Hole

While there is a fairly comprehensive overview available here of the induction of several exceptional experiences with psychedelic substances it is clear that systematic study in this area is at a nascent stage or, as with extra-dimensional percepts, barely even started. This is somewhat unfortunate because by exploring psychedelics there may be a lot to be learned about the neurobiology involved in these various exceptional experiences, as is proposed by the DMT and ketamine models of NDE. And indeed a lot we can learn about the limits of human consciousness.

However, one important thing seems apparent from the data, and that is that altered states of consciousness, as opposed to psychedelic chemicals *per se*, seem to be key in the induction of such experiences, at least where they are not congenital: for every experience presented here, and more, can also occur in non-psychedelic states – although psychedelics have the relative benefit of immediacy and repeatability. As such, it may well be the states produced by psychedelics and other means of inducing ASCs that are primary, not the neurochemical action. Of course all states of consciousness probably involve changes in brain chemistry, such as occurs with the simple change of O_2 and CO_2 in blood and brain induced by breathing techniques (e.g., holotropic; Grof & Grof 2010) or carbogen (Meduna, 1950), but whilst there are many states and many neurochemical pathways so many of these can give rise to the same experience syndromes as described in this book. Indeed, it should be remembered that the experiential outcome of an ASC is determined not just by substance (which could be any ASC technique) but by set and setting too (Leary, Litwin & Metzner, 1963, Vayne, 2017).

Curiously, recent brain imaging research with psilocybin has demonstrated that, counter to the received neuroscientific wisdom, no region of the brain was more active under the influence of this substance but rather several key hub regions of the cortex – the thalamus, anterior and posterior cingulate cortex (ACC & PCC), and medial prefrontal cortex (mPFC); collectively termed the Default Mode Network (DMN) – demonstrated *reduced* cerebral blood flow (Carhart-Harris et al., 2012). Similar findings of reduced DMN activity have been demonstrated with other ASCs, such as with ayahuasca (Palhano-Fontes et al., 2015), hypnosis (McGeown, Mazzoni, Venneri & Kirsch, 2009), meditation (Brewer et al., 2011; Garrison et al., 2015), and with experienced automatic writing trance mediums (Peres et al., 2012).

These findings seem to support Dietrich's (2003) proposal that all ASCs are mediated by a transient decrease in prefrontal cortex activity, and that the different induction methods – be it drugs, drumming, dreaming, dancing or diet – affect how the various prefontal neural pathways steer the experience. In this sense then, there are many mechanisms for a general altered state, in which many exceptional experiences are possible, but which ultimately have their own flavour in line with the specific method of induction (combining set, setting *and* substance) wherein specific exceptional experiences become more prevalent (e.g, OBEs are possible with all psychedelics but are most common with high doses of ketamine).

These brain imaging studies and other evidence (e.g., see Kastrup, 2012; Kelly et al., 2007), also support Aldous Huxley's (1954) extension of Henri Bergson's idea that the brain is a filter of consciousness and, according to Huxley, that psychedelics inhibit the brain's default filtering process thereby giving access to mystical and psychical states. In any case, even if specific neurobiological processes can be identified in the induction of specific exceptional experiences and states does not mean to say that a reductionistic argument has prevailed, because as Huxley also stated, psychedelics are the occasion not the cause – the ontology of the ensuing experience still needs fathoming whether the neurobiological *mediating* factors are determined or not.

Ultimately, the importance of these psychedelically-induced exceptional experiences may be determined by what we can learn about ontology, consciousness and our identity as living organisms, and by what use they may be in ecopsychology, psychotherapy, one's own spiritual quest, and as catalysts for personal transformation and healing (Roberts & Winkelman, 2013).

References

Aardvark, D. (Ed.) (2002). *Salvia divinorum and Salvinorin A: The best of The Entheogen Review: ER monograph series, No 2* (2nd ed.). Sacramento, CA: The Entheogen Review.

Abraham, H. D. (1983). Visual phenomenology of the LSD flashback. *Archives of General Psychiatry, 40*, 884-889.

Addy, P. (2007). Facilitating transpersonal experiences with dextromethorphan: potential, cautions, and caveats. *The Journal of Transpersonal Psychology, 39(1)*, 1-22.

Addy, P. H. (2010). *That deep internal voice: Controlled administration of Salvia divinorum.* Unpublished doctoral thesis, Institute of Transpersonal Psychology, Palo Alto, California.

Afra, P., Funke, M., & Matsuo, F. (2009). Acquired auditory-visual synesthesia: a window to early cross-modal sensory interactions. *Psychology Research and Behavior Management, 2*, 31-37.

Ahmadi, J., Keshtkar, M., & Pridmore, S. (2011). Methamphetamin induced synaesthesia: A case report. *American Journal Addictions, 20*, 306.

Alvarado, C. S. (1995). Emilio Servadio at ninety: A tribute. *Journal of the Society for Psychical Research, 60*, 122-128.

Alvarado, C. S. (1998). ESP and altered states of consciousness: An overview of conceptual research trends. *Journal of Parapsychology, 62*, 27-63.

Alvarado, C. S. (2000). Out-of-body experiences. In E. Cardeña, S. J. Lynn, & S. Krippner (Eds.), *Varieties of anomalous experience: Examining the scientific evidence* (pp. 183-218). Washington, DC: American Psychological Association.

American Psychiatric Association (2000). *Diagnostic and statistical manual of mental disorders* (4th ed., text revision). Washington, DC: Author.

Anderson, E. F. (1980). *Peyote: The divine cactus.* Tuscon, AZ: University of Arizona Press.

Andrews, G. (Ed.). (1997). *Drugs and magic.* Lilburn, GA: IllumiNet Press.

Andritzky, W. (1989). Sociopsychotherapeutic functions of ayahuasca healing in Amazonia. *Journal of Psychoactive Drugs, 21*, 77-90.

Anonymous. (2004a). *Baby Woodrose telepathy: LSA and MDMA.* Retrieved January 27, 2004, from http://leda.lycaeum.org/?ID=5297

Anonymous. (2004b). *Dream from Hell: Telepathy, time travel, and assorted craziness.* Retrieved January 27, 2004, from http://leda.lycaeum.org/?ID=5964

Anonymous. (2004c). *Salvia divinorum: Diviner's sage.* Retrieved January 27, 2004, from http://leda.lycaeum.org/?ID=269

Anonymous. (2004d). *Telepathy: Strange Aztec designs.* Retrieved January 27, 2004, from http://leda.lycaeum.org/?ID=5823

Anonymous. (2004e). *Word telepathy: We're back from cuckoo land.* Retrieved January 27, 2004, from http://leda.lycaeum.org/?ID=5278

Anonymous. (2005). *Message 19019 – Salvia Divinorum Alliance*. Retrieved November 25, 2005, from http://groups.yahoo.com/group/SalviaD_Alliance/message/19019

Araújo, W. S. (2006). The Barquinha: Symbolic space of cosmology in the making. *Fieldwork in Religion, 2*(3), 350-362.

Arthur, J. D. (2010). *Salvia divinorum: Doorway to thought-free awareness*. Rochester, VT: Park Street Press.

Asperen de Boer, S. R. van., Barkema, P. R., & Kappers, J. (1966). Is it possible to induce ESP with psilocybin? An exploratory investigation. *International Journal of Neuropsychiatry, 2*, 447-473.

Assailly, A. (1961). Biochemical elements of mediumship. In Anon., *Proceedings of Two Conferences on Parapsychology and Pharmacology* (pp. 53-55). New York: Parapsychology Foundation.

Atwater, P. M. H. (1994). *Beyond the light: What isn't being said about near-death experience*. New York. Carol Publishing Corporation.

Australian Institute of Parapsychological Research (2004). *AIPR fact sheet: Psychic and mystical experiences of the Aborigines*. Retrieved January 12, 2004, from http://www.aiprinc.org/aborig.html

Averill, R. L., & Rhine, J. B. (1945). The effect of alcohol upon performance in PK tests. *Journal of Parapsychology, 9*, 32.

Avramopoulos, D., Stefanis, N.C., Hantoumi, I., Smyrnis, N., Evdokimidis, I., & Stefanis, C.N. (2002). Higher scores of self reported schizotypy in healthy young males carrying the COMT high activity allele. *Molecular Psychiatry, 7*, 706-711.

Bahn, P. (1988). Comment on: The signs of all times: Lewis-Williams and Dowson. *Current Anthropology, 29*(2), 217-8.

Bahn, P. (1997). *Journey through the Ice Age*. Berkeley, CA: University of California Press.

Ballesteros, S., Ramón, M. F., Iturralde, M. J., & Martínez-Arrieta, R. (2006). National source of drugs of abuse: Magic mushrooms In S. M. Cole (Ed.), *New Research on Street Drugs* (pp. 167-186). New York: Nova Science Publishers.

Banissy, M. J., Holle, H., Cassell, J., Annett, L., Tsakanikos, E., Walsh, V., Spiller, M. J., & Ward, J. (2013). Personality traits in people with synaesthesia: Do synaesthetes have an atypical personality profile? *Personality and Individual Differences, 54*, 828-831.

Barbosa, P. C. R., Giglio, J. S., & Dalgalarrondo, P. (2005). Altered status of consciousness and short-term psychological after-affects induced by the first time ritual use of ayahuasca in an urban context in Brazil. *Journal of Psychoactive Drugs, 37*, 193-201.

Barker, S. A., Borjigin, J., Lomnicka, I., & Strassman, R. (2013). LC/MS/MS analysis of the endogenous dimethyltryptamine hallucinogens, their precursors, and major metabolites in rat pineal gland microdialysate. *Biomedical Chromatography, 27*, 1690-1700.

Barker, S. A., McIlhenny, E. H., Strassman, R. (2012). A critical review of reports of endogenous psychedelic N, N-dimethyltryptamines in humans: 1955-2010. *Drug Testing and Analysis, 7-8*, 617-635.

Baruss, I. (2003). *Alterations of consciousness: An empirical analysis for social scientists*. Washington, DC: American Psychological Association.

Bednarik, R.G. (1988). Comment on: The signs of all times: Lewis-Williams and Dowson. *Current Anthropology, 29*(2), 218-9.

Bednarik, R.G. (1990). On neuropsychology and shamanism in rock art. *Current Anthropology, 31*(1), 77-85.

Bell, J.S. (1964). On the Einstein Podolsky Rosen Paradox. *Physics, 1,* 195-200.

Beloff, J. (1968). Summary. In R. Cavanna, & M. Ullman (Eds.), *Psi and Altered States of Consciousness: Proceedings of an International Conference on Hypnosis, Drugs, Dreams, and Psi* (pp. 2020-208). New York: Parapsychology Foundation.

Bergson, H. (1990). *Matter and memory* (N. M. Paul & W. S. Palmer, Trans). New York: Zone Books. (original work published 1896).

Besmer, F. E. (1983). *Horses, musicians, and Gods. The Hausa cult of possession-trance.* New York: Greenwoood.

Beyer, S. [V.](1974). *Magic and ritual in Tibet: The cult of Tara.* Berkeley and Los Angeles: University of California Press.

Beyer, S. V. (2009). *Singing to the plants: A guide to mestizo shamanism in the Upper Amazon.* Albuquerque, NM: University of New Mexico Press.

Bianchi, A. (1994). I mistici del vegetale: Piante psicotrope e stati alterati di coscienza nella selva Amazzonica [A mystical vegetation: Psychotropic plants and altered states of consciousness in the Amazon jungle]. *Quaderni de Parapsychologia, 25*(2), 43-58.

Bianchi, A. (1997). Comments on "The ketamine model of the near-death experience: A central role for the *N*-methyl-D-aspartate receptor". *Journal of Near-Death Studies, 16,* 71-78.

Bibra, Baron, E. von (1994). *Plant intoxicants.* Rochester, Vermont: Healing Arts Press. (originally published 1855).

Bierman, D. J. (1998, October). *The effects of THC and psilocybin on paranormal phenomena.* Paper presented at Psychoactivity: A Multidisciplinary Conference on Plants, Shamanism, and States of Consciousness, Amsterdam.

Billcock, V. A., & Tsou, B. H. (2012). Elementary visual hallucinations and their relationship to neural pattern formation. *Psychological Bulletin, 138,* 744-774.

Black, D. (2001). *Acid: A new secret history of LSD.* London: Vision Paperbacks.

Blackmore, S. J. (1982). Have you ever had an OBE: The wording of the question. *Journal of the Society for Psychical Research, 51,* 292-302.

Blackmore, S. J. (1984). A postal survey of OBEs and other experiences. *Journal of the Society for Psychical Research, 52,* 225-244.

Blackmore, S. J. (1986). Spontaneous and deliberate OBEs: A questionnaire survey. *Journal of the Society for Psychical Research, 53,* 218-224.

Blackmore, S. J. (1992). *Beyond the body: An investigation of out-of-the-body experiences.* Chicago, Illinois: Academy Chicago.

Blackmore, S. J. (2003). *Consciousness: An introduction.* London: Hodder & Stoughton.

Blackmore, S. J. (2005, May 21). I take illegal drugs for inspiration. *Daily Telegraph.*

Blackmore, S. J., & Harris, J. (1983). OBEs and perceptual distortions in schizophrenic patients and students. In W. G. Roll, J. Bellof, & R. A. White (Eds.), *Research in Parapsychology: Abstracts and Papers from the combined 25th Annual Convention of the Parapsychological Association and the Centenary Conference of the Society for Psychical Research, 1982* (pp. 232-234). Metuchen, NJ: Scarecrow Press.

Blake, W. (1906). *The marriage of heaven and hell.* Boston, MA: John W. Luce and Company. (Originally published 1973).

Blanke, O., & Dieguez, S. (2009). Leaving body and life behind: Out-of-body and near-death experience. In S. Laureys & G. Tononi (Eds.) *The neurology of consciousness: Cognitive neuroscience and neuropathology* (pp.303-325). New York: Academic Press.

Blewett, D. (1961a). Investigating the psychedelic experience. In Anon., *Proceedings on Two Conferences on Parapsychology and Pharmacology* (pp. 8-9). New York: Parapsychology Foundation.

Blewett, D. (1961b). LSD in psychiatric treatment. In Anon., *Proceedings of Two Conferences on Parapsychology and Pharmacology* (pp. 56-58). New York: Parapsychology Foundation.

Blewett, D. (1963). Psychedelic drugs in parapsychological research. *International Journal of Parapsychology, 5* (1), 43-74.

Blewett, D. (1965). ESP and LSD. *International Journal of Parapsychology, 7* (3), 306-311.

Blewett, D. B., & Chwelos, M. D. (1959). *A handbook for the therapeutic use of LSD-25: Individual and group procedures.* Saskatchewan, Canada: Published privately by the authors.

Bong Man (2006). *Take the Third Toke.* Retrieved on 9th June, 2009 from http://www.erowid.org/experiences/exp.php?ID=52797

Bonta, I. L. (2004). Schizophrenia, dissociative anesthesia and near-death experience: Three events meeting at the NMDA receptor. *Medical Hypotheses, 62,* 23-28.

Bourguignon, E. (1976). *Possession.* San Francisco, CA: Chandler & Sharp.

Boyce, M. (1975). *History of Zoroastrianism, Vol. I.* Leiden: Brill.

Brang, D., & Ramachandran, V. S. (2008). Psychopharmacology of synesthesia: The role of serotonin S2a receptor activation. *Medical Hypotheses, 70,* 903-904.

Brang, D., & Ramachandran, V. S. (2011). Survival of the synaesthesia gene: Why do people hear colors and taste words? *PLoS Biology, 9,* 11, e1001205.

Braude, S. E. (2002). The problem of super-psi. In F. Steinkamp (Ed.), *Parapsychology, philosophy and the mind: Essays honouring John Beloff* (pp. 91-111). Jefferson, NC: McFarland.

Braud, W. (2002). Psi favorable conditions. In V. G. Rammohan (Ed.), *New frontiers of human science: A festschrift for K. Ramakrishna Rao* (pp. 95-118). Jefferson, NC: McFarland.

Breederveld, H. (1976). Towards reproducible experiments in psychokinesis II: Experiments with a roulette apparatus. *Research Letter of the Parapsychology Laboratory of Utrecht, 7,* 6-9.

Breederveld, H. (2001). An adventure in casino gaming. *Paranormal Review, 19,* 34.

Breederveld, H. (2008). Chess with the dead? [letter to the editor]. *Journal of the Society for Psychical Research, 72,* 62.

Breslaw, D. (1961). A year of drug-taking. In D. Ebin (Ed.), *The drug experience: first-person accounts of addicts, writers, scientists and others.* New York: Orion.

Bresloff, P.C., Cowan, J.D., Golubitsky, M., Thomas, P.J., & Weiner, M.C. (2001). Geometric visual hallucinations, Euclidean symmetry and the functional architecture of the striate cortex. *Philosophical Transactions of the Royal Society London, 356,* 299-330.

Bressloff, P. C., Cowan, J. D., Golubitsky, M., Thomas, P. J., & Wiener, M. C. (2002). What geometric hallucinations tell us about the visual cortex? *Neural Computation, 14,* 473- 491.

Brewer, J. A., Worhunsky, P. D., Gray, J. R., Tang, Y-Y., Weber, J., & Kober, H. (2011). Meditation experience is associated with differences in default mode network activity and connectivity. *Proceedings of the National Academy of Sciences of the United States of America, 108*, 20254-20259.

Britton, W. B., & Bootzin, R. R. (2004). Near-death experience and the temporal lobe. *Psychological Science, 15*, 254-258.

Broad, C. D. (1962). *Lectures on psychical research.* London: Routledge & Kegen Paul.

Brown, D., DeG., (1994). *Umbanda: Religion and politics in urban Brazil.* New york: Columbia University Press.

Brown, D. J. (Ed.)(2009). Special issue: Psychedelics and ecology. *Bulletin of the Multidisciplinary Association for Psychedelic Studies, 19 (1).*

Brown, D. J. (2012a). LSD & ESP: Scientists study psychic phenomena and psychedelic drugs. *Santa Cruz Patch* (online), posted on 9 June, 2012, at http://santacruz.patch.com/articles/lsd-esp-scientists-study-psychic-phenomena-and-psychedelic-drugs

Brown, D. J. (2012b). Psychedelic medicines of the future: More undiscovered drugs than stars in the sky. *Santa Cruz Patch* (online), posted on 28 June, 2012, at http://santacruz.patch.com/articles/psychedelic-medicines-of-the-future-more-undiscovered-drugs-than-stars-in-the-sky

Brugger, P., & Mohr, C. (2008). The paranormal mind: How the study of anomalous experiences and beliefs may inform cognitive neuroscience. *Cortex, 44*, 1291-1298.

Bruhn, J. G., El-Seedi, H. R., Stephanson, N., Beck, O., & Shulgin, A.T. (2008). Ecstasy analogues found in cacti. *Journal of Psychoactive Drugs, 40* (2), 219-22.

Bruhn, J. G., Lindgren, J. E., Holmstedt, B., & Adovasio, J. M. (1978). Peyote alkaloids: Identification in a prehistoric specimen of *Lophophora* from Coahuila, Mexico. *Science, 199*, 1437-1438.

Burger, R. (1992). *Chavín and the origins of Andean civilisation.* London: Thames and Hudson.

Butt, A., Wavell, S., & Epton, N. (1966). *Trances.* London: George Allen & Unwin.

Cadoret, R. J. (1953). The effect of amytal and dexadrine on ESP performance. *Journal of Parapsychology, 17*, 259-274.

Callaway, J. C. (1988). A proposed mechanism for the visions of dream sleep. *Medical Hypotheses, 26*, 119-24.

Callaway, J. C. (2005). Various alkaloid profiles in decoctions of *Banisteriopsis caapi. Journal of Psychoactive Drugs, 37* (2), 151-155.

Callaway, J. C. (2006). Phytochemistry and neuropharmacology of ayahuasca. In R. Metzner (Eds.), *Sacred vine of the spirits: Ayahuasca* (pp. 94-116). Rochester, VT: Park Street.

Carbonaro, T. M., & Gatch, M. B. (2016). Neuropharmacology of *N,N*-dimethyltryptamine. *Brain Research Bulletin, 126*(1), 74-88.

Carbonaro, T. M., Johnson, M. W., & Griffiths, R. R. (2017). Comparison of anomalous experiences after ingesting mushrooms in research and non-research settings. *Drug and Alcohol Dependence, 171*, e34.

Cardeña, E. (2009). Anomalous experiences during deep hypnosis. In M. Smith (Ed.), *Anomalous experiences: Essays from parapsychological and psychological perspectives* (pp. 93-107). New York: Praeger.

Cardeña, E., Lynn, S. J., & Krippner, S. (2014). Introduction: Anomalous experiences in perspective. In E. Cardeña, S. J. Lynn and S. Krippner (Eds.), *Varieties of Anomalous Experience: Examining the Scientific Evidence* (2nd ed.)(pp.3-20). Washington, DC: American Psychological Association.

Carhart-Harris, R. (2011). *Using fMRI to investigate the effects of psilocybin on brain function*. Abstracts of papers presented at Breaking Convention: A Multidisciplinary Meeting on Psychedelic Consciousness, University of Kent, p.5.

Carhart-Harris, R. L., Erritzoe, D., Williams, T., Stone, J. M., Reed, L. J., Colasanti, A., Tyacke, R. J., Leech, R., Malizia, A. L., Murphy, K., Hobden, P., Evans, J., Feilding, A., Wise, R. G., & Nutt, D. J. (2012) Neural correlates of the psychedelic state as determined by fMRI studies with psilocybin. *Proceedings of the National Academy of Science, 109,* 2138- 2143.

Carhart-Harris, R.L., Williams, T. M., Sessa, B., Tyacke, R. J., Rich, A. S., Feilding, A., & Nutt, D. J. (2011). The administration of psilocybin to healthy, hallucinogen-experienced volunteers in a mock-functional magnetic resonance imaging environment: a preliminary investigation of tolerability. *Journal of Psychopharmacology, 25,* 1562-1567.

Carpenter, D. (2006). *A psychonaut's guide to the invisible landscape: The topography of the psychedelic experience*. Rochester, VT: Park Street Press.

Carr, B. (2008). Worlds apart?: Can psychical research bridge the gulf between matter and mind? *Proceedings of the Society for Psychical Research, 59*(221), 1-96.

Carroll, P. J. (1987). *Liber null and psychonaut: An introduction to chaos magic*. York Beach, Maine: Samuel Weiser.

Case, J. (2003). The community K-hole. *Entheogen Review, 12* (2), 58.

Castle, D, & Murray, R. (2004). *Marijuana and madness*. Cambridge: Cambridge University Press.

Cavanna, R. (1961). Biochemical factors of personality states. In Anon., *Proceedings of Two Conferences on Parapsychology and Pharmacology* (pp. 59-60). New York: Parapsychology Foundation.

Cavanna, R., & Servadio, E. (1964). *ESP experiments with LSD 25 and psilocybin. A methodological approach: Parapsychological monographs 5*. New York: Parapsychology Foundation.

Cemin, A. (1998). *Ordem, xamanismo e dádiva: o poder do Santo Daime*. Unpublished PhD thesis, Department of Anthropology, University of São Paulo.

Chagnon, N. A. (1992). *Case Studies in cultural anthropology: Yąnomamö*. Fort Worth, TX: Harcourt Brace Jovanovich.

Cheesman, J., & Merikle, P. M. (1986). Distinguishing conscious from unconscious visual processes. *Canadian Journal of Psychology, 40,* 343-367.

Cheyne, J. A. (2001). The ominous numinous: Sensed presence and 'other' hallucinations. *Journal of Consciousness Studies, 8* (5-7), 133-150.

Clark, M. (2017). *Soma, haoma, and ayahuasca*. London: Muswell Hill Press.

Cohen, E. (2008). What is spirit possession? Defining, comparing and explaining two possession forms. *Ethnos, 73*(1), 101-126.

Cohen, S. (1970). *Drugs of hallucination*. St. Albans, Herts., UK: Paladin.

Cohen Kadosh, R., Gertner, L., & Terhune, D. B. (2012). Exceptional abilities in the spatial representation of numbers and time: Insights from synaesthesia. *Neuroscientist, 18,* 208-215.

Conan Doyle. A. (1890). *The sign of the four*. London: Spencer Blackett.

Conrad, K. (1958). *Die beginnende Schizophrenie: Versuch einer gestaltanalyse des Wahns [The onset of schizophrenia: An experimental analysis of creative madness]*. Thieme, Stuttgart.

Constable, J. (1999). *The Southwark mysteries*. London: Oberon Books.

Conway, R. (1989). Lysergic acid and transpersonal experience. In G. K. Zollachan, J. F. Schumaker, & G. F. Walsh (Eds.), *Exploring the paranormal: Perspectives on belief and experience* (pp. 97-104). Dorset, UK: Prism Press.

Cooles, P. (1980). Abuse of the mushroom *Panaeolus foenisecii. British Medical Journal, 280,* 446-447.

Copley, B. (1962). *Hallucinogenic drugs and their application to extra-sensory perception.* Joshua Tree, CA: Hypnosophic Institute.

Corazza, O. (2002). Contributo alla discussione sulle potenzialità paranormali sviluppate da sostanze psicoattive: Uno studio sull'uso contemporeneo di ketamina [Contribution to the discussion of the paranormal potential of psychoactive substances: A study in contemporary use of ketamine]. *Quaderni de Parapsicologia, 33,* (2), 39-43.

Corazza, O. (2008). *Near-death experiences: Exploring the mind-body connection.* London: Routledge.

Corazza, O., & Schifano, F. (2010). Near-death states reported in a sample of 50 misusers. *Substance Use & Misuse, 45,* 916-924.

Cott, C., & Rock, A. J. (2008). Phenomenology of N,N-dimethyltryptamine use: A thematic analysis. *Journal of Scientific Exploration. 22*(3), 359-370.

Cowan, J. (2013*). A model of how geometric hallucinations are generated in the brain.* Invited lecture for the Imperial College and Beckley Foundation conference on Scientific Research with Psychedelic Drugs, Imperial College, London. 12th June.

Cozzi, N.V., Mavlyutov, T.A., Thompson, M.A., & Ruoho A.E. (2011). Indolethylamine N- methyltransferase expression in primate nervous tissue. *Society for Neuroscience Abstracts, 37,* 840.19.

Crookall. R. (1961). *Astral projection.* London: Aquarian Books.

Crookall, R. (1964). *More astral projections.* London: Aquarian Books.

Crookall. R. (1972). *A casebook of astral projection.* New Jersey: University Books.

Crosby, D. M., & McLaughlin, J. L. (1973). Cactus alkaloids XIX: Crystallization of mescaline HCl and 3-methoxytryptamine HCl from *Trichocereus pachanoi. Lloydia, 36* (4), 416-418.

Crowley, M. (1996). When the gods drank urine: A Tibetan myth may help solve the riddle of soma, sacred drug of ancient India. *Fortean Studies,* vol. 3.

Curran, H. V., & Morgan, C. (2000). Cognitive, dissociative and psychotogenic effects of ketamine in recreational users on the night of drug use and 3 days later. *Addiction, 95*(4), 575-590.

Cytowic, R. E. (1993). *The man who tasted shapes: A bizarre medical mystery offers revolutionary insights into emotions, reasoning, and consciousness.* New York: Tarcher/Putnam.

Cytowic, R. E., & Eagleman, D. M. (2009). *Wednesday is indigo blue: Discovering the brain of synaesthesia.* Cambridge, MA: MIT Press.

Daniels, M. (2005). *Shadow, self, spirit: Essays in transpersonal psychology.* Exeter: Imprint Academic.

Dawson, A. (2010). Taking possession of Santo Daime: The growth of Umbanda within a Brazilian new religion. In B. Schmidt and L. Huskinson (Eds.), *Spirit possession and trance: new interdisciplinary perspectives* (pp.134-150). London: Continuum.

Dawson, A. (2011). Spirit, self, society in the Brazilian new religion of Santo Daime. In A. Dawson (Ed.), *Summoning the spirits: Possession and invocation in contemporary religion* (pp.143-161). London: I. B. Taurus & Co.

Dawson, A. (2012). Spirit possession in a new religious context: The Umbandaization of Santo Daime. *Nova Religio: The Journal of Alternative and Emergent Religions, 15* (4), 60-84.

Dawson, D., & Encel, N. (2007). Melatonin and sleep in humans. *Journal of Pineal Research, 15,* 1-12.

Dawson, K. A. (2005). A psychedelic neurochemistry of time. *Bulletin of the Multidisciplinary Association for Psychedelic Studies, 15* (1), 27-29.

Dean, D. (1967). Parapsychological Association presidential address: Parapsychology and Dr. Einstein. *Journal of Parapsychology, 31*, 327-329.

De Feo, V. (1992). Medicinal and magical plants in the northern Peruvian Andes. *Fitotherapia, 63* (5), 417-440.

DeGracia, D. J. (1995). *Do psychedelic drugs mimic awakened kundalini? Hallucinogen survey results.* Retrieved October 27, 2004, from http://www.csp.org/practices/entheogens/docs/kundalini_survey.html

Dennett, D.C. (1991). *Consciousness explained.* Boston, MA: Little Brown.

Department of Health (2004). *The score: Facts about drugs.* London: Department of Health Publications.

de Rios, M. D., & Janiger, O. (2003). *LSD, spirituality and the creative process.* Rochester, VT: Park Street Press.

Deroy, O., & Spence, C. (2013). Why we are not all synesthetes (not even weakly so). *Psychonomic Bulletin and Review, 20*, 643-664.

Devereux, P. (1997). *The long trip: A prehistory of psychedelia.* New York: Penguin/ Arkana.

Devereux, P. (2008). *The long trip: A prehistory of psychedelia* (2nd ed.). Brisbane: Daily Grail Publishing.

Diamond Joe (2000). *Hyperspatial crossroads.* Retrieved on 9th June, 2009 from http:// www.erowid.org/experiences/exp.php?ID=2205

Díaz, J. L. (1979). Ethnopharmacology and taxonomy of Mexican psychodysleptic plants. *Journal of Psychedelic Drugs, 11* (1-2), 71-101.

Diaz-Mataix, L., Scorza, M. C., Bortolozzi, A., Toth, M., Celada, P., & Artigas, F. (2005). Involvement of 5-HT1A receptors in prefrontal cortex modulation of dopaminergic activity. *Journal of Neuroscience, 25*, 10831-10843.

Dietrich, A. (2003). Functional neuroanatomy of altered states of consciousness: The transient hypofrontality hypothesis. *Consciousness and Cognition, 12*, 231-156.

Ditman, K.S., Moss, T., Forgy, E.W., Zunin, L.M., Lynch, R.D., Funk, W.A. (1969). Dimensions of the LSD, methylphenidate and chlordiazepoxide experiences. *Psychopharmacologia, 14*, 1-11.

Dobkin de Rios, M. (1968). *Trichocereus pachanoi*: A mescaline cactus used in folk healing in Peru. *Economic Botany, 22*(2), 191-194.

Dobkin de Rios, M. (1977). Plant hallucinogens and the religion of the Mochica: An ancient Peruvian people. *Economic Botany, 31*, 189-203.

Dobkin de Rios, M. (1978). A psi approach to love magic, witchcraft and psychedelics in the Peruvian Amazon. *Phoenix: New Directions in the Study of Ma*n, 2, 22-27.

Dobkin de Rios, M. (1981). Saladerra: A culture-bound misfortune syndrome in the Peruvian Amazon. *Culture, Medicine and Psychiatry*, 5, 193-213.

Dobkin de Rios, M. (1984). The vidente phenomenon in third world traditional healing: An Amazonian example. *Medical Anthropology, 8*, 60-70.

Dobkin de Rios, M. (1996). *Hallucinogens: Cross-cultural perspectives.* Prospect Heights, IL: Waveland Press.

Dobkin de Rios, M., & Janiger, O. (2003). *LSD, spirituality, and the creative process*: *Based on the groundbreaking research of Oscar Janiger, M.D..* Rochester, VT: Park Street Press.

Dobkin de Rios, M., & Rumrrill, R. (2008). *A hallucinogenic tea, laced with controversy: Ayahuasca in the Amazon and the United States.* Westport, CT: Greenwood Press.

Doblin, R. (1991). Pahnke's Good Friday experiment: A long-term follow-up and methodological critique. *Journal of Transpersonal Psychology, 23*(1), 1-28.

Doblin, R. (2004, June). *Psychedelic and marijuana research: Politics and promise.* (Audio CDROM). Paper presented at the international conference Exploring Consciousness: With What Intent?, Bath Spa University, UK.

Domino, E. F., Warner, D. S. (2010). Taming the ketamine tiger. *Anesthesiology, 113,* 678-684.

Don, N. S., McDonough, B. E., Warren, C. A., & Moura, G. (1996). Psi, brain function, and "Ayahuasca" (telepathine). *Proceedings of Papers Presented at the 39th Parapsychology Association Annual Convention, San Diego,* 315-334.

Dowson, T.A. (2007). Debating shamanism in southern African rock art: Time to move on... *South African Archaeological Bulletin, 62*(185), 49-61.

Doyle, R. (2012). Healing with plant intelligence: A report from ayahuasca. *Anthropology of consciousness, 23,* 28-43.

Driver, H. (1969). *Indians of North America* (2nd ed., rev.). Chicago: University of Chicago Press.

Dronfield, J. (1996). The vision thing: Diagnosis of endogenous derivation in abstract arts. *Current Anthropology, 37*(2), 373-391.

Dunbar, E. (1905). Light thrown on psychological processes by the action of drugs. *Proceedings of the Society for Psychical Research, 19,* 62-77.

Dunne, B.J., & Jahn, R.G. (2003). Information and uncertainty in remote perception research. *Journal of Scientific Exploration, 17*(2), 207-41.

Durwin, J. (2001). *Dreamtime: Psycho-biological methodology and morphogenesis in the shamanic tradition.* Unpublished manuscript, Arizona State University.

Eagleman, D. M., Kagan, A. D., Nelson, S. S., Sagaram, D., & Sarma, A. K. (2007). A standardized test battery for the study of synesthesia. *Journal of Neuroscience Methods, 159,* 139-145.

Eastman, M. (1962). Out-of-the-body experiences. *Proceedings of the Society for Psychical Research, 53,* 287-309.

Echenhofer, F. (2005). Ayahuasca/EEG research progress report and invitation to donate. *Bulletin of the Multidisciplinary Association for Psychedelic Studies, 15* (1), 19-20.

Eckblad, M., & Chapman, L. J. (1983). Magical ideation as an indicator of schizotypy. *Journal of Consulting and Clinical Psychology, 51,* 215-225.

Edge, H. L., Morris, R. L., Palmer, J., & Rush, J. H. (1986). *Foundations of parapsychology: Exploring the boundaries of human capability.* London: Routledge and Kegan Paul.

Eisenbeiss, W., & Hassler, D. (2006). An assessment of ostensible communications with a deceased grandmaster as evidence for survival. *Journal of the Society for Psychical Research, 70,* 65-97.

Eisner, Betty G. (1995). Physical and psychical loading (Abstract from the Fourteenth Annual Meeting of the Society for Scientific Exploration). *Journal of Scientific Exploration, 9,* 45.

Eisner, Bruce (1989). *Ecstasy: The MDMA story.* Berkeley, CA: Ronin Publishing.

Eliade, M. (1972). *Shamanism: Archaic techniques of ecstasy.* Princeton, NJ: Princeton University Press. (Originally published in French in 1951).

Ellis, H. (1898). Mescal: A new artificial paradise. *The Contemporary Review, 73,* 130-141.

El-Seedi, H. R., De Smet, P. A., Beck, O, Possnert, G., & Bruhn, J. G. (2005). Prehistoric peyote use: Alkaloid analysis and rediocarbon dating of archaeological specimens of Lophophora from Texas. *Journal of Enthnopharmacology, 101*(1-3), *238-242.*

Ermentrout, G. B., & Cowan, J. D. (1979). A mathematical theory of visual hallucination patterns. *Biological Cybernetics, 34,* 137-150.

Erowid, F. (2001). A look at the mescaline content of *T. peruvianus* and *T. panchanoi. Erowid Extracts, 2,* 20-21.

Erowid (2008). The distillation. *Erowid Extracts, 15* (November), 22-5.

Erowid, E., & Erowid, F. (2006). The value of experience. Erowid's collection of first-person psychoactive reports. *Erowid Extracts, 10* (June), 14-9.

Esterman, M., Verstynen, T., Ivry, R. B., & Robertson, L. C. (2006). Coming unbound: disrupting automatic integration of synesthetic color and graphemes by transcranial magnetic stimulation of the right parietal lobe. *Journal of Cognitive Neuroscience, 18,* 1570-1576.

Evans, S., Almahdi, B., Sultan, P., Sohanpal, I., Brandner, B., Collier, T., Shergill, S. S., Cregg, R., & Averbeck, B. B. (2012). Performance on a probabilistic inference task in healthy subjects receiving ketamine compared with patients with schizophrenia. *Journal of Psychopharmacology 26,* 1211, (published online 2 March 2012).

Evans-Wentz, W. Y. (2004). *The fairy-faith in Celtic countries.* Franklin Lakes, NJ: Career Press (originally published in 1911).

Exman, E. (1961). Individual and group experiences. In Anon., *Proceedings of Two Conferences on Parapsychology and Pharmacology* (pp. 10-13). New York: Parapsychology Foundation.

Farber, P. (2000). MDMA and hypnotic anchoring. In T. Lyttle. (Ed.), *Psychedelics reimagined* (pp.87-90). Brooklyn, NY: Autonomedia.

Fenwick, P. (1997). Is the near-death experience only *N*-methyl-D-aspartate blocking? *Journal of Near-Death Studies, 16,* 42-53.

Fontanilla, D., Johannessen, M., Hajipour, A., Cozzi, N. V., Jackson, M. B., & Ruoho, A. E. (2009). The hallucinogen N,N-diemthyltryptamine (DMT) is an endogenous sigma-1 receptor regulator. *Science, 323,* 934-937.

Fotiou, E. (2012). Working with "la medicina": Elements of healing in contemporary ayahuasca rituals. *Anthropology of Consciousness, 23,* 6-27.

Fracasso, C., & Friedman, H. (2011). Near-death experiences and the possibility of disembodied consciousness: Challenges to prevailing neurobiological and psychosocial theories. *NeuroQuantology, 9,* 41-53.

Frecska, E. (2008). The shaman's journey: Supernatural or natural? A neuro-ontological interpretation of spiritual experiences. In R. Strassman, S. Wojtowicz, L.E. Luna and E. Frecska, *Inner paths to outer space: Journeys to alien worlds through psychedelics and other spiritual technologies* (pp.162-206.). Rochester, VT: Park Street Press.

Frecska, E., Móré, C. E., Vargha, A., & Luna, L. E. (2012). Enhancement of creative expression and entoptic phenomena as after-effects of repeated ayahuasca ceremonies. *Journal of Psychoactive Drugs, 44*(3), 191-199.

Frecska, E., Szabo, A., Winkelman, M. J., Luna, L. E., & McKenna, D. J. (2013). A possibly sigma-1 receptor mediated role of dimethyltryptamine in tissue protection, regeneration, and immunity. *Journal of Neural Transmission, 120,* 1295-1303.

Frederiks, J. A. M. (1963). Macrosomatognosia and microsomatognosia. *Psychiatria, Neurologia, Neurochirurgia, 66,* 531-536.

Frenopoulo, C. (2006). Healing in the Barquinha religion. *Fieldwork in Religion, 2*(3), 363-392.

Friedberg, C. (1959). Rapport sommaire sur une mission au Pérou. *Journal d'Agriculture Tropicale et de Botanique Appliquée, 6*, 439-450.

Friedman, H. (1983). The Self-Expansiveness Level Form: A conceptualization and measurement of a transpersonal construct. *The Journal of Transpersonal Psychology, 15*, 37-50.

Friedman, H. (2006). The renewal of psychedelic research: Implications for humanistic and transpersonal psychology. *The Humanistic Psychologist, 34*(1), 39-58.

Friedman, S. M., & Fisher, C. (1960). Further observations of on primary modes of perception: The use of a masking technique for subliminal visual stimulation. *Journal of the American Psychoanalytic Association, 8*, 100-129.

Froese, T., Woodward, A., & Isegami, T. (2013). Turing instabilities in biology, culture, and consciousness? On the enactive origins of symbolic material culture. *Adaptive Behaviour, 21*(3), 199-214.

Gaiman, N., Keith, S., Dringenberg, M., & Jones III, M. (1991). The *Sandman: Preludes and nocturnes*. New York: DC Comics

Gallagher, C., Kumar, V. K., & Pekala, R. J. (1994). The anomalous experiences inventory: Reliability and validity. *Journal of Parapsychology, 58*, 402-428.

Gallimore, A. (2013). Building alien worlds: The neuropsychological and evolutionary implications of the astonishing psychoactive effects of *N,N*-dimethyltryptamine (DMT). *Journal of Scientific Exploration, 27* (3), 455-503.

Gallimore, A., & Luke, D. (2015). DMT research from 1956 to the end of time. In D. King, D. Luke, B. Sessa, C. Adams and A. Tollen (Eds), *Neurotransmissions: Psychedelic essays from Breaking Convention* (pp.291-316). London: Strange Attractor Press.

Garrett, E. J. (1961a). Patterns of clairvoyance. In Anon., *Proceedings on Two Conferences on Parapsychology and Pharmacology* (pp. 14-16). New York: Parapsychology Foundation.

Garrett, E. J. (1961b). Psychopharmacological parallels to mediumship. *Proceedings on Two Conferences on Parapsychology and Pharmacology* (pp. 61-63). New York: Parapsychology Foundation.

Garrison, K. A., Zeffiro, T. A., Scheinost, D., Constable, R. T., & Brewer, J. A. (2015). Meditation leads to reduced default mode network activity beyond an active task. *Cognitive Affective Behavioural Neuroscience, 15*(3), 712-720.

Gaskin, S. (1990). *Haight-Ashbury flashbacks* (2nd ed.). Berkeley, CA: Ronin Publishing.

Gauld, A. (1983). *Mediumship and survival: A century of investigations*. London: Paladin.

Gautier, T. (1843, July 10). Le club des hachichins. *La Presse.*

Gelfer, J. (2007). Towards a sacramental understanding of dextromethorphan. *Journal of Alternative Spiritualities and New Age Studies, 3*, 80-96.

Giesler, P. (1984). Parapsychological anthropology: I. Multi-method approaches to the study of psi in the field setting. *Journal of the American Society for Psychical Research, 78*, 287-328.

Giesler, P. (1985). Parapsychological anthropology: II. A multi-method study of psi and psi-related processes in the Umbanda ritual trance consultation. *Journal of the American Society for Psychical Research, 79*, 113-66.

Glass-Coffin, B. (1999). Engendering Peruvian shamanism through time: Insights from ethnohistory and ethnography. *Ethnohistory, 46* (2), 205-238.

Glass-Coffin, B. (2000). The meaning of experience: Theoretical dilemmas in depicting a Peruvian curandera's philosophy of healing. *Method and Theory in the Study of Religion, 12*, 226-237.

González, D., Riba, J., Bouso, J. C., Gómez-Jaraboa, G., & Barbanoj, M. J. (2006). Pattern of use and subjective effects of *Salvia divinorum* among recreational users. *Drug and Alcohol Dependence, 85*, 157-162.

González-Maeso, J., Ang, R. L., Yuen, T., Chan, P., Weisstaub, N. V., López-Giménez, J. F., Zhou, M., Okawa, Y., Callado, L. F., Milligan, G., Gingrich, J. A., Filizola, M., Meana, J. J., & Sealfon, S. C. (2008). Identification of a serotonin/glutamate receptor complex implicated in psychosis (letter to editor). *Nature (online), 24 February, 2008.*

Gorman, P. (1992). Journeys with ayahuasca, the vine of the little death. *Shaman's Drum, 29*, 49-58.

Goulart, S. L. (2006). Religious matrices of the União do Vegetal. *Fieldwork in Religion, 2*(3), 286-318.

Goutarel, R., Gollnhofer, O., & Sillans, R. (1993). Pharmacodynamics and therapeutic applications of iboga and ibogaine. *Psychedelic Monographs & Essays, 6*, 70-111.

Gowan, J. C. (1975). *Trance, art, and creativity*. Buffalo, NY: State University College.

Graves, R. (1961). *The white goddess: A historical grammar of poetic myth*. London: Faber and Faber.

Greeley, A. M. (1974). *Ecstasy: A way of knowing*. Englewood Cliffs, NJ: Prentice-Hall.

Grey, A. (2007). *Chapel of sacred mirrors: COSM tour book*. Wappingers Falls, NY: CoSM Press.

Greyson, B. (2000). Near-death experiences. In E. Cardeña, S. J. Lynn, & S. Krippner (Eds.), *Varieties of anomalous experience: Examining the scientific evidence* (pp. 315-352). Washington, DC: American Psychological Association.

Griffiths, R. R., Johnson, M. W., Richards, W. A., Richards, B. D. McCann, U., & Jesse, R. (2011). Psilocybin occasioned mystical-type experiences: Immediate and persisting dose-related effects. *Psychopharmacology, 218*(4), 649-665.

Griffiths, R. R., Richards, W. A., McCann, U., & Jesse, R. (2006). Psilocybin can occasion mystical-type experiences having substantial and sustained personal meaning and spiritual significance. *Psychopharmacology, 187*, 268-83.

Grinspoon, L., & Bakalar, J. (1979). *Psychedelic drugs reconsidered*. New York: Basic Books.

Grinspoon, L., & Bakalar, J. B. (1998) *Psychedelic drugs reconsidered* (2nd ed.). New York: The Lindesmith Centre.

Grob, C., & Harman. W. (1995). Making sense of the psychedelic issue: Federal approval for research into psychedelics resumes. *Noetic Sciences Review, 35*, 4-19.

Grof, S. (1970). *Subjective experiences during the LSD training session*. Unpublished manuscript, available at http://www.maps.org/research/cluster/psilo-lsd/grof1970.pdf

Grof, S. (1975). *Realms of the human unconscious: Observations from LSD research*. NY: Viking Press.

Grof, S. (1980). *LSD psychotherapy*. CA: Hunter House.

Grof, S. (1990). Survival after death: Observations from modern consciousness research. In G. Doore (Ed.), *What survives? Contemporary explanations of life after death*. (pp. 22-33). Los Angeles: Tarcher.

Grof, S. (1994). Alternative cosmologies and altered states. *Noetic Sciences Review, 32*, 21.

Grof, S. (2001). *LSD psychotherapy* (3rd ed.). Sarasota, FL: Multidisciplinary Association for Psychedelic Studies.

Grof, S. (2004). Stanislav Grof interviewing Dr. Albert Hofmann at the Esalen Institute in Big Sur, California, 1984. In P. Peet (Ed.), *Under the influence: The disinformation guide to drugs* (pp. 284-295). New York: The Disinformation Company.

Grof, S., & Grof, C. (2010). *Holotropic breathwork: A new approach to self-exploration and therapy*. Albany, New York: State University of New York Press.

Groisman, A. (2013). *Ayahuasca religions, mediumship and religious agency: Health and the fluency of social relations*. Paper presented at Breaking Convention: The 2nd Multidisciplinary Conference on Psychedelic Consciousness, University of Greenwich, London, 12-14 July.

Grosso, M. (1976). Some varieties of out-of-body experience. *Journal of American Society for Psychical Research, 70*, 179-193.

Hagenbach, D., & Wertmüller, L. (2013). *Mystic chemist: The life of Albert Hofmann and his discovery of LSD*. Santa Fe, NM: Synergetic Press.

Halliday, J. L. (1961). The practice of active introversion. In Anon., *Proceedings of Two Conferences on Parapsychology and Pharmacology* (pp. 64-66). New York: Parapsychology Foundation.

Hameroff, S., & Chopra, D. (2010). End-of-life brain activity: A sign of the soul? *Huffington Post*, 16 August, 2012 - http://www.huffingtonpost.com/deepak-chopra/end-of-life-brain-activit_b_684176.html

Hancock, G. (2005). *Supernatural: Meetings with the ancient teachers of mankind*. London: Century.

Hanna, J. (1998). Alex Grey speaks... *The Entheogen Review, 7* (4), 17-22.

Hanna, J. (2003). *Drug inspired metaphysical concepts*. Talk given at Burning Man festival, available on audio from http://www.matrixmasters.com/podcasts/Jon-Hanna/JonHanna-BurningMan2003.mp3

Hanna, J. (2010). *DMT and the pineal: Fact or fiction?* Uploaded 3rd June 2010 on www.erowid.org/chemicals/dmt/dmt_article2.shtml

Harman, W. (1963). Some aspects of the psychedelic drug controversy. *Journal of Humanistic Psychology, 3*, 93-107.

Harman, W. W. (1993). Towards an adequate epistemology for the scientific exploration of consciousness. *Journal of Scientific Exploration, 7*, 133-143.

Harner, M. (1972). *The Jivaro: People of the sacred waterfalls*. Berkeley, CA: University of California Press.

Harner, M. J. (1973a). Common themes in South American Indian yagé experiences. In M. J. Harner (Ed.), *Hallucinogens and shamanism* (pp.155-175). New York: Oxford University Press.

Harner, M. J. (1973b). The role of hallucinogenic plants in European witchcraft. In M. J. Harner (Ed.), *Hallucinogens and shamanism* (pp.125-150). New York: Oxford University Press.

Harrison, K., Straight, J., Pendell, D., & Stamets, P. (2007). Plant spirit. In J. P. Harpingnies (Ed.), *Visionary plant consciousness: The shamanic teachings of the plant world* (pp. 133-145). Rochester, VT: Park Street Press.

Hartman, A. M., & Hollister, L. E. (1963). Effect of mescaline, lysergic acid diethylamide and psilocybin on color perception. *Psychopharmacologia, 4*, 441-451.

Harvey, G. (2005). An Animist manifesto. *Strange Attractor Journal, 2*, 124-129

Harvey-Wilson, S. (2001). Shamanism and alien abductions: A comparative study. *Australian Journal of Parapsychology, 1*, 103-116.

Hastings, A. C. (1973). *Psychical Research*. Menlo Park, CA: Center for the Study of Social Policy, Stanford Research Institute.

Hastings, A. (2006). An extended nondrug MDMA-like experience evoked through posthypnotic suggestion. *Journal of Psychoactive Drugs, 38*, 273-283.

Hastings, A., Berk, I., Cougar, M., Ferguson, E., Giles, S., Steinbach-Humphrey, S., McLellan, K., Mitchell, C, & Viglizzo, B. (2000). An extended non-drug MD-MA-like experience evoked through hypnotic suggestion. *Bulletin of the Multidisciplinary Association for Psychedelic Studies, 10* (1), 10.

Hausner, S. L. (2016). *The spirits of Crossbones graveyard.* Bloomington, IN: Indiana University Press.

Heaven, R. (2009). *The hummingbird's journey to God: Perspectives on San Pedro, the cactus of vision.* Poole, Dorset: O Books.

Heffter, A. (1898). Über pellote. Beiträge zur chemicschen und pharmacologischen Kenntnis der Cacteen. Zweite Mittheilung. *Archiv für Experimentelle Pathologie und Pharmacologie, 40,* 385-429.

Heim, R., & Wasson, R. G. (1958). *Les champignons hallucinogènes du Mexique: études ethnologiques, taxinomiques, biologiques, physiologiques et chimiques.* Paris: Muséum national d'histoire naturelle

Helmholtz, H., von. (1925). Helmholtz's treatise on physiological optics (Translated from the third German edition of *Handbuch der physiologischen optik*, by J. P.C. Southall). Washington, DC: The Optical Society of America.

Hermans, H. G. M. (1998). *Memories of a maverick.* Maassluis, Netherlands: Pi.

Heywood, R. (1961). Personality changes under mescaline. In Anon., *Proceedings of Two Conferences on Parapsychology and Pharmacology* (pp. 72-73). New York: Parapsychology Foundation.

Heywood, R. (1978). *The sixth sense: An inquiry into extra-sensory perception* (2nd ed.). Harmondsworth, Middlesex, UK: Penguin Books.

Hill, D. R., & Persinger, M. A. (2003). Application of transcerebral, weak (1 microT) complex magnetic fields and mystical experiences: Are they generated by field-induced dimethyltryptamine release from the pineal organ? *Perceptual and Motor Skills, 97,* 1049-1050.

Hirst, M. (2000). Root, dream and myth. The use of the oneirogenic plant *Silene capensis* among the Xhosa of South Africa. *Eleusis: Journal of Psychoactive Plants and Compounds, 4,* 121-149.

Hirst, M. (2005). Dreams and medicines: The perspective of Xhosa diviners and novices in the Eastern Cape, South Africa. *Indo-Pacific Journal of Phenomenology, 5* (2), 1-22.

Hirukawa, T., Hiraoka, R., da Silva, F. E., Pilato, S., & Kokubo, H. (2006). Field REG experiments of religious rituals and other group events in Paraná, Brazil. *Livro de Registro de Trabalhos Apresentados, 3 Encontro Psi, Implicações e Aplicações da Psi [Proceedings of Presented Papers, 3rd Psi Meeting: Implications and Applications of Psi],* Curitiba: Faculdades Integradas "Espírita", Curitiba, Brazil, 17-26.

Ho, B. T. (1977). Pharmacological and biochemical studies with beta-carboline analogs. *Current Developments in Psychopharmacology, 4,* 151-177.

Hochel, M., & Milán, E. G. (2008). Synaesthesia: the existing state of affairs *Cognitive Neuropsychology, 25,* 93-117.

Hoffer, A. (1961a). Non-statistical research techniques. In Anon., *Proceedings of Two Conferences on Parapsychology and Pharmacology* (pp. 17-18). New York: Parapsychology Foundation.

Hoffer, A. (1961b). Pharmacological stimuli to sensitivity. *Proceedings of Two Conferences on Parapsychology and Pharmacology* (pp. 69-71). New York: Parapsychology Foundation.

Hofmann, A. (1983). *LSD my problem child: Reflections on sacred drugs, mysticism, and science.* Los Angeles: Jeremy P. Tarcher.

Hofmann, A., Broeckers, M., & Liggenstorfer, R. (2009). When one lives in paradise one is in no hurry to leave. In A. Feilding (Ed.), *Hofmann's elixir: LSD and the new Eleusis: Talks and essays by Albert Hofmann and others* (pp. 1-14). Oxford: Beckley Foundation / Strange Attractor Press.

Hollister, L. E., & Hartman, A. M. (1962). Mescaline, lysergic acid diethylamide and psilocybin: comparison of clinical syndromes, effects on colour perception and biochemical measures. *Comprehensive Psychiatry, 3(4)*, 235-241.

Holt, N. J., Simmonds-Moore, C., Luke, D., & French, C. C. (2012). *Anomalistic psychology.* Basingstoke, UK: Palgrave Macmillan.

Holt, N.J., Simmonds-Moore, C.A., & Moore, S.L. (2008). *Psi, belief in the paranormal, attentional filters and mental health.* Paper presented at the Bial Foundation Convention, Porto, Portugal.

Holzinger, R. (1964). LSD 25: A tool in psychotherapy. *Journal of General Psychology, 71*, 9-20.

Honorton, C. (1977). Psi and internal attention states. In B. B. Wolman (Ed.), *Handbook of Parapsychology* (pp. 435-72). New York: Van Nostrand Rheinhold.

Honorton, C., & Ferrari, D.C. (1989). Future telling: A meta-analysis of forced choice precognition experiments, 1935-1987. *Journal of Parapsychology, 53*, 281-308.

Horn, S. (2009). *Unbelievable: Investigations into ghosts, poltergeists, telepathy, and other unseen phenomena, from the Duke parapsychology laboratory.* New York: Ecco Press.

Horner, C. (2012). *The university of the forest: Plant spirits in ayahuasca shamanism.* Unpublished masters thesis, University of Colorado, CO.

Houran, J., & Lange, R. (2001). Support for the construct validity of the two-factor conceptualization of paranormal belief: A complement to Thalbourne. *European Journal of Parapsychology, 16*, 53-61.

Houran, J., & Williams, C. (1998). Relation of tolerance of ambiguity to global and specific paranormal experience. *Psychological Reports, 83*, 807-818.

Hubbard, E. M., Brang, D., & Ramachandran, V. S. (2011). The cross-activation theory at 10. *Journal of Neuropsychology, 5*, 152-177.

Hubbard, E. M., & Ramachandran, V. S. (2003). Refining the experimental lever: A reply to Shanon & Pibram. *Journal of Consciousness Studies, 10* (3), 77-84.

Huby, P. M., & Wilson, C. W. M. (1961). The effects of centrally acting drugs on ESP ability in normal subjects. *Journal of the Society for Psychical Research, 41*, 60-67.

Hurst, W. (1994). Report from the Telluride mushroom conference, Colorado, August 26-29, 1994. *Bulletin of the Multidisciplinary Association for Psychedelic Studies, 5 (3)*, 33-38.

Huxley, A. (1954). *The doors of perception.* London: Chatto & Windus, Ltd.

Huxley, F. (1961a). Increase in awareness and suggestibility. In Anon., *Proceedings of Two Conferences on Parapsychology and Pharmacology* (pp. 72-73). New York: Parapsychology Foundation.

Huxley, F. (1961b). States of suggestibility. In Anon., *Proceedings of Two Conferences on Parapsychology and Pharmacology* (pp. 19-21). New York: Parapsychology Foundation.

Huxley, F. (1966). *The invisibles: Voodoo Gods in Haiti.* New York: McGraw-Hill.

Hyman, R. (1995). Evaluation of the program on anomalous mental phenomena. *Journal of Parapsychology, 59*(4), 321-51.

International Foundation for Advanced Study. (1962). *Research report No. 1: Questionnaire study of the psychedelic experience.* Menlo Park, CA: Author.

Irwin, H. J. (1985). *Flight of mind: A psychological study of the out-of-body experience*. Metuchen, NJ: Scarecrow Press.

Irwin, H. J. (1994). *An introduction to parapsychology* (2nd ed.). NC: McFarland & Co.

Irwin, H. (2009). *The psychology of paranormal belief: A researcher's handbook*. Hatfield: University of Hertfordshire Press.

Jackson, N., & Howard, M. (2000). *The pillars of Tubal Cain*. Somerset, UK: Capall Bann.

Jacob, M. S., & Presti, D. E. (2005). Endogenous psychoactive tryptamines reconsidered: An anxiolytic role for dimethyltryptamine. *Medical Hypotheses, 64*, 930-937.

James, W. (1902/1985). *Varieties of religious experience*. Cambridge, MA: Harvard University Press.

James, W. (2003). *Essays in radical empiricism*. Mineola, New York: Dover. (originally published in 1912).

Jansen, K. L. R. (1990). Neuroscience and the near-death experience: Roles for the NMDA-PCP receptor, the sigma receptor, and the endopsychosins. *Medical Hypotheses, 31*, 25-29.

Jansen, K. L. R. (1997a). The ketamine model of the near-death experience: A central role for the NMDA receptor. *Journal of Near-Death Studies, 16*, 5-26.

Jansen, K. L. R. (1997b). Response to commentaries on "The ketamine model of the near-death experience…". *Journal of Near-Death Studies, 16*, 79-95.

Jansen, K. L. R. (1999). Ketamine (K) and quantum psychiatry. *Asylum: The Journal for Democratic Psychiatry, 11* (3), 19-21.

Jansen, K. [L. R.] (2001). *Ketamine: Dreams and realities*. Sarasota, FL: Multidisciplinary Association for Psychedelic Studies.

Jansen, K. [L. R.] (2004). What can ketamine teach us about ordinary and altered states of consciousness? *Consciousness Research Abstracts from the Toward a Science of Consciousness Conference, Tucson, Arizona*, 90.

Jay, M. (2005). Enter the jaguar: Psychedelic temple cults of ancient Peru. *Strange Attractor Journal, 2*, 17-34.

Jocik, Z. (2008a). The wrath of the forgotton Ongons: Shamanic sickness, spirit embodiment and fragmentary trancescape in contemporary Buriat shamanism. *Sibirica, 7* (1), 23-50.

Jokic, Z. (2008b). Yanomami shamanic initiation: The meaning of death and postmortem consciousness in transformation. *Anthropology of Consciousness, 19* (1), 33-59.

Johns, L. C., Cannon, M. S., Singleton, N., Murray, R. M., Farrell, M., Brugha, T., Bebbington, P., Jenkins, R., & Meltzer, H. (2004). Prevalence and correlates of self-reported psychotic symptoms in the British population. *British Journal of Psychiatry, 185* (10), 298-305.

Johnson, R. C. (1955). *Psychical research*. London: English Universities Press.

Jungle Girl (2008). *When light exists in darkness*. Retrieved on 9th June, 2009 from http://www.erowid.org/experiences/exp.php?ID=70143

Juszczak, G. R. (2012). Hallucinatory telepathic experiences induced by *Salvia divinorum*. *Journal of Scientific Exploration, 26*(2), 33-43.

Kaiser, D. (2011). *How the hippies saved physics: Science, counterculture and the quantum revival*. New York: W. W. Norton & Company.

Kappers, J. (1983). Screening for good ESP subjects with object-reading. In W. G. Roll, J. Bellof, & R. A. White (Eds.), *Research in Parapsychology: Abstracts and Papers from the combined 25th Annual Convention of the Parapsychological*

Association and the Centenary Conference of the Society for Psychical Research, 1982 (pp. 150-151). Metuchen, NJ: Scarecrow Press.

Kapur, S., & Seeman, P. (2002). NMDA receptor antagonists ketamine and PCP have direct effects on the dopamine D(2) and serotonin 5-HT(2) receptors: Implications for models of schizophrenia. *Molecular Psychiatry, 7*, 837-844.

Kärkkäinen J., Forsström T., Tornaeus J., Wähälä K., Kiuru P., Honkanen A., Stenman U.-H., Turpeinen U., & Hesso A. (2005). Potentially hallucinogenic 5-hydroxytryptamine receptor ligands bufotenine and dimethyltryptamine in blood and tissues. *Scandinavian Journal of Clinical and Laboratory Investigation, 65*(3), 189-199.

Kastrup, B. (2012). A paradigm-breaking hypothesis for solving the mind-body problem. *Paranthropology, 3*(3), 4-12.

Katzung, B. G., Masters, S. B., & Trevor, A. J. (2012). *Basic and clinical pharmacology (12th ed.)*. New York: McGraw-Hill Medical

Kehoe, A. B., & Giletti, D. H. (1981). Women's preponderance in possession cults: The calcium deficiency hypothesis extended. *American Anthropologist New Series, 83*(3), 549-561

Kelly, E. L. (1934). An experimental attempt to produce artificial chromaesthesia by the technique of conditioned response. *Journal of Experimental Psychology, 17*, 315-341.

Kelly, E. F., Kelly, E. W., Crabtree, A., Gauld, A., Grosso, M., & Greyson, B. (2007). *Irreducible mind: Toward a psychology for the 21st century*. Plymouth, UK: Rowman & Littlefield.

Kensinger, K. M. (1973). Banisteriopsis usage among the Peruvian Cashinahua. In M. J. Harner (Ed.), *Hallucinogens and shamanism* (pp. 9-14). Oxford: Oxford University Press.

Kent, J. (2005). The case against DMT elves. In C. Pickover (Ed.), *Sex, drugs Einstein, and elves* (pp.102-105). Smart Publications: Petaluma, CA.

Kent, J. L. (2010) *Psychedelic information theory: Shamanism in the age of reason.* Seattle, WA: PIT Press.

Kern, M.D. (1964). The University of California Extension Division Liberal Arts Conference: Seminar on psychical research and the psychedelic drugs. *Journal of the American Society for Psychical Research, 58*, 75-76.

Kjellgren, A., & Norlander, T. (2000-2001). Psychedelic drugs: A study of drug-induced experiences obtained by illegal drug users in relation to Stanislav Grof's model of altered states of consciousness. *Imagination, Cognition and Personality, 20*(1), 41-57.

Kjellgren, A., & Soussan, C. (2011). Heaven and Hell: A phenomenological study of recreational use of 4-HO-MET in Sweden. *Journal of Psychoactive Drugs, 43*, 211-219.

Klass, M. (2003). *Mind over mind: The anthropology and psychology of spirit possession.* Lanham, MD: Rowman & Littlefield.

Kohr, R. L. (1980). A survey of psi experiences among members of a special population. *Journal of the American Society for Psychical Research, 74*, 395-411.

Klüver, H., (1926). Mescal visions and eidetic vision. *American Journal of Psychology, 37*(4), October, 502-15.

Klüver, H. (1966). *Mescal and mechanisms of hallucinations*. Chicago, IL: University of Chicago Press.

Kottmeyer, M. S. (1999). Graying mantis. *The REALL News* (online), 7 (5) - retrieved 17 September, 2010 from http://www.reall.org/newsletter/v07/n05/graying-mantis.html

Kolp, E., Young, M. S., Friedman, H., Krupitsky, E., Jansen, K., & O'Connor L. (2007). Ketamine enhanced psychotherapy: Preliminary clinical observations on its effectiveness in treating death anxiety. *International Journal of Transpersonal Studies, 26*, 1-17.

Krebs, T.S. & Johansen, P.Ø. (2013). Over 30 million psychedelic users in the United States. *F1000 Research, 2*, 98.

Krill, A.E., Alpert, H.J., & Ostfeld, A.M. (1963). Effects of a hallucinogenic agent in totally blind subjects. *Archives of Ophthalmology, 69*, February, 180-5.

Krippner, S. (1967). The cycle of deaths among U.S. presidents elected at twenty-year intervals. *International Journal of Parapsychology, 9* (3), 145-153.

Krippner, S. (1985). Psychedelic drugs and creativity. *Journal of Psychoactive Drugs, 17* (4), 235-245.

Krippner, S. (1999). A pilot study in dream telepathy with the Grateful Dead. In R. G. Weiner (Ed.), *Perspectives on the Grateful Dead: Critical writings* (pp. 11-17). Westport, CT: Greenwood Press.

Krippner, S. (2000). The epistemology and technologies of shamanic states of consciousness. *Journal of Consciousness Studies, 7*(11-12), 93-118.

Krippner, S. (2006a, January). *LSD and parapsychological experiences.* Paper presented at LSD: Problem Child and Wonder Drug, an International Symposium on the Occasion of the 100th Birthday of Albert Hofmann, 13-15 January, Basel, Switzerland.

Krippner, S. (2006b, January). *The Future of Religion.* Paper presented at LSD: Problem Child and Wonder Drug, an International Symposium on the Occasion of the 100th Birthday of Albert Hofmann, 13-15 January, Basel, Switzerland.

Krippner, S., & Davidson, R. (1970). Religious implications of paranormal events occurring during chemically-induced 'psychedelic' experience. *Pastoral Psychology, 21*, 27-34.

Krippner, S., & Davidson, R. (1974). Paranormal events occurring during chemically-induced psychedelic experience and their implications for religion. *Journal of Altered States of Consciousness, 1*, 175-184.

Krippner, S., & Fersch, D. (1970). Paranormal experiences among members of American contra-cultural groups. *Journal of Psychedelic Drugs, 3*, 109-114.

Krippner, S., Honorton, C., & Ullman, M. (1973). An experiment in dream telepathy with "The Grateful Dead". *Journal of the American Society for Psychosomatic Dentistry and Medicine, 20*, 9-18.

Krippner, S., & Luke, D. (2009). Psychedelics and species connectedness. *Bulletin of the Multidisciplinary Association for Psychedelic Studies, 19 (1)*, 12-15.

Krummenacher, P., Brugger, P., Fahti, M., Mohr, C. (2002). *Dopamine, paranormal ideation, and the detection of meaningful stimuli.* Poster presented at the 3rd Forum of European Neuroscience, Paris, France.

Krummenacher, P., Mohr, C., Haker, H., & Brugger, P. (2009). Dopamine, paranormal belief, and the detection of meaningful stimuli. *Journal of Cognitive Neuroscience, 22*, 1670-1681.

Kugel, W. (1977). Call-time as a new parameter in statistical ESP experiments. In J. D. Morris, W. G. Roll, & R L. Morris (Eds.), *Research in Parapsychology 1976: Abstracts and Papers from the Nineteenth Annual Convention of the Parapsychological Association*, (pp. 138-140). Metuchen, NJ: Scarecrow Press.

Kumar, V. K., Pekala, R. J., & Cummings, J. (1992). Sensation seeking, drug use, and reported paranormal beliefs and experiences. In E. W. Cook (Ed.), *Research in Parapsychology: Abstracts and Papers from the 34th Annual Convention of the Parapsychological Association, 1992* (pp. 35-40). Metuchen, NJ: Scarecrow Press.

Kumar, V. K., Pekala., R. J., & Gallagher, C. (1994). *The anomalous experiences inventory (AEI)*. Unpublished psychological test. West Chester University of Pennsylvania.

La Barre, W. (1938). *The peyote cult: Yale University publications in anthropology, no. 19*. New Haven: Yale University Press

La Barre, W. (1975). Anthropological perspectives on hallucination and hallucinogens. In R. K. Siegel and L. J. West (Eds.), *Hallucinations; behavior, experience, and theory* (pp.9-52). New York: Wiley.

Labate, B. C. (2006). Brazilian literature on ayahuasca religions. *Fieldwork in Religion, 2*(3), 200-234.

Lagrou, E. (2000). Two ayahuasca myths from the Cashinahua of northwestern Brazil. In L. E. Luna. and S. F. White (Eds.) *Ayahuasca reader. Encounters with the Amazon's sacred vine* (pp.31-35). Santa Fe, NM: Synergetic Press.

Lahti, A. C., Weiler, M. A., Michaelidis, T., Parwani, A., & Tamminga, C. A. (2001). Effects of ketamine in normal and schizophrenic volunteers. *Neuropsychopharmacology, 25(4),* 455-467.

Laidlaw, R. W. (1961). New understanding of mediumistic phenomena. In Anon., *Proceedings on Two Conferences on Parapsychology and Pharmacology* (pp. 25-26). New York: Parapsychology Foundation.

Lajoie, D. H., & Shapiro, S. I. (1992). Definitions of transpersonal psychology: The first twenty-three years. *The Journal of Transpersonal Psychology, 24*(1), 79-98.

Lang, A. (1893). *The secret commonwealth of elves, fauns & fairies: A study in folklore & psychical research*. London: David Nutt.

Langdon-Davies, J. (1961). *On the nature of man*. New York: New American Library.

Lange, R., Thalbourne, M. A., Houran, J., & Storm, L. (2000). The revised transliminality scale: Reliability and validity data using a top-down purification procedure. *Consciousness and Cognition, 9*, 591-617.

Larcher, H. (1958). Parapsychochimie da la divination [Parapsychochemistry of divination]. *Revue métapsychique, 2*(8), 5-13.

Leary, T. (1966). Programmed communication during experiences with DMT (dimethyltryptamine). *Psychedelic Review, 8*, 83-95.

Leary, T., Litwin. G. H., & Metzner, R. (1963). Reactions to psilocybin administered in a supportive environment. *Journal of Nervous and Mental Disease, 137*, 561-573.

Leary, T., Metzner, R., & Alpert, R. (1964). *The psychedelic experience: A manual based on the Tibetan book of the dead*. New York: University Books.

Lee, H-M., & Roth, B. L. (2012). Hallucinogen actions on human brain revealed. *Proceedings of the National Academy of Science, 109*, 1820-1821.

Lerner, M., & Lyvers, M. (2006). Values and beliefs of psychedelic drug-users: A cross-cultural study. *Journal of Psychoactive Drugs, 38*, 143-147.

LeShan, L. (1968). Psi and altered states of consciousness. In R. Cavanna & M. Ullman (Eds.), *Psi and Altered States of Consciousness: Proceedings of an International Conference on Hypnosis, Drugs, Dreams, and Psi* (pp. 129-131). New York: Parapsychology Foundation.

Letcher, A. (2004, June). *Mad thoughts on mushrooms: Discourse and power in the study of psychedelic consciousness*. (Audio CDROM). Paper presented at the international conference Exploring Consciousness: With What Intent?, Bath Spa University, UK.

Letcher, A. (2007) Mad thoughts on mushrooms: Discourse and power in the study of psychedelic consciousness. *Anthropology of Consciousness, 18*(2), 74-98.

Levine, J. (1968). Psychopharmacology: Implications for psi research. In R. Cavanna & M. Ullman (Eds.), *Psi and Altered States of Consciousness: Proceedings of an International Conference on Hypnosis, Drugs, Dreams, and Psi* (pp.88-106). New York: Parapsychology Foundation.

Levine, J., & Ludwig, A. M. (1965). Alterations in consciousness produced by combinations of LSD, hypnosis, and psychotherapy. *Psychopharmacologia, 7*, 123-137.

Lewis, I. M. (1978). *Ecstatic religion: An anthropological study of spirit possession and shamanism* (2nd ed.). Harmondsworth, Middlesex, UK: Penguin.

Lewis-Williams, J.D. (2002). *The mind in the cave: Consciousness and the origins of art.* London: Thames & Hudson.

Lewis-Williams, J.D., & Dowson, T.A. (1988). The signs of all times: Entoptic phenomena in Upper Paleolithic art. *Current Anthropology, 29*, 201-45.

Lewis-Williams, J.D. & Pearce, D. (2005). *Inside the Neolithic mind: Consciousness, cosmos and the realm of the gods.* London: Thames & Hudson.

Liberman, J. (1995). *Take off your glasses and see.* New York: Crown.

Liester, M. B. (2013). Near-death experiences and ayahuasca-induced experiences: Two unique pathways to a phenomenologically similar state of consciousness. *Journal of Transpersonal Psychology, 45*(1), 24-48.

Lilly, J. C. (1967). *The human biocomputer.* London: Abacus.

Lilly, J. C. (1969). Parapsychological Association convention dinner address: Inner space and para-psychology [abstract]. *Journal of Parapsychology, 33*, 349.

Lilly, J. C. (1978). *The scientist.* Philadelphia: Lippincott.

Lizot, J. (1991). *Tales of the Yanomami: Daily life in the Venezuelan forest.* Cambridge: Cambridge University Press. (trans. E. Simon).

Lommel, P., van. (2004). About the continuity of our consciousness. In C. Machado and D.A. Shewmon (Eds.), *Brain death and disorders of consciousness: Advances in experimental medicine and biology* (vol. 550)(pp.115-132). New York: Kluwer Academic/ Plenum Publishers.

Louv, J. (Ed). (2005). *Generation hex.* New York: The Disinformation Company.

Ludwig, A. M. (1968). The hypnodelic state. In R. Cavanna & M. Ullman (Eds.), *Psi and Altered States of Consciousness: Proceedings of an International Conference on Hypnosis, Drugs, Dreams, and Psi* (pp. 68-87). New York: Parapsychology Foundation.

Ludwig, A. M., & Lyle, W. H. (1964). The experimental production of narcotic drug effects and withdrawal symptoms through hypnosis. *International Journal of Clinical and Experimental Hypnosis, 12*, 1-17.

Luke, D. (2004a). *Altered states of psi: A neurochemical perspective.* (audiocassette). London: The Society for Psychical Research Invited Lecture Series.

Luke, D. (2004b). Paranormal experiences and psychoactive drugs: A literature review project. *Bulletin of the Multidisciplinary Association for Psychedelic Studies, 14* (1), 11.

Luke, D. (2004c, June). *Psi-chedelics and science. Looking for the lost field of parapsycho-pharmacology.* (Audio CDROM). Paper presented at the international conference Exploring Consciousness: With What Intent?, Bath Spa University, UK.

Luke, D. (2005). *Transpersonal and paranormal experiences with entheogenic substances: A parapsychological first-person perspective.* Unpublished manuscript.

Luke, D. (2006). A tribute to Albert Hofmann on his 100th birthday: The mysterious discovery of LSD and the impact of psychedelics on parapsychology. *Paranormal Review, 37*, 3-8.

Luke, D. (2007). Lecture report: Inducing near-death states through the use of chemicals – Dr. Ornella Corazza. *Paranormal Review, 43*, 28-29.

Luke, D. (2008a). Disembodied eyes revisited: An investigation into the ontology of entheogenic entity encounters. *Entheogen Review: The Journal of Unauthorized Research on Visionary Plants and Drugs, 17*(1), 1-9 & 38-40.

Luke, D. P. (2008b). Inner paths to outer space: Journeys to alien worlds through psychedelics and other spiritual technologies by Rick Strassman et al. [book review]. *Journal of Scientific Exploration, 22*, 564-569.

Luke, D. P. (2008c). Psychedelic substances and paranormal phenomena: A review of the research. *Journal of Parapsychology, 72*, 77-107.

Luke, D. (2009a). Cleansing the doors of perception: Introduction. In R. Heaven, *The hummingbird's journey to God: Perspectives on San Pedro, the cactus of vision* (pp.1-7). Poole, Dorset: O Books.

Luke, D. (2009b). Near-death experiences: Exploring the mind-body connection, by Ornella Corazza [book review]. *Journal of Parapsychology, 73, 175-180.*

Luke, D. (2010a). Anthropology and parapsychology: Still hostile sisters in science? *Time and Mind: The Journal of Archaeology, Consciousness & Culture, 3*, 245-266.

Luke, D. (2010b). Connecting, diverging and reconnecting. Putting the psi back into psychedelic research. *Journal of Parapsychology, 74, 219-234.*

Luke, D. P. (2010c). Rock art or Rorschach: Is there more to entoptics than meets the eye? *Time & Mind: The Journal of Archaeology, Consciousness & Culture, 3*, 9-2.

Luke, D. (2011a). Anomalous phenomena, psi and altered consciousness. In E. Cardeña & M. Winkelman (Eds.), *Altering consciousness: A multidisciplinary perspective, volume 2- Biological and psychological perspectives* (pp.355-374). Westport, CT: Praeger.

Luke, D. (2011b). Discarnate entities and dimethyltryptamine (DMT): Psychopharmacology, phenomenology and ontology. *Journal of the Society for Psychical Research, 75*, 26-42.

Luke, D. (2011c). Experiential reclamation and first person parapsychology. *Journal of Parapsychology, 75*, 185-199.

Luke, D. (2011d). The light from the forest: The ritual use of ayahuasca in Brazil: Special issue of Fieldwork in Religion 2(3), by B.C. Labate & E. MacRae [book review]. *Time & Mind: The Journal of Archaeology, Consciousness & Culture 4*(3), 361-364.

Luke, D. (2012a). Altered states of consciousness, mental imagery and healing. In C. Simmonds-Moore (Ed.), *Exceptional experience and health: Essays on mind, body and human potential* (pp.64-80). Jefferson, NC: McFarland.

Luke, D. (2012b). Holy mountain or holey mountain? *Psychedelic Press UK Journal, 1*, 24-25.

Luke, D. (2012c). Notes on getting cactus lodged in your reducing valve: San Pedro and psychic abilities. In R. Heaven (Ed.). *Cactus of mystery: The shamanic powers of the Peruvian San Pedro cactus* (pp.167-195). Rochester, VT: Inner Traditions.

Luke, D. (2012d). Psychoactive substances and paranormal phenomena: A comprehensive review. *International Journal of Transpersonal Studies, 31*, 97-156.

Luke, D. (2013a). Ecopsychology and the psychedelic experience. *European Journal of Ecopsychology, 4,* 1-8.

Luke, D. (2013b). So long as you've got your elf: Death, DMT and discarnate entities. In A. Voss and W. Rowlandson (Eds.), *Daimonic imagination: Uncanny intelligence* (pp.282-291). Cambridge: Cambridge Scholars Publishing.

Luke, D. (2014). Psychedelic possession: The growing incorporation of incorporation into ayahuasca use. In J. Hunter and D. Luke (Eds.) *Talking with the spirits: Ethnographies from between the worlds* (pp.229-254). Brisbane, Australia: Daily Grail Publishing.

Luke, D. (2015). Drugs and psi phenomena. In E. Cardeña, J. Palmer, and D. Marcusson-Clavertz (Eds.), *Parapsychology: A handbook for the 21ˢᵗ century.* (pp.149-164). Jefferson, NC: McFarland.

Luke, D. (2017). The big dream and archeo-geo-neuro-pharmaco-parapsychological theories. *Paranthropology: Journal of Anthropological Approaches to the Paranormal, 7*(2), 13-14.

Luke, D., Delanoy, D., & Sherwood. S. J. (2008). Psi may look like luck: Perceived luckiness and beliefs about luck in relation to precognition. *Journal of the Society for Psychical Research, 72*(4), *193-207.*

Luke, D., & Friedman, H. (2010). The speculated neurochemistry of psi and associated processes. In S. Krippner & H. Friedman (Eds.), *Mysterious minds: The neurobiology of psychics, mediums and other extraordinary people.* (pp.163-185). Westport, CT: Greenwood / Praeger.

Luke, D., & Kittenis, M. (2005). A preliminary survey of paranormal experiences with psychoactive drugs. *Journal of Parapsychology, 69*(2), 305-327.

Luke, D., & Spowers, R. (Eds.)(2018). *Divine molecule talks: Exploring entheogenic entity encounters.* Rochester, VT: Park Street Press.

Luke, D., & Terhune, D. B. (2013). The induction of synaesthesia with chemical agents: A systematic review. *Frontiers in Psychology, 4,* 753.

Luke, D., Terhune, D., & Friday, R. (2012*).* Psychedelic synaesthesia: Evidence for a serotonergic role in synaesthesia. *Seeing and Perceiving, 25,* 74.

Luke, D., & Yanakieva, S. (2016, June). *The transpersonal psychedelic experience and change in ecological attitude and behaviour.* Paper presented at the International Conference on Psychedelics Research, Stichting Open, Amsterdam, 3ʳᵈ-5ᵗʰ June.

Luke, D., & Zychowicz, K. (2014). Working the graveyard shift at the witching hour: Further exploration of dreams, psi and circadian rhythms. *International Journal of Dream Research, 7*(2), 105-112.

Luke, D., Zychowicz, K., Richterova, O., Tjurina, I., & Polonnikova, J. (2012). A sideways look at the neurobiology of psi: Precognition and circadian rhythms. *NeuroQuantology: An Interdisciplinary Journal of Neuroscience and Quantum Physics, 10*(3), 580-590.

Luna, L. E. (1986). *Vegetalismo: Shamanism among the Mestizo population of the Peruvian Amazon.* Stockholm: Almquist & Wiksell International.

Luna, L. E. (2008). The varieties of ayahuasca experience. In R. Strassman, S. Wojtowicz, L.E. Luna and E. Frecska, *Inner paths to outer space: Journeys to alien worlds through psychedelics and other spiritual technologies* (pp.120-142). Rochester, VT: Park Street Press.

Luna, L. E., & White, S. F. (Eds.). (2000). *Ayahuasca reader: Encounters with the Amazon's sacred vine.* Sante Fe, New Mexico: Synergetic Press.

Luna, L. E., & White, S. F. (Eds.). (2016). *Ayahuasca reader: Encounters with the Amazon's sacred vine.* Sante Fe, New Mexico: Synergetic Press.

Maas, U., & Strubelt, S. (2003). Music in the Iboga initiation ceremony in Gabon: Polyrhythms supporting a pharmacotherapy. *Music Therapy Today (online)*, *4*(3), available at http://musictherapyworld.net

Mack, J. E. (1999). *Passport to the cosmos: Human transformation and alien encounters*. New York: Three Rivers.

Maher, B. (2008). The case of the missing heritability. *Nature, 456*, 18-21.

Mandel, L.R., Prasad, R., Lopez-Ramos, B., & Walker, R.W. (1977). The biosynthesis of dimethyltryptamine in vivo. *Research Communications in Chemical Pathology and Pharmacology, 16*(1), 47-58.

Marks, L. E. (1975). On coloured-hearing synaesthesia: cross-modal translations of sensory dimensions. *Psychological Bulletin, 82*, 303-331.

Marks, L. (2014). Synesthesia: A teeming multiplicity. In E. Cardeña, S. J. Lynn and S. Krippner (Eds.), *Varieties of Anomalous Experience: Examining the Scientific Evidence* (2nd ed.)(pp.79-108). Washington, DC: American Psychological Association.

Marques, A. A., Jnr. (2007). *The incorporation of Umbanda by Santo Daime. Unpublished article extracted* (trans. D. Thornton) from "Tambores pará a Rainha da Floresta: a inserção da Umbanda nenhuma Santo Daime" [Drums for the Queen of the Forest: the insertion of Umbanda in Santo Daime], unpublished masters thesis, Pontifícia Universidade Católica de São Paulo, Brazil.

Marti-Ibanez, F. (1965, June). The gates to paradise. *MD Medical News-magazine*, 11.

Masters, R. E. L., & Houston, J. (1966). *The varieties of psychedelic experience*. London: Turnstone.

Mavromatis, A. (1987). *Hypnogogia: The unique state of consciousness between wakefulness and sleep*. London: Routledge & Kegan Paul.

Mayagoitia, L., Díaz, J-L., & Contreras, C. M. (1986). Psychopharmacologic analysis of an alleged oneirogenic plant: *Calea zacatechichi. Journal of Ethnopharmacology, 18*, 229-243.

Mayhew, C. (1956, October 26). An excursion out of time. *The London Observer*.

McCreery, C., & Claridge, G. (1995). Out-of-the-body experiences and personality. *Journal of the Society for Psychical Research, 60*, 129-148.

McGeown, W. J., Mazzoni, G., Venneri, A., & Kirsch, I. (2009). Hypnotic induction decreases anterior default mode activity. *Consciousness and Cognition, 18*, 848-855.

McGovern, W. (1927). *Jungle paths and Inca ruins*. New York: Grosset & Dunlap.

McIlhenny, E. H. (2012). *Ayahuasca characterization, metabolism in humans, and relevance to endogenous N,N-dimethyltryptamines*. Unpublished doctoral thesis, Louisiana State University. Available from http://www.neip.info/downloads/McIlhenny_Ayahuasca.pdf

McKellar, P. (1957). *Imagination and thinking*. New York: Basic Books

McKenna, D. (2004). Clinical investigations of the therapeutic potential of ayahuasca: Rationale and regulatory challenges. *Pharmacology and Therapeutics, 102*, 111-129.

McKenna, D. (2018). Is DMT a chemical messenger from an extra-terrestrial civilisation? In D. Luke and R. Spowers (Eds.), *Divine molecule talks: Exploring entheogenic entity encounters*. Rochester, VT: Park Street Press.

McKenna, T. (1982). *Food of the gods*. London: Bantam.

McKenna, T. (1991). *The archaic revival: Speculations on psychedelic mushrooms, the Amazon, virtual reality, UFOs, evolution, shamanism, the rebirth of the Goddess, and the end of history*. San Francisco: Harper.

McKenna, T. (1992). *Food of the gods: The search for the original tree of knowledge - A radical history of plants, drugs, and human evolution.* New York: Bantam.

McKenna, T, & McKenna, D. (1994). *The invisible landscape: Mind, hallucinogens, and the I Ching.* Pymble, NSW: Harper Collins Australia.

Meduna, L. J. (1950). The effect of carbon dioxide upon the functions of the brain. In L. J. Meduna (Ed.), *Carbon dioxide therapy.* Springfield, Illinois: Charles Thomas.

Mercury, D., & Feelodd, D. (2008). First look at a new psychoactive drug: Symmetry (salvinorin B ethoxymethyl ether). *The Entheogen Review, 16,* 136-145.

Metzner, R. (1992). Divinatory dreams induced by tree datura. In C. Rätsch, *Yearbook for Ethnomedicine and the Study of Consciousness (1991-0)* (pp.193-198). Berlin: VWB.

Metzner, R. (2005a). Psychedelic, psychoactive and addictive drugs and states of consciousness. In M. Earlywine (Ed.), *Mind-altering drugs: The science of subjective experience* (Pp. 27-48). New York: Oxford University Press.

Metzner, R. (Ed.)(2005b). *Sacred vine of spirits: Ayahuasca.* Rochesta, VT: Park Street Press.

Meyer, P. (1994). Apparent communication with discarnate entities induced by dimethyltryptamine (DMT). In T. Lyttle (Ed.), *Psychedelics* (Pp. 161-203). New York: Barricade Books.

Michelot, D., & Melendez-Howell, L. M. (2003). *Amanita muscaria*: Chemistry, biology, toxicology, and ethnomycology. *Mycological Research, 107,* 131-146.

Milán, E.G., Iborra, O., Hochel, M., Rodríguez Artacho, M. A., Delgado-Pastor, L. C., Salazar, E., & González-Hernández, A. (2012). Auras in mysticism and synaesthesia: A comparison. *Consciousness and Cognition, 21*(1), 258.

Millay, J. (1999). *Multidimensional mind: Remote viewing in hyperspace.* Berkeley, CA: North Atlantic Books.

Millay, J. (2001). The influence of psychedelics on remote viewing. *Bulletin of the Multidisciplinary Association for Psychedelic Studies, 11* (1), 43-44.

Millay, J. (2004a, May). *Psi and psychedelics: Stories from the underground.* Presentation given at the Conference of the Association for Scientific and Spiritual Advancement, San Francisco, CA.

Millay, J. (2004b). Psi and entheogens. *Proceedings of the 20th Annual International Conference on the Study of Shamanism and Alternative Modes of Healing, San Rafael, CA.*

Millay, J. (2005, September). *Psychedelics, psychics, and psi* (Part 1 of 2). Paper presented at the 21st Annual International Conference on Study of Shamanism and Alternative Modes of Healing, San Rafael, CA.

Millay, J. (2006, September). *Psychedelics, psychics, and psi* (Part 2 of 2). Paper presented at the 22nd Annual International Conference on the Study of Shamanism and Alternative Modes of Healing, San Rafael, CA.

Millay, J. (2010). Psychic gifts from entheogens. In J. Millay (Ed.). *Radiant minds: Scientists explore the dimensions of consciousness* (pp.217-226). Doyle, CA: Millay.

Miller, I. (1994). *Becoming the vine: An anecdotal account of ayahuasca initiation.* Unpublished manuscript, available at www.mishkitaki.org/main/wp.../07/Becoming-the-Vine.pdf

Miller, R. A. (1978). The biological function of the third eye. *The Continuum, 2* (3).

Milton, J., & Wiseman, R. (1997). *Guidelines for extrasensory perception research.* Hatfield, UK: University of Herefordshire.

Minsky, M. (1987). *Society of mind*. New York: Simon and Schuster.

MoDu (2003). Shared experiences and fields of consciousness. *Entheogen Review, 12*(2), 56-58.

Mogar, R. E. (1965). Current status and future trends in psychedelic (LSD) research. *Journal of Humanistic Psychology, 5*, 147-166.

Montanelli, D. G., & Parra, A. (2000). Conflictive psi experiences: A survey with implications for clinical parapsychology [Abstract]. *Journal of Parapsychology, 64*, 248.

Moody, R. (1989). *The light beyond*. New York: Bantam.

Moreira-Almeida, A., & Lotufo-Neto, F. (2017). Methodological guidelines to investigate altered states of consciousness and anomalous experiences. *International Review of Psychiatry* (online), 1-10.

Morse, M. L. (1997). Commentary on Jansen's paper. *Journal of Near-Death Studies, 16*, 59-62.

Morse, M. L., Venecia, D., & Milstein, J. (1989). Near-death experiences: A neurophysiologic explanatory model. *Journal of Near-Death Studies, 8*, 45-53.

Motoyama, H. (2001). *Theories of the chakras: Bridge to higher consciousness*. New Delhi, India: New Age Books.

Muetzelfeldt, L., Kamboj, S. K., Rees, H., Taylor, J., Morgan, C. J. A., & Curran, H. V. (2008). Journey through the K-hole: Phenomenological aspects of ketamine use. *Drug and Alcohol Dependence, 95*(3), 219-229.

Muggleton, N., Tsakanikos, E., Walsh, V., & Ward, J. (2007). Disruption of synaesthesia following TMS of the right posterior parietal cortex. *Neuropsychologia, 45*, 1582-1585.

Müller-Ebeling, C., Rätsch, C., & Storl, W-D. (2003). *Witchcraft medicine: Healing arts, shamanic practices, and forbidden plants*. Rochester, Vermont: Inner Traditions.

Mullis, K. (1998). *Dancing naked in the mind field*. New York: Pantheon Books.

Murphy, G. (1961). *The challenge of psychical research*. New York: Harper Colophon.

Myers, S. A., Austrin, H. R., Grisso, J. T., & Nickeson, R. C. (1983). Personality characteristics as related to the out-of-body experience. *Journal of Parapsychology, 47*, 131-144.

Naranjo, C. (1967). Psychotropic properties of the harmala alkaloids. In D. Efron (Ed.), *Ethnopharmacologic Search for Psychoactive Drugs: Proceedings of Symposium held in San Francisco, January 28-30, 1967* (pp. 385-391). Public Health Service Publication No 1645. Washington, DC: US Department of Health, Education, and Welfare.

Naranjo, C. (1973a). Psychological aspects of the yagé experience in an experimental setting. In M. J. (Ed.), *Hallucinogens and shamanism* (pp.176-190). New York: Oxford University Press.

Naranjo, C. (1973b). *The healing journey: New approaches to consciousness*. New York: Ballantine Books.

Naranjo, C. (1987). "Ayahuasca" imagery and the therapeutic property of the harmala alkaloids. *Journal of Mental Imagery, 11*, 131-136.

Narby, J. (1998). *The cosmic serpent, DNA, and the origins of knowledge*. London: Tarcher/ Putnum.

Narby, J. (2000). Shamans and scientists. In J. Narby & F. Huxley (Eds.), *Shamans through time: 500 years on the path to knowledge* (pp.301-305). London: Thames and Hudson.

Narby, J. (2006). *Intelligence in nature: An inquiry into knowledge.* NY: Jeremy P. Tarcher / Penguin.

Nebesky-Wojkowitz, R. (1956). *Oracles and demons of Tibet: The cult and iconography of the Tibetan protective deities.* London: Oxford University Press.

Neppe, V. M. (1989). Near-death experiences: A new challenge in temporal lobe phenomenology? Comments on "A neurobiological model for near-death experiences." *Journal of Near-Death Studies, 7,* 243-248.

Neppe, V. M. (2006). A detailed analysis of an important chess game: Revisiting ' Marcóczy versus Korchnoi.' *Journal of the Society for Psychical Research, 71,* 129-147.

Newcombe, R. (2008). Ketamine case study: The phenomenology of the ketamine experience. *Addiction Research and Theory, 16,* 209-215.

Nichols, D. E. (2004). Hallucinogens. *Pharmacology and Therapeutics, 101,* 131-181.

Nichols, D. E. (2016). Psychedelics. *Pharmacological Reviews, 68,* 264-355.

Nicol, J. F., & Nicol, B. H. (1961). Experimental uses of chemical compounds. In Anon., *Proceedings of Two Conferences on Parapsychology and Pharmacology* (pp. 27-29). New York: Parapsychology Foundation.

Nunn, J. A., Rizza, F., & Peters, E. R. (2001). The incidence of schizotypy among cannabis and alcohol users. *Journal of Nervous and Mental Disease, 189,* 741-748.

Nuttal, J. (1970). *Bomb culture.* London: Paladin.

Oesterreich, T. K. (1966). *Possession, demoniacal and other, among primitive races, in antiquity, the Middle Ages, and modern times.* New Hyde Park, NY: University Books. (Trans. D. Ibberson. Originally published in German, 1921).

Ogalde, J.P., Arriaza, B.T., & Soto, E.C. (2008). Identification of psychoactive alkaloids in ancient Andean human hair by gas chromatography/mass spectrometry. *Journal of Archaeological Science, 36*(2), 467-72.

Orne, M. T. (1962). On the social psychology of the psychological experiment with particular reference to demand characteristics and their implications. *American Psychologist, 17,* 776-783.

Osis, K. (1961a). A pharmacological approach to parapsychological experimentation. In Anon., *Proceedings of Two Conferences on Parapsychology and Pharmacology* (pp. 74-75). New York: Parapsychology Foundation.

Osis, K. (1961b). Psychobiological research possibilities. In Anon., *Proceedings of Two Conferences on Parapsychology and Pharmacology* (pp. 30-32). New York: Parapsychology Foundation.

Osmond, H. (1961a). New techniques of investigation. In Anon., *Proceedings of Two Conferences on Parapsychology and Pharmacology* (pp. 76-78). New York: Parapsychology Foundation.

Osmond, H. (1961b). Variables in the LSD setting. In Anon., *Proceedings of Two Conferences on Parapsychology and Pharmacology* (pp. 33-35). New York: Parapsychology Foundation.

Osmond, H. (1968). Psi and the psychedelic movement. In R. Cavanna, & M. Ullman (Eds.), *Psi and Altered States of Consciousness: Proceedings of an International Conference on Hypnosis, Drugs, Dreams, and Psi* (pp. 107-114). New York: Parapsychology Foundation.

Osmond, H., & Smythies, J. (1952). Schizophrenia: A new approach. *Journal of Mental Science, 98,* 309-315.

Ostrander, O., & Schroeder, L. (1997). *Psychic discoveries: The iron curtain lifted.* London: Souvenir Press.

Ott, J. (1993). *Pharmacotheon: Entheogenic drugs, their plant sources and history.* Kennewick, WA: Natural Products Co.

Ott, J. (1996a). Entheogens II: On entheology and ethnobotany. *Journal of Psychoactive Drugs, 28*, 205-209.

Ott, J. (1996b). *Pharmacotheon: Entheogenic drugs, their plant sources and history* (2nd ed.). Kennewick, WA: Natural Products Co.

Ott, J. (2001). Pharmanopo-psychonautics: Human intranasal, sublingual, intrarectal, pulmonary and oral pharmacology of bufotenine. *The Journal of Psychoactive Drugs, 33*, 273-281.

Ott, U. (2007). States of absorption: in search of neurobiological foundations. In G. Jamieson (Ed.), *Hypnosis and conscious states: The cognitive neuroscience perspective* (pp. 29-50). Oxford: Oxford University Press.

Owl (1995). A mushroom entity. *The Entheogen Review, 4* (2), 5-6.

Pablos, F. de. (2002). Enhancement of precognitive dreaming by cholinesterase inhibition: A pilot study. *Journal of the Society for Psychical Research, 66*, 88-105.

Pablos, F. de. (2004). Spontaneous precognition during dreams: A theoretical model. *Journal of the Society for Psychical Research, 68*, 226-244.

Pahnke, W. N. (1966). Drugs and mysticism. *The International Journal of Parapsychology, 8*(2), 295-313.

Pahnke, W. N. (1968). The psychedelic mystical experience in terminal cancer patients and its possible implications for psi research. In R. Cavanna & M. Ullman (Eds.), *Psi and Altered States of Consciousness: Proceedings of an International Conference on Hypnosis, Drugs, Dreams, and Psi* (pp. 115-128). New York: Parapsychology Foundation.

Pahnke, W. N. (1971). The use of psychedelic drugs in parapsychological research. *Parapsychology Review, 2*(4), 5-6 & 12-14.

Pahnke, W. N., & Richards, W.A. (1966). Implications of LSD and experimental mysticism. *Journal of Religion and Health, 5*, 175-208.

Palhano-Fontes, F., Andrade, K. C., Tofoli, L. F., Santos, A. C., Crippa, J. A. S., Hallak, J. E. C., Ribeiro, S., & de Araujo, D. B. (2015). The psychedelic state induced by ayahuasca modulates the activity and connectivity of the Default Mode Network. *PLoS ONE, 10*(2), e0118143.

Palmer, J. (1978). Extrasensory perception: Research findings. In S. Krippner (Ed.), *Advances in parapsychological research: 2 Extrasensory perception* (pp. 59-243). New York: Plenum Press.

Palmer, J. (1979). A community mail survey of psychic experiences. *Journal of the American Society for Psychical Research, 73*, 221-251.

Palmer, J. (1982). ESP research findings: 1976-1978. In S. Krippner (Ed.), *Advances in parapsychological research 3* (pp. 41-82). New York: Plenum Press.

Palmer, J., & Neppe, V. M. (2003). A controlled analysis of the subjective paranormal experiences in temporal lobe dysfunction in a neuropsychiatric population. *Journal of Parapsychology, 67*, 75-97.

Palmer, J., & Neppe, V. M. (2004). Exploratory analysis of refined predictors of subjective ESP experiences and temporal lobe dysfunctiond in a neuropsychiatric population. *European Journal of Parapsychology, 19*, 44-65.

Palmer, J., Tart, C. T., & Redington, D. (1976). A large-sample classroom ESP card-guessing experiment. *European Journal of Parapsychology, 1*, 40-56.

Pappas, J., & Friedman, H. (2007). The construct of self-expansiveness and the validity of the Transpersonal Scale of the Self-Expansiveness Level Form. *The Humanistic Psychologist, 35*(4), 323-347.

Paqueron, X., Leguen, M., Rosenthal, D., Coriat, P., Willer, J. C., & Danziger, N. (2003). The phenomenology of body image distortions induced by regional anaesthesia. *Brain, 126*, 702-712.

Pardanani, J.H., McLaughlin, J.L., Kondrat, R.W., & Cooks, R.G. (1977). Cactus alkaloids XXXVII: Mescaline and related compounds from *Trichocereus peruvianus*. *Lloydia, 40*(3), 286-288.

Parker, A. (1975). *States of mind: ESP and altered states of consciousness*. London: Malaby Press.

Parker, A. (2001). What can cognitive psychology and parapsychology tell us about near-death experiences? *Journal of the Society for Psychical Research, 65*, 225-240.

Paterson, T. T. (1961a). Development and testing of hypotheses. In Anon., *Proceedings of Two Conferences on Parapsychology and Pharmacology* (pp. 36-39). New York: Parapsychology Foundation.

Paterson, T. T. (1961b). Frontiers of experimentation. In Anon., *Proceedings on Two Conferences of Parapsychology and Pharmacology* (pp. 79-81). New York: Parapsychology Foundation.

Paul, M. A. (1966). Two cases of altered consciousness with amnesia apparently telepathically induced. *Psychedelic Review, 8*, 4-8.

Pekala, R., & Cardeña, E. (2000). Methodological issues in the study of altered states of consciousness and anomalous experiences. In E. Cardeña, S. J. Lynn & S. Krippner (Eds.), *Varieties of anomalous experience* (pp. 47-81). Washington, DC: American Psychological Association.

Pekala, R. J., Kumar, V. K., & Marcano, G. (1995a). Anomalous/paranormal experiences, hypnotic susceptibility, and dissociation. *Journal of the American Society for Psychical Research, 89*, 313-331.

Pekala, R. J., Kumar, V. K., & Marcano, G. (1995b, March). *Hypnotic susceptibility, dissociation, and marijuana use: A relationship between high hypnotic susceptibility, marijuana use, and dissociative ability*. Paper presented at the annual meeting of the American Society of Clinical Hypnosis, San Diego, CA.

Peres, J. F., Moreira-Almeida, A., Caixeta, L., Leao, F., Newburg, A. (2012). Neuroimaging during trance state: A contribution to the study of dissociation. *PloS ONE, 7*(11), e49360.

Persinger, M. A. (1988). Increased geomagnetic activity and the occurrence of bereavement hallucinations: Evidence for melatonin-mediated microseizuring in the temporal lobe? *Neuroscience Letters, 88*, 271-274.

Persinger, M. A., & Makarec, K. (1987). Temporal lobe epileptic signs and correlative behaviors displayed by normal populations. *The Journal of General Psychiatry, 114*, 179-195.

Peters, L., & Price-Williams, D. (1980). Toward an experiential analysis of shamanism. *American Ethnologist, 7*, 397-418.

Pickover, C. (2005). *Sex, drugs, Einstein, and elves*. Petaluma, CA: Smart Publications.

Pimm, S. L., Russell, G. J., Gittleman, J. L. Brooks, T. M. (1995). The future of biodiversity. *Science, 269*, 347-350.

Pitman, J. A., & Owens, N. E. (2004). The effect of manipulating expectations before and during a test of ESP. *Journal of Parapsychology, 68*(1), 45-63.

Pizzagalli, D., Lehmann, D., & Brugger, P. (2001). Lateralized direct and indirect semantic priming effects in subjects with paranormal experiences and beliefs. *Psychopathology, 34*, 75-80.

Polari de Alverga, A. (1999). *Forest of visions: Ayahuasca, Amazonian spirituality and the Santo Daime Tradition*. Rochester, VT: Park Street Press.

Polari de Alverga, A. (2000). The book of visions: Journey to Santo Daime (excerpt). In L.E. Luna and S.F. White (Eds.), *Ayahuasca reader: Encounters with the Amazon's sacred vine* (pp.145-53). Santa Fe, NM: Synergetic Press.

Pomarol-Clotet, E., Honey, G. D., Murray, G. K., Corlett, P. R., Absalom, A. R., Lee, M., McKenna, P. J., Bullmore, E. T., & Fletcher, P. C. (2006). Psychological effects of ketamine in healthy volunteers: Phenomenological study. *British Journal of Psychiatry, 189,* 173-179.

Popik, P., Layer, R., & Skolnick, P. (1995). 100 years of ibogaine: Neurochemical and pharmacological actions of a putative anti-addictive drug. *Pharmacological Reviews, 47,* 235-253.

Potts, M. (2012). Does N,N-dimethyltryptamine (DMT) adequately explain near-death experiences? *Journal of Near-death Studies, 31*(1), 3-23.

Presti, D. E. (2011). Neurochemisry and altered consciousness. In E. Cardeña, and Winkelman, M. (Eds.), *Altering consciousness: A multidisciplinary perspective, vol 2– Biological and psychological perspectives.* (pp.21-41). Westport, CT: Praeger.

Previc, F. (2011). Dopamine, altered consciousness, and distant space with special reference to shamanic ecstasy. In E. Cardeña & M. Winkelman (Eds.), *Altering consciousness: A multidisciplinary perspective, volume 2- Biological and psychological perspectives (pp.43-61).* Westport, CT: Praeger.

Price, H. H. (1948). Future work in parapsychology: Some suggestions. *Journal of Parapsychology, 12,* 25-31.

Price, H. H. (1964). A mescalin experience. *Journal of the American Society for Psychical Research, 58,* 3-20.

Price, L. H., & Lebel, J. (2000). Dextromethorphan-induced psychosis. *American Journal of Psychiatry, 157,* 304.

Progoff, I. (1961). Depth psychological potentialities of psychedelics. In Anon., *Proceedings of Two Conferences on Parapsychology and Pharmacology* (p. 40). New York: Parapsychology Foundation.

Psychedelicious (2008). *The spicy saga of Psychedelicious.* Retrieved on 9th June, 2009 from http://www.erowid.org/experiences/exp.php?ID=68549

Puharich, A. (1959). *The sacred mushroom: Key to the door of eternity.* Garden City, NY: Doubleday.

Puharich, A. (1962). *Beyond telepathy.* Garden City, NY: Doubleday & Co.

Pup (2006). *DMT trip accounts.* posted on February 10, 2006 at http://dmt.tribe.net/thread/9e832018-5fbc-4ff6-b4e5-e314184f687c (number 246)

Radin, D. (1989). Parapsychological Association presidential address: The Tao of psi. In L. A. Henkel & R. E. Berger (Eds), *Research in Parapsychology 1988: Abstracts and Papers from the Thirty-First Annual Convention of the Parapsychological Association* (pp.157-174). Metuchen, NJ: Scarecrow Press.

Radin, D. (1997). *The conscious universe.* San Francisco, CA: HarperEdge.

Ramakrishna Rao, K. (1966). *Experimental parapsychology: A review and interpretation.* Springfield, IL: Charles Thomas.

Rätsch, C. (2004, June). *Psychedelics and enlightenment.* (Audio CDR). Paper presented at the international conference Exploring Consciousness: With What Intent?, Bath Spa University, UK

Ray, T.S. (2010). Psychedelics and the human receptorome. *PLoS ONE 5*(2), e9019.

Raz, A., Hines, T., Fossella, J., & Castro, D. (2008). Paranormal experience and the COMT dopaminergic gene: A preliminary attempt to associate phenotype with genotype using an underlying brain theory. *Cortex, 44,* 1336-1341.

Rees, A. (2004, August 8). Nobel Prize genius Crick was high on LSD when he discovered the secret of life. *Mail on Sunday*.

Reichel-Dolmatoff, G. (1975). *The shaman and the jaguar: A study of narcotic drugs among the Indians of Colombia*. Philadelphia, PA: Temple University Press.

Reverend Raw, The. (2009). *DMT cleans my clocks*. Retrieved on 9th June, 2009 from http://www.erowid.org/experiences/exp.php?ID=77760

Reymond, J-L., Awale, M. (2012). Exploring chemical space for drug discovery using the chemical universe database. *ACS Chemical Neuroscience* (published online 25 April, 2012).

Rhine, J. B. (1934). *Extra-sensory perception*. Oxford: Boston Society for Psychical Research.

Rhine, J. B., Humphrey, B. M., & Averill, R. L. (1945). An exploratory experiment on the effect of caffeine upon performance in PK tests. *Journal of Parapsychology, 9*, 80.

Rhue, J. W., & Lynn, S. J. (1989). Fantasy proneness, hypnotizability, and absorption—a re-examination: a brief communication. *International Journal of Clinical and Experimental Hypnosis, 37*, 100-106.

Riba, J., Anderer, P., Jané, F., Saletu, B., & Barbanoj, M. J. (2004). Effects of the South American psychoactive beverage *ayahuasca* on regional brain electrical activity in humans: A functional neuroimaging study using low-resolution electromagnetic tomography. *Neuropsychobiology, 50*, 89-101.

Richardson, A. (1990). Recollections of R. Gordon Wasson's 'friend and photographer'. In T. J. Riedlinger (Ed.), *The sacred mushroom seeker* (pp. 193-204). Portland, Oregon: Dioscorides Press.

Ring, K., & Cooper, S. (2008). *Mindsight: Near-death and out-of-body experiences in the blind* (2nd ed.). New York: iUniverse.

Ring, K. (1989). Near-death and UFO encounters as shamanic initiations: Some conceptual and evolutionary implications. *ReVision, 11*(3), 14-22.

Ring, K. (1992). *The Omega Project: Near-death experiences, UFO encounters and mind at large*. New York: William Morrow & Co.

Ro, T., Farne, A., Johnson, R. M., Wedeen, V., Chu, Z., Wang, Z. J., Hunter, J. V., & Beauchamp, M. S. (2007). Feeling sounds after a thalamic lesion. *Annals of Neurology, 62*, 433-441.

Roberts, A. (2004, February). An acid test for ESP. *Fortean Times, 180*.

Roberts, T. B. (Ed.). (2001). *Psychoactive sacramentals: Essays on entheogens and religion*. San Francisco: Council on Spiritual Practices.

Roberts, T. B., & Winkelman, M. J. (2013). Psychedelic induced transpersonal experiences, therapies, and their implications for transpersonal psychology. In H. L. Friedman and G. Hartelius (Eds.), *The Wiley-Blackwell handbook of transpersonal psychology* (pp.459-479). Hoboken, NJ: John Wiley and Sons.

Rock, A. J., & Krippner, S. (2012). States of consciousness or states of phenomenology? In A. E. Cavanna & A. Nani (Eds.), *Consciousness: States, mechanisms and disorders*. Hauppauge, NY: Nova Science.

Rodriguez, M. A. (2007). A methodology for studying various interpretations of the N,N-dimethyltryptamine-induced alternate reality. *Journal of Scientific Exploration, 21*(1), 67-84.

Rogo, D. S. (1975). *Parapsychology: A century of inquiry*. New York: Taplinger.

Rogo, D. S. (1976). *Exploring psychic phenomena: Beyond mind and matter*. Wheaton, Illinois. The Theosophical Society in America.

Rogo, D. S. (1982). ESP and Schizophrenia: An analysis from two perspectives. *Journal of the Society for Psychical Research, 51*, 329-342.

Rogo, D. S. (1984). Ketamine and the near-death experience. *Anabiosis: The Journal of Near-Death Studies, 4*, 87-96.

Roll, W. G., & Montagno, E. de A. (1985). Neurophysical aspects of psi. In R. A. White & J. Solfvin (Eds.), *Research in Parapsychology: Abstracts and Papers from the 27th Annual Convention of the Parapsychological Association, 1984* (pp. 35-40). Metuchen, NJ: Scarecrow Press.

Roney-Dougal, S. M. (1984). Occult conference questionnaire. *Journal of the Society for Psychical Research, 52*, 379-382.

Roney-Dougal, S. M. (1986). Some speculations on a possible psychic effect of harmaline. In D. H. Weiner & D. H. Radin (Eds.), *Research in Parapsychology: Abstracts and Papers from the 28th Annual Convention of the Parapsychological Association, 1985* (pp.120-123). Metuchen, NJ: Scarecrow Press.

Roney-Dougal, S. M. (1989). Recent findings relating to the possible role of the pineal gland in affecting psychic ability. *Journal of the Society for Psychical Research, 55*, 313-328.

Roney-Dougal, S.M. (1990). Geomagnetism and the pineal gland: Some speculations. In L.A. Henkel and J. Palmer (Eds.), *Research in Parapsychology 1989* (pp. 57-61). Metuchen, NJ: Scarecrow Press.

Roney-Dougal, S. M. (1991). *Where science and magic meet.* London: Element Books.

Roney-Dougal, S. [M.] (2001). *Walking between the worlds: Links between psi, psychedelics, shamanism, and psychosis.* Unpublished manuscript, Psi Research Centre, Glastonbury, UK.

Roney-Dougal, S. M., Ryan, A., & Luke, D. (2013). The relationship between local geomagnetic activity, meditation and psi. Part I: Literature review and theoretical model. *Journal of the Society for Psychical Research, 77*(2), 72-88.

Roney-Dougal, S., Ryan, A., & Luke, D. (2014). The relationship between local geomagnetic activity and psychic awareness. *Journal of Parapsychology, 78*(2), 235-254.

Roney-Dougal, S.M., & Vögl, G. (1993). Some speculations on the effect of geomagnetism on the pineal gland. *Journal of the Society for Psychical Research, 59*, 1-15.

Rothen, N., Nyffeler, T., von Wartburg, R., Muri, R., & Meier, B. (2010). Parieto-occipital suppression eliminates implicit bidirectionality in grapheme-colour synaesthesia. *Neuropsychologia, 48*, 3482-3487.

Rouhier, A. (1925). Phénomènes de Matagnomie expérimentale observés au cours d'une expérience faite avec le "peyotl" (*Echinocactus Williamsii*). *Revue Métaphysique,* May-June, 144-154.

Rouhier, A. (1927). *La plante qui faite les yeux émerveillés: Le peyotl.* Paris: Doin.

Ruck, C., Bigwood, J., Staples, R., Wasson, R., & Ott, J. (1979). Entheogens. *Journal of Psychedelic Drugs, 11*, 145-146.

Rudgley, R. (2000). *The encyclopedia of psychoactive substances.* New York: Thomas Dunne.

Rush, J. H., & Cahn, H. A. (1958). Physiological conditioning for psi performance [Abstract from the Proceedings of the first convention of the Parapsychological Association, August, 1958, New York]. *Journal of Parapsychology, 22*, 300.

Ryzl, M. (1968). Training methods for psi induction. In R. Cavanna & M. Ullman (Eds.), *Psi and Altered States of Consciousness: Proceedings of an International*

Conference on Hypnosis, Drugs, Dreams, and Psi (pp. 55-67). New York: Parapsychology Foundation.

Saavedra-Aguilar, J., & Gómez-Jeria, J. (1989). A neurobiological model for near-death experiences. *Journal of Near-Death Studies, 7*, 205-222.

Sakellarios, S. (2005). *Another view of near-death experiences and reincarnation: How to respond to reductionistic thinking.* Retrieved November 25, 2005, from http://www.omplace.com/articles/Reductionist_thinking.html

Salway. C. (2015). *Psychonauts going psychonuts.* Paper presented to the 3rd Breaking Convention: International Conference on Psychededelic Consciousness, University of Greenwich, London, 10-12th July.

Sargant, W. (1973). *The mind possessed: A physiology of possession, mysticism and faith healing.* London: Heinemann.

Satori (2003). *Golden salamanders.* Retrieved on 9th June, 2009 from http://www.erowid.org/experiences/exp.php?ID=24260

Satyananda Saraswati, Swami. (1972). *The pineal gland (ajna chakra).* Bihar, India: Bihar School of Yoga.

Satyananda Saraswati, Swami. (1996). *Kundalini tantra* (2nd ed.). Munger, Bihar, India: Yoga Publications Trust.

Satyanarayana, M., Rao, P. V. K., & Vijaylakshmi, S. (1993). Role of pineal activity in ESP performance: A preliminary study. *Journal of Indian Psychology, 11*, 44-56.

Saunders, N. (1993). *E for ecstasy.* London: Nicholas Saunders.

Savage, C., Harman, W. W., & Fadiman, J. (1969). *Ipomoea purpurea*: A naturally occurring psychedelic. In C. T. Tart (Ed.), *Altered states of consciousness: A book of readings* (pp. 441-443). New York: John Wiley & Sons

Savigny, J.B.H. (1838). Phosphenes ou sensations loumineuses. *Archives Générale de Médecine, 3*(2), 495-497.

S., C. (1999). A vision of the fabric that is woven by us all. In R. Metzner (Ed.), *Sacred vine of the spirits: Ayahuasca* (pp.171-173). Rochester, VT: Park Street Press.

Schmeidler, G. R. (1994). ESP experiments 1978-1992: The glass is half full. In S. Krippner (Ed.), *Advances in parapsychological research 7* (pp.104-197). Jefferson, NC: McFarland.

Schroll. M. (2011). Out-of-body-experience, the dentist and nitrous oxide. *Paranthropology: Journal of Anthropological Approaches to the Paranormal, 2*(2), 40-42.

Schultes, R. E., & Hofmann, A. (1992). *Plants of the Gods: Their sacred, healing, and hallucinogenic powers.* Rochester, Vermont: Healing Arts Press.

Scotto (2000). *A very intense education.* Retrieved on 9th June, 2009 from http://www.erowid.org/experiences/exp.php?ID=1767

Scully, T. (2010). Some anecdotes regarding LSD, biofeedback and consciousness. In J. Millay (Ed.). *Radiant minds: Scientists explore the dimensions of consciousness* (pp.208-216). Doyle, CA: Millay.

Servadio, E. (1961). Psychological criteria and testing methods. In Anon., *Proceedings of Two Conferences on Parapsychology and Pharmacology* (pp.84-86). New York: Parapsychology Foundation.

Severi, B. (1996). Ayahuasca, la medicina dell'anima: Viaggio ed esperienze tra gli sciamani Shipibo-Conibo del Perù [Ayahuasca, the drug of the soul: Journey and experience among the Shipibo-Conibo shamans of Peru]. *Quaderni de Parapsychologia, 27*, 15-27.

Severi, B. (1999). *A very impressive experience with a 'teacher plant'.* Submission 21 from http://www.issc-taste.org/main

Severi, B. (2003). Sciamani e psichedelia. [Shamans and psychedelics]. *Quaderni de Parapsychologia, 34*, 36.

SFos (2000a). *Otherworldly bewilderness.* Retrieved on 9th June, 2009 from http://www.erowid.org/experiences/exp.php?ID=1851

SFos (2000b). *The elven antics annex.* Retrieved on 9th June, 2009 from http://www.erowid.org/experiences/exp.php?ID=1841

Shanon, B. (2001). Altered temporality. *Journal of Consciousness Studies, 8*(1), 35-58.

Shanon, B. (2002). *The antipodes of the mind: Charting the phenomena of the ayahuasca experience.* Oxford: Oxford University Press.

Shanon, B. (2003a). Hallucinations. *Journal of Consciousness Studies, 10*(2), 3-31.

Shanon, B. (2003b). Three stories concerning synaesthesia: A commentary on Ramachandran and Hubbard. *Journal of Consciousness Studies, 10*(3), 69-74.

Sharon, D. (1978). *Wizard of the four winds: A shaman's story.* New York: The Free Press.

Sharon, D. (1990). The San Pedro cactus in Peruvian folk healing. In P.T. Furst. (Ed.). *Flesh of the Gods: The ritual use of hallucinogens* (pp. 114-135). Illinois: Waveland Press.

Sheldrake, R. (1988). *The presence of the past.* London: Fontana / Collins.

Sheldrake, R. (2018). Morphic resonance, psychedelic experiences and collective memory. In D. Luke and R. Spowers (Eds.), *Divine molecule talks: Exploring entheogenic entity encounters.* Rochester, VT: Park Street Press.

Sherwood, S. (2002). Relationship between the hypnogogic/hypnopompic states and reports of anomalous experiences. *Journal of Parapsychology, 66*, 127-150.

Sherwood, S.J., & Roe, C.A. (2003). A review of dream ESP studies conducted since the Maimonides dream ESP programme. *Journal of Consciousness Studies 10*, 85-109.

Shulgin, A. [T.](2004, June). *Investigating consciousness.* (Audio CDROM). Paper presented at the international conference Exploring Consciousness: With What Intent?, Bath Spa University, UK.

Shulgin, A. [T.](2010). Chemistry and memory. In J. Millay (Ed.). *Radiant minds: Scientists explore the dimensions of consciousness* (pp.190-197). Doyle, CA: Millay.

Shulgin, A. T., Manning, T., Daley, P. F. (2011). *The Shulgin index (vol.1): Psychedelic phenethylamines and related compounds.* Berkeley, CA: Transform Press.

Shulgin, A. T, & Shulgin, A. (1991). *PIHKAL: A chemical love story.* Berkeley, CA: Transform Press.

Shulgin, A. T, & Shulgin, A. (1997). *TIHKAL: The continuation.* Berkeley, CA: Transform Press.

Siegel, R. K. (1980). The psychology of life after death. *American Psychologist, 35*, 911-931.

Siegel, R.K., Brewster, J.M., Johnson, C.A., & Jarvik, M.E. (1976). The Effects of hallucinogens on blind monkeys. *International Pharmacopsychiatry, 11*, 150-156.

Siegel, R. K., & Hirschman. A. E. (1984). Hashish near-death experiences. *Anabiosis: The Journal of Near-Death Studies, 4*, 70-86.

Simmonds-Moore, C. A. (2013). *Exploring the relationship between the synaesthesias and anomalous experiences.* Unpublished report for the Bial Foundation. University of West Georgia, USA.

Simmonds, C. A., & Roe, C. A. (2000). Personality correlates of anomalous experiences, perceived ability and beliefs: Schizotypy, temporal lobe signs and gender.

Proceedings of presented papers from the 43rd annual convention of the Parapsychology Association, 2000, Frieburg, Germany, 272-291.

Simner, J., Harrold, J., Creed, H., Monro, L., & Foulkes, L. (2009). Early detection of markers for synaesthesia in childhood populations. *Brain, 132,* 57-64.

Simner, J., Mulvenna, C., Sagiv, N., Tsakanikos, E., Witherby, S. A., Fraser, C., Scott, K., & Ward, J. (2006). Synaesthesia: The prevalence of atypical cross-modal experiences. *Perception, 35,* 1024-1033.

Simpson, L., & McKellar, P. (1955). Types of synaesthesia. *Journal of Mental Science, 101,* 141-147.

Sinel, J. (1927). *The sixth sense: A physical explanation for clairvoyance, telepathy, hypnotism, dreams and other phenomena usually considered occult.* London: T. Werner Laurie.

Sinke, C., Halpern, J. H., Zedler, M., Neufeld, J., Emrich, H. M., & Passie, T. (2012). Genuine and drug-induced synesthesia: A comparison. *Consciousness and Cognition, 21,* 1419-1434.

Siskind, J. (1973). Visions and cures among the Sharanahua. In M. J. Harner (Ed.), *Hallucinogens and shamanism* (pp.28-39). New York: Oxford University Press.

Slotkin, J. S. (1956). The peyote way. *Tomorrow, 4,* 96-105.

Smith, H. (2000). *Cleansing the doors of perception: The religious significance of entheogenic plants and substances.* New York: Jeremy P. Tarcher/Putnum.

Smith, L. A., & Tart. C. T. (1998). Cosmic consciousness experience and psychedelic experience: A first person comparison. *Journal of Consciousness Studies, 5*(1), 97-107.

Smythies, J. R. (1953). The mescaline experience. *The British Journal for the Philosophy of Science, 3,* 339-347.

Smythies, J.R. (1956). *Analysis of perception.* London: Routledge and Kegan Paul.

Smythies, J. R. (1960). New research frontiers in parapsychology and pharmacology. *International Journal of Parapsychology, 2*(2), 28-38.

Smythies, J. R. (1961a). Images as mind functions. In Anon., *Proceedings of Two Conferences on Parapsychology and Pharmacology* (p. 86). New York: Parapsychology Foundation.

Smythies, J. R. (1961b). Spontaneous activity of the human psyche. In Anon., *Proceedings of Two Conferences on Parapsychology and Pharmacology* (pp.41-42). New York: Parapsychology Foundation.

Smythies, J. R. (1965). ESP experiments with LSD 25 and psilocybin, by R. Cavanna & E. Servadio [book review]. *Journal of the Society for Psychical Research, 43,* 149-150.

Smythies, J. R. (1983). The impact of psychedelic drugs on philosophy and psychical research. *Journal of the Society for Psychical Research, 52,* 194-200.

Smythies, J. R. (1987). Psychometry and mescaline. *Journal of the Society for Psychical Research, 54,* 266-268.

Smythies, J. R. (2011). Ketamine, Bergson and NDEs. *Journal of the Society for Psychical Research, 75,* 148-150.

Soal, S. G., & Bateman, F. (1954). *Modern experiments in telepathy.* London: Faber.

Sobiecki, J. F. (2008). A review of plants used in divination in southern Africa and their psychoactive effects. *Southern African Humanities, 20,* 1-19.

Sobiecki, J. F. (2012). Psychoactive ubulawu spiritual medicines and healing dynamics in the initiation process of southern Bantu diviners. *Journal of Psychoactive Drugs, 44,* 216-223.

Soutar, I. (2001). Ska pastora – leaves of the shepherdess: Conference at Breitenbush Hot Springs, Dec 7-10, 2000. *Bulletin of the Multidisciplinary Association for Psychedelic Studies, 11*(1), 32-40.

Spess, D. L. (2000). *Soma: The divine hallucinogen.* Rochester, VT: Park Street Press.

Stafford, P. [G.](1977). *Psychedelics encyclopedia.* Berkeley, CA: And / Or Press

Stafford, P. G., & Golightly, B. H. (1967). *LSD the problem-solving psychedelic.* London: Tandem.

Stamets, P. (1996). *Psilocybin mushrooms of the world: An identification guide.* Berkeley, CA: Ten Speed Press.

Stanford, R. G. (1990). An experimentally testable model for spontaneous psi events: A review of related evidence and concepts from parapsychology and other sciences. In S. Krippner (Ed.). *Advances in parapsychological research Vol. 6* (pp. 54-167). Jefferson, NC: McFarland.

Steinkamp, F., Milton, J., & Morris, R.L. (1998). Meta-analysis of forced-choice experiments comparing clairvoyance and precognition. *Journal of Parapsychology, 62,* 193-218.

Stevens, J. (1988). *Storming heaven: LSD and the American dream.* London: William Heinemann.

Stevenson, I. (1981). Presidential address: Can we describe the mind. In W.G. Roll & J. Beloff (Eds.), *Research in Parapsychology: Abstracts and Papers from the 23rd Annual Convention of the Parapsychological Association, 1980* (pp. 130-147). Metuchen, NJ: Scarecrow Press.

Strieber, W. (1987). *Communion: A true story.* New York: Avon Books.

Stokes, D. M. (1997). Spontaneous psi phenomena. In S. Krippner (Ed.), *Advances in parapsychological research 8* (pp. 6-87). Jefferson, NC: McFarland.

Stolaroff, M. J. (2004). *The secret chief revealed: Conversations with a pioneer of the underground psychedelic therapy movement.* Sarasota, FL: Multidisciplinary Association for Psychedelic Studies.

Stoll, W.A. (1947). LSD, Ein phantastikum aus der mutterkorngruppe. *Schweizer Archiv für Neurologie und Psychiatrie, 60,* 279.

Stone, R. E. (2011). *The jaguar within: Shamanic trance in ancient Central and South American art.* Austin, TX: University of Texas Press.

Storm, L., & Rock, A. J. (2009). Imagery cultivation vs. noise reduction: Shamanic-like journeying as a psi-conducive alternative to the ganzfeld protocol. *Australian Journal of Parapsychology, 9*(1), 5-31.

Storm, L., & Rock, A. J. (2011). *Shamanism and psi: Imagery cultivation as an alternative to the ganzfeld protocol.* Gladesville, New South Wales: Australian Institute of Parapsychological Research.

Strassman, R.J. (1994). *Hallucinogen Rating Scale (version 3.06).* Unpublished instrument, Department of Psychiatry, University of New Mexico, Albuquerque, NM.

Strassman, R. J. (1997). Endogenous ketamine-like compounds and the NDE: If so, so what? *Journal of Near-Death Studies, 16,* 27-41.

Strassman, R. [J.] (2001). *DMT: The spirit molecule: A doctor's revolutionary research into the biology of near-death and mystical experiences.* Rochester, VT: Park Street Press.

Strassman, R. [J.] (2008a). *ASC Query.* Personal Communication, 6th October

Strassman, R. [J.](2008b). The varieties of the DMT experience. In R. [J.] Strassman, S. Wojtowicz, L. E. Luna & E. Frecska (Eds.), *Inner paths to outer space: Journeys to alien worlds through psychedelics and other spiritual technologies* (pp.51-80). Rochester, VT: Park Street Press.

Strassman, R. J., Qualls, C. R., Uhlenhuth, E. H., & Kellner, R. (1994). Dose-response study of N,N-dimethyltryptamine in humans. II Subjective effects and preliminary results of a new rating scale. *Archives of General Psychiatry, 51*, 98-108.

Stuckey, D. E., Lawson, R., & Luna, L. E. (2005). EEG Gamma coherence and other correlates of subjective reports during ayahuasca experiences. *Journal of Psychoactive Drugs, 37*, 163-178.

Studerus, E. (2013). *Psilocybin-induced altered states of consciousness: Tolerability, assessment, and prediction.* Saarbrücken, Germany: Südwestdeutscher Verlag für Hochschulschriften.

Studerus, E., Gamma, A., Kometer, M., & Vollenweider, F. X. (2012). Prediction of psilocybin response in healthy volunteers. *PloS ONE, 7*, 2, e30800.

Studerus, E., Gamma, A., & Vollenweider, F. X. (2010). Psychometric evaluation of the Altered States of Consciousness Rating Scale (OAV). *PLoS ONE, 5*(8), e12412.

Studerus, E., Kometer, M., Hasler, F., & Vollenweider, F. X. (2011). Acute, subacute and long-term subjective effects of psilocybin in healthy humans: A pooled analysis of experimental studies. *Journal of Psychopharmacology, 25*, 1434-1452.

Szára, S. (1957). The comparison of the psychotic effects of tryptamine derivatives with the effects of mescaline and LSD-25 in self-experiments. In W. Garattini and V. Ghetti (Eds.) *Psychotropic Drugs* (pp.460-467). New York: Elsevier.

Targ, R. (1994). Remote viewing replication evaluated by concept analysis. *Journal of Parapsychology, 58*, 271-84.

Tart, C. T. (1967). Psychedelic experiences associated with a novel hypnotic procedure, mutual hypnosis. *American Journal of Clinical Hypnosis, 10*, 65-78.

Tart, C. T. (1968). Hypnosis, psychedelics, and psi: Conceptual models. In R. Cavanna & M. Ullman. *Psi and Altered States of Consciousness: Proceedings an International Conference on Hypnosis, Drugs, Dreams, and Psi* (pp. 24-41). NY: Parapsychology Foundation.

Tart, C. T. (1970). Marijuana intoxication: Common experiences. *Nature, 226*, 701-704.

Tart, C. [T.](1971). *On being stoned: A psychological study of marijuana intoxication.* Palo Alto, CA: Science and Behavior Books.

Tart, C. T. (1972a). Considering the scientific study of the human aura. *Journal of the Society for Psychical Research, 46*, 1-21.

Tart, C. T. (1972b). States of consciousness and state-specific sciences. *Science, 176*, 1203-1210.

Tart, C. T. (1975). *States of consciousness.* New York: E. P. Dutton.

Tart, C. T. (1977). Drug-induced states of consciousness. In B. Wolman (Ed.), *Handbook of Parapsychology* (pp. 500-525). New York: Van Nostrand Reinhold.

Tart, C. T. (1993). Marijuana intoxication, psi, and spiritual experiences. *The Journal of the American Society for Psychical Research, 87*, 149-170.

Tart. C. T. (1994). Marijuana, psi, and mystical experiences. In E. W. Cook & D. L. Delanoy (Eds.), *Research in Parapsychology: Abstracts and Papers from the 34th Annual Convention of the Parapsychological Association, 1991* (pp. 120-122). Metuchen, NJ: Scarecrow Press.

Tart, C. T. (1998). Investigating altered states of consciousness on their own terms: A proposal for the creation of state-specific sciences. *Journal of the Brazilian Association for the Advancement of Science, 50*, 103-116.

Tart, C. T. (2000). Investigating altered states of consciousness on their own terms: A proposal for the creation of state-specific sciences. *International Journal of Parapsychology, 11*(1), 7-41.

Tart, C. T. (2001). Psychoactive sacramentals: What must be said. In T. B. Roberts (Ed.). *Psychoactive sacramentals: Essays on entheogens and religion* (pp. 47-56). San Francisco: Council on Spiritual Practices.

Tart, C. (2002). Parapsychology and transpersonal psychology: "Anomalies" to be explained away or spirit to manifest? *Journal of Parapsychology, 66,* 31-47.

Tart, C. T., Palmer, J., & Redington, D. J. (1979). Effects of immediate feedback on ESP performance: A second study. *Journal of the American Society for Psychical Research, 73,* 151-165.

Tellegen, A., & Atkinson, G. (1974). Openness to absorbing and self-altering experiences ("absorption"), a trait related to hypnotic susceptibility. *Journal of Abnormal Psychology, 83,* 268-277.

Terhune, D. B., Luke, D. P., & Cohen Kadosh, R. (2017). The induction of synaesthesia in non-synaesthetes. In O. Deroy (Ed.), *Sensory blending: On synaesthesia and related phenomena* (pp.215-247). Oxford: Oxford University Press.

Terhune, D. B., Luke, D. P., Kaelen, M., Bolstridge, M., Feilding, A., Nutt, D., Carhart-Harris, R., Ward, J. (2016). A placebo-controlled investigation of synaesthesia-like experiences under LSD. *Neuropsychologia, 88,* 28-34.

Thalbourne, M. A. (1998). Transliminality: Further correlates and a short measure. *Journal of the American Society for Psychical Research, 92,* 402-419.

Thalbourne, M. (2000). Transliminality and creativity. *The Journal of Creative Behavior, 34,* 193-202.

Thalbourne, M. A. (2001). Measures of the sheep goat variable, transliminality, and their correlates. *Psychological Reports, 88,* 339-350.

Thalbourne, M.A. (2003). *A glossary of terms used in parapsychology* (2nd ed.). Charlottesville, VA: Puente Publications.

Thalbourne, M. A., & Delin, P. S. (1993). A new instrument for measuring the sheepgoat variable: Its psychometric properties and factor structure. *Journal of the American Society for Psychical Research, 59,* 172-186.

Thalbourne, M. A., & Fox, B. (1999). Paranormal and mystical experience: The role of panic attacks and kundalini. *Journal of the American Society for Psychical Research, 93,* 99-115.

Thalbourne, M. A., & Houran , J. (2005). Patterns of self-reported happiness and substance use in the context of transliminality. *Personality and Individual Differences, 38,* 327-336.

Thomas, S. (2004). Agmatine and near-death experiences. Retrieved November 25, 2005, from http://www.neurotransmitter.net/neardeath.html

Thouless, R. H. (1960). Where does parapsychology go next? *Journal of the Society for Psychical Research, 40,* 207-219.

Tibbs, M. (1963). Hallucinogens and extra-sensory perception. *Tomorrow, 11,* 165-167.

Tinoco, C. A. (1994). Testa de ESP empacientes sob efeito da ayahuasca [Controlled ESP test in patients under the influence of ayahuasca]. *Revista de Brasileira de Parapsicologia, 14,* 42-48.

Tinoco, C. A. (2011). *Teste de persepção extrassensorial com respostas livres em pessoas sob efeito da ayahuasca* [Free response extrasensory perception tests with people under the effects of ayahuasca]. Unpublished manuscript, Department of Parapsychology, UniBem, Curitiba, Brazil.

Toad (1999a). DPT primer. *The Entheogen Review, 8*(1), 4-10.

Toad (1999b). 4-Acetoxy-DIPT primer. *The Entheogen Review, 8*(4), 126-131.

Tobacyk, J. J. (1988). *A revised Paranormal Belief Scale*. Unpublished manuscript, Louisiana Tech University, Ruston, LA.

Tornatore, N.V. (1977a). The paranormal event in psychotherapy as a psychotherapeutic tool: A survey of 609 psychiatrists. In J. D. Morris, W. G. Roll & R. L. Morris (Eds.), *Research in parapsychology, 1976: Abstracts and papers from the nineteenth Annual Convention of Parapsychological Association* (pp. 114-116). Metuchen, NJ: Scarecrow Press.

Tornatore, N. [V.](1977b). The paranormal event in psychotherapy: A survey of 609 psychiatrists. *Psychic Magazine (July)*, 34-37.

Torres, C. M., & Repke, D. B. (2006). *Anadenanthera: Visionary plant of ancient South America*. New York: Haworth Herbal Press.

Trip333 (2007). *A choice between worms and stars*. Retrieved on January 8, 2007, from http://www.erowid.org/experiences/exp.php?ID=6217

Trungpa, C. (1982). Sacred outlook: The Vajrayogini shrine and practice. In D. E. Klimburg-Salter (Ed.), *The silk route and the diamond path*. Los Angeles: UCLA Art Council.

Turner, D. M. (1994). *The essential psychedelic guide*. San Francisco: Panther Press.

Turner, D. M. (1995). Exploring hyperspace. *Entheogen Review: The Journal of Unauthorized Research on Visionary Plants and Drugs, 4*(4), 4-6.

Ullman, M., Krippner, S., & Vaughan, A. (2002). *Dream telepathy: Experiments in extrasensory perception* (3rd ed). Charlottesville, VA: Hampton Roads Publishing.

Unger, S. M. (1963). Mescaline, LSD, psilocybin and personality change. *Psychiatry: Journal for the Study of Interpersonal Processes, 26*, 111-125.

Usha, S., & Pasricha, S. (1989a). Claims of paranormal experiences: I. Survey of psi and psi-related experiences. *Journal of the National Institute of Mental Health and Neurosciences (India), 7*(2), 143-150.

Usha, S., & Pasricha, S. (1989b). Claims of paranormal experiences: II. Attitudes toward psychical research and factors associated with psi and psi-related experiences. *Journal of the National Institute of Mental Health and Neurosciences (India), 7*(2), 151-157.

Utts, J.M. (1995a). An assessment of the evidence for psychic functioning. *Journal of Parapsychology, 59*(4), 289-320.

Utts, J.M. (1995b). Response to Ray Hyman's report of September 11, 1995, 'Evaluation of program on anomalous mental phenomena.' *Journal of Parapsychology, 59*(4), 353-356.

Vallee, J. (1969). *Passport to Magonia*. Chicago: Henry Regnery Company.

Vayne, J. (2001). *Pharmakon: Drugs and the imagination*. London: Liminalspace/El Cheapo.

Vayne, J. (2017). *Getting higher: The manual of psychedelic ceremony*. London: Psychedelic Press UK.

Velmans, M. (2009). *Understanding consciousness* (2nd ed.). Hove, East Sussex, UK: Routledge.

Vollenweider, F. X. (2001). Brain mechanisms of hallucinogens and entactogens. *Dialogues in Clinical Neurosceince, 3*(4), 265-279.

Vollenweider, F. X. (2004). Brain mechanisms of hallucinogens. *Consciousness Research Abstracts from the Toward a Science of Consciousness Conference, Tucson, Arizona*, 91-92.

Vollenweider, F. X., & Geyer, M. A. (2001). A systems model of altered consciousness: Integrating natural and drug-induced psychoses. *Brain Research Bulletin, 56*, 495-507.

Wackerman, J., Pütz, P., Büchi, S., Strauch, I., & Lehmann, D. (2000). A comparison of ganzfeld and hypnogogic state in terms of electrophysiological measures and subjective experience. *Proceedings of the 43rd Annual Convention of the Parapsychology Association, Freiburg, Germany*, 302-315.

Wackerman, J., Wittman, M., Hasler, F., & Vollenweider., F. X. (2008). Effects of varied does of psilocybin on time interval reproduction in human subjects. *Neuroscience Letters, 435*, 51-55.

Walker, J. (1981). The amateur scientist: About phosphenes. *Scientific American 244*(5), 142-52.

Wallach, J.V. (2009). Endogenous hallucinogens as ligands of the trace amine receptors: A possible role in sensory perception. *Medical Hypotheses, 72*(1), 91-94.

Wallis, R.J. (2009). Animism, ancestors and adjusted atyles of communication: Hidden art in Irish passage tombs. In T. Meier and P. Tillessen (Eds.), *Archaeological imaginations of religion*: Budapest: Archaeolingua.

Walsh, R. (2003). Entheogens: True or false? *International Journal of Transpersonal Studies, 22*, 1-6.

Ward, J. (2008). *The frog who croaked blue: Synesthesia and the mixing of the senses.* Hove, UK: Routledge.

Ward, J. (2013). Synesthesia. *Annual Review of Psychology, 64*, 49-75.

Ward, J., & Mattingley, J. B. (2006). Synaesthesia: An overview of contemporary findings and controversies. *Cortex, 42*, 129-136.

Ward, J., Li, R., Salih, S., & Sagiv, N. (2007). Varieties of grapheme-colour synaesthesia: A new theory of phenomenological and behavioural differences. *Consciousness and Cognition, 16*, 913-931.

Wasson, R. G. (1962). Hallucinogenic fungi of Mexico. *International Journal of Parapsychology, 4*(4), 41-58.

Wasson, G. (1964). Notes on the present status of ololiuhqui and the other hallucinogens of Mexico. *Psychedelic Review, 1*(3), 275-301.

Wasson, R. G. (1979). Traditional use in North America of *Amanita muscaria* for divinatory purposes. *Journal of Psychedelic Drugs, 11*, 25-28.

Wasson, R. G., & Wasson, V. P. (1957). *Mushrooms, Russia, and history* (2 vols.). New York: Pantheon.

Watts, A. (1968). Psychedelics and religious experience. *California Law Review, 56*, 74-85.

Weil, A. (1972). *The natural mind: A new way of looking at drugs and higher consciousness.* Boston: Houghton Mifflin.

Weil, A. (1980). *The marriage of the sun and the moon.* Boston: Houghton Mifflin.

Weil, G. M., Metzner, R., & Leary, T. (Eds.). (1965). *The psychedelic reader.* New York: University Books.

West, D. (1965). SPR Presidential Address: ESP, the next step. *Proceedings of the Society for Psychical Research, 54*, 185-202.

Wezelman, R., & Bierman, D. J. (1997). Process orientated ganzfeld research in Amsterdam. *Proceedings of the 40th Parapsychology Association Annual Convention held in conjunction with the Society for Psychical Research*, 477-492.

Whalley, M. G., & Brooks, G. B. (2009). Enhancement of suggestibility and imaginative ability with nitrous oxide. *Psychopharmacology, 203*, 745-752.

White, R. [A]. (1997). Dissociation, narrative, and exceptional human experience. In S. Krippner and S. M. Powers (Eds.), *Broken images, broken selves: Dissociative narratives in clinical practice* (pp.88-124). Washington, DC: Brunner/Mazel.

White, R. [A]. (1999). Exceptional Human Experiences: A Brief Overview. EHE Network, online publication http://www.ehe.org/display/ehe-page3439.html?ID=6

White, R. A., & Brown, S. V. (1997). Classes of EEs/EHEs. In R. A. White (Ed.), *Exceptional human experience: Background papers II* (pp.43-45). New Bern, NC: EHE Network.

White, W. E. (1997). Altered states and paranormal experiences. In W. E. White, *The Dextromethorphan FAQ: Answers to frequently asked questions about DXM,* (version 4). Retrieved April 2, 2002, from http://www.erowid.org/chemical/dxm/faq/dxm_paranormal.shtml

Whiteman, J. H. M. (1956). The process of separation and return in experiences out of the body. *Proceedings of the Society for Psychical Research, 50,* 240-274.

Whiteman, J. H. M. (1965). Psychical effects of mescalin and LSD considered in light of experimental mysticism. *Parapsychologia (South African Society for Psychical Research), 6,* 4-20.

Whiteman, J. H. M. (1995). Short-term precognition, time-skills and the world-plan for physical events. *Journal of the Society for Psychical Research, 60,* 300-316.

Whittlesey, J. R. B. (1960). Some curious ESP results in terms of variance. *Journal of Parapsychology, 24,* 220-222.

Wikipedia (2005). *Levels of psychedelic experience.* Retrieved November 25, 2005, from http://en.wikipedia.org/wiki/Psychedelic_experience

Wilkins, L. K., Girard, T. A., & Cheyne, J. A. (2011). Ketamine as a primary predictor of out-of-body experiences associated with multiple substance use. *Consciousness and Cognition, 20,* 943-950.

Wilson, A. J. C. (1949). Ayahuasca, peyotl, yage. *Proceedings of the Society for Psychical Research, 49,* 353-363.

Wilson, C. W. M. (1961). Possible influence of drugs on ESP Ability. In Anon., *Proceedings on Two Conferences on Parapsychology and Pharmacology* (pp. 43-44). New York: Parapsychology Foundation.

Wilson, C. W. M. (1962). The physiological basis of paranormal phenomena. *International Journal of Parapsychology, 4*(2), 57-96.

Wilson, K., & French, C. C. (2006). The relationship between susceptibility to false memories, dissociativity, and paranormal belief and experience. *Personality and Individual Differences, 41,* 1493-1502.

Winkelman, M. (1983). The anthropology of magic and parapsychological research. *Parapsychological Review, 14*(2), 13-19.

Winkelman, M. (1989). A cross-cultural study of shamanistic healers. *Journal of Psychoactive Drugs, 21,* 17-24.

Winkelman, M. (1990). Shamans and other "magico-religious" healers: A cross-cultural study of their origins, nature and social transformations. *Ethos, 18*(3), 308-352.

Winkelman, M. (2008). *Psychedelics and human evolution. A view from evolutionary psychology.* Paper presented at the World Psychedelic Forum, Basel, Switzerland.

Witthoft, N., & Winawer, J. (2013). Learning, memory, and synaesthesia. *Psychological Science, 24,* 258-265.

Wolfe, T. (1971). *The electric Kool-Aid acid test.* London: Bantam.

Woodruff, J. L. (1943). ESP tests under various physiological conditions. *Journal of Parapsychology, 7,* 264-271.

Wulff, D. M. (1997). *Psychology of religion: Classic and contemporary* (2nd ed.). New York: Wiley.

Wulff, D. M. (2000). Mystical experiences. In E. Cardeña, S. J. Lynn & S. Krippner (Eds.), *Varieties of anomalous experience: Examining the scientific evidence* (pp. 387-440). Washington, DC: American Psychological Association.

Wyllie. T. (1981). *Phencyclidine and ketamine: A view from the street.* Unpublished manuscript, available at http://www.timothywyllie.com/PCP.htm

Wyllie, T. (1999). *The entheogen impulse: An artist's viewpoint.* Unpublished manuscript, available at http://www.timothywyllie.com/Entheogenic%20Impulse.htm

Xeper (2005). DXM and entity contact. *Silver Star: A Journal of New Magick, 4*, 20.

Zaehner, R. C. (1957). *Mysticism: Sacred and Profane.* Oxford: Clarendon Press, Oxford University.

Zelnick, R. R. (2005). *Psi-chedelics: Hallucinogens and ESP.* Unpublished manuscript, University of Philosophical Research, Los Angeles, CA.

Zerda Bayon, R. (1912, August 27). The yage plant. A supposed cure for beri-beri. *The Times South American Supplement,* 8.

Index

Made in the USA
San Bernardino, CA
27 August 2017